T0235357

Lecture Notes in Computer Science 9265

Commenced Publication in 1973
Founding and Former Series Editors:
Gerhard Goos, Juris Hartmanis, and Jan van Leeuwen

Editorial Board

David Hutchison
Lancaster University, Lancaster, UK
Takeo Kanade
Carnegie Mellon University, Pittsburgh, PA, USA
Josef Kittler
University of Surrey, Guildford, UK
Jon M. Kleinberg
Cornell University, Ithaca, NY, USA
Friedemann Mattern
ETH Zurich, Zürich, Switzerland
John C. Mitchell
Stanford University, Stanford, CA, USA
Moni Naor
Weizmann Institute of Science, Rehovot, Israel
C. Pandu Rangan
Indian Institute of Technology, Madras, India
Bernhard Steffen
TU Dortmund University, Dortmund, Germany
Demetri Terzopoulos
University of California, Los Angeles, CA, USA
Doug Tygar
University of California, Berkeley, CA, USA
Gerhard Weikum
Max Planck Institute for Informatics, Saarbrücken, Germany

More information about this series at http://www.springer.com/series/7409

Andrea Kő · Enrico Francesconi (Eds.)

Electronic Government and the Information Systems Perspective

4th International Conference, EGOVIS 2015
Valencia, Spain, September 1–3, 2015
Proceedings

Editors
Andrea Kő
Corvinus University of Budapest
Budapest
Hungary

Enrico Francesconi
Institute of Legal Information Theory and Techniques
Florence
Italy

ISSN 0302-9743 ISSN 1611-3349 (electronic)
Lecture Notes in Computer Science
ISBN 978-3-319-22388-9 ISBN 978-3-319-22389-6 (eBook)
DOI 10.1007/978-3-319-22389-6

Library of Congress Control Number: 2015945127

LNCS Sublibrary: SL3 – Information Systems and Applications, incl. Internet/Web, and HCI

Springer Cham Heidelberg New York Dordrecht London
© Springer International Publishing Switzerland 2015
This work is subject to copyright. All rights are reserved by the Publisher, whether the whole or part of the material is concerned, specifically the rights of translation, reprinting, reuse of illustrations, recitation, broadcasting, reproduction on microfilms or in any other physical way, and transmission or information storage and retrieval, electronic adaptation, computer software, or by similar or dissimilar methodology now known or hereafter developed.
The use of general descriptive names, registered names, trademarks, service marks, etc. in this publication does not imply, even in the absence of a specific statement, that such names are exempt from the relevant protective laws and regulations and therefore free for general use.
The publisher, the authors and the editors are safe to assume that the advice and information in this book are believed to be true and accurate at the date of publication. Neither the publisher nor the authors or the editors give a warranty, express or implied, with respect to the material contained herein or for any errors or omissions that may have been made.

Printed on acid-free paper

Springer International Publishing AG Switzerland is part of Springer Science+Business Media
(www.springer.com)

Preface

The 4th International Conference on Electronic Government and the Information Systems Perspective, EGOVIS 2015, took place in Valencia, Spain, during September 1–3, 2015. The conference belongs to the 26th DEXA Conference Series.

The international conference cycle EGOVIS focuses on information systems and ICT aspects of e-government. Information systems are a core enabler for e-government/governance in all its dimensions: e-administration, e-democracy, e-participation, and e-voting. EGOVIS brought together experts from academia, public administrations, and industry to discuss e-government and e-democracy from different perspectives and disciplines, i.e., technology, policy and/or governance and public administration. This year the OpenLaws workshop was organized as a related event, with a focus on open innovation.

The Program Committee accepted 26 papers from recent research fields such as government cloud, identity management and e-government architectures, collaborative innovation, open government, open and linked data, intelligent systems, and semantic technologies applications. Beyond theoretical contributions, papers cover e-government experiences from all over the world; cases are presented from Europe and South America.

This proceedings volume is organized into nine sections according to the conference sessions.

We were honored that the EGOVIS 2015 keynote speech was given by Prof. Ronald Traunmüller: He is one of the pioneers in e-government studies and has contributed for years to identify limits and opportunities in the field. Prof. Traunmüller's speech discussed the previous 15 years of e-government research directions covered by the DEXA and EGOVIS conference series.

The chairs of the Program Committee wish to thank all the reviewers for their valuable work, the reviews raised several research questions that were discussed at the conference. We would like to thank Gabriela Wagner for the administrative support and for assisting us with the scheduling.

We wish our readers pleasant and beneficial learning experiences and we hope that the discussion between researchers will continue after the conference and contribute to building a global community in the field of e-government.

June 2015

Enrico Francesconi
Andrea Kő

Organization

General Chair

Roland Traunmüller	University of Linz, Austria

Program Committee Co-chairs

Enrico Francesconi	Italian National Research Council, Italy
Andrea Kő	Corvinus University Budapest, Hungary

Honorary Chairs

Wichian Chutimaskul	King Mongkut's University of Technology, Thailand
Fernando Galindo	University of Zaragoza, Spain

Program Committee

Luis Álvarez Sabucedo	Universidade de Vigo, Spain
Francesco Buccafurri	Università degli Studi Mediterranea di Reggio Calabria, Italy
Alejandra Cechich	Universidad Nacional del Comahue, Argentina
Wojciech Cellary	Poznan University of Economics, Poland
Wichian Chutimaskul	King Mongkut's University of Technology, Thailand
Flavio Corradini	University of Camerino, Italy
Peter Cruickshank	Edinburgh Napier University, UK
Vytautas Cyras	Vilnius University, Lithuania
Enrico Francesconi	Italian National Research Council, Italy
Ivan Futo	National Tax and Customs Administration, Hungary
András Gábor	Corvinus University of Budapest, Hungary
Fernando Galindo	University of Zaragoza, Spain
Johann Gamper	Free University of Bozen, Italy
Francisco Javier García Marco	University of Zaragoza, Spain
Stefanos Gritzalis	University of the Aegean, Greece
Patrik Hitzelberger	Centre de Recherche Public - Gabriel Lippmann, Luxembourg
Christos Kalloniatis	University of the Aegean, Greece
Nikos Karacapilidis	University of Patras, Greece
Andrea Kő	Corvinus University Budapest, Hungary
Christine Leitner	Centre for Economics and Public Administration Ltd. (CEPA), UK

Herbert Leitold	E-Government Innovation Center EGIZ, Austria
Marian Mach	Technical University of Kosice, Slovakia
Peter Mambrey	University of Duisburg-Essen, Germany
Mara Nikolaidou	Harokopio University of Athens, Greece
Javier Nogueras	University of Zaragoza, Spain
Aljosa Pasic	Atos, Spain
Andrea Polini	UNICAM, Italy
Reinhard Posch	Technical University Graz, Austria
Aires J. Rover	Federal University of Santa Catarina, Brazil
Christian Rupp	Federal Chancellery of Austria/Federal Platform Digital Austria, Austria
Erich Schweighofer	University of Vienna, Austria
A. Min Tjoa	Vienna University of Technology, Austria
Julian Valero	iDertec - Innovation, Law and Technology Research Group University of Murcia, Spain
Costas Vassilakis	University of the Peloponnese, Greece
Gianluigi Viscusi	EPFL-CDM-CSI, Switzerland
Roland Wagner	University Linz, Austria
Frank Wilson	Interaction Design, UK
Robert Woitsch	BOC Asset Management, Austria
Chien-Chih Yu	National ChengChi University, China (Taiwan Province)

External Reviewers

Agustina Buccella	University of Comahue, Argentina
Andrés Flores	University of Comahue, Argentina
Elmar Kiesling	Vienna University of Technology
Evangelos Goggolidis	University of the Aegean, Greece
Stavros Simou	University of the Aegean, Greece
Barbara Re	University of Camerino, Italy

Contents

Keynote Talk

DEXA Covering 15 Years of E-Government Research

Roland Traunmüller(✉)

Johannes Kepler Universität Linz, Altenbergerstraße 69, 4040 Linz, Austria
traunm@ifs.uni-linz.ac.at

Abstract. The term "Electronic Government" became a common label fifteen years ago and since then DEXA has covered the development of E-Government within its Conference Cluster. Such an anniversary offers an opportunity for reflexion. DEXA Aix conference 2002 was the first big international conference dedicated to e-Government R&D and brought together the European community exerting considerable influence on outlining e-Government. First this defining phase is sketched; then reflexion turns to future prospects.

Keywords: Electronic Government · Electronic governance · e-Transformation

1 A Suitable Moment for Reflexion

Nineties turning a new century the term "Electronic Government" became a common tag. Having employed that label for fifteen years DEXA Valencia can be regarded as a proper forum to recall the beginning and to reflect perspectives. The sweeping success of e-Government was due to the strong appeal for the use of information technologies in Government. Substantial improvements were achieved in the ways in which Government works and interacts with the addressees of its action. Change became pervasive and Government went through a permanent "e-Transformation". Entirely new ways became apparent in which public governance can be exercised.

From the very beginning DEXA has covered the development of e-Government within its Conference Cluster, first with workshops and then with founding a particular Conference series dedicated to R&D in e-Government. The first such conference was within DEXA 2002 in Aix-en-Provence [6]. The Aix conference was successful in convening the scientific community and the "Aix Declaration" exerted considerable influence on defining e-Government. One year later the EU promulgated the Como Vademecum which was heavily based on the Aix declaration. Aix became the beginning of a line of e-Government conferences within DEXA. The label EGOV was later changed to EGOVIS which accentuates the Information Systems aspect.

2 The Aix Declaration on E-Government

The Aix Conference was more than a convening of the scientific community; it brought in addition a consolidated view on e-Government. So the declaration adopted at the conference is worth to be cited. The following theses were proclaimed to the public:

© Springer International Publishing Switzerland 2015
A. Kő and E. Francesconi (Eds.): EGOVIS 2015, LNCS 9265, pp. 3–10, 2015.
DOI: 10.1007/978-3-319-22389-6_1

1. A holistic view: Moving ahead means having an integral view. Clear strategies and perceptions are a prerequisite to facing the challenges and making the best of the opportunities created by technological progress and its intellectual mastery. E-Government is more than a new wave of administrative modernisation, e-Government means a permanent e-transformation that enables governance on a comprehensive scale.
2. Service provision as focus: Citizen portals and service delivery to business, to individual citizens and to communities reflect the viewpoints of individual citizens or of companies, looking at government and administration from outside. So the portal part is of prime concern, yet is should be noted that communicating with agencies is only the tip of an iceberg: the entire scope of administrative action has to be involved.
3. Redefining governmental processes: Thus, a thorough rethinking of the machinery of Government is mandatory. It will reveal many more situations where IT as an enabling force can enhance effectiveness, quality and efficiency of public action as well as its legitimacy. In many respects the legal framework of these processes has to be changed, and new institutions will emerge which fit the new ways of producing and delivering public services.
4. Knowledge enhanced government: A shift of focus from structures and processes towards content reaches the very heart of administrative work: taking decisions. Management of legal/administrative domain knowledge is a decisive driver in governance. In addition, understanding the connections between processes and knowledge will improve design. In the agency of the future human and software expertise become totally interwoven – knowledge enhancement at its best.
5. An engineering approach: A sound engineering approach is indispensable. At bottom level this means a suitable IT infrastructure - unhampered communication and cooperation, availability, security, data protection, etc. At the application level it means smooth cooperation, high usability and a design integrating important perspectives: citizen service, process reorganisation, knowledge enhancement.
6. Reference models and administrative standards: Reference models and pilot projects give an idea about the full extent of the possibilities available. Above all, issues of standards have to be tackled: establishing a common understanding of processes, building on widespread administrative concepts, ensuring interoperable platforms; providing definitions for data interchange.
7. Change Management: Success can only be achieved if a quantum leap in the innovative capacity of the public sector is achieved. Critical success factors include strategic thinking and a farsighted allocation of funds for creating infrastructures and avoiding reinventing the wheel in different places. Best practice and guidelines derived from landmark projects will have to replace the attitude of curious but indiscriminate trying out of different approaches. Competent change management will have to place people first, and an unprecedented qualification offensive is needed to communicate the necessary know-how.

3 DEXA Aix and Defining E-Government

The Aix declaration can be regarded as a culmination in the line of efforts defining e-Government. A precursor part was initiated by the Special Committee on Governmental Informatics of the German Computer Society (GI). So in 1999 a collective volume on e-Government was published on behalf of the GI Committee. Then the year 2000 brought the Memorandum "Electronic Government for Modernizing State and Public Administration" (sustained by GI together with VDE). Concerning citations see [5] respectively [1].

DEXA Aix was the first international e-Government conference with R&D Design and convened the scientific community in a critical mass. No wonder that the Aix declaration exerted heavy influence on defining e-Government. Shaping the EU Como Vademecum 2003 described in next section. Other impact concerned influencing various events. As example the conferences in Schiras and Damascus are quoted [3, 4]. Quite important was an incessant spurring of the internal discussion within the scientific community. Especially, the subsequent DEXA conferences in Zaragoza and Prague were places of a broad discussion (as documented in the proceedings [7, 8]).

In that way additional topics came in the limelight. Quite important was the focus on public governance. This meant considering the whole governance cycle which includes many activities: democratic deliberation, policy formulation, citizen involvement, law making, execution of policies, evaluation etc. It is worth noting that herewith some old ideas formulated in the Sixties as "political cybernetics" by Luhmann were recalled. Ten years ago the definition phase came to a provisional close and so we cite the official EU definition: "e-Government is the use of information and communication technologies in public administrations - combined with organisational change and new skills - to improve public services and democratic processes and to strengthen support to public policies."

4 Impact for the EU: Shaping the Como Vademecum

The Aix declaration drew a lot of visibility and subsequently Klaus Lenk and I were both invited by the EU to join a small drafting team for a Vademecum to be presented at the EU Ministerial Conference on e-Government in Como 2003 [3]. Under the management of EIPA (Cristine Leitner) such a "Vademecum" was created and the content was heavily shaped by the ideas and concepts discussed in the sections before. The title was "eGovernment in Europe: State of affaires". These endeavours have to be seen in the perspective of the European Commission intending to influence the course of e-Government. Although from a legal point of view the EC has no direct influence on the administrations of the Member States, in an indirect way considerable influence is exerted. For the most part, the EC finances a lot of multinational projects within the Research Framework Programmes.

The explicit goal of the Como Vademecum was giving an overview of the vision and reality of e-Government in order to help decision makers in the conceptualisation and implementation phases of e-Government projects. The Como Conference was quite big and promulgated also a portfolio of project cases and three winners honoured by the biennial “eEurope Award”. In the awards competition projects were sought that would be declared as model cases. Such projects have to provide a valuable and sufficiently detailed list of advice which can be given to others in e-Government. By the way, one of the 2003 Como winners was an Austrian project, namely Help.gv.at. All in all, the Como event brought high attention.

5 E-Government as Permanent Transformation: A Vision and a Construction Site

Como was also quite successful in building a general awareness what e-Government is. The idea of good governance leads to the concept good government. The following demands are key marks: citizen-centric in attitude; cooperative in nature; seamless and joined up seen from the clients; multilevel and polycentric in composition. Simultaneously basic qualities are enhanced, so the effectiveness and efficiency of public actions. Thus, e-Government is closely linked to permanent change; it is a persistent process of transforming public governance and administration. On the whole, it is both, a vision and a construction site.

Progress is no easy grasp as in Government we deal with a rather complex system. Regarded in a systemic view we consider several subsystems. Basic is the governmental arrangement: public authorities, pubic services, political decision making, legislation, jurisdiction and executive bodies. Next view concerns the surrounding conditions such as society, economy, environment and culture. Then the focus shifts to technological and political drivers, just as to mention societal needs, political decisions, ICT innovations. All this has to be directed by particular goal functions such as efficiency, effectiveness, economic and public value.

Transformation starts with a thorough rethinking of the machinery of Government. This leads to fundamentally redefining the production processes. Thereby the entire range of relationships of public bodies to clients and partners is transformed. E-Transformation takes place in many domains and the core patterns are alike in their basic composition. Principal feature is using telecooperation as prime mode of work. Set off is creating appropriate activity/business models and integrating flows of information. Fundamental needs have to be met such as providing a protected and trustworthy environment and safeguarding secure and legally binding transactions. Concerning the governmental domain, transformation has three main goals:

1. Striving to improve public services
2. Aiding democratic processes
3. Strengthening the support to public policies.

Reflexion means both, analysing the roots and deliberating the future. Progress builds on solid trends that already now can be observed emerging. Here some relevant issues are sketched.

6 Proactive and Borderless Government

Key for progress is proactive Government which means providing additional services to citizens. Data collected for several purposes could be merged and utilized to build additional systems. For example, public administration is already helping citizen access data from banks, employers, and pension funds to make their tax declarations easier. In the same way, local government may inform citizens on entitlements or possible fee reductions etc.

Another important point is having services crossing borders. For example, a classical case is encountered when a European citizen works in multiple European states throughout his career, and ultimately retires in and asks for his pension from yet another state. In this situation, which is faced by an increasing number of European citizens, the pension organisations from the various states must cooperate.

7 Enhanced Usability

For e-Government achieving a high up take is central. Thus, a major concern has to be directed towards enhancement of the user-interface. General deficiencies occur quite often: a lack in targeting the audience; an inadequate and inconsistent design; lacking of comments and adequate examples; sloppiness in maintenance with outdated pieces of information. Improvements go several ways and even plain rules will contribute to usability such as "Less is more" and "Keep it straight and simple". More complicated interaction processes need a deeper analysis. Essential enhancements comprise both static and dynamic help. A static support may include describing clearer scenarios or having better help-functions. Instruments for dynamic help are software agents.

Administrative applications can often be improved through the addition of knowledge-based components, which increase the capacity to understand the meaning of queries. In particular, semantic-based technologies show great promise. Ontologies are standardized representation of knowledge as a set of concepts within a domain, and the relationships between those concepts. A particular ontology provides a shared vocabulary and taxonomy. So a domain can be modelled by defining objects and their properties and relations. For intelligent modules process knowledge is collected based on expert experience from different cases.

8 Decision Making and Meeting Support

A broad range of methods and tools are available to support decision-making, so analytical models, information retrieval, simulation and knowledge-based systems. Decision models have to be regarded with a grain of salt. Usually information is oriented to a special and restricted purpose and must be tuned with respect to user and aim. Therefore, decision models are in some way restricted. Another problem is that decision models combine diverse categories of data which makes data integration central. The collections of data comprise data of diverse type format originated from different sources, so files, databases, legacy system etc. Another critical point is getting key numbers as output and having data visualised. Usually information gets abstracted in some schematic form. Focus is put on getting results which flow into the actual decisions of an enterprise. In consequence, proper abstraction turns out to be a central question in decision making: "Which data to take and which data to neglect".

Meeting support can be useful in negotiations and mediation procedures as well as in policy formulation. Such support systems aid the meeting process itself as well as various sub tasks, including agenda setting, problem structuring, evaluation of solutions and assisting mediation. Additional auxiliary functions concern facilitating brainstorming and guiding argumentation. Argumentation systems (IBIS as precursor) structure arguments in establishing and connecting issues, positions, pro- and contra-arguments.

9 Handling Legal Information

Legal drafting needs instruments, so tools for modelling norms and information retrieval. There exists a long history of modelling norms. Sixties was the time of the precursors with cybernetic thinking en vogue. In the Seventies legal databases and information retrieval blossomed and first applications of artificial intelligence came in. Nineties have brought a sound methodological basis including essential work on ontologies and building tools.

Information retrieval has not changed since decades and is still keyword-oriented. Urgently needed are devices for case based retrieval. There are research systems using deontic logic, probabilistic measures and neuronal nets; yet they have not matured to praxis. Another point is handling the information flow between stakeholders from the beginning to the authentic publication. Stakeholders are ministries, parliaments, political parties and consulting bodies.

Some problems appear in cross border usage needing equivalent legal terms in different languages. It is difficult to find an adequate meaning as legal terms are often left vague on purpose. Hence the nature of the administrative process allows some openness and discretionary power of street level bureaucrats. This is a common feature found in domains such as intellectual property, licensing, certificates and academic degrees. To improve the situation the EU started "openlaws activities" aiming at obtaining legal information more easily. This comprises in concrete several efforts, namely creating a network of legislation, case law, legal literature and legal experts, as well on a national and a European level.

10 Knowledge Management

Competition is growing everywhere among countries, companies and people. With increased pressure from competition knowledge is seen as panacea or at least as part of a remedy. The role of knowledge in institutions is vast so as intellectual capital, as productive resource or as instrument of power. Even when knowledge eludes clear cut definitions, in an constructive approach knowledge can be comprehended as "arranging pieces of information and offering correlated interpretations". According to such interpretations knowledge is an abstract issue which is goal-oriented, context-related and subject-relevant. In design knowledge is converted, so in analysis from implicit to explicit and in constructing from explicit to explicit.

Technical handling of knowledge requires storability. Formalisation is the basis for storage, transfer (and if applicable automatic processing). For being formalized knowledge has to be made explicit. The range of formalization is broad reaching from simple structures and hypertext to rules in expert systems and software agents. Knowledge Management Systems (KMS) contain several components so repositories, ontologies, instruments for data integration as well as functions for collecting and dissemination. KMS emerged as a scientific discipline in the earlier Nineties. Many systems are techno-centric quasi built around a tool and focussed on improving knowledge sharing.

11 Open Government

Origin of the concept goes back to the American and French Revolution when Freedom of Press was proclaimed. Goals are quite diverse yet the universal focus is public value which is linked to several individual and societal interests. The range of objectives goes from improving transparency and using Open Software unto making public value from governmental data and heightening the quality of life by useful applications.

Open Source governance is a political philosophy with focus on decision-making methods that better cover public interest (more open, less antagonistic). Open Source software should enable any interested citizen to add to the creation of policy. A prevalent issue is Open Government Data. The fan of Open Government Data is broad: micro-census, geographical data, regulations, traffic data. A number of institutions provide open data creating an e-Government demand pull. Successful applications are created in cooperation of agencies with private enterprises.

12 Mobile Government

The widespread use of mobile devices makes access to the Internet quasi-ubiquitous. The fact that such a large proportion of citizens use mobile devices such as smartphones and tablets to access the Internet has serious consequences. Mobile devices support keeping in touch, prolong availability and change patterns of communication. Additional impact is enforced via synergies, so location functions bring quite useful services.

Especially, Mobile Government and social media reinforce each other in a co-evolutionary manner. The general administrative realm is improved by obtaining feedback from citizens, an increased contact with the public and a better cross agency cooperation. Quite substantial is the impact on participation aiding democratic deliberation, advising of other citizens, assisting monitoring and law enforcement. Thus citizen involvement achieves the aim of improving public responsiveness and reconnecting voters with politics and policy making.

References

1. GI/VDE 2000: Electronic Government als Schlüssel zur Modernisierung von Staat und Verwaltung. Ein Memorandum des Fachausschusses Verwaltungsinformatik der Gesellschaft für Informatik e.V. und des Fachbereichs 1 der Informationstechnischen Gesellschaft im VDE, Stuttgart/Frankfurt a.M. http://www.gi-ev.org/fileadmin/redaktion/Download/presse_memorandum.pdf
2. Leitner, C. (ed.).: EU Como Vademecum: eGovernment in Europe: The State of Affairs. Presented at the EU e-Government Conference Como, EIPA, Maastricht (2003)
3. Far, B., Shafazand, M., Takizawa, M., Wagner, R. (eds.): EurAsia: Proceedings of the Workshops EurAsia-ICT 2002 – Advances in Information and Communication Technology, Österreichische Computer Gesellschaft, Schriftenreihe der OCG Band 161, Wien (2002)
4. ICCTA: International Conference on Information & Communication Technologies: From Theory to Applications, Damascus, Syria (2006). ISBN 0-7803-9521-2
5. Lenk, K., Traunmüller, R. (Hrsg.): Öffentliche Verwaltung und Informationstechnik: Perspektiven einer radikalen Neugestaltung der öffentlichen Verwaltung mit Informationstechnik. Schriftenreihe Verwaltungsinformatik Bd. 20, im R. v. Decker´s Verlag, Heidelberg (1999)
6. Traunmüller, R., Lenk, K. (eds.): First International Conference on Electronic Government. EGOV 2002, Aix-en-Provence, France, September 2002. Springer (2002). (ISBN: 3-540-44121-2)
7. Traunmüller, R. (ed.): EGOV 2003. LNCS, vol. 2739. Springer, Heidelberg (2003)
8. Traunmüller, R. (ed.): EGOV 2004. LNCS, vol. 3183. Springer, Heidelberg (2004)

Semantic Technologies in E-Government

Using the Semantic Web for the Integration and Publication of Public Procurement Data

José Félix Muñoz[1,2(✉)] and Guillermo Esteban[2]

[1] Aragonese Foundation for Research and Development (ARAID), Huesca, Spain

[2] University of Zaragoza, Walqa Technological Park, 22197 Huesca, Spain

{jfm, gesteban}@unizar.es

Abstract. Public procurement is an activity that is common to all administrations, with a major impact on their functioning and that also affects the economy as a whole. This paper presents an experience that shows how the Semantic Web provides appropriate resources to develop data models that can be used both for the management of public contracts and for the publication of information about them. And within that, with a dual objective of improving efficiency by facilitating competitive tendering, and of making easy the monitoring of public contracts by citizens. Firstly, we developed the PPROC ontology in said experience, with the domain of the ontology being the legal institution of public contracting, which includes the procedure for the preparation of contracts. Next, we used the ontology as a basis for the integration and publication of data from various Spanish administrations.

Keywords: Public procurement · Semantic web · Ontologies · Open government · Freedom of information

1 Introduction

1.1 The Right to Free Access to Public Sector Information

One of the third-generation human rights is free access to public sector information, which is now included in the laws of many of the most developed countries [1]. To justify this, it would be sufficient to recognize that this information is created using resources contributed by the general public as a whole through taxes, but that the exercise of this right is usually linked to the following specific purposes:

- The defense of the interests of the affected parties, in the access to administrative files.
- Academic, in the access to historic archives.
- Political, in the transparency conceived as an instrument for the control of the activities of public authorities.
- Economical, in the re-use of public information by the private sector (generally, Open Government Data (OGD) projects form part of this latter purpose).

© Springer International Publishing Switzerland 2015

A. Kő and E. Francesconi (Eds.): EGOVIS 2015, LNCS 9265, pp. 13–28, 2015.
DOI: 10.1007/978-3-319-22389-6_2

Nowadays, access to information is regulated by differents laws and regulations depending on how it is linked to one purpose or another. This situation is meaningless as the exercise of the right of access has become independent of the purpose and must always be allowed, inasmuch as one of the limitations provided by the law is not applicable. Therefore, it is necessary to draft one unified regulation so that public information spans these four perspectives. This legislation should also encompass the entire life cycle of information and not just access to it [2].

Depending on the purpose of the access, different laws might be applied and the authority might be given to different bodies and institutions. One of the consequences of this fact is that numerous redundancies are generated that, as well as leading to an unnecessary consumption of resources, cause confusion between users and public servants (as can be seen in the case of Italy, in [3]). Another consequence is that very inconsistent strategies and standards will be produced. For example, it is in the access for the re-use of information in which technological tools—such as the Semantic Web—are used to a greater extent, since it is assumed that one of the main objectives is that the re-users can exploit the information by using computerized means. However, as we will see in this paper, the Semantic Web could be a very useful tool for administrations to help the public exercise its right of access to information in all its aspects, and not just from the re-use perspective.

1.2 Transparency and Public Procurement

Advertising has always been an essential part of public procurement, in which it must fulfil a dual purpose: on one hand, it is a resource to improve competitive tendering and, on the other, it constitutes an instrument for transparency and for the monitoring of the behavior of the contracting authorities [4]. With the progress of electronic government, the publication of information regarding contracting procedures increasingly began to be performed using electronic means. In 2004, European directives[1] created a specific mechanism called the buyer profile. All public sector entities must have one and publish certain information on it about the contracts that they put out to tender, and therefore, it has become the central information point for companies and the public. However, its use has been severely limited by the major functional and technical differences between the different profiles and the lack of interoperability between them, which makes the integrated processing of the information published on them nearly impossible.

Faced with this problem, the solution that is usually adopted is to make the publication of announcements regarding tender procedures of all administrations mandatory on a single web site. For example, within the scope of the EU there is the Tenders Electronic Daily (TED), which is the online version of the "Supplement to the Official Journal of the EU", dedicated to European public procurement. In Spain, this is the

[1] Today replaced by the directives of the European Parliament and of the Council: 2014/24/EU, of 26 February 2014 on public procurement and repealing Directive 2004/18/EC; and 2014/25/EU, of 26 February 2014, on procurement by entities operating in the water, energy, transport and postal services sectors and repealing Directive 2004/17/EC.

Public Sector Contracting Platform (PSCP). However, only part of the problem is solved using this measure. This is the part related to competitive tendering and, therefore, to economic efficiency since, in order to comply with this objective, it is enough to publish a limited set of announcements. However, transparency requires much more information and, in addition, transparency practices can be very different depending on the policies followed by each authority. Therefore, from the perspective of transparency, the solution involves preparing standards that could be used by administrations to publish all the information that they consider appropriate.

Below we will describe an experience that includes the integration and publication of data about public contracts and the procurement procedures of various Spanish Administrations following this strategy. We carried out the experience within the framework of the ContSem project[2]—led by the company iASoft (Oesia)—and we based it on semantic technology (Sect. 2). Their main objective has been publish the information as linked RDF, which holds the five stars level from the rating system for open data established by the W3C.[3] To do this we developed the PPROC ontology,[4] the principal characteristics of which are described in Sect. 3. Using this ontology, we integrated (Sect. 4) and semantically labeled and published (Sect. 5) the data of two local administrations and of the entire state administration of Spain. Finally, as a conclusion, we present some observations drawn from the experience.

2 Data Models in Electronic Administration

2.1 Management and Interoperability

Over the short history of electronic administration, new purposes or objectives for the processing of data by administrations have been added, which has led to changes in the methodology used in the design of data models.

We can assume that the first reason why public administrations used computers was management. If we analyze the data models prepared for management applications, we can see that their designs meant that their structure was closely related to the temporal succession in which the information was being generated or received by the management bodies. This was due to the way that the computer analysts obtain information from the administrative managers, as these latter tend to request that the different fields be incorporated sequentially, in the order that they are required to record certain information. This leads to an organization of data that we could call "procedural", as it is closely connected to the procedure and, therefore, to the way of working of each administrative service. Its reflection in the applications consists of a succession of screens where the entire sequence of a specific case (of a public contract, for example) can be followed from start to finish.

---

[2] Financed by the Spanish Ministry of Industry, Commerce and Tourism through the project "Optimization of public procurement using semantic technologies", TSI-020606-2012-4.

[3] http://www.w3.org/DesignIssues/LinkedData.html.

[4] http://contsem.unizar.es/def/sector-publico/pproc.

The objective of interoperability was later requested from the information systems of public administrations, which led to the development of data models whose objective was to achieve interoperability, by addressing communication between systems. Public procurement is a good example of this, as the announcements that are published on these web sites that, as we have just seen, both the EU and national governments have created to centrally publish information about public tenders are among the first exchanges of information performed electronically using structured messages. There are various initiatives whose purpose is to create standards for electronic procurement, including, within the scope of the EU, OpenPEPPOL[5] and CEN BII.[6] In both cases, XML formats that make it possible to structure the messages exchanged by the various agents involved in electronic procurement are defined. However, the administrations chose to create "de facto" standards, such as the one established for the TED eSenders[7] or CODICE,[8] defined for the Spanish PSCP. In the design of these standards, computer analysts use documents (messages) that are exchanged between organizations as their reference, and these determine the structure of the information. Consequently, we can call these XML standards "document-oriented".

2.2 Re-Use

Recently, laws highlight the re-use of information, both by the different bodies of each administration and by the administrations as a whole, as one of the principles that should govern electronic administration. From a technical perspective, this objective relates to the application of the principles of unique data and shared data. However, while interoperability solely addresses communication between systems and ignores how information is organized inside each of them, re-use requires consistency between the parts of a system and between the various systems themselves, so that information can be shared between multiple agents and for various purposes.

One of the purposes will be to facilitate the exercise of the right of free access to public sector information. From the first moment, this right must be considered as a basic requirement in the design of systems and, therefore, public access will have to be considered as one of the possible uses of the information in the design of data models. Consequently, it will not be enough to propose common data structure for public organizations; instead it will be necessary to define models which includes all the information that citizens may require. Going further, the final objective must be that the information used for management and the information for public access be the same, which does not mean it is necessary to publish all information, but does mean that no conversion process be required for publication.

Numerous projects are being developed within the context of the Semantic Web, with the objective of creating models that will make it possible to represent legal concepts. It is calculated that in 2011 over 60 ontologies focused on legal knowledge

[5] http://www.peppol.eu.

[6] http://www.cenbii.eu.

[7] http://simap.europa.eu/ojs_esenders/sending_xml_notices/index_en.htm.

[8] https://contrataciondelestado.es/wps/portal/codice.

had been completed. These are very varied ontologies, both from a granularity point of view and regarding their degree of formalization and the methods used for their development [5]. Regarding the sources of knowledge used, the main legal concepts prepared by the philosophy of law have been used as a basis for representations of legal knowledge. Therefore, some place legal texts at the heart of representation, and others are focused on the activity of legal experts, while there are also those focused on the modeling of discourse, which is the basis of legal argument.

Ontologies also differ regarding their objectives. In some, called core ontologies, the objective is the creation of models of general legal concepts [6]. In other cases, the objective is not to describe general concepts but to design a specific social mechanism. This is the case with our project, in which the intention is to represent the social mechanism used to connect the contracting process of public sector entities. For the development of these models we consider that an approach based on the "theory of the institution" is appropriate. According to this approach, the central focus of the model would be public procurement, considered as a legal institution whose purpose is the attainment of a "product": a public contract [7]. This approach helps to demarcate the field of knowledge to be represented, as the institutions can also be seen as systems with a well-defined interface with an environment [8].

It seems logical that a closely studied formalization of a certain legal institution—an "institution-oriented" model—could be useful for its representation within the information system, both for management and publication requirements. Although these do not totally coincide, there are no differences in terms of the organization and the high-level entities; instead they appear, above all, because the management requires certain additional, internal information. This information has not been included in the ontology, as it is not its objective to describe all of the entities and properties that are required in management. These data are not of interest to the public and it is sufficient to carry out an extension of the ontology to incorporate the data that are necessary in the back-office.

3 The PPROC Ontology

3.1 Structure and Sources of Knowledge

The perspective focused on the "institution" firstly determines the semantic relationships of the model. Some systems of legal concepts are organized vertically from the most general concepts to the most specific ones. In this case, the relationships are about belonging. Other systems, known as operational families, gather together the elements related to a specific item [9]. An institution-based model belongs to this second type and its semantic relationships are organized according to the role that each concept plays within the institution that is represented. In order to identify and define these relationships, the science of the law can be used, which is devoted to studying and organizing the legal elements that comprise institutions and the relationships between them.

Secondly, considering an institution as the scope of the model will help us to establish the nature of the entities that will be able to form part of the model, as all the realities involved in the public contract formation process will have to be included, and these comprise theoretical, social and physical realities [10]. This varied nature of the entities also means that the sources of knowledge will be different. We will firstly need to use legal texts, as public procurement forms part of public law, and within this, of administrative law. In this respect, it is necessary to consider that the durability of the representation contained in the model could be severely reduced through excessive connection to legal texts as, in general, administrative laws vary much more over time than those of private law—especially those of civil law, where many of the core figures of the legal system are defined with a greater degree of generalization and abstraction. In this sense, by focusing the model on the "legal institution", it will be possible to identify the elements of the institution that have become established over the years, remaining constant in successive regulations. Likewise, this strategy is also consistent with the objective of the ontology—the publication of information thereby facilitating understanding by the public—as, in order to achieve the objective, not only is it unnecessary to strictly adhere to details by reflecting the literal contents of laws, it could even prove to be counterproductive.

According to Ferraris, social realities are always related to documents, so much so that being a document is sufficient to be a social fact [10]. Given that the publication of public information is always performed through documents, each of the acts that comprise contracting procedures will be a social reality. Therefore, the second source of knowledge to be used will be the documents through which administrations publish information about these procedures and contracts. Laws establish part of their content but above all, it is determined by the practices of the various administrations and, within the scope of e-procurement, by the standardization needs. Finally, the third source of knowledge to be used is that regarding physical realities, and the most important for the model are those that appear within the object of the contracts. It is also necessary to include other physical facts that we could call secondary (such as the physical location of an office, for example).

3.2 Use of Semantic Technology in Public Procurement

The growth in procurement by electronic means has led to what is called e-procurement, in which both XML standards and semantic technology are widely used [11]. Among the developments in the European context, there are some that consist of the preparation of ontologies for the representation of knowledge about public procurement.

One of these experiences is LOTED2 [12], which bases most of its content on the two directives (2004/17/EC and 2004/18/EC) that at the time of development regulated public contracts in Europe. The result is a thorough study of legal documents. This means that the legal content of European procurement is heavily present and rigorously represented in LOTED2. Another initiative focused on public procurement is MOLDEAS (Methods On Linked Data for E-procurement Applying Semantics) [13], an ontology focused on the representation of information contained in the announcements about public tenders. The objective of this ontology was to provide a pan-European standard about public procurement data, enriching it with the classifications of already-existing products and publishing it by following established open data guidelines.

A third initiative in the EU is the Public Contracts Ontology (PCO), implemented within the framework of the LOD2 Project [14]. PCO models the main aspects of public contracts, although not in great depth. The ontology considers "only the information that is publicly available in existing systems on the Web […], mainly produced during the tendering phase". Hence, the result is a lightweight ontology that re-uses widely accepted ontologies and vocabularies such as VCard, Payments Ontology, schema.org, Call for Anything vocabulary and GoodRelations.

PCO and MOLDEAS describe the main concepts of public procurement without examining details very much and, as a consequence, some specific relations, roles or behaviors are not strictly represented (e.g. the contracting body or distinguish between objective and subjective award criteria). On the other hand, LOTED2 represents almost every aspect of public procurement with the result that his the model is closely related to the text of the 2004 directives. None of the three ontologies studied had transparency as its primary goal and the main objective we chased with the use of the ontology was to improve the transparency of public contracting processes. Consequently, although taking PCO as our basis, we decided to develop the PPROC ontology, the main objective of which is to facilitate access for all parties interested in information regarding public contracts, which means that not only contracting powers and tenderer companies, but also the general public as a whole has been considered in its design.

3.3 Description of the Ontology

The PPROC ontology is composed of 78 classes and 129 properties that are divided into four blocks, each one of which includes the classes that are directly related to the following points of the contract: (1) the object, which is the supply that the contract covers; (2) the parts, which are the agents that participate in the procurement process and, when appropriate, in the contract—the contracting authority, tender, awarded tender, etc.; (3) the procedure, composed of the steps taken until the end of the contract; and (4) the fulfilment, which includes actions that must be taken after the contract formalization.

The class `pproc:Contract` is the main class all contracts begin with (see Fig. 1). It contains the basic information about the contract and serves as an entry point to link to other classes. In order to define the object of the contract, PPROC can use two different (non- exclusive) approaches. The first way to define the object is to use `pproc:object` or `pc:mainObject`, properties that are especially appropriate for using the Common Procurement Vocabulary (CPV).[9] It is exclusively used in EU procurement and consists of a main vocabulary for defining the object of a contract without entering into great detail, and a supplementary vocabulary for adding further qualitative information. However, the object in public contracts is not different from the object in other business situations, and therefore vocabularies developed for business can be re-used. Consequently, we have established a second way, and to further define

[9] http://simap.europa.eu/codes-and-nomenclatures/codes-cpv/codes-cpv_en.htm.

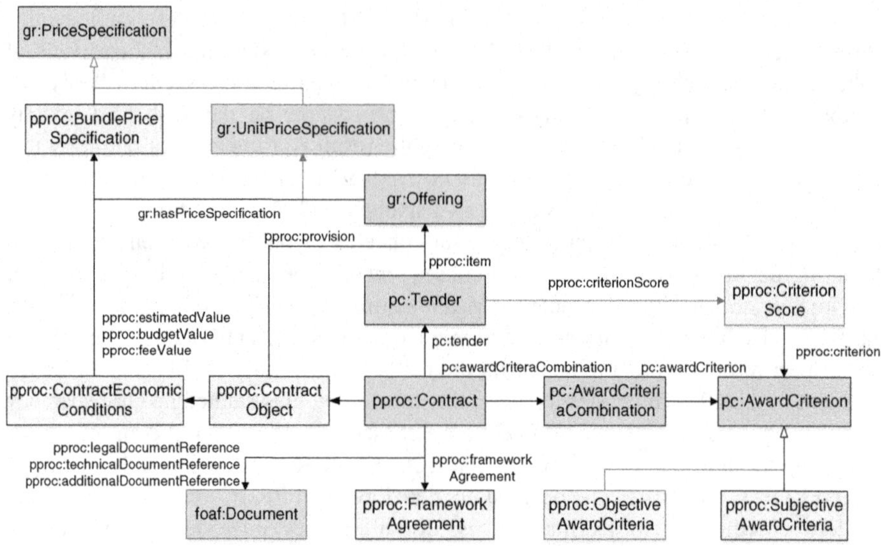

Fig. 1. Contract directly related classes

the object of a contract, we use GoodRelations [15], an ontology that makes it possible to describe products and services, prices and payment options in greater detail.

Apart from describing the contract and its objects, we also need to describe the parts involved in a public procurement procedure (see Fig. 2). In order to define them we use the Organization Ontology,[10] which includes the classes and properties needed to describe organizational structures and their hierarchy. The role that an organization plays in a given procedure or contract—contracting authority, delegating authority, the organization on whose behalf of a contract is being made, the contracting body, managing department and the specific supplier of a tender (tenderer)—is established by the property used to link it with the contract.

To describe the persons grouped together to perform a task of the procedure, we can use the `pproc:Committee` class. These committees are known as contract bodies and could have different functions in the procedure. We could state the members belonging to a concrete organization or committee by using membership properties such as `s:member` or `org:memberOf`. To further describe these organizations, committees and persons we point out properties belonging to other ontologies and vocabularies, such as Organization Ontology itself, Schema, Friend Of A Friend (FOAF)[11] or SKOS [16]. There are several contents where the location or a specific place should be known (e.g. the office of the contracting authority or a tenderer, the location where the goods should be left or the place of a meeting), and to define them we could use the `s:Place` class and properties of the Schema vocabulary.

[10] http://w3.org/TR/2014/REC-vocab-org-20140116/.

[11] http://www.foaf-project.org/.

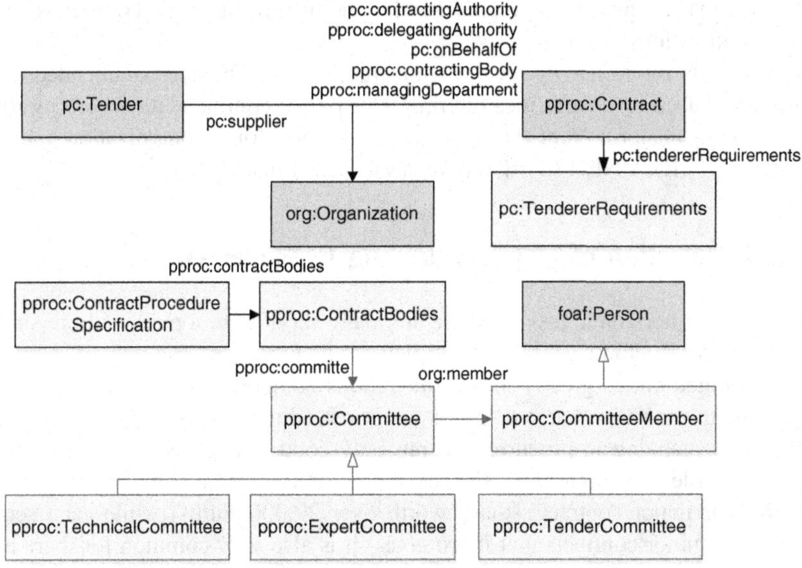

Fig. 2. Parties of the contract

Next, to describe proposals made by the suppliers, the class `pc:Tender` is re-used. PCO uses two properties to link tenders to their related contract: `pc:tender` and `pc:awardedTender`. We created subclasses to further define a `pc:Tender` (`pproc:AwardedTender`, `pproc:AcceptedTender`, `pproc:ExcludedTender` and `pproc:FormalizedTender`). Finally, tenderers are also defined through the Organization Ontology and linked using the `pc:supplier` property from a `pc:Tender`.

Another block of information is referred to the procedure. This includes the kind of procedure and all the information about it that could be useful to any party and the public, such as the tender requirements, briefing meetings or information about remedies. However, the information about the procedure is very important for the control of contracting and, therefore, the ontology also includes classes to describe other points, such as the people that participate in the procedure or possible resources and their result. It is also necessary to know if the type of procedure used is the one related to the contract, and the ontology has specific properties to do this, such as `pproc:assumptionProtectingProcedureType`.

Also, the term of the contract does not end with the formalization, which is the time when the contracting procedure is considered as finished. Contracts are often modified at a later time through specific procedures, which often change points such as the price or the term for completion. These modifications can be used to breach the principles of the contracting and, therefore, a fourth block is dedicated to this phase, which we call fulfilment. This contains classes that make it possible to represent the conditions and limits that possible modifications to the contract are subject to. Finally, clauses are also included that make it possible to represent what the final result of the contract is, if one or more modifications are made.

Regarding its future use by local administrations, PPROC is recommended as the ontology to be used by smart cities offering their public contract data according to the proposed technical norm from the Spanish Association for Standardization and Certification (AENOR), UNE 178301 on Open Data for Smart Cities.

4 The Integration of Data Regarding Procurement

Procurement is a horizontal task, as there are many services of a public administration that require contracts to be prepared to implement its functions. The way in which this task is distributed varies greatly in administrations composed of various departments and services. In the cases that we studied we observed that there is normally a central department specializing in procurement, but only contracts that exceed a determined figure are handled through this. For example, in Zaragoza City, the Council is responsible for major contracts (those worth over 20,000 Euros) while each service deals with the minor contracts that it promotes. It is also very common for there to be bodies that are linked to the administration but that act autonomously, in the form of foundations, state companies, etc. These entities manage their own contracts, regardless of their figures. The result is that there is little control over procurement, not only by the public but also by the managers and politicians responsible for this.

In the last two years, Zaragoza City Council has developed a project for the implementation of a workflow tool for the management of procurement files, which replaces the management applications used in recent years. This platform is unique for all services that handle contracts and for all contract types, meaning that only autonomous bodies are omitted from integration in this first phase. The decision taken by the parties responsible for this process was to use the PPROC ontology as a basis for the data structure of the new tool. This was also done by the Provincial Government of Huesca for the development of its contracting platform. In both cases it was considered that the use of the ontology as a starting point for the design of the data structure would enable the data organization to be independent of any temporal or secondary aspect, and instead would be related to the entities that comprise the "institution" and the relationships between them.

The data integration starts discovering the relevant public procurement data aimed to transparency and, as explained in Sect. 3, capturing its model as an ontology. Afterwards comes the matching of the data from different sources, mapping the classes and properties of the ontology with the entities of the relational databases that were being used for the management of contracts and for the publication of announcements in the buyer profile. This step is the most expensive, as requires knowledge of both the original database and ontology schemas. The W3C has a language recommendation that express customized mappings from relational databases to RDF called R2RML[12] which we used in both our use cases. Finally, the data is transformed using the

[12] http://www.w3.org/TR/r2rml/.

generated map and an existing R2RML implementation that automatically connects to the given relational database and retrieves the information as RDF.

The object of another integration task was the announcements published on the PSCP. All contracts from the state public sector already had to be necessarily published on this online platform, and the Single Market Guarantee Act 20/2013 of 9th December broadened its scope to include contracts from all Spanish public administrations, that is, autonomous and local administrations are now also included. As we already mentioned, the PSCP uses its own XML dialect, named CODICE, to enable administrations to publish data on their website. We therefore prepared a mapping between CODICE and the PPROC ontology, the purpose of which is to serve as a basis for the translation of XML messages into RDF triples.[13]

Additionally, we carry out monitoring of the classes used by each entity, with the document "PPROC usage", which describes the classes and properties of the ontology that are used by each authority.[14] According to this monitoring, of the three cases studied 58 classes or properties (28 %) of the ontology are used. One of the reason is that contracting authorities still publish an important part of the information in non-structured formats (mainly PDF documents). Moreover, there are other information that they do not publish nowadays. But, the final goal of transparency regulations is to improve transparency through the publication of all the information regarding public contracts. And, from the open data perspective, the aim is to publish all this information using linked RDF. In consequence the PPROC domain covers all the data that can be published by a contracting authority. In next years, we hope that the progressive implementation of electronic processing in public procurement increases the ratio of structured data which could be directly published using the ontology.

Also, as a result of this monitoring, we have been able to confirm that the information available in the different administrations varies greatly, given that of these 58 elements only 11 are used by the three administrations, 32 are used by two and 15 by just one. Obviously, this represents a major obstacle when integrating data for the realization of queries and for their analysis. We therefore consider that this monitoring could help to improve this situation, as its purpose is that it will be used as a source of guidance for user administrations regarding entities to be published on their profiles—thereby creating a kind of core vocabulary based on the practices of administrations—and also used as a source of information for the public regarding information points and the content of each of them. And, in short, to encourage re-use by creating a common information archive regarding public contracting.

5 The Publication of Data Regarding Procurement

Once the PPROC was prepared, the following task was the publication in RDF of the buyer profiles of Zaragoza City Council and of the Provincial Government of Huesca. When it comes to the release of structured data already published on the website (as

[13] http://dx.doi.org/10.6084/m9.figshare.1327549.

[14] http://contsem.unizar.es/def/sector-publico/usage.html.

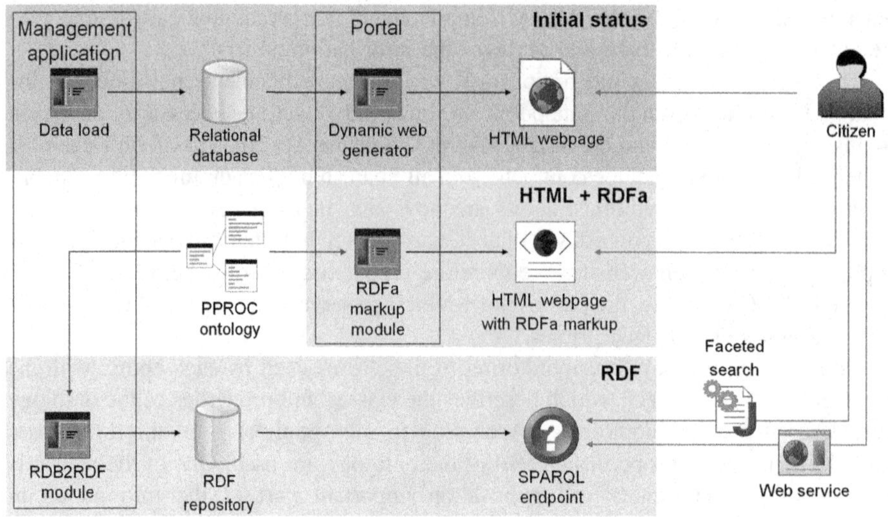

Fig. 3. Options for the publication of the contracting party profile

buyer profiles), a decision has to be made between two non-exclusive alternatives (see Fig. 3). The first is to publish an endpoint that enables users to perform queries directly to the data graph, using SPARQL query language. The second is to semantically label the content of the web pages, using the RDFa markup,[15] which provides a specification to express structured data directly in any markup language (e.g. HTML). Both administrations chose the first option. We installed the SPARQL endpoints[16] into the servers of the administrations, using a Virtuoso Universal Server.[17]

As we have already mentioned, the contracts of the PSCP have also been published, for which we developed software that generates RDF triples based on the CODICE format using the R2RML specification. This information has been made publicly available in a SPARQL endpoint[18] that, at the time of the drafting of this paper, contains approximately 12 million RDF triples, including information about 199,611 contracts.

One of the benefits of the integration task is that multiple contracting authorities can publish its own set of contracts through a SPARQL endpoint. As all these data follows PPROC model, it is possible to build agents that retrieve and aggregate this information. As an example, we have developed a web service that can recover and add information from various SPARQL endpoints, which are indicated in a file that contains the URL of each of them. The web service is implemented using REST architecture and has two different calls, which are made using JSON messages. The first call

[15] http://www.w3.org/TR/rdfa-syntax/.

[16] http://www.zaragoza.es/ciudad/risp/sparql.html and http://www.dphuesca.es/sparql.

[17] http://semanticweb.org/wiki/Virtuoso.

[18] http://pproc.unizar.es:8890/sparql/.

(facetQuery) uses the set of facet-value pairs chosen by the user as input, returning a list of contracts (identifiers and some basic information) that match these facet-value pairs. The second call (contractQuery) uses the contract identifier provided by the first call as input, and returns all the information about the contract in a JSON-LD format. Based on this service we have published a faceted search web that is also kept active in a public URL, available to whoever wished to use it.[19]

The set of facets was defined by the experts in procurement and some of them are representative of the difficulty entailed in obtaining valid results when managing information from different sources and where different policies have been followed for data entry and management. For example, the first facet is the object of the contract, that is, the provision (product or service) that is contracted. As we have said, there is a specific code (the CPV), but often this field is not completed and other times it is completed with a very low disaggregate level. To do this, we also implemented a search for words describing the object. Although in the ontology there is a specific field for the textual description of the object, this search is performed not only in this field but also in the title and in the description of the contract, as very often these fields are the only places where the object is specified.

The second facet refers to the economic aspects, where it is necessary to consider that there are several sums associated with just one contract. One is the estimated value, which is included in the announcement prior to the tendering (provided that this is published, as it is optional). In all cases there is a tender budget, which is the sum for which the tender is published, a sum for which the contract is awarded and a final sum that may be the same or different from this depending on whether there have been changes made or not. The final amount is also higher in contracts that accept possible extensions. The third facet is the status of the procedure, which is determined by searching to ascertain if certain steps have been performed, such as the approval of the case, the publication of the tender announcement and the awarding or formalization of the contract. The fourth and fifth facets refer to the parties of the contract, as these are the contracting authority and the provider. Finally, the sixth facet comprises the dates of some steps and milestones and the seventh is the type of procedure.

Based on these tools, our group has begun to analyze some aspects of the public procurement in Spain. One of these aspects refers to the companies that are contracted by administrations. For example, Fig. 4 shows the main Zaragoza City Council suppliers and the number of contracts that were awarded from 2008 to 2014. In this regard, one of the next planned actions is to integrate this information with that from databases that contain information about the companies, in order to inter-relate the companies that belong to the same groups. In this first steps, we do not use semantic web tools such as reasoning, agents or logic, but, as a basis for future works, we are now identifying some questions about public contracts which can be studied using these tools. Also, our group collaborates with other groups and re-users interested in the exploitation of the linked open data about publics contracts.

[19] http://contsem.unizar.es/docs/facetedsearch/.

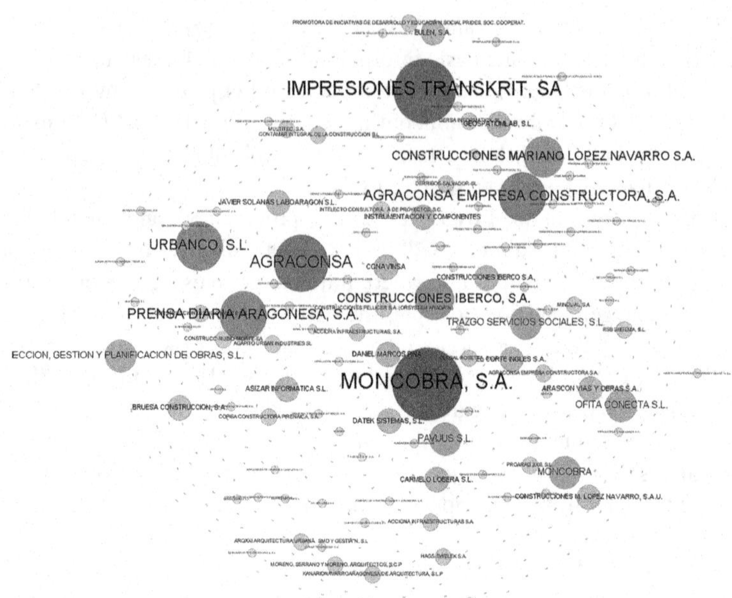

Fig. 4. Zaragoza City Council suppliers according to the number of contracts awarded (2008–2014)

6 Conclusion

The Semantic Web provides the opportunity to agree upon models that will represent the various realities and "institutions". In this way, the data structures used for various functions within the same system and between different information systems can be progressively harmonized. In addition, it is possible that the distinction between the information that administrations use to perform their work and the information that it prepares (currently) to make it available to the public will disappear, or at least lessen significantly. Both circumstances are conducive to the progressive implementation in public administrations of the principles of unique data and shared data.

In the experience that we have described, we have seen how the work initially carried out to facilitate public access to information can have a direct influence on a major improvement to the information system as a whole and, therefore, to the business intelligence within the organization itself. This represents one more piece of evidence that the design and development of information systems must be done in such a way that one sole set of data is used for different purposes, both current and future.

These purposes include that of facilitating citizens' access to information. From a legal perspective, this access, which is a fundamental right, should be regulated as a single unit and, therefore, regardless of the use that is to be made of the information. In order for the legislation that regulates administrations to be consistent with all these objectives, it is necessary to have new laws based on a unique and comprehensive concept of public information. Thus, based on this concept, these new laws will regulate all aspects related to the obtaining, management and exploitation of public information. If this is done, not only could the right to free access to public information be greatly strengthened, but so could the efficiency and quality of the information systems of administrations as a whole.

Finally, we should state that from the point of view of interaction between information technology and law, that the application of the Semantic Web to public information could lead to numerous scenarios—as has been shown in this article—in which the representations of legal knowledge will be truly useful in practical terms. This fact would help to reduce the lack of trust that in some (or many) cases legal experts have regarding the applications of artificial intelligence to their field of knowledge.

Acknowledgements. The authors would like to thank Miguel Angel Bernal and Francisco Serón (co-authors of the PPROC ontology), and Oscar Corcho, Carlos Bobed and Carlos Becana (contributors). Also to those responsible for procurement and the buyer's profile and the technicians of the participating administrations in the project: the Zaragoza City Council (Maria Jesús Fernandez, Ana Budría, Laura Fernando, Victor Morlán and Rubén Notivol), the Provincial Government of Huesca (Cristina de la Hera, Montserrat Rodríguez and Javier Casado) and the Regional Government of Aragón (Ricardo Cantabrana, José María Subero and Eva Sanz).

References

1. Ackerman, J.M., Sandoval-Ballesteros, I.E.: The global explosion of freedom of information laws. Adm. Law Rev. **58**(1), 85–130 (2006)
2. Muñoz Soro, J.F., Bermejo Latre, J.L.: The redefinition of the objetive scope of transparency and the right of access to public sector information. In: Valero Torrijos, J., Fernandez Salmeron, M. (eds.) Legal Regime of Transparency in the Public Sector, pp. 189–239. Aranzadi, Cizur Menor (2014)
3. Palmirani, M., Martoni, M., Girardi, D.: Open government data beyond transparency. In: Andrea, K., Francesconi, E. (eds.) EGOVIS 2014. LNCS, vol. 8650, pp. 275–291. Springer, Heidelberg (2014)
4. Miroslav, M., Miloš, M., Velimir, Š., Božo, D., Đorđe, L.: Semantic technologies on the mission: preventing corruption in public procurement. Comput. Ind. **65**(5), 878–890 (2014)
5. Casellas, N.: Legal Ontology Engineering. Springer, Dordrecht (2011)
6. Agnoloni, T., Fernández Barrera, M., Sagri, M.T., Tiscorni, D., Venturi, G.: When a framenet-style knowledge description meets an ontological characterization of fundamental legal concepts. In: Casanovas, P., Pagallo, U., Sartor, G., Ajani, G. (eds.) AICOL-II/JURIX 2009. LNCS, vol. 6237, pp. 93–112. Springer, Heidelberg (2010)
7. MacCormick, N.: Norms. Institutions, and Institutional Facts, Law and Philosophy **17**, 301–345 (1998)
8. Boer, A.: Legal Theory, Sources of Law and the Semantic Web. IOS Press, Amsterdam (2009)
9. Fernandez-Barrera, M., Sartor, G.: The legal theory perspective: doctrinal, conceptual systems vs. computational ontologies. In: Sartor, G., Casanovas, P., Biasiotti M.A., Fernandez-Barrera M. (eds.) Approaches to Legal Ontologies, pp. 15–47. Springer, Dordrecht (2011)

10. Ferraris, M.: Social ontology and documentality. In: Sartor, G., Casanovas, P., Biasiotti, M. A., Fernandez-Barrera, M. (eds.) Approaches to Legal Ontologies, pp. 83–97. Springer, Dordrecht (2011)
11. Alvarez-Rodríguez, J.M., Labra, J.E., Ordoñez de Pablos, P.: New Trends on e-Procurement Applying Semantic Technologies. Current Status and Future Challenges. Comput. Ind. **65**, 800–820 (2014)
12. Distinto, I., d'Aquin, M., Motta, E.: LOTED2: An Ontology of European Public Procurement Notices (2012). http://www.semantic-web-journal.net/content/loted2-ontology-european-public-procurement-notices-1
13. Alvarez-Rodríguez, J.M., Labra, J.E., Cifuentes, F., Alor-Hernandez, G., Sánchez, C., Luna, J.A.G.: Towards a pan-European e-procurement platform to aggregate, publish and search public procurement notices powered by linked open data: the MOLDEAS approach. Int. J. Software Eng. Knowl. Eng. **22**(03), 365–383 (2012)
14. Nečaský, M., Klímek, J., Mynarz, J., Knap, T., Svátek, V., Stárka, J.: Linked data support for filing public contracts. Comput. Ind. **65**(5), 862–877 (2014)
15. Hepp, M.: GoodRelations: an ontology for describing products and services offers on the web. In: Gangemi, A., Euzenat, J. (eds.) EKAW 2008. LNCS (LNAI), vol. 5268, pp. 329–346. Springer, Heidelberg (2008)
16. Miles, A., Matthews, B., Wilson, M., Brickley, D.: SKOS Core: simple knowledge organisation for the web. In: International Conference on Dublin Core and Metadata Applications, pp. 3–10 (2005)

The Ontology-Based Approach of the Publications Office of the EU for Document Accessibility and Open Data Services

Enrico Francesconi[1(✉)], Marc W. Küster[1], Patrick Gratz[2], and Sebastian Thelen[2]

[1] Publications Office of the EU, Luxembourg City, Luxembourg
enrico.francesconi@publications.europa.eu
[2] Infeurope S.A., Luxembourg City, Luxembourg

Abstract. The Publications Office of the European Union is responsible to make available and disseminate the official publications and bibliographic resources produced by the institutions of the European Union. The central component of its information system is the CELLAR repository, providing semantic indexing, advanced search and data retrieval for multilingual resources. This paper gives an overview of the semantic modeling approach for CELLAR, based on semantic web technologies. Moreover, a proposal for a possible evolution aiming to improve the modularity and facilitating the general management of the model is shown.

Keywords: Multilingual documents · Semantic indexing · Knowledge modeling

1 Introduction

The dissemination of the official documents as well as other bibliographic resources produced by the European Union institutions is the main mandate of the Publications Office of the European Union, in its role of inter-institutional body of the European Commission in charge to inform about government procedures and legal framework.

As for official publications[1], this right is guaranteed by the availability of such resources in the 24 official languages spoken in the 28 member states of the European Union, while other publications (like tendering documents, general publications and information on EU-funded research projects) are mainly available in the 3 fundamental languages (English, French and German). With the authentic and legally binding publication of the electronic edition of the Official

[1] Treaties, International agreements, Legislation, Complementary legislation, Preparatory acts, Case-law, National implementing measures, References to national case-law concerning EU law, Parliamentary questions, Consolidated legislation, Other documents published in the Official Journal C series, EFTA documents.

© Springer International Publishing Switzerland 2015
A. Kő and E. Francesconi (Eds.): EGOVIS 2015, LNCS 9265, pp. 29–39, 2015.
DOI: 10.1007/978-3-319-22389-6_3

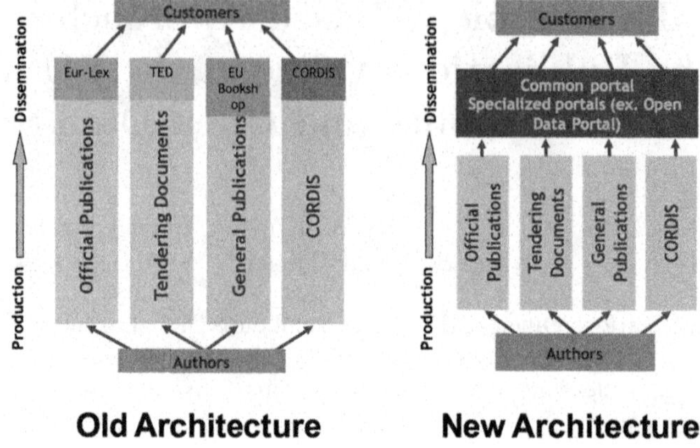

Fig. 1. The Publications Office archival and dissemination transformation programme

Journal (e-OJ) from 1 July 2013, the on-line accessibility of legal resources has become an essential requirement, guaranteed by the Eur-lex service[2].

In the last couple of years most efforts of the Publications Office (OP) were focusing on a project aiming to transform the archival and dissemination architecture, based on different systems, into a federative architecture based on a common archival service, providing also a common interface for disseminating materials to the users (Fig. 1). The central component of this architecture is CELLAR, a content and metadata repository containing documents coming from the production and postproduction services (including content validation and metadata production). They are available for long term preservation, open data, indexing, as well as advanced search and retrieval services. CELLAR resources are semantically described by an ontology, which represents the Common Metadata Model (CDM) of the OP resources. This paper is focused on the description of this ontology as well as on possible developments. It is organized as follows: in Sect. 2 the architecture of the CELLAR platform is described; in Sect. 3 the CELLAR multilingual semantic approach, represented by CDM, is presented; in Sect. 4 a possible evolution of CDM is illustrated and in Sect. 5 the advantages of the proposed evolution are discussed. Finally in Sect. 6 some conclusions are reported.

2 The CELLAR Architecture

CELLAR represents the central hub of the whole information system of the OP. It is based on a Fedora digital objects repository[3], organized in two logical units including Oracle database technologies: content is stored in the CELLAR Common Content Repository (CCR) currently[4] including about 152 million documents in 24 languages; metadata in as many languages are stored in the CELLAR Common

[2] http://eur-lex.europa.eu.

[3] http://www.fedora-commons.org.

[4] March 2015.

Metadata Repository (CMR) described by semantic web technologies, resulting in about 1100 million triples, stored in an RDF triple store. Currently CELLAR receives about 5 million requests per day, providing information results for the EUR-Lex service and for the query service (SPARQL endpoint) recently exposed in order to complement linked open data services to potential consumers. Other services and types of resources, like TED for tendering documents, EU Bookshop for general publications, CORDIS for information on EU-funded research projects will be served by CELLAR in the near future (Fig. 2). Concerning disaster recovery and emergency management a proper data replication service for the production database has been put in place as shown in Fig. 2.

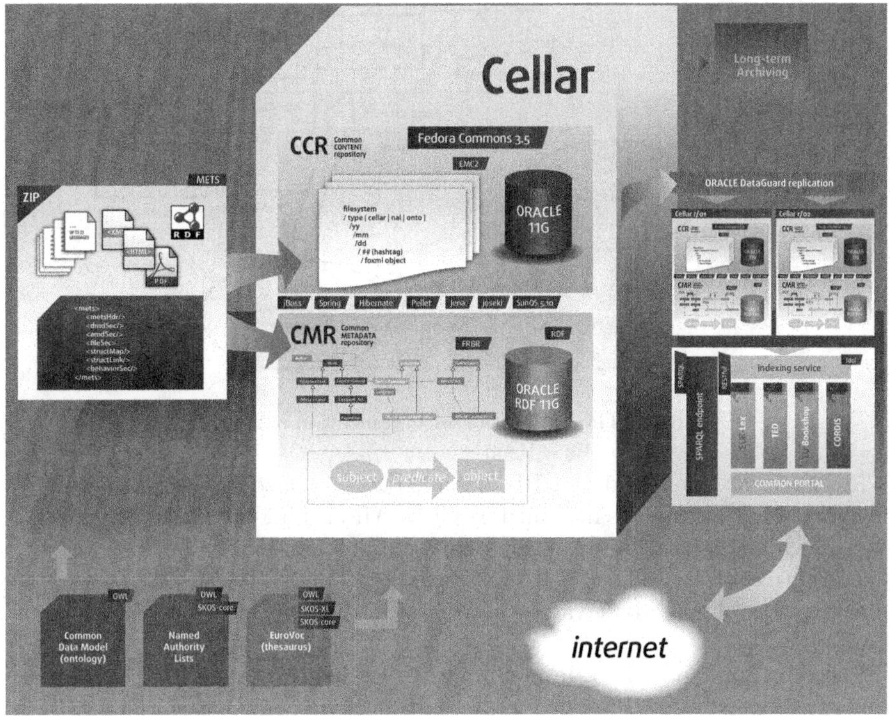

Fig. 2. The CELLAR architecture and services (courtesy F. Sanmartin.)

Based on CDM, the Common Metadata Repository (CMR) represents the essential asset to guarantee multilingual semantic access services to the CELLAR contents. The following section depicts how the CDM allows to describe, from a semantic point of view, all the OP resources.

3 Common Metadata Model (CDM)

The current CDM is an ontology based on the FRBR[5] model [1], described by RDF(S)/OWL technologies, able to represent the relationships between the

[5] Functional Requirements for Bibliographic Records.

resource types managed by the OP and their views according to the FRBR model in terms of Work, Expression, Manifestation and Item. In the current CDM organization, the FRBR hierarchy represents a sort of pivot knowledge organization system, according to which resource types (general publications, legal resources, legislation, case law, etc.) and FRBR views (ex: general publication expression, case law expression, official journal manifestation, etc.) are organized through sub-class relationships (Fig. 3).

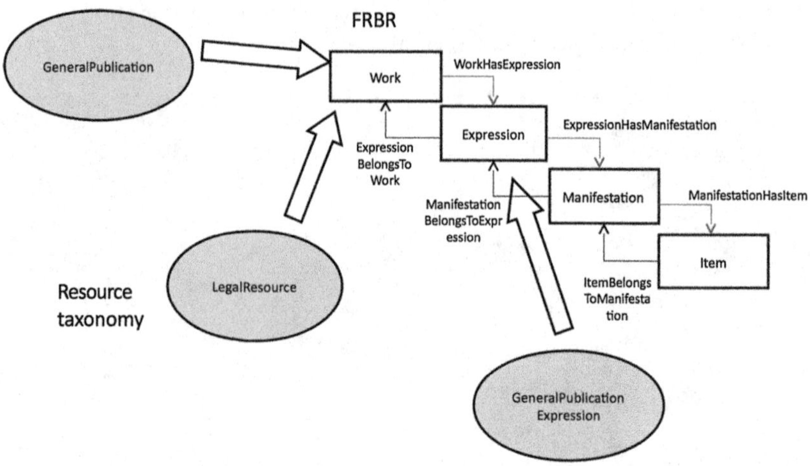

Fig. 3. The current CDM organization system

Resources are identified by URIs classified according to the FRBR hierarchy, thus organizing the objects managed by CELLAR at different FRBR abstraction levels. Such URIs have for example http://publications.europa.eu/resource/oj/ as namespace of the official journal resources, followed by an ID created as concatenation of metadata values at each FRBR level (see Table 1 for some examples).

Based on commonly known best practices for linked data, CELLAR enables clients to retrieve various resource representations via content negotiation. Each resource that represents an entity of the FRBR hierarchy can be considered a non-information resource, redirecting clients to one of its specific representations based on parameters (i.e., Accept header, Accept-Language, etc.) passed in the request.

Of all existing representations, the so called tree notice of a FRBR hierarchy is the representation that best describes the bibliographic record from a "web of data" point of view, since it provides the entire set of metadata at each level of the FRBR hierarchy in a single RDF serialization. In CELLAR, tree notice URIs follow the pattern `cellar:[hash-value]/rdf/tree/full`.[6]

[6] Where `cellar:` represents the CELLAR namespace http://publications.europa.eu/resource/cellar/.

Table 1. URIs at different FRBR levels

Resource FRBR type	Resource ID
Work (Regular OJ publication n. 26 of 2015)	JOL_2015_026_R_0001
Expression (english variation)	JOL_2015_026_R_0001.ENG
Manifestation (PDF/A-1a format)	JOL_2015_026_R_0001.FRA.pdfa1a
Item	JOL_2015_026_R_0001.FRA.pdfa1a. l_02620150131fr00010002.pdf

This CDM version is currently in production providing detailed views, in particular regarding language versions and formats, of the OP resources, for both documents and metadata search and retrieval services, as well as for the OP common portal.

In the context of a recent activity a review of the current CDM in order to reduce complexity of the query framework was performed. During this review the following shortcomings of the current model have been revealed:

1. the mixture in the same taxonomy of resource types and FRBR classes
2. the need to follow complex paths to reach different FRBR views of the same resource type (see General Publication type: GeneralPublication → Work → Expression → GeneralPublicationExpression).

These issues result in certain limitations of the framework. For instance that, given a resource type, the access to the different levels of the FRBR model is not direct. Moreover, it is necessary to know the type of a resource at query level in order to retrieve metadata at each level of the FRBR model, while it would be more simple that, given a resource, there is a common query to access metadata at different FRBR levels, irrespective of the resource type.

In the next sections an overview of the current discussion about a possible CDM evolvement is presented.

4 Proposal for CDM Evolvement

A proposal for possible evolvement of the current CDM approach aims firstly to keep a distinction between the taxonomy of the resources and the FRBR model.

A *Resource* in the ISBD[7] sense is defined as "*an entity, tangible or intangible, that comprises intellectual and/or artistic content and is conceived, produced and/or issued as a unit, forming the basis of a single bibliographic description*". Therefore, resources are actually not equivalent to, or sub-class of, any individual FRBR classes [2]. As pointed out in [3] each FRBR classes *reflects* one aspect of a resource, seen as a bibliographic entity at different levels of abstraction.

A *Resource* (in the ISBD sense) has the same intention as the combined attributes of the FRBR model [3], therefore it can be considered as the disjoint

[7] International Standard Bibliographic Description.

union of the Work, Expression, Manifestation and Item levels in FRBR model, as expressed by (1).

$$Resource = Work + Expression + Manifestation + Item \quad (1)$$

The relationship between the two domains (resource taxonomy and FRBR model) is therefore of *part-of/aspect*. In this context, every FRBR level is an *aspect* of a current resource and can be considered as collector of the metadata able to describe a resource at that level.

Therefore, a resource and its FRBR model can be viewed as aspects of the same reality in two perspectives [2]:

1. The "web of data" perspective
2. The "bibliographic data" perspective

A resource identified by a specific URI represents an entity of the "web of data". The resources published by the OP are basically bibliographic entities. Therefore, they can be described according to the FRBR model. Works, Expressions, Manifestations and Items of the FRBR model are also type of entities of the web of data, but they can also be viewed as a specific aspects of a bibliographic resource, therefore viewed in the "bibliographic data" perspective.

This distinction provides the main motivation for improving CDM with the goal to simplify the query framework, thus improving the accessibility of the resources. To achieve this goal, the following actions have been undertaken:

1. Introduction of a logical separation between the taxonomy of the OP resources and the FRBR model, therefore avoiding any subClass relations between them;
2. Introduction of cdm:has[FrbrClass]Aspect[8] relations between a classes of the OP resource taxonomy and their aspects as FRBR classes (e.g.: cdm:hasWorkAspect, cdm:hasExpressionAspect, etc.);
3. Introduction of a rdfs:subPropertyOf relation between cdm:has[ResourceTypeFrbrClass]Aspect at different levels of the taxonomies.

In Fig. 4 a sketch of the OP resource taxonomy (limited, for simplicity, to the root and one subclass) and its relationships with the FRBR model at each taxonomy level is represented. In particular the generic class of OPBibliographicResource is linked with cdm:hasWorkAspect, cdm:hasExpressionAspect, cdm:hasManifestationAspect, cdm:hasItemAspect to the corresponding classes of the FRBR model. Sub classes in the resource taxonomy, like SourceOfLaw, are linked to the corresponding classes of the FRBR model with similar specific properties (as cdm:hasSourceOfLawWorkAspect, cdm:hasSourceOfLawExpressionAspect, etc.). Such "aspect" properties are organized in pure taxonomic relationships (subPropertyOf) for each level of the FRBR model (cdm:hasSourceOfLawWorkAspect is a sub property of cdm:hasWorkAspect, and so on).

---

[8] where cdm: is the CDM namespace and [FrbrClass] is one of Work, Expression, Manifestation or Item classes.

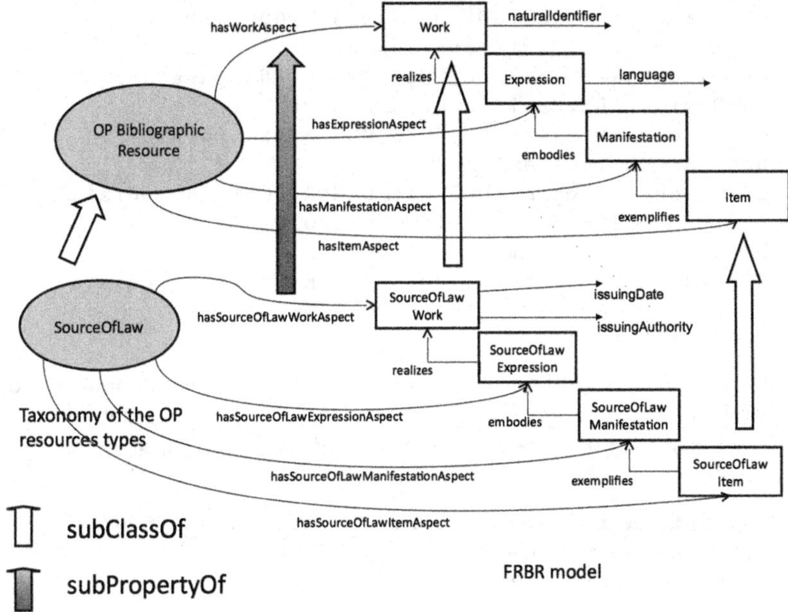

Fig. 4. A proposal for CDM organization system development

The FRBR classes are collectors of resource metadata at their specific taxonomy level: for example (see Fig. 4) at Work aspect level, a resource will have for example cdm:naturalIdentifier as generic metadata, described by object or datatype properties, shared by all the OP bibliographic resources. Similarly at SourceOfLawWork aspect level, specific metadata shared by all the sources of law, are given, as for example cdm:issuingDate and cdm:issuingAuthority of a legal measure. The same holds for the other FRBR classes at each level of the OP resource taxonomy.

In this CDM model, CELLAR tree notice URIs are the identifiers of the resource taxonomy entities linked with cdm:has[ResourceTypeFrbrClass]Aspect relation to the FRBR classes, since they provide the entire set of FRBR metadata in a single RDF serialization (an excerpt of it for a SourceOfLaw is the following[9]):

```
<rdf:Description rdf:about=
"cellar:58da3a99-a91d-11e4-8e01-01aa75ed71a1/rdf/tree/full">
 <rdf:type rdf:resource="cdm:SourceOfLaw"/>
 <cdm:hasSourceOfLawWorkAspect
     rdf:resource="ojns:JOL_2015_026_R_0001"/>
 <cdm:hasSourceOfLawExpressionAspect
     rdf:resource="ojns:JOL_2015_026_R_0001.ENG"/>
 <cdm:hasSourceOfLawExpressionAspect
```

[9] ojns: is the namespace http://publications.europa.eu/resource/oj/.

```
      rdf:resource="ojns:JOL_2015_026_R_0001.FRA"/>
 <cdm:hasSourceOfLawManifestationAspect
      rdf:resource="ojns:JOL_2015_026_R.ENG.pdfa1a"/>
 <cdm:hasSourceOfLawManifestationAspect
      rdf:resource="ojns:JOL_2015_026_R.FRA.pdfa1a"/>
 <cdm:hasSourceOfLawItemAspect
      rdf:resource="ojns:JOL_2015_026_R_0001.ENG.pdfa1a.
                 1_02620150131en00010002.pdf"/>
 <cdm:hasSourceOfLawItemAspect
      rdf:resource="ojns:JOL_2015_026_R_0001.FRA.pdfa1a.
                 1_02620150131fr00010002.pdf"/>
</rdf:Description>
```

Moreover, the SourceOfLaw in the previous example has metadata (properties) related to its corresponding FRBR aspects, as well as the metadata of the FRBR aspects of its superclasses. An excerpt of its metadata at its Work level is the following:

```
<rdf:Description rdf:about="ojns:JOL_2015_026_R_0001">
 <rdf:type rdf:resource="cdm:SourceOfLawWork"/>
 <cdm:naturalIdentifier>
    L 26/1
 </cdm:naturalIdentifier>
 <cdm:issuingDate rdf:datatype="&xsd;dateTime">
    2015-01-26T00:00:00
 </cdm:issuingDate>
 <cdm:issuingAuthority>
    Council of the European Union
 </cdm:issuingAuthority>
</rdf:Description>
```

The described approach has been implemented as proof of concepts in RDF(S)/ OWL, resulting in the OWL-DL profile, thus available for deriving inferences by using DL reasoners like Pellet[10] or HermiT[11].

5 Benefits of the Approach

The proposed CDM modeling approach has several advantages with respect to the existing one.

First of all it allows a direct constant access to the FRBR levels through the properties cdm:has[ResourceTypeFrbrClass]Aspect, while in the existing CDM the FRBR levels have to be navigated until reaching the expected one. In the existing CDM in fact there is no resource in the metadata that identifies the actual bibliographic entity (SourceOfLaw), therefore the resource can be either a work, expression, manifestation or item. Consequently a complex property path is necessary to navigate to the suitable FRBR entity and, in order to access to the Expression of a SourceOfLaw, for example, the following query is needed:

[10] http://clarkparsia.com/pellet/.

[11] http://hermit-reasoner.com.

```
SELECT ?uri  WHERE
{
   ?resource cdm:item_belongs_to_manifestation?/
   cdm:manifestation_manifests_expression?/
   cdm:expression_belongs_to_work?/
   ^cdm:expression_belongs_to_work ?uri
}
```

On the contrary, in the new model the same result can be obtained by the following, more simple query:

```
SELECT ?uri WHERE
{
   ?resource rdf:type cdm:SourceOfLaw .
   ?resource cdm:hasSourceOfLawExpressionAspect ?uri
}
```

A similar query can be created to access all the FRBR aspects of an OP resource.

Another important advantage of this architecture is that the queries for retrieving metadata of a resource are independent of its resource type. In fact, the inheritance mechanism on properties allows us to express queries at the top level of the hierarchy, independently of the resource type, while in the existing model the resource type is to be known to retrieve its metadata, having as many queries as resource types.

For example, in the existing model the following query can be run for accessing metadata at the level of Work of a SourceOfLaw:

```
SELECT * WHERE
{
   <RESOURCE_URI> cdm:item_belongs_to_manifestation ?/
   cdm:manifestation_manifests_expression ?/
   cdm:expression_belongs_to_work? ?uri .
   ?uri ?p ?o
}
```

This query retrieves all metadata at work level, regardless of the starting point in the FRBR hierarchy.

On the other hand in the new model given the SourceOfLaw URI considered in Sect. 4, the following query will retrieve the URI of its Work aspect:

```
SELECT DISTINCT ?uri WHERE
{
   cellar:58da3a99-a91d-11e4-8e01-01aa75ed71a1/rdf/tree/full
   cdm:hasWorkAspect  ?uri
}
```

Note that this query does not contain any reference to the OP resource type, therefore it is valid for every type of resources and the query framework of the system becomes more simple. Therefore, given a URI of a resource represented by its tree notice, the problem of accessing its metadata at different levels of the

FRBR hierarchy is a matter of accessing FRBR levels of abstraction at the top of the resource taxonomy.

Similarly, a query in the existing model able to retrieve the English expression of a resource is the following

```
SELECT ?uri WHERE
{
   ?resource cdm: item_belongs_to_manifestation ?/
   cdm: manifestation_manifests_expression ?/
   cdm: expression_belongs_to_work?/
   ^cdm:expression_belongs_to_work ?uri.
   ?uri cdm:language"en"^^xsd:string.
}
```

This query retrieves the uri of the English expression, regardless of the starting point in the FRBR hierarchy.

On the other hand in the new model the same result can be obtained by accessing the Expression aspect of the given resource, in particular its English expression, as follows:

```
SELECT DISTINCT ?uri WHERE
{
   cellar:58da3a99-a91d-11e4-8e01-01aa75ed71a1/rdf/tree/full
   cdm:hasExpressionAspect ?uri .
   ?uri cdm:language"en"^^xsd:string
}
```

Also in this case no reference to OP resource type is contained in the query.

An additional advantage of this modeling approach is the possibility to obtain a simplified management of the resource metadata, since they are organized in terms of properties of the FRBR classes, distributed at different levels of the resource taxonomy. This allows us, for example, to query the CDM model asking for all the Work metadata (i.e. owl:DatatypeProperties) of a generic SourceOfLaw, as follows:

```
SELECT DISTINCT ?property WHERE
{
   ?property rdf:type owl:DatatypeProperty .
   ?property rdfs:domain ?class .
   cdm:SourceOfLawWork rdfs:subClassOf* ?class
}
```

or to query the CDM model just selecting the specific metadata at SourceOfLaw-Work level:

```
SELECT DISTINCT ?property WHERE
{
   ?property rdf:type owl:DatatypeProperty .
   ?property rdfs:domain cdm:SourceOfLawWork
}
```

6 Conclusions

CELLAR represents the central information system of the OP, providing storage as well as advanced semantic indexing and access facilities to all the dissemination portals. The CDM semantic approach for the CELLAR resources is able to greatly improve accessibility of the OP multilingual documents. The proposed revision of the current CDM architecture, in particular, has the benefit of providing modularity and flexibility to the CDM approach, thus facilitating the management and extension of such knowledge organization system, as well as to simplify the query framework.

References

1. Study group on IFLA. Functional requirements for bibliographic records. Technical report, International Federation of Library Associations and Institutions (1998). http://www.ifla.org/VII/s13/frbr/frbr.pdf
2. Bianchini, C., Willer, M.: ISBD resource and its description in the context of the semantic web. Cataloging Classif. Q. **52**, 869–887 (2014)
3. Dunsire, G.: Resource and work, expression, manifestation, item. Amended October 6, 2013, following comments by Patrick Le Boeuf and discussion at IFLA 2013, July 28 2013

Engineering Semantic Web Services for Government Business Processes Automation

Jean Vincent Fonou-Dombeu[1](✉) and Magda Huisman[2]

[1] Department of Software Studies, Vaal University of Technology, Private Bag X021, Andries Potgieter Blvd, Vanderbijlpark 1900, South Africa
fonoudombeu@gmail.com

[2] School of Computer, Statistical and Mathematical Sciences, North-West University, Private Bag X6001, Potchefstroom 2520, South Africa
Magda.Huisman@nwu.ac.za

Abstract. Web Services (WS) technology does not allow automatic discovery and execution of services in the current distributed and complex business environments. Semantic Web Services (SWS) overcome this limitation by adding semantic descriptions to WS, enabling automatic discovery, selection, composition and execution of services for intelligent interoperable machine-to-machine interactions over the World Wide Web (WWW). These capabilities of SWS are useful in distributed environments such as that of e-government. On the other hand, existing SWS solutions assume the existence of dedicated service providers of WS to be semantically described. However, government operations and processes may require a certain amount of prior re-engineering (conceptualization, design, modeling, specification, etc.). This study proposed an infrastructure for Semantic Web Services-enabled e-government that integrates Business Process Modelling (BPM) and Semantic Annotation into existing SWS solutions as tools for the modeling and engineering of SWS for non-automated government operations and processes. The proposed infrastructure leverages SWS technology in e-government while enabling continuous re-engineering and automation of government processes. The study presents an example of the application of the proposed infrastructure with emphasis on the modeling and semantic annotation of business processes for SWS design.

Keywords: E-government · Web service · Semantic web service · Business process modeling · Semantic annotation

1 Introduction

E-government is not only about implementing technologies; it also entails re-engineering and automating government processes [1]. The re-engineering consists of analysing, reorganizing, conceptualizing and redesigning government processes in a way that is easily understood by public authorities and civil servants and can be automated for online services delivery to citizens and

© Springer International Publishing Switzerland 2015
A. Kő and E. Francesconi (Eds.): EGOVIS 2015, LNCS 9265, pp. 40–54, 2015.
DOI: 10.1007/978-3-319-22389-6_4

businesses. Business Process Modeling (BPM) is a commonly used method for re-engineering government processes [1–3]. It is the task of designing, modeling and optimizing government processes in such a way that they can be understood, analysed and improved [4]. BPM uses various formalisms including Business Process Modeling Notation (BPMN), Event-Driven Process Chains (EPCs), etc. to represent the business processes of an organization. The resulting process models must be further converted into software artefacts to enable the automation and ICT-based execution of the business processes. In the case of governments the resulting process models must be converted into electronic services (e-services) for online delivery of related government processes. Web Services (WS) technology is commonly used to convert process models into software artefacts [4–7].

WS are software modules that can be described, published, located, and invoked over the WWW [8]. They enable web-based applications to exchange information on the WWW through Internet connections [9]. Several WS are available on the WWW to users; each of them has its purposes that match the kind of services needed by users [10]. However, Web service operations and exchanged messages are described at a syntactic level; their meaning is not described semantically [4]. Therefore, programmers need to understand how existing WS work and perform manual selection and composition of appropriate WS for given operations. These weaknesses of WS are addressed with Semantic Web Services (SWS). SWS add semantic descriptions to WS based on ontology, making them machine-readable. This enables the automatic discovery, selection, composition and execution of services for intelligent interoperable machine-to-machine interactions over the WWW. These capabilities of SWS are useful in distributing environments. This is witnessed by the growing interest in the adoption of SWS technology in various e-business domains, supported by two existing frameworks for creating and executing SWS, namely, Internet Reasoning Services (IRS-III) [11] and Web Service Execution Environment (WSMX) [12].

In [13], the IRS-III framework is presented as well as its application in three domains including Business Process Management, e-Leaning and e-Science. Another study in [14] proposed a solution for SWS adoption in the telecommunication industry based on the IRS-III and WSMX frameworks. Other Semantic Web Service-oriented models for project management and e-commerce are presented in [15] and [16], respectively. The model in [15] is based on the IRS-III framework, whereas, that in [16] is based on WSMX. An interesting application of SWS in digital libraries based on WSMX is presented in [17]. SWS solutions for e-government based on the IRS-III framework are proposed in [18–21].

In all of the above SWS-oriented e-business solutions, SWS are built from pre-existing WS supplied by dedicated service providers; no provision is made for the design and engineering of SWS for non-automated business processes of organizations in general and governments in particular. Furthermore, research on the conceptual modeling and design of SWS is still at its early stages [7,22–24] and requires more empirical studies to validate the approaches and methods proposed. This study proposes an infrastructure for Semantic Web Services-enabled e-government that integrates Business Process Modeling (BPM) and

Semantic Annotation into existing SWS solutions as tools for the modeling and engineering of SWS for non-automated government operations and processes. The proposed infrastructure differs from that of previous studies [18–21] in that it leverages SWS technology in e-government while enabling continuous re-engineering and automation of government processes. In fact, previous studies do not provide solution for the design and engineering of SWS for non-automated business processes as it is done in this study. The study presents an example of the application of the proposed infrastructure with emphasis on the modeling and semantic annotation of business processes for SWS design. The proposed infrastructure can also be applied in other domains such as e-commerce, e-learning, e-Science, etc.

The rest of the paper is organized as follows. Section 2 presents the materials and methods used in the study. The proposed infrastructure is presented in detail in Sect. 3. An example of the application of the infrastructure as well as the modeling and semantic annotation of business processes of a government domain is described in Sect. 4. The future direction of the research is also presented in Sect. 4. A conclusion ends the paper in Sect. 5.

2 Materials and Methods

The key technologies employed in the proposed infrastructure including Business Process Modelling, Semantic Annotation, Web Service Modelling Ontology (WSMO) and WSMO reference implementations are presented in this section.

2.1 Business Process Modeling

Business Process Modeling (BPM) is a discipline that enables the definition and description of the business operations and processes of an organization through information flows, data and systems [25]. It consists of designing, modeling and optimizing government processes in a way that can be understood, analyzed and improved [4]. It is an important tool for understanding how an organization works, the activities of the organization and the nature of information required to carry out these activities. BPM uses various techniques to model the business processes of an organization; these include BPMN, EPCs, Petri Nets, Workflow Nets and Unified Modeling Language (UML) [4,24,25]. Several studies reported the use of BPM as a tool for re-engineering and re-organizing government processes [1–3]; however, none of the studies has integrated BPM into SWS-enabled infrastructure for e-government.

2.2 Semantic Annotation

At present, the process models that describe business processes of organizations are not machine-readable, due to the lack of formal definitions of (1) the terminology employed, and (2) the dynamic semantics of process models [22,24,26]. As a consequence, it is challenging to automatically process or query existing process models of organizations. To overcome this challenge, authors in [7,22–24] proposed the semantic annotation of process models. This entails adding semantic descriptions to process models with ontologies that describe process model constructs as well as domain ontologies [7,22].

Formally, a semantic annotation S_A is a 4-tuple $(\Phi, \Delta, \Theta, \Omega)$, where Φ is the set of elements of the process model to be annotated, Δ a semantic process annotation model (SPAM) [23] or semantic annotation structured model (SASM) [27], Θ a set of domain ontologies describing the knowledge domain and Ω the set of mappings between the elements of Φ and Δ on the one hand and between Δ and the concepts of Ω on the other hand. A semantic annotation S_A is defined as in Eq. 1 [27].

$$S_A = \{\Phi, \Delta, \Theta, \Omega(\Phi, \Delta), \Omega(\Delta, \Theta)\} \tag{1}$$

The SPAM/SASM (Δ) is an ontology of the modeling language constructs in which elements of Φ are represented [23,27]. Equation 2 defines the mapping between the elements of Φ and Δ as a set of products of subsets of Φ and Δ.

$$\Omega(\Phi, \Delta) = \{\prod_{i=1}^{k} \partial(\sigma(\Phi), \sigma(\Delta)) | \sigma(\Phi) \in \Phi \wedge \sigma(\Delta) \in \Delta\} \tag{2}$$

where, $\sigma(\Phi)$ and $\sigma(\Delta)$ are subsets of Φ and Δ, respectively. The mapping ∂ of $\sigma(\Phi)$ to $\sigma(\Delta)$ is defined as in Eq. 3; it is a set of cartesian products of elements of $\sigma(\Phi)$ and $\sigma(\Delta)$.

$$\partial(\sigma(\Phi), \sigma(\Delta)) = \{m_a\langle a_i, b_j\rangle | a_{i,1 \leq i \leq n} \in \sigma(\Phi) \wedge b_{j,1 \leq j \leq m} \in \sigma(\Delta)\} \tag{3}$$

where a_i are elements of $\sigma(\Phi)$ to be annotated and b_j their semantic descriptions in $\sigma(\Delta)$. m_a is the type of mappings between a_i and b_j. Similarly, the mapping between Δ and the concepts of domain ontologies in Θ is defined in Eq. 4.

$$\Omega(\Delta, \Theta) = \{\prod_{i=1}^{k} \partial(\sigma(\Delta), \sigma(\Theta)) | \sigma(\Delta) \in \Delta \wedge \sigma(\Theta) \in o_k, o_k \in \Theta\} \tag{4}$$

where, $\sigma(\Delta)$ and $\sigma(\Theta)$ are subsets of Δ and an ontology o_k belonging to Θ, respectively. The mapping ∂ of $\sigma(\Delta)$ to $\sigma(\Theta)$ is defined as in Eq. 5.

$$\partial(\sigma(\Delta), \sigma(\Theta)) = \{m_b\langle b_j, e_l\rangle | b_{j,1 \leq j \leq m} \in \sigma(\Delta) \wedge e_{l,1 \leq l \leq k} \in \sigma(\Theta)\} \tag{5}$$

where b_j are the semantic descriptions of the elements of Φ in $\sigma(\Delta)$ and e_l the concepts they are mapped to in the domain ontologies o_k in Θ. The mappings m_a and m_b in Eqs. 3 and 4, respectively, are of three types [27]:

- The equivalent relationship $m_{\sim}\langle x, y\rangle$ - x is semantically equivalent to y.
- The subsume relationship $m_{\supset/\subset}\langle x, y\rangle$ - x is a superclass of y, i.e., the semantics of x is inherited by y or y is a superclass of x, i.e., the semantics of y is inherited by x.
- The intersection relationship $m_{\cap}\langle x, y\rangle$ - the semantics of x intersects with the semantics of y.

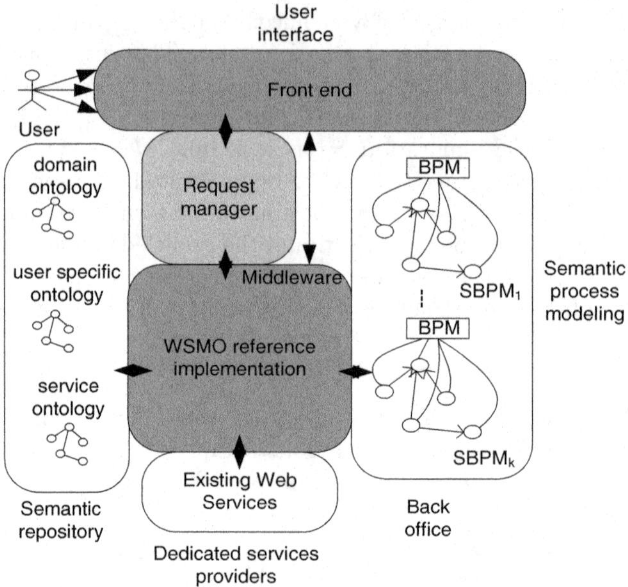

Fig. 1. Infrastructure for semantic web services enabled E-government

The resulting semantic enhanced process models may be directly implemented into Semantic Web Services [22,26] via Web Service Modelling Ontology (WSMO) reference implementations such as IRS-III and WSMX.

2.3 Web Service Modeling Ontology (WSMO)

WSMO is a framework for modeling and describing Semantic Web Services. It makes use of four main elements to describe SWS including: ontologies, Web services, goals and mediators [18]. The ontologies provide domain specific descriptions of information to be used by other elements; they are formal explicit specifications of shared conceptualizations [17]. Web services descriptions provide the functional behaviour of an existing Web service; they also specify how Web services communicate (choreography) and are composed (orchestration). Goals specify the objectives the user (service requester) expects to achieve with a Web service. The mediators establish links between ontologies, goals and Web services, and specify the mapping mechanisms between them, thereby, addressing the mismatches that may occur amongst WSMO components. WSMO has been extended with two reference implementations, namely, IRS-III [11] and WSMX [12] that enable the creation and execution of SWS. The two WSMO reference implementations form part of the proposed infrastructure to enable the direct implementation of newly designed SWS for non-automated business processes of government domains. The next section presents the proposed infrastructure.

3 Infrastructure for Semantic Web Services Enabled E-Government

The proposed infrastructure is depicted in Fig. 1. It is constituted of five main components including the front end, request manager, middleware, semantic repository and back office. The abovementioned components are explained in detail below.

- **Front end** - Provides the interface for the interaction with users. Through this layer, users may submit various requests for services to the middleware via the request manager and receive responses. These requests are used by the middleware to invoke and execute suitable services.
- **The request manager** - Receives user requests, processes and submits them to the middleware. Upon receiving a user request, all related events are discovered and the user is allowed to select the suitable event. The selected event matches information and goals described in the domain and service ontologies. In fact, domain information is described in the domain ontology, whereas, goals are described in the service ontology. The invocation of a goal by a user's request triggers a call to the middleware which retrieves its semantic description. This semantic description is used to identify, invoke and execute the suitable Web service(s) to provide results to the user's request. The semantic descriptions of Web services are stored in the service ontology.
- **Semantic repository** - Stores the domain, user specific and service ontologies. Domain knowledge is described in the domain ontology. The user specific ontology describes the common terms of users such as linguistic terms [20]. The definitions of SWS are kept in the service ontology; these include the goals, semantic descriptions of Web services and instances of mediator classes. The semantic descriptions of Web services are created either from the newly semantically annotated process models of the government domain or from pre-existing Web services obtained from dedicated service providers. In the latter, semantic descriptions are added to the existing Web services to build SWS.
- **Middleware** - Reference implementation(s) of WSMO, i.e., IRS-II and/or WSMX. WSMO is a framework for modeling SWS. Its reference implementations provide the software environments for building full applications based on SWS; they enable the description, publication and execution of SWS [11].
- **Back office** - Deals with the modeling and semantic annotation of business processes of the e-government domain as well as the supply of existing Web services from dedicated service providers. Various techniques including BPM and Semantic Annotation (Sects. 2.1 and 2.2) are used to build the semantic descriptions of process models. The resulting semantic descriptions are used to build SWS in the middleware. The definitions of SWS including goals, web service descriptions and instances of mediators' classes are kept in the service ontology.

An example of the application of the proposed infrastructure is presented in the next section. Emphasis is placed on the modeling and semantic annotation of process models to illustrate how government processes and operations could be designed and re-engineered into SWS at the back office component of the infrastructure.

4 Application in the Development Projects Monitoring Knowledge Domain in Developing Countries

In this section, a scenario of the application of the proposed infrastructure in the domain of development projects monitoring in developing countries is presented. The business processes of the domain are identified and modeled in BPMN formalism. The semantic annotation structure presented in Sect. 2.2 is applied to perform the annotation of the process models' elements. Finally, a part of the resulting semantic descriptions of process models in a machine readable form is presented, in a OWL-S like syntax.

4.1 Scenario of Application of the Infrastructure

Developing countries receive international assistance from donors in the form of formal projects that deal with the problems of communities [28]. These types of projects are called development projects (DPs); they are projects or programmes specifically designed for economic and social needs of developing countries [29]. The objectives of DPs are mainly concerned with poverty alleviation, improvement of living standards, environmental and basic human rights protection, assistance to victims of natural or people caused disasters, capacity building and the development of basic physical and social infrastructures [29]. DPs are funded by multilateral development agencies and bilateral agreements between developed and developing countries [28].

Development projects implementation is a very complex task that involves many processes and actors. Further, the implementation processes may be distributed across several government divisions, requiring many legacy systems to interoperate for better efficiency. This makes it challenging to monitor and evaluate the implementation processes of these projects to ensure their efficiency and effectiveness. A Semantic Web Services-enabled infrastructure like that proposed in Fig. 1 would enable the automation of DPs monitoring processes. DPs monitoring processes would be modeled and re-engineered into several process models at the back office. These process models would be semantically annotated based on the domain and user specific ontologies and implemented into SWS through the middleware. Pre-existing Web services from existing government systems (tender and procurement, tax return, certification, permitting, payment, identification, etc.) would be semantically described in the middleware and saved into the service ontology. The front office will provide all actors with a user specific interface for introducing various requests to the system. Domain and user specific ontologies would be built to capture relevant concepts and terminologies of DPs monitoring processes. The semantic descriptions of process models and existing Web services will be saved in the service ontology. The virtual community of actors formed of: government authorities, civil servants, donor organizations,

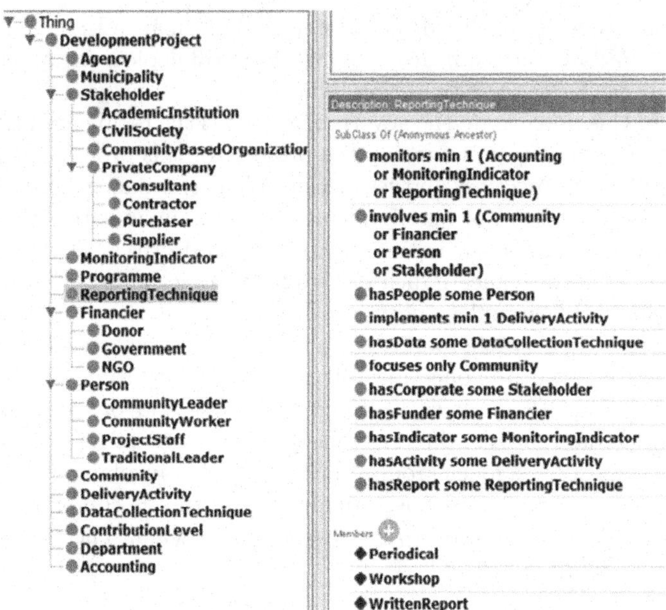

Fig. 2. Ontology of development projects monitoring in developing countries

NGOs, project staff, private companies, community members, etc. would share projects data (technical, financial, statistical, etc.) and available Web services transparently and efficiently. The middleware would assist with technical tasks such as finding, composing, and resolving mismatches between Web services from different heterogeneous systems of government departments involved in projects, as well as providing reasoning capacities necessary for addressing technical issues such as data security and privacy, computational power for processing users' requests, etc. The identification, semantic modeling and annotation of DPs monitoring processes are presented in the next subsections.

4.2 Domain Ontology for Development Projects Monitoring

As a starting point for building SWS for e-government monitoring of DPs in developing countries, the authors developed a domain ontology [30] as in Fig. 2. The domain ontology describes the key concepts of the domain (people, stakeholder, financier, monitoring/performance indicator, reporting technique, etc.), the activities carried out in the domain (training, discussion, fieldwork, visit, meeting, etc.) and the relationships between the constituents of the domain.

4.3 Business Process Modeling of Development Projects Monitoring Processes

Three processes of DPs monitoring were identified and modeled into process models with the BPMN formalism; these processes include (1) Development of Performance Indicators, (2) Measurement of Performance Indicators and (3) Evaluation of Performance Indicators [31,32]. Figure 3 depicts the process model for developing performance monitoring indicators during project planning. The main actors of this process are the government who is the recipient of the project and the donor(s) who is/are financing the project. In this process, both parties agree on key project objectives and set measurable performance monitoring indicators that would help the project implementation team/unit to measure at all time the progress of project activities toward these objectives. At the end of this process, a list of performance indicators is compiled to be used during project implementation. During implementation, government and the project implementation team/unit monitor the performance indicators developed during project planning. This is done by collecting relevant data (1) during regular project supervision missions, (2) after each project milestone and/or (3) at the end of the project. The data may be directly collected from project reports or through survey techniques such as focus groups, interviews, etc., involving recipient communities. A summary report on performance indicators is compiled after each data collecting process for the project management team. The BPMN of this process is provided in Fig. 4.

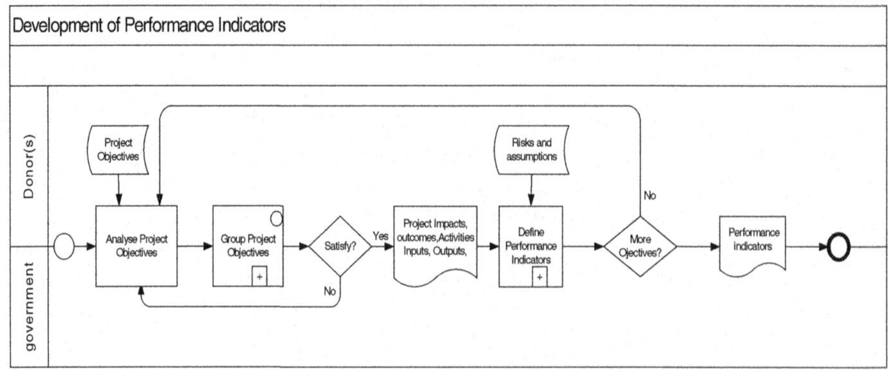

Fig. 3. BPMN for the development of performance indicators process

Figure 5 depicts the process model for evaluating the performance indicators collected during project implementation. In this process, each summary report of performance indicators produced by the project implementation team/unit is analyzed by both government and donor(s) against the project objectives to ascertain whether the project is meeting its targeted outcomes and impacts. This is done at the midterm review or at the end of the project. Corrective actions are taken in cases there are concerns.

4.4 Semantic Annotation of Development Projects Monitoring Process Models

Figures 3, 4 and 5 are the process models of the DPs monitoring domain represented in BPMN. As explained in Sect. 2.2, the Semantic Annotation of these

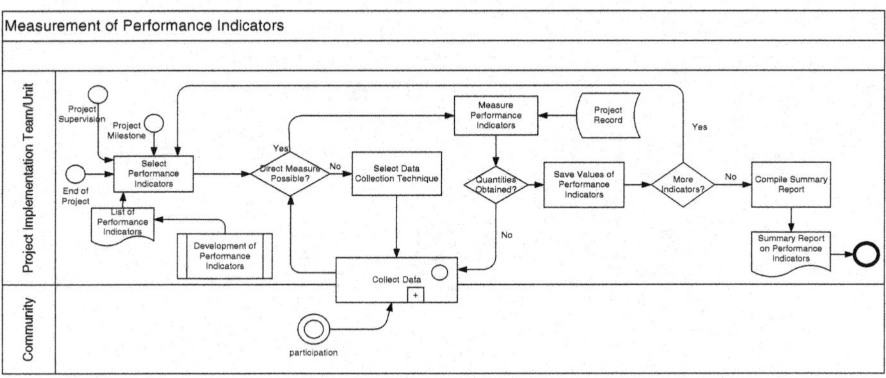

Fig. 4. BPMN for the measurement of performance indicators process

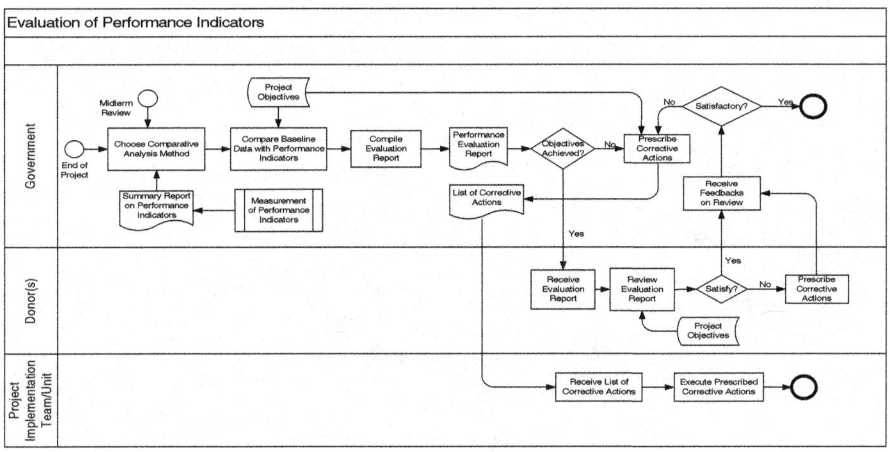

Fig. 5. BPMN for the evaluation of performance indicators process

process models requires a semantic process annotation model (SPAM) and a domain ontology [22,23]. The SPAM is an abstract description of the modeling language constructs for representing process models, whereas, the domain ontology describes the concepts of the domain. In this study, the SPAM is the general process ontology (GPO) proposed in [23] and the domain ontology is the one in Fig. 2. Both the GPO and the domain ontology in Fig. 2 are used to semantically annotate the process models of the DPs monitoring domain in Figs. 3, 4 and 5. Due to space constraint, only the Semantic Annotation of the process model in Fig. 3 is presented in this study.

Fig. 6 depicts the Semantic Annotation of the process model in Fig. 3 with the corresponding instance of the GPO ontology; it shows the links between the process model elements and the corresponding instances of the GPO ontology. In fact each element of the process model in Fig. 3 is an instance of a concept in the GPO ontology. The bottom part of Fig. 6 shows the full instance of the GPO

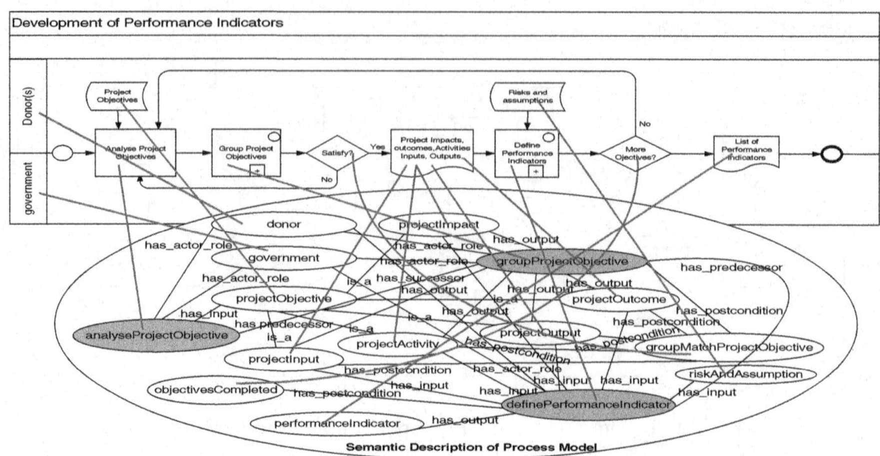

Fig. 6. Semantic a nnotation of the development of performance indicators process model

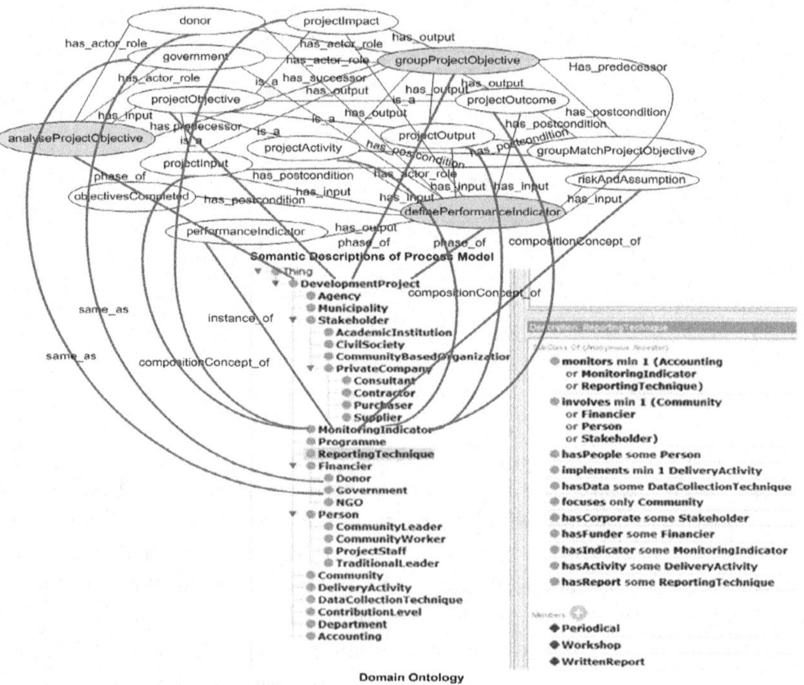

Fig. 7. Semantic annotation of semantic descriptions of process model with domain ontology

ontology representing the semantic description of the process model in Fig. 3. This semantic description is comparable to a Web service description in OWL-S [23]. This makes the process model machine readable. However, the semantic

Table 1. Part of Semantic Description of the Development of Performance Indicators Process Model

$analyseProjectObjective \sqsubseteq \exists\ has\_actor\_role.(donor \sqcup government)$
$analyseProjectObjective \sqsubseteq \exists\ has\_input.projectObjective$
$analyseProjectObjective \sqsubseteq \exists\ has\_successor.groupProjectObjective$
$\mathbf{analyseProjectObjective \sqsubseteq \exists phase\_of.developmentProject}$
$groupProjectObjective \sqsubseteq \exists\ has\_predecessor.analyseProjectObjective$
$groupProjectObjective \sqsubseteq \exists\ has\_actor\_role.(donor \sqcup government)$
$groupProjectObjective \sqsubseteq \exists\ has\_output.(projectImpact \sqcup projectOutcome \sqcup$
$projectActivity \sqcup projectInput \sqcup projectOutput)$
$\mathbf{groupProjectObjective \sqsubseteq \exists phase\_of.developmentProject}$
$groupProjectObjective \sqsubseteq \exists\ has\_postcondition.groupMatchProjectObjective$
$projectImpact \sqsubseteq \exists\ has\_postcondition.groupMatchProjectObjective$
$projectOutcome \sqsubseteq \exists\ has\_postcondition.groupMatchProjectObjective$
$projectActivity \sqsubseteq \exists\ has\_postcondition.groupMatchProjectObjective$
$\mathbf{government \sqsubseteq \exists same\_as.government}$
$\mathbf{donor \sqsubseteq \exists same\_as.donor}$
$\mathbf{projectInput \sqsubseteq \exists compositionConcept\_of.monitoringIndicator}$
$\mathbf{projectOutcome \sqsubseteq \exists compositionConcept\_of.monitoringIndicator}$
$definePerformanceIndicator \sqsubseteq \exists\ has\_actor\_role.(donor \sqcup government)$
$definePerformanceIndicator \sqsubseteq \exists\ has\_input.(projectImpact \sqcup projectOutcome \sqcup$
$projectActivity \sqcup projectInput \sqcup projectOutput)$
$definePerformanceIndicator \sqsubseteq \exists\ has\_output.performanceIndicator$
$\mathbf{performanceIndicator \sqsubseteq \exists instance\_of.MonitoringIndicator}$

description of the process model in Fig. 6 contains only instances of abstract constructs of the process model such as activity, input, output, etc. Relationships need to be further established between the concretes domain information in the semantic description of the process model and the domain ontology [23].

Figure 7 depicts the Semantic Annotation of the semantic description of process model components in Fig. 6 with concepts of the domain ontology in Fig. 2. This Semantic Annotation establishes the relationships between the semantic description of process model elements and concepts of the domain ontology, making it possible to reason, discover and navigate the process model fragments [23]. The properties between the components of the semantic description of process model and concepts of the domain ontology include $same\_as$, $instance\_of$, $phase\_of$, $componentConcept\_of$, etc., as prescribed in [23].

Table 1 shows a part of the semantic description of the annotated process model in a machine readable form. The lines in bold form part of the semantic relationships between the semantic description of the process model and concepts of the domain ontology. The code in Table 1 is very similar to that of a Web service description in OWL-S [23]. Let's recall that the proposed infrastructure in

Fig. 1 is suitable for implementing SWS that are WSMO compliant, i.e., formed of ontologies, Web Services, goals and mediators. Therefore, with the domain ontology in Fig. 2 and the Web service descriptions of process models obtained (example in Table 1), the study is getting close to the complete design of semantic web services for e-government monitoring of development projects in developing countries. The future direction of the study would be to model the goals of process activities based on the goal ontology proposed in [23].

5 Conclusion

This paper presented an approach for designing and engineering SWS for non-automated government processes as part of an infrastructure for Semantic Web Services adoption in e-government. The infrastructure differs from that of related studies in that it enables the continuous design and engineering of SWS for non-automated government processes. The design and engineering of government processes into SWS rely on BPM and Semantic Annotation techniques. Web services from dedicated service providers form part of the infrastructure in order to fit it into existing systems. An example of the application of the proposed approach that illustrate the modeling and Semantic Annotation of business processes for SWS design in the domain of development projects monitoring in developing countries was presented. The proposed approach for engineering SWS as part of an infrastructure for SWS adoption can also be applied in other e-business domains such as e-commerce, e-learning, e-Science, etc.

References

1. Moreira, E. Fillies, C.: A business process analysis and modelling architecture for E-government. In: AAAI Spring Symposium 2006, Technical report SS-06-06 (2006)
2. Palkovits, S., Orensanz, D., Karagiannis, D.: Process modelling in Egovernment - living process modelling within a public organisation. In: IADIS International e-Society, pp. 3–10 (2004)
3. Liu, Z., Le Calve, A., Cretton, F., Evequoz, F., Mugellini, E.: A framework for semantic business process management in E-government. In: Proceedings of the IADIS International Conference WWW/INTERNET 2013, Texas, USA (2013)
4. Grolinger, K., Capretz, M.A.M., Cunha, A., Tazi, S.: Integration of business process modelling and web services : A survey. Serv. Oriented Comput. Appl. **8**, 105–128 (2013)
5. Papazoglou, M.P., Yang, J.: Design methodology for web services and business processes. In: Buchmann, A.P., Casati, F., Fiege, L., Hsu, M.-C., Shan, M.-C. (eds.) TES 2002. LNCS, vol. 2444, pp. 54–64. Springer, Heidelberg (2002)
6. Leynman, F., Schmidt, M.T.: Web services and business process management. IBM Syst. J. **41**, 198–211 (2002)
7. Abramowicz, W., Filipowska, A., Kaczmarek, M., Kaczmarek, T.: Semantically enhanced business process modelling notation. In: Workshop on Semantic Business Process and Product Lifecycle Management (SBPM), Innsbruck, Austria (2007)

8. Mcilraith, S.A., Martin, D.L.: Bringing semantics to web services. IEEE Intel. Syst. **18**, 90–93 (2003)
9. Fensel, D., Facca, M.F., Simperl, E., Toma, I.: Semantic Web Services. Springer, Heidelberg (2011)
10. Bouguettaya, A., Medjahed, B., Rezgui, A., Ouzzani, M., Liu, X., Yu, Q.: WebDG – a platform for E-government web services. In: Wang, S., Tanaka, K., Zhou, S., Ling, T.-W., Guan, J., Yang, D., Grandi, F., Mangina, E.E., Song, I.-Y., Mayr, H.C. (eds.) ER Workshops 2004. LNCS, vol. 3289, pp. 553–565. Springer, Heidelberg (2004)
11. Cabral, L., Domingue, J., Galizia, S., Gugliotta, A., Tanasescu, V., Pedrinaci, C., Norton, B.: IRS-III: a broker for semantic web services based applications. In: Cruz, I., Decker, S., Allemang, D., Preist, C., Schwabe, D., Mika, P., Uschold, M., Aroyo, L.M. (eds.) ISWC 2006. LNCS, vol. 4273, pp. 201–214. Springer, Heidelberg (2006)
12. Herold, M.: WSMX Documentation. http://www.wsmx.org/papers/documentation/WSMXDocumentation.pdf (last Access 6 January 2015)
13. Galizia, S., Gugliotta, A., Pedrinaci, C., Domingue, J.: Applying semantic web services. In: 4th Workshop on Semantic Web Applications and Perspectives (SWAP 2007), Bari, Italy (2007)
14. Khan, A.N., Asghar, S., Fong, S.: Framework of integrated semantic web services and ontology development for telecommunication industry. J. Emerg. Technol. Web Intell. **3**, 110–119 (2011)
15. Ni, J., Zhao, X., Zhu, L.: A semantic web service-oriented model for E-commerce. In: International Conference Service Systems and Service Management, Chengdu, China (2007)
16. Mohammadi, S., Khalili, A.: A semantic web service-oriented model for project management. In: IEEE 8th International Conference on Computer and Information Technology Workshops, Sydney, Australia, pp. 667–672 (2008)
17. Kruk, S.R., Mocan, A., Sapkota, B., Zaremba, M.: Building semantic web services infrastructure for digital libraries. In: European Semantic Web Conference: ESWC 2005, Heraklion, Crete, Greece (2005)
18. Gugliotta, A., Cabral, L., Domingue, J. and Roberto, V.: A Conceptual Model for Semantically-Based E-government Portal. In: International Conference on e-Government 2005 (ICEG 2005), Ottawa, Canada (2005)
19. Roberto, V., Rowlatt, M., Davies, R., Gugliotta, A., Cabral, L., Domingue, J.: A semantic web service-based architecture for the interoperability of e-Government services. In: Web Information Systems Modeling Workshop (WISM 2005) / 5th International Conference on Web Engineering (ICWE 2005), Sydney, Australia (2005)
20. Dutta, B.: Semantic web service infrastructure for e-Governance. In: International Conference on Semantic Web and Digital Libraries: ICSD-2007, Bagalore, India, pp. 144–153 (2007)
21. Marjit, U., Roy, R., Santra, S., Biswas, U.: A semantic web service based approach E-government. In: 2nd International Conference on Application of Digital Information and Web Technologies 2009 (ICADIWT 2009), London, UK, pp. 232–237 (2009)
22. Born, M., Dorr, F., Weber, I.: User-friendly semantic annotation in business process modelling. In: Web Information Systems Engineering - WISE 2007 Workshops (2007)

23. Lin, Y.: Semantic annotation for process models: facilitating process knowledge management via semantic interoperability. Ph.D. thesis, Department of Computer and Information Science Norwegian University of Science and Technology, Trondheim, Norway (2008)
24. Lautenbacher, F., Bauer, B., Seitz, C.: Semantic business process modelling - benefits and capability. In: AAAI Spring Symposium, Stanford University, California, USA
25. Aydinli, O.F., Brinkkermper, S., Revestyn, P.: Business process improvement in organization design of e-Government services. Electr. J. e-Government **7**, 123–134 (2009)
26. Hepp, M., Leymann, F., Bussler, C., Domingue, J., Wahler, A., Fensel, D.: Semantic business process management: a vision towards using semantic web services for business process management. In: IEEE ICEBE 2005, Beijing, China, pp. 535–540 (2005)
27. Liao, Y., Lezoche, M., Loures, E., Panetto, H., Boudjlida, N.: Formalization of semantic annotation for systems interoperability in a PLM environment. In: Herrero, P., Panetto, H., Meersman, R., Dillon, T. (eds.) OTM-WS 2012. LNCS, vol. 7567, pp. 207–218. Springer, Heidelberg (2012)
28. Diallo, A., Thuillier, D.: The success dimensions of international development projects: the perceptions of african project coordinators. Int. J. Proj. Manage. **22**, 19–31 (2004)
29. Ahsan, K., Gunawan, I.: Analysis of cost and schedule performance of international development projects. Int. J. Proj. Manage. **28**, 68–78 (2010)
30. Fonou-Dombeu, J.V., Huisman, M.: Semantic-driven E-government: application of uschold and king ontology building methodology for semantic ontology models development. Int. J. Web Semant. Technol. (IJWesT) **4**, 1–20 (2011)
31. Mosse, R., Sontbeimer, L.E.: Performance monitoring indicators handbook. World Bank Technical Paper No. 334, WTP334 September (1996)
32. Menon, S., Karl, J., Wignaraja, K.: Handbook on Planning. Monitoring and Evaluating for Developments Results, United Nations Development Programmes (2009)

Identity Management in E-Government

Enhancing Public Digital Identity System (SPID) to Prevent Information Leakage

Francesco Buccafurri[1](✉), Lidia Fotia[1], Gianluca Lax[1], and Rocco Mammoliti[2]

[1] DIIES, University Mediterranea of Reggio Calabria, Via Graziella, Località Feo di Vito, 89122 Reggio Calabria, Italy
{bucca,lidia.fotia,lax}@unirc.it

[2] Security and Safety, Poste Italiane S.p.A, viale Europa 175, 00144 Roma, Italy
mammoliti.rocco@posteitaliane.it

Abstract. Public Digital Identity System (SPID) is the Italian government framework compliant with the EU eIDAS regulatory environment, aimed at implementing electronic identification and trust services in e-government and business applications. According to this federated identity management framework, digital identities are issued, upon application of the interested party, by digital identity providers. This way, users authenticate to service providers, which are public or private organizations providing a service to authorized users, provided that they adhere to SPID. A drawback that could limit the real diffusion of this framework is that, despite the fact that identity and service providers might be competitor private companies, SPID authentication results in information leakage about customers of identity providers. To overcome this potential limitation, in this paper, we propose a modification of SPID to allow user authentication by preserving the anonymity of the identity provider that grants the authentication credentials. This way, information leakage about customers of identity providers is fully prevented.

1 Introduction

Following a number of normative provisions, aimed at favoring the spread of network services in e-government and business settings, the Agency for Digital Italy (AGID) [1] has introduced the public system for the management of the digital identity of citizens and businesses, named SPID, for short. SPID is compliant with the EU regulatory environment called eIDAS [3] (even though its introduction has in fact anticipated the European initiative), aimed at implementing electronic identification and trust services to enable secure and seamless electronic interactions between businesses, citizens and public authorities. As reported in the official site, the eIDAS regulation aims at boosting the user convenience, trust and confidence in the digital world, while keeping pace with technological developments, promoting innovation and stimulating competition. In particular, the fragmentation of the market intended as the existence of different rules applying to service providers of Member States is one of the drawbacks that should

© Springer International Publishing Switzerland 2015
A. Kő and E. Francesconi (Eds.): EGOVIS 2015, LNCS 9265, pp. 57–70, 2015.
DOI: 10.1007/978-3-319-22389-6_5

be overcome thanks to the adoption of a common regulatory system. Another serious issue is the lack of trust and confidence in electronic systems. Indeed, the tools provided and the legal framework can often create the impression that there are fewer legal safeguards than with physical interaction. The adoption of standardization-based approaches to implement technical interoperability must be accompanied by clear rules and responsibilities to ensure legal certainty and reciprocal recognition of trust services and electronic identification.

The Italian system SPID is an open system thanks to which public and private entities, provided that they are accredited by the Agency for Digital Italy, can offer services of electronic identification for citizens and businesses. The providers of such services have to ensure a suitable procedure for the initial identification and have to implement the authentication of citizens to service providers, which are public or private organizations, provided that they adhere to SPID. SPID is based on the technical specifications widely accepted in Europe and already adopted by experimental projects as Stork and Stork2 (Secure Identity Across Borders Linked) [20,21]. Italy has also already notified the Commission the institution of SPID. Thus, according to the provisions of eIDAS, from July 1, 2016, SPID will be recognized and accepted by all other EU Member States.

A drawback that could limit the real diffusion of SPID, and, in principles, of other similar systems adopted in different Countries, is that SPID authentication results in information leakage about customers of identity providers (despite the fact that identity and service providers might be competitor private companies). We remark that this is not an abstract problem, as it comes from a careful analysis conducted in an industrial research project (partially supporting this research), where just industrial partners have highlighted this potential criticality. Consider this simple example. Suppose that `Alice` is a customer of the company `Bob&C`. Obviously, personal data of `Alice` together with all the information regarding the whole customer base of `Bob&C` are a crucial asset of the company, which reluctantly wants to yield to other potential competitors. Unfortunately, in the current federated authentication framework of SPID, if `Bob&C` decides to play the role of Identity Provider, by relying on its customer base presumably prone to avail this new service, the authentication of `Alice` to a competitor company `Trudy&C` (playing the role of Service Provider) discloses to `Trudy&C` that `Alice` is a customer of `Bob&C`. This, for example, might enable more specific and effective strategies to acquire `Alice` in its customer base.

To overcome this drawback, in this paper, we propose a modification of SPID based on a cooperative approach to allow user authentication by preserving the anonymity of the identity provider which grants the authentication credentials. The whole architecture and security of SPID is preserved, thus guaranteeing backward compatibility, but information leakage about customers of identity providers is fully prevented.

The paper is organized as follows. In the next Section, the Public Digital Identity System (SPID) framework is presented. In Sect. 3, we present an overview of our solution to the problem of information leakage in SPID. In Sect. 4, we describe the technical implementation of the proposed enhanced SPID protocol.

Then, in Sect. 5, we survey the related work of the recent literature. Finally, in Sect. 6, we discuss some aspects relating to the setting of the parameters of the system and draw our conclusions.

2 The SPID Framework

In this section, we present the Public Digital Identity System (SPID) framework and the technical details necessary to understand our proposal [5]. Preliminarily, we describe the Security Assertion Markup Language (SAML) as the implementation of the framework is based upon SAML.

SAML [4] is an XML-based, open-standard data format for exchanging authentication and authorization data between an identity provider and a service provider. It uses security tokens containing assertions to pass information and enables web-based authentication and authorization scenarios including cross-domain single sign-on, which helps reduce the administrative overhead of distributing multiple authentication tokens to the user. Short SAML messages are carried directly in the URL query string of an HTTP GET request. Due to the limit of URL length, longer messages are transmitted via HTTP POST Binding. Although SAML allows the use of SSL or TLS for the communications, in SPID, it is mandatory the use of TLS.

The architecture of SPID involves the following entities:

1. *Users*, physical or legal people, using SPID to authenticate. Each user can be associated with one or more IDs, contain sensitive information, such as social security number, name, surname, place of birth, date of birth and sex.
2. *Identity Providers*, which create and manage IDs. They are private or public subjects certified by a trusted third party.
3. *Service Providers*, public or private organizations providing a service to authorized users.
4. a *Trusted Third Party (TTP)*, which guarantees the standard levels of security required by SPID and certifies the involved entities (e.g., in Italy it is the Agency for Digital Italy).

Observe that, the framework provides for the presence of another type of entity, the *Attribute Authority*, which can certify some attributes, such as possession of a degree, membership of a professional body, etc. As this entity has not a relevant role in our proposal, it is neglected here.

To obtain an ID, a user must be registered to one of the *Identity Providers*, which is responsible of the verification of the user identity before issuing the ID and the security credentials. Observe that different levels of sophistication are allowed for security credentials. This derives from the need to have a technologically neutral model, which fits the technological evolution without continuous remodeling.

The presence of a *Federation Registry*, a repository of all information related to *Identity Providers* managed by the *TTP*, guarantees the authenticity of certified *Identity Providers*, and, thus, provides the trust associated with the framework [2]. For each entity, the register contains an entry `AuthorityInfo` defined as follows:

Definition 1. `AuthorityInfo` is an element consisting of:

- ⟨`EntityId`⟩: identifier (URI) of the entity;
- ⟨`AuthorityType`⟩: type of the identity (i.e., Identity Provider, Attribute Provider);
- ⟨`MetadataProviderURL`⟩: URL of the service returning the characteristics of the entity. They are defined through metadata available through the interface `IMetadataRetrive` and are signed by *TTP*;
- ⟨`AttributeList`⟩: list of attributes certified by the entity.

The access to the register is done through the interface `IRegistryAccess`, a HTTP-GET method that allows the search of entities giving as input an `entityId`, or an `authorityType`, or an `attributeType` to select an entity that can certify a particular qualified attribute. The result is an XML file signed by *TTP*.

When the user needs to access a service given by *Service Provider*, he runs the authentication mechanism, which is summarized in Fig. 1. First, the user using a browser (`User Agent`) sends to *Service Provider* a request for accessing the service (Step 1). Then, *Service Provider* replies to `User Agent` with an authentication request to be forwarded to *Identity Provider* (Step 2).

The authentication request `AuthnRequest` is defined as:

Definition 2. `AuthnRequest` is a message that contains the following fields:

- an unique attribute `ID`. This is generally obtained by a combination of origin and timestamp, such as ID = Assertion-uuidae7136e4-0118-18d8-999d-cff934ae63db;
- an attribute `Version`, which indicates the version of SAML of the message;
- an attribute `IssueInstant`, which specifies the instant at which the request was issued;
- an attribute `ProtocolBinding`, a URI that identifies the binding (GET or POST) to be used to forward the response message;
- an attribute `Destination`, the address to which the request is sent;
- an attribute `AssertionConsumerServiceURL`, which is the URL of the destination of the response message (i.e., the URL of *Service Provider*);
- an element ⟨`Issuer`⟩, the `EntityID` of the *Service Provider*;
- an element ⟨`RequestedAuthnContext`⟩, which indicates the robustness of the required credentials.

If the received request is valid, *Identity Provider* performs a challenge authentication with the user (Steps 3 and 4). In case of successful user authentication, *Identity Provider* prepares the *assertion* containing the statement of user authentication for *Service Provider*. The `Assertion` is defined as:

Definition 3. `Assertion` contains the following elements:

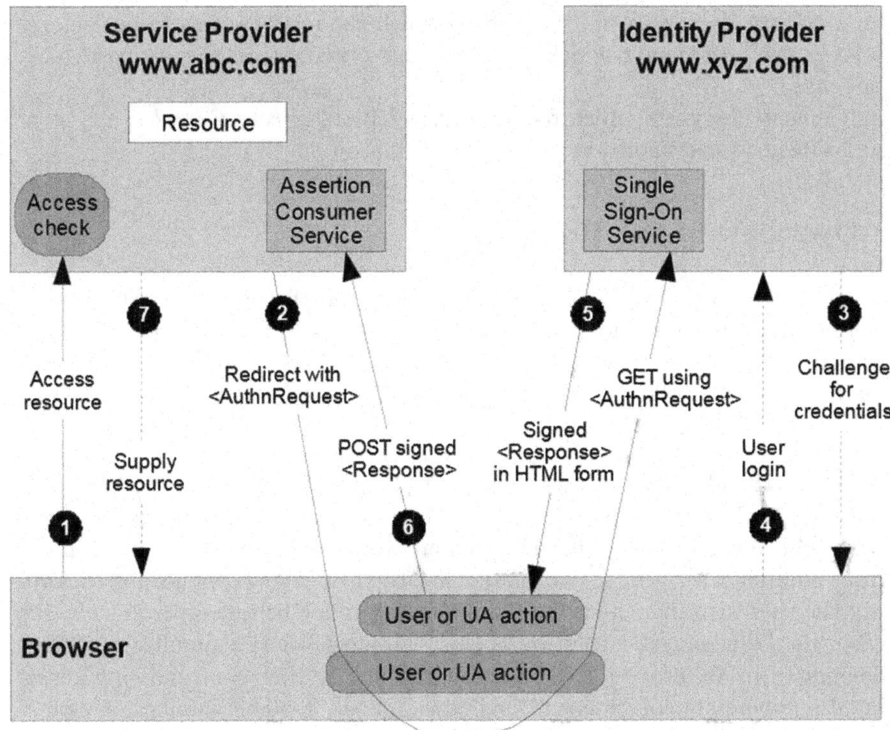

Fig. 1. Data flow during an authentication request in SPID.

- ⟨`Subject`⟩, which identifies the authenticated user;
- ⟨`Issuer`⟩, which specifies the `EntityID` of *Identity Provider*;
- ⟨`Conditions`⟩, which define the temporal range of validity;
- ⟨`AuthnContext`⟩, which is the description of the authentication's context;
- ⟨`AttributeStatement`⟩, which contains the SPID identification code of the authenticated user;
- ⟨`Signature`⟩, the *Identity Provider* signature on the assertion.

Now, *Identity Provider* returns to `User Agent` the message `Response` containing `Assertion` (Step 5), which is forwarded to the *Service Provider* via HTTP POST Binding (see Step 6).

The message `Response` is defined as:

Definition 4. `Response` contains the following fields:

- an unique attribute `ID`;
- an attribute `Version`, which indicates the version of SAML of the message;
- an attribute `IssueInstant`, which specifies the instant at which the request was issued;
- an attribute `InResponceTo`, containing the value of the attribute `ID` of `AuthnRequest`;

- an attribute Destination, the URI to which the response has to be sent;
- an element ⟨Status⟩, which specifies the outcome of the request (e.g., success);
- an element ⟨Issuer⟩, which reports EntityID of *Identity Provider*;
- an element ⟨Assertion⟩, as defined in Definition 3.

3 Overview of the Proposal

With reference to the protocol of SPID described in the previous section, now, we briefly describe the modifications that we propose to apply to the SPID system to overcome the privacy issues dealt with in the introduction. Specifically, we individuate the following three changes to the current version of the SPID protocol.

1. In SPID, the identifier of a user reports the reference to the *Identity Provider* that identified and registered him. But the connection between user and *Identity Provider* is just the information that we want to keep hidden when the user requires a service. As a consequence, the first change we need is to modify the user identifier in such a way that it can not be linked to the *Identity Provider.* The simplest solution is that the identifier is a number randomly generated in an interval such that the probability that two randomly generated numbers are coincident is negligible, for any realistic number of users.
2. Recall that in the phase of authentication, the message AuthnRequest includes the attribute Destination that contains the address of the specific *Identity Provider* to which such request must to be sent, taken from the user identifier. With the first change introduced above, the destination cannot be known from the service provider. To reach the right provider, our proposal is that the authentication request is sent from the service provider to a (first) randomly selected *Identity Provider.* If this provider is the one responsible of the authentication of this user, then it starts the authentication process. Otherwise it forwards the request to another randomly selected identity provider, which, recursively, will process the request in the same way. Eventually, a message of type Response is generated, stating if the authentication succeeded or not.
3. The third change is necessary to avoid that the *Service Provider* can infer the identity provider of the user looking at the sender of the Response. In our proposal, to hide the identity of the provider that processes the request, we require that also the Response is forwarded to several providers before it reaches the service provider.

Clearly, suitable solutions are adopted to solve the problem arising from the change in the protocol, such as how to prevent a message from circulating indefinitely among providers, how to build the AuthnRequest and Response messages and how to select the identity providers. These issues along with the technical details of the proposal are the subject of the next sections.

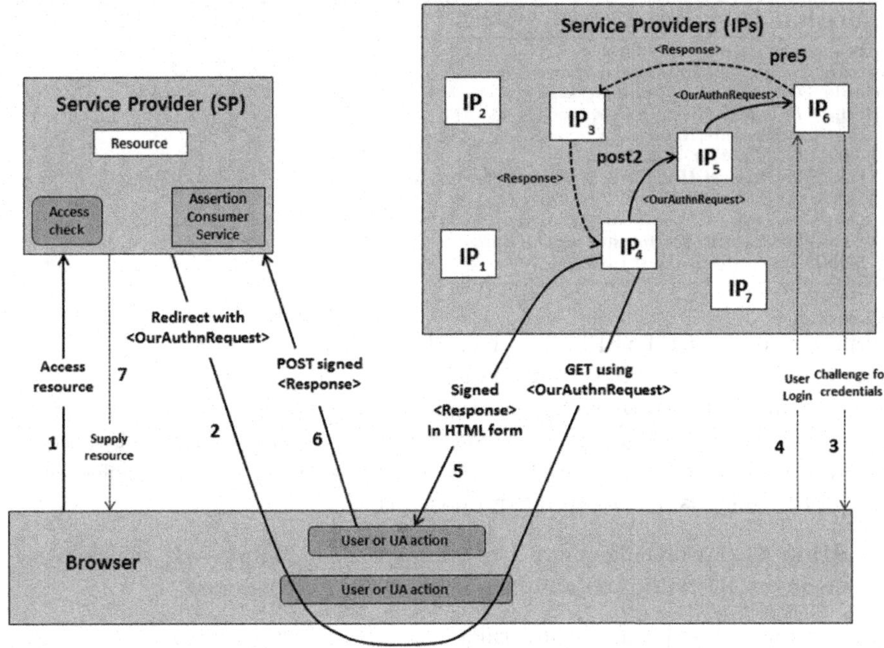

Fig. 2. Data flow during an authentication request in our proposal.

4 Implementation

In this section, we describe the technical implementation of the proposed enhanced SPID protocol.

First, we recall that the first change our proposal requires is that the ID of the user is not linked to the identity provider that issued him the credential. For this purpose, we propose that the ID assigned to the user is randomly generated as a 1024-bit string. This choice allows us to guarantee that the probability of assigning the same ID to two different users is practically zero, for any realistic overall number of users. Indeed, yet assuming to have a population of 100 billion people, this probability is less than 2^{-900}.

Now, we describe the enhance SPID protocol, which is illustrated in Fig. 2. The request that the user sends to the *Service Provider* for accessing the service (i.e., `Access resource` at Step 1 of Fig. 2), contains this randomly generated ID of the user.

Service Provider processes the received request `Access Resource` according to the code shown in Algorithm 1. Observe that the algorithm is parametric w.r.t. the value `TTLmax`, a non-negative integer number used as time-to-live to prevent messages from circulating indefinitely among providers (how to set up this parameter is discussed in Sect. 6).

First, the algorithm randomly selects an identity provider by using the interface `IProviderRandom`, which is included in our proposal (Line 1). Indeed, this

Algorithm 1. *Process AccessResource*

Input *Access Resource*: a message
Constant *TTLmax*: an integer number
Variable *OurAuthnRequest*: a message
Variable *Entry*: an Identity Provider
1: Entry := IProviderRandom();
2: *CREATE new OurAuthnRequest*
3: *OurAuthnRequest.UserID := AccessResource.ID*
4: *OurAuthnRequest.TTL := TTLmax*
5: *OurAuthnRequest.FirstIdentityProvider := Entry.EntityId*
6: *OurAuthnRequest.Destination := OurAuthnRequest.FirstIdentityProvider*
7: **SEND** *OurAuthnRequest* to *Entry*

interface is similar to the SPID interface `IRegistryAccess` presented in Sect. 2, with the difference that, `IRegistryAccess` returns all identity providers, instead `IProviderRandom` returns only one provider randomly selected by TTP from the *Federation Registry*. `IProviderRandom` returns an entry `AuthorityInfo` as defined in Definition 1. Then, it creates a message of the type `OurAuthnRequest` (Lines 2-6), which is defined in our proposal as:

Definition 5. `OurAuthnRequest` is a message that contains all the fields of `AuthnRequest` (Definition 2) and in addition the following ones:

- the attribute `UserID`, a user identifier;
- the attribute `FirstIdentityProvider`, the URL of an identity provider;
- the attribute `TTL`, a non-negative integer.

Specifically, in the created message, `UserID` is the randomly generated user's identification number contained in the request `Access Resource`, `TTL` is initialized to `TTLmax` (the system parameter introduced above), and `FirstIdentityPro-vider` is the URL of the provider obtained through the interface `IProviderRandom` (i.e., `Entry`). Note that, we need to save in this message the reference to this provider because it will send to the service provider the outcome of the authentication request, in order to hide the identity of the actual provider that processes the request. The attribute `Destination` is updated every time the message is forwarded to another provider. Moreover, the attribute `Destination`, which is inherited from `AuthnRequest` (which `OurAuthnRequest` extends), is set to `FirstIdentityProvider`. The remaining elements of the message are set as done in the standard SPID protocol. Finally, `OurAuthnRequest` is sent to the identity provider returned from the interface `IProviderRandom` (Line 7).

The message `OurAuthnRequest` reaches the identity provider, say IP, (Step 2 of Fig. 2), which processes it according to the code shown in Algorithm 2. As done by the service provider previously, first, IP calls the interface `IProviderRandom` to obtain the reference to another random identity provider (Line 1). Then, IP verifies whether the ID of the user, which is stored in *OurAuthnRequest. UserID*, is in the lists of the IDs it issued (Line 2). In this case, the provider creates the message `Response` (Definition 4).

This message is obtained by inserting, as destination of the response, the URL of the service provider (Line 4) and storing also the reference to the (first)

Algorithm 2. *Process OurAuthnRequest*

```
Input OurAuthnRequest: a message
Variable Response: a message
Variable Entry: an Identity Provider
1: entry := IProviderRandom();
2: if (OurAuthnRequest.UserID is my client) then
3:    CREATE new Response
4:    Response.Destination := OurAuthnRequest.AssertionConsumerURL
5:    Response.Issuer := OurAuthnRequest.FirstIdentityProvider
6:    ChallengeCredential()
7:    UserLogin()
8:    if (UserLogin successes) then
9:       Response.Status := "Success"
10:   else
11:      Response.Status := "AuthnFailed"
12:   end if
13:   SEND Response to entry
14: else
15:   if (OurAuthnRequest.TTL > 0) then
16:      OurAuthnRequest.TTL := OurAuthnRequest.TTL - 1
17:      SEND OurAuthnRequest to Entry
18:   else
19:      CREATE new Response
20:      Response.Status := "RequestDenied"
21:      Response.Destination := OurAuthnRequest.AssertionConsumerURL
22:      Response.Issuer := OurAuthnRequest.FirstIdentityProvider
23:      SEND Response to OurAuthnRequest.FirstIdentityProvider
24:   end if
25: end if
```

identity provider that received the `OurAuthnRequest` from *Service Provider* (Line 5). Moreover, the challenge authentication with the user (Steps 3 and 4) is performed by using the (standard) methods `ChallengeCredential` and `UserLogin`, respectively (Lines 6-7). The response contains the result of the user authentication, named `Status`, which can be "Success" or "AuthnFailed" (Lines 8-12). In both cases, the response is sent (Steps 5 and 6) to the randomly selected *Identity Provider* (Line 13).

In the case the user has not been registered by IP, if the message is not expired (Line 15), it is forwarded with decreased TTL (Line 16) to another identity provider (Line 17), which will process this input recursively by this algorithm. When the message is expired, a new message `Response` with `Status` equal to "RequestDenied" is generated (Lines 19-22) and sent to the (first) identity provider that received the `OurAuthnRequest` from *Service Provider* (Line 23).

An identity provider IP' that receives a message `Response` processes it according to the code shown in Algorithm 3. This algorithm is parametric w.r.t. the real value p ranging from 0 to 1. First, it verifies if this response is relative to a request `OurAuthnRequest` that it (i.e. IP') has received directly from *Service Provider* (Line 1). In this case, IP' creates the `Assertion`, as defined in Definition 3, for this response (Line 2), thus appearing as the executor of the user authentication. The response is then sent to the *Service Provider* (Line 3). Otherwise, with probability p (Lines 5-6), the received message is directly sent to the *Service Provider*, whereas with a probability $1-p$, the message is forwarded to another random identity provider (Lines 9-10).

Algorithm 3. *Process Response*

```
Input     Response: a message
Constant  p: a real number
Variable  Assertion: a message
Variable  Entry: an Identity Provider
if (Response.FirstIdentityProvider is my URL) then
   Response.Assertion := CREATE Assertion
   SEND Response to Response.Destination
else
   GENERATE a random real number x in [0,1]
   if (x ≤ p) then
      SEND Response to Response.FirstIdentityProvider
   else
      Entry := IProviderRandom();
      SEND Response to Entry
   end if
end if
```

Finally, we provide a short example about the message routing to handle an access resource request. We consider again the scenario in Fig. 2, in which we assume the presence of seven identity providers (`IPs`). Steps 1 and 2 are the same as in SPID, thus follow the procedure discussed in Sect. 2. In our example, *Service Provider* (`SP`) receives the reference to $\texttt{IP}_4$ calling the interface `IProviderRandom`. As the identity provider that registered the user is $\texttt{IP}_6$, `OurAuthnRequest` is forwarded randomly among several identity providers (only $\texttt{IP}_5$) until it reaches $\texttt{IP}_6$ (Step post2). Observe that this additional routing of the authentication request is not present in SPID. Once $\texttt{IP}_6$ receives the request, performs the user login and challenge authentication tasks with the user (Steps 3 and 4, as in SPID). The result of the user authentication (i.e., the `Response` message) is again forwarded among several identity providers (only $\texttt{IP}_3$) until it reaches the identity provider $\texttt{IP}_4$, which started the routing (Step pre5). Also this step for handling the response delivery is not present in SPID. Finally, $\texttt{IP}_4$ forwards `Response` as well as the `Assertion` to `SP` (Steps 5 and 6, as in SPID), so that the user may access the resource (Step 7, as in SPID).

5 Related Work

Our paper is contextualized in the topic of electronic identification, authentication and trust services (eIDAS), where there exists a wide literature.

In [15], the authors present the main principles of eIDAS and analyze whether these principles are a positive evolution from the currently existing legal framework for electronic seals, time stamping, electronic document acceptability, electronic delivery and web site authentication. However, the authors demonstrate that the European Commission may have moved too hastily in drafting this proposal, resulting in a number of unclarities, inconsistencies and ambiguities.

In [11], a mechanism to provide authenticity and integrity of documents based on Twitter is proposed. The problem of the information leakage derived from the expression of opinions in social networks is dealt with in [7–10, 12]. A recent survey on attacks and vulnerability of digital signature is provided in [18].

Massacci et al. [19] discuss potential security and privacy issues related to electronic IDs and trust service providers, and proposes recommendations for the eIDAS draft based on the innovative technological contributions of EU Trust and Security Programme projects.

Also, in [14], the authors describe eIDAS and the three UE projects related to it (Stork, Stork 2.0 and FutureID). In particular, they analyze whether eIDAS provides requirements that need to be implemented in the FutureID infrastructure. For this purpose, the description of eIDAS and the analysis of its main requirements for technical developers are in general relevant to the development of online identification and authentication schemes.

Now, we consider some applications of eIDAS in cloud computing and e-banking systems. Cloud computing promises to provide great advantages and many analysts expect a significant growth of the cloud services market. In a similar manner, the forthcoming European regulation on electronic identification and trusted services for electronic transactions in the internal market is expected to ease electronic identification, authentication and signatures (eIDAS) in Europe. Hühnlein [16] discusses whether and how the two approaches can be combined in order to provide services for electronic identification and authentication of entities, the creation, verification, validation and preservation of electronic signatures and the registered delivery of documents in an efficient manner using cloud computing techniques.

Jordan et al. [17] believe that the technology used by the Mobile, Social and Cloud triad can greatly boost the deployment of applications and, therefore, may accelerate the achievement of the eIDAS vision. Mobile devices have become the something-you-have authentication factor that has been generally delegated to hardware tokens. Smartphones allow deploying highly-secure yet user-friendly mechanisms that can complement existing national eIDs and overcome user-experience drawbacks. Furthermore, they explain that the identity services are not solely useful for backing up identities provisioned and managed by Member States but can also enhance services by federating and elevating trust on social and other consumer identities.

In [6], the authors analyze the weaknesses of the current e-banking system. Nowadays, millions of consumers are now able to conduct financial transactions using a wide range of mobile devices. This growth exposes the system not only to the set of known threats that are now migrating from traditional PC-based e-banking to the mobile-based scenario, but, to emerging threats specifically targeting mobile devices. To provide transaction security, and minimize the potential threats, e-banking systems must implement robust identification and authentication systems (eIDAS). Therefore, the authors present a brief review on the current state of the art analyzing the most popular eIDAS implemented in Europe. In particular, they assess the most common eIDAS approaches for e-banking and their suitability against the known threats in terms of related incidents and financial loss. Finally, they propose a set of challenges and recommendations to be considered in any eIDAS implementation.

Buchmann et al. [13] discuss the adaption of the upcoming eIDAS standard towards trusted banking transactions and outline resulting security and privacy enhancements. In particular, they extend the eIDAS standard by biometric authenticated transactions which not only boost user convenience, trust and confidence towards eBanking and eBusiness, but suggest to integrate state-of-the-art privacy compliant biometric technologies into the security ecosystem. As a result, they demonstrate that eIDAS is highly suitable for banking transactions since it is solely based on security protocols and infrastructure which have been for more than ten years proven secure in the civil aviation domain.

6 Discussion and Conclusion

In this paper, we proposed a modification of SPID based on a cooperative approach to allow user authentication by preserving the anonymity of the identity provider that grants the authentication credentials.

For this purpose, we introduced in the protocol used by service and identity providers two mechanisms of message routing by means of which both the service provider and the identity provider are not aware of the association between the authenticated user and the provider that guarantees his identity. The first routing mechanism moves the authentication request among several identity providers and a TTL-based strategy is adopted to prevent a message from circulating indefinitely among providers. By suitably setting the initial value of message TTL (i.e., TTLmax), which acts as a first system parameter, it is possible to guarantee with a given probability the delivery of the request to the right identity provider.

A second routing mechanism, which relies on a second system parameter p, is used to deliver the response to the service provider guaranteeing no information leakage. Concerning the setting of TTLmax, it should be high to avoid that a short life time does not allow the message to reach the target identity provider. On the other hand, a too high TTLmax can increase the traffic in case of a request with no valid user ID. As a consequence, a trade-off has to be solved. Also the second parameter should be set. Again, the trade-off to solve is fast response delivery (i.e., high p) versus the high level of obfuscation of the path followed by the message (i.e., low p).

The setting of the two system parameters is left as future work. Moreover, we plan to study the use of eIDAS in interactions between users without the presence of a bank or government entities.

Acknowledgment. This work has been partially supported by the TENACE PRIN Project (n. 20103P34XC) funded by the Italian Ministry of Education, University and Research and by the Program "Programma Operativo Nazionale Ricerca e Competitività" 2007-2013, Distretto Tecnologico CyberSecurity funded by the Italian Ministry of Education, University and Research.

References

1. Agency for Digital Italy (AGID) (2015). http://www.agid.gov.it/
2. Art. 3 DPCM of 24 October 2014 (2015). http://www.agid.gov.it/sites/default/files/leggi_decreti_direttive/dpcm_24_ottobre_2014.pdf
3. Electronic identification and trust services (eIDAS) (2015). http://ec.europa.eu/dgs/connect/en/content/electronic-identification-and-trust-services-eidas-regulatory-environment-and-beyond
4. Security Assertion Markup Language (SAML) (2015). http://it.wikipedia.org/wiki/Security_Assertion_Markup_Language
5. SPID-Agenzia per l'Italia Digitale (2015). http://www.agid.gov.it/sites/default/files/regole_tecniche/spid_regole_tecniche_v0_1.pdf
6. Vila, J.A., Serna-Olvera, J., Fernandez, L., Medina, M., Sfakianakis, A.: A professional view on ebanking authentication: challenges and recommendations. In: 2013 9th International Conference on Information Assurance and Security (IAS), pp. 43–48. IEEE (2013)
7. Buccafurri, F., Fotia, L., Lax, G.: Allowing continuous evaluation of citizen opinions through social networks. In: Kő, A., Leitner, C., Leitold, H., Prosser, A. (eds.) EDEM 2012 and EGOVIS 2012. LNCS, vol. 7452, pp. 242–253. Springer, Heidelberg (2012)
8. Buccafurri, F., Fotia, L., Lax, G.: Privacy-preserving resource evaluation in social networks. In: Proceedings of the 2012 Tenth Annual International Conference on Privacy, Security and Trust (PST 2012), pp. 51–58. IEEE Computer Society (2012)
9. Buccafurri, F., Fotia, L., Lax, G.: Allowing non-identifying information disclosure in citizen opinion evaluation. In: Kő, A., Leitner, C., Leitold, H., Prosser, A. (eds.) EDEM 2013 and EGOVIS 2013. LNCS, vol. 8061, pp. 241–254. Springer, Heidelberg (2013)
10. Buccafurri, F., Fotia, L., Lax, G.: Allowing privacy-preserving analysis of social network likes. In: Privacy, Security and Trust (PST), 2013 Eleventh Annual International Conference on, pp. 36–43. IEEE (2013)
11. Buccafurri, F., Fotia, L., Lax, G.: Social signature: signing by tweeting. In: Kő, A., Francesconi, E. (eds.) EGOVIS 2014. LNCS, vol. 8650, pp. 1–14. Springer, Heidelberg (2014)
12. Buccafurri, F., Fotia, L., Lax, G.: A privacy-preserving e-participation framework allowing citizen opinion analysis. Electron. Gov. An Int. J. **11**, 185–206 (2015)
13. Buchmann, N., Rathgeb, C., Baier, H., Busch, C.: Towards electronic identification and trusted services for biometric authenticated transactions in the single euro payments area. In: Preneel, B., Ikonomou, D. (eds.) APF 2014. LNCS, vol. 8450, pp. 172–190. Springer, Heidelberg (2014)
14. Cuijpers, C., Schroers, J.: eIDAS as guideline for the development of a pan European eID framework in FutureID. Open Identity Summit **2014**(237), 23–38 (2014)
15. Dumortier, J., Vandezande, N.: Critical Observations on the Proposed Regulation for Electronic Identification and Trust Services for Electronic Transactions in the Internal Market. ICRI Research Paper, 9 (2012)
16. Hühnlein, D.: Towards eIDAS as a Service. In: Reimer, H., Pohlmann, N., Schneider, W. (eds.) ISSE 2014 Securing Electronic Business Processes, pp. 241–248. Springer, Heidelberg (2014)
17. Jordan, F., Pujol, H., Ruana, D.: Achieving the eIDAS vision through the mobile, social and cloud triad. In: Reimer, H., Pohlmann, N., Schneider, W. (eds.) ISSE 2014 Securing Electronic Business Processes, pp. 81–93. Springer, Heidelberg (2014)

18. Lax, G., Buccafurri, F., Caminiti, G.: Digital document signing: Vulnerabilities and solutions. A Global Perspective, Information Security Journal (2015)
19. Massacci, F., Gadyatskaya, O.: How to get better EID and Trust Services by leveraging eIDAS legislation on EU funded research results (2013)
20. Navarro, V.A., Gumbau, J., Santapau, P., Marzal, A.: Stork project results: Pan-european eid interoperability demonstrated (2011)
21. Wessels, B.: Identification and the practices of identity and privacy in everyday digital communication. New Media Soc. **14**, 1251–1268 (2012)

Encryption-Based Second Authentication Factor Solutions for Qualified Server-Side Signature Creation

Christof Rath(✉), Simon Roth, Harald Bratko, and Thomas Zefferer

Institute for Applied Information Processing and Communications, Graz University of Technology, Graz 8010, Austria
{christof.rath,simon.roth,harald.bratko,thomas.zefferer}@iaik.tugraz.at
http://www.iaik.tugraz.at

Abstract. Electronic identity (eID) and electronic signature (e-signature) are key concepts of transactional e-government solutions. Especially in Europe, server-based eID and e-signature solutions have recently gained popularity, as they provide enhanced usability while still complying with strict security requirements. To implement obligatory two-factor user-authentication schemes, current server-based eID and e-signature solutions typically rely on one-time passwords delivered to the user via short message service (SMS). This raises several issues in practice, as the use of SMS technology can be cost-effective and insecure. To address these issues, we propose an alternative two-factor user-authentication scheme following a challenge-response approach. The feasibility and applicability of the proposed user-authentication scheme is evaluated by means of two concrete implementations. This way, we show that the proposed authentication scheme and its implementations improve both the cost effectiveness and the security of server-based eID and e-signature solutions.

Keywords: Electronic identity · Electronic signature · Server signature · User authentication · Challenge response · Two-factor authentication

1 Introduction

The concepts of electronic identity (eID) and electronic signature (e-signature) are crucial for transactional e-government services. They enable users to securely and reliably authenticate at services and to create electronic signatures. Their relevance is especially given in the European Union (EU), where so-called qualified electronic signatures are legally equivalent to handwritten signatures [10]. This enables users to remotely provide written consent in transactional services.

During the past years, different approaches for the realization of eID and e-signature concepts have been studied, implemented, and deployed. First approaches to provide users eID and e-signature functionality have been based on

© Springer International Publishing Switzerland 2015
A. Kő and E. Francesconi (Eds.): EGOVIS 2015, LNCS 9265, pp. 71–85, 2015.
DOI: 10.1007/978-3-319-22389-6_6

smart-card technology [4,5]. However, these approaches have turned out to suffer from several usability-related limitations and hence from limited user acceptance [11]. As an alternative, mobile eID and e-signature solutions have emerged early. These solution remove the need for smart-card usage by making use of the user's mobile phone instead. Two approaches can be distinguished. The first approach employs the mobile phone's SIM card to store eID data and to implement cryptographic functions required for the creation of electronic signatures. The second approach instead relies on a central hardware security module (HSM) to store eID data and to carry out required cryptographic functions.

During the past years, the second approach, i.e., server-based solutions, has gained relevance and popularity, mainly because it defines fewer requirements for the mobile end-user device and mobile network operators (MNO), which in turn improves applicability, feasibility and usability. The main challenge in designing and developing server-based eID and e-signature solutions is the provision of appropriately secure user-authentication schemes. These schemes are required to restrict access to centrally stored eID data and cryptographic signing keys to the legitimate user. In order to assure a sufficient level of security, two-factor authentication (2FA) is typically the approach of choice.

Current mobile eID and e-signature solutions following the sever-based approach implement 2FA schemes by means of one-time passwords (OTPs) delivered by SMS messages [8,9]. After the user has entered a secret password covering the authentication factor knowledge, he or she receives a OTP via SMS. By proving reception of the OTP, the user proves possession of the mobile phone. This way, the authentication factor possession is covered and the 2FA process is completed.

Unfortunately, reliance on SMS technology raises several issues [6]. First, SMS must not be regarded as secure. This especially applies to smartphones, on which incoming SMS messages can be intercepted by third party applications. Second, the sending of SMS messages containing OTPs can cause significant costs for the service operator, as mobile network operators (MNOs) typically charge the delivery of SMS messages. To overcome these issues, we propose an alternative 2FA scheme for server-based mobile signature solutions. Our proposed scheme renders the use of SMS technology unnecessary. This way, it provides higher cost efficiency and better security compared to existing approaches.

2 Related Work

Two-factor authentication has been a topic of interest for many years. This does not only apply to eID and e-signature solutions but basically to any e-service that requires a secure and reliable remote authentication of users. Numerous approaches and solutions to authenticate users by means of 2FA have been proposed and developed during the past years. Although these approaches and solutions rely on different technologies and communication protocols, they can be classified in a few basic categories, whereas the implementation of the authentication factor possession is used as key classification criterion. Relevant categories of 2FA schemes are briefly sketched in this section.

Client-generated OTPs represent the first relevant category of 2FA schemes. The basic idea behind this scheme is simple. The user creates a OTP using some kind of hardware token. As creation of the correct OTP is infeasible without this token, proving knowledge of the OTP proves possession of the respective hardware token. This way, the authentication factor possession is covered. During the past years, different implementations of authentication schemes relying on client-generated OTP have been proposed. Examples are SecurID[1] or DIGIPASS[2], which incorporate the current time for the derivation of OTPs. A related standard for the generation of OTPs based on the current time has been proposed in RFC 6238[3]. Alternatively, a counter synchronized between the remote entity and the user's local hardware token can also be used to derive unambiguous OTPs. This has been described in RFC 4226[4]. Recently, OTP-based authentication solutions have been developed that rely on personalized mobile apps instead of hardware tokens. Examples of such app-based approaches are Google Authenticator[5] or a solution developed by the Barada project[6]. In general, client-generated OTPs are a relatively old and hence time-tested approach. However, they have several disadvantages when being used for server-based signature solutions. For example, they do not allow an unambiguous binding between the current transaction and the generated OTP.

To overcome limitations of client-generated OTPs, current server-based signature solutions follow the SMS-OTP Approach, where the authentication factor possession is covered by the user's SIM. Possession of the SIM is verified by sending an OTP to the user's mobile phone via SMS. By proving knowledge of the OTP, the user proves possession of the SIM. Although the SMS-OTP Approach makes use of OTPs as well, there are conceptual differences to solutions relying on client-generated OTPs. Client-generated solutions require only one communication step, in which the locally created OTP is transferred to the remote entity. In contrast, the SMS-OTP Approach implements two consecutive communication steps. A centrally created OTP is first sent to the user's mobile phone. Subsequently, the OTP must be transmitted back to the remote entity. The central generation of the OTP is an important conceptual advantage, as it enables the remote entity to unambiguously bind the OTP to a specific authentication run and hence to a certain transaction. Unfortunately, the central OTP generation also bears a considerable drawback. The SMS-OTP approach demands that the OTP is transferred to the user's mobile end-user device via SMS. Unfortunately, SMS technology cannot guarantee secure data transmissions. This especially applies to modern smartphones, on which incoming SMS messages can be compromised by malware [2]. Still, the SMS-OTP Approach is frequently used in practice. Examples are e-banking solutions and the mobile signature solutions

[1] http://www.emc.com/security/rsa-securid.htm.
[2] https://www.vasco.com/products/products.aspx.
[3] http://tools.ietf.org/html/rfc6238.
[4] http://tools.ietf.org/html/rfc4226.
[5] https://code.google.com/p/google-authenticator/.
[6] http://barada.sourceforge.net/.

Austrian Mobile Phone Signature[7] and ServerBKU [9]. The latter two rely on a concept by Orthacker et al. [8] in order to assure a sufficient level of security to create qualified electronic signatures.

As an alternative to OTP-based approaches, challenge-response approaches have emerged as 2FA schemes during the past years. They represent the third category, in which current 2FA solutions can be classified. Challenge-response approaches resemble the SMS-OTP Approach, as they also rely on two consecutive communication steps. First, the remote entity generates a random challenge, which is transmitted to the user's mobile phone. The mobile phone creates a response from this challenge using cryptographic methods. These methods employ a device-specific cryptographic key. Thus, the capability to create responses from received challenges with this particular key proves possession of the device. Created responses are then returned to the remote entity. The remote entity cryptographically verifies the obtained response. Therefore, it must be aware of the cryptographic key used to create the response. Hence, challenge-response approaches require a pairing process to exchange relevant key material. During the past years, several authentication solutions following challenge-response approaches have been introduced for powerful mobile end-user devices such as smartphones. These solutions can again be classified into two categories. Software-based solutions store required cryptographic key material and implement cryptographic functionality in software. Such a software-based authentication solutions following a challenge-response approach is for instance SQRL[8]. In contrast, hardware-based solutions implement cryptographic functionality in secure hardware elements. While this provides a higher level of security, it also requires mobile end-user devices to provide appropriate hardware components. A well-known example for a hardware-based authentication solution following the challenge-response approach is U2F proposed by the FIDO Alliance[9].

All of the mentioned 2FA schemes come with various pros and cons. However, none of them has been explicitly designed for a use with server-based eID and e-signature solutions. Hence, these schemes are not tailored to the special requirements of this use cases. To address this issue, we propose a new 2FA scheme that explicitly takes into account special requirements and characteristic of server-based eID and e-signature solutions. These requirements are identified and discussed in the following section.

3 Requirements

Relevant requirements for the proposed 2FA scheme have been derived from current state-of-the-art solutions, i.e., SMS message-based two-factor authentication, and from requirements defined by relevant legislations. Derived requirements are listed and described below in more detail. Derived requirements will also serve as basis for the evaluation of the proposed solution.

[7] http://www.handy-signatur.at.

[8] http://sqrl.pl.

[9] https://fidoalliance.org/.

R1: Platform independence
In order to avoid exclusion of certain user groups, the proposed solution must be platform independent.

R2: Transaction binding
It must be possible to unambiguously link the document to be signed to the authentication data used to authorize the transaction.

R3: Security
The proposed solution must be at least as secure as established SMS-based solutions.

R4: Usability
User acceptance is a key factor for any eID solution [11]. In general, an alternative 2FA approach must not reduce the usability and, thus, user acceptance. Furthermore, a new solution should be self-explanatory for users and necessary changes and benefits should be easy to communicate from the operator side.

R5: Feasibility
For operators, the proposed solution must be easy to integrate and flexible in its operation. External dependencies should be minimized.

R6: Cost efficiency
The solution must be cost efficient, i.e., investments must pay off and the operation must be cheaper than SMS-based solutions. At the same time, costs must not be transferred to the users.

Based on these requirements, we propose an alternative 2FA scheme for server-based eID and e-signature solutions in the next section.

4 Proposed Solution

Over the time, several different approaches as alternatives for the widely used SMS-OTP procedure have been developed. Apart from economical reasons, i.e., the costs for the huge amount of SMS messages to be sent, security considerations were the most important factor to look for a new two-factor authentication approach. Trivially, one could simply change the direction of the SMS message from *being-received* to *has-to-be-sent* by the user. However, this greatly reduces the usability of the system and, thus, the willingness to use such a solution.

The growing popularity of smartphones enables novel solutions that do not rely on SMS messages to prove the possession of an authentication token. Accordingly, our proposed solution does not rely on a separate communication channel, i.e. the GSM protocol and the MNO, but uses a standard network connection and cryptographic key material that is bound to the device.

Overall, the proposed solution consists of two distinct phases, the pairing phase and the authentication phase. The basic concept of the solution and its two phases is depicted in Fig. 1 and detailed in the following subsections.

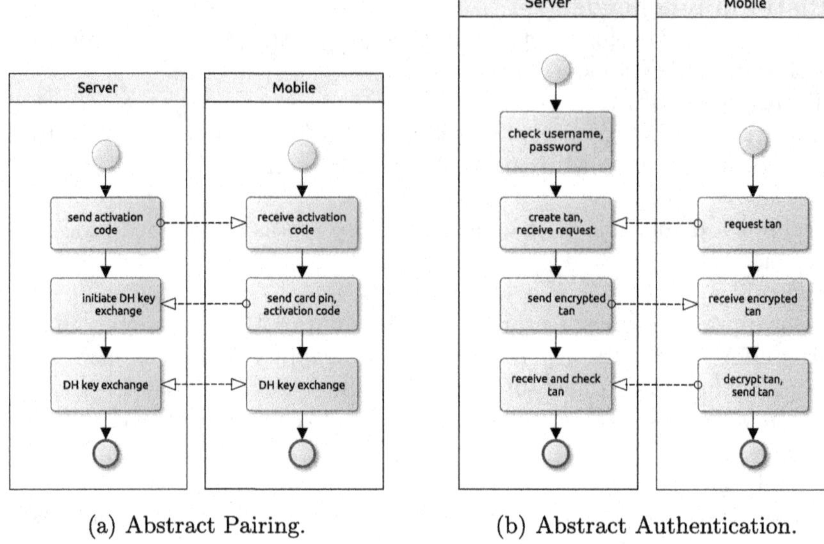

(a) Abstract Pairing. (b) Abstract Authentication.

Fig. 1. Abstract basic concept of the solution.

4.1 Pairing

Initially, a mobile device, which is later used for authentication, must be bound to a user account by the so-called pairing process. This is shown in Fig. 1(a). After initiating this pairing process, the server component, which maintains the respective user account, generates a random activation code. The activation code gets embedded into an URL that references the server's pairing component and is sent via SMS message to the user's phone. Once this URL gets dereferenced, the user is asked to authenticate by entering his or her personal password that is assigned to his or her user account. If the entered password is correct, the active pairing session can be identified via the embedded activation code and a symmetric key is exchanged between the mobile device and the server component using the Diffie-Hellman key exchange protocol [3]. The exchanged key is securely stored by both the server component and the mobile device and is used in subsequent authentication phases.

4.2 Authentication

The authentication process is shown in Fig. 1(b). It starts with a conventional user name and password authentication to cover the first authentication factor. If this step succeeds, the server component prepares a challenge by generating a random OTP t. The OTP is encrypted using the shared symmetric key ssk generated during the pairing phase.

$$t_{\mathsf{enc}} = \mathrm{encrypt}(t;\ ssk) \tag{1}$$

Upon user interaction, the mobile phone requests the encrypted OTP t_{enc}. On the mobile phone, the OTP is decrypted using the same shared secret ssk'.

$$t' = \text{decrypt}(t_{\mathsf{enc}};\ ssk') \tag{2}$$

By proving the capability to decrypt the OTP t, the user proves possession of the mobile device. This covers the second authentication factor. The decrypted OTP t' is returned to the server component. The server component verifies the correctness of the received OTP t'. If the received OTP t' is correct, the authentication is regarded as successful.

5 Evaluation

The solution proposed in Sect. 4 has been evaluated by means of two concrete implementations. In this section we introduce these two implementations in more detail. Our first implementation has been based on HTML5 and is discussed in Subsect. 5.1. To further increase usability, we have also developed a solution that makes use of QR tags. This solution is described in detail in Subsect. 5.2. Both implementations increase cost efficiency R6 in comparison to traditional SMS-OTP solutions by superseding the need for sending SMS messages every time a signature is created.

To test our approach, we integrated both implementations in the *ServerBKU* [9]. The *ServerBKU* is a secure and flexible server-based mobile eID and e-signature solution. It uses the classical SMS-OTP approach to authenticate users and to authorize the creation of server-side signatures. We have enhanced the *ServerBKU* by replacing its SMS-based user-authentication scheme with the two implementations of the proposed solution. The two developed implementations and their integration into the *ServerBKU* is detailed in the following subsections.

5.1 *TanApp*

Our first implementation of the concept proposed in Sect. 4 is called *TanApp*. The *TanApp* implements all required client functionality by means of HTML5 and JavaScript functionality. According to the proposed concept, the *TanApp* retrieves AES-encrypted [7] OTPs from the *ServerBKU*, decrypts these OTPs and displays them to the user. To further improve security, the *TanApp* additionally features an elaborate sequencing mechanisms. This means, that communication between the *TanApp* and the *ServerBKU* is sequence controlled. Before the first user-authentication process, *ServerBKU* and *TanApp* negotiate an initialization vector (IV), which acts as sequence counter. The sequence counter, i.e. the IV, changes after each user-authentication process.

In total, the *TanApp* implements two use cases: paring and signature creation. During the pairing process, *ServerBKU* and *TanApp* negotiate a secret AES key that is used to encrypt and decrypt OTPs. Furthermore, the IV, which is required for the implemented sequencing mechanism, is negotiated. During signature creation, the *TanApp* is used to authenticate the user at the *ServerBKU* and to authorize a signature-creation process. Both use cases are described in the following subsections in more detail.

Pairing: After the user is registered at the *ServerBKU* and has activated an eID, in the context of the Austrian e-government also known as mobile citizen card (MCC), he or she may pair this eID to the *TanApp* on his smartphone to use this approach instead of the SMS-based method henceforth.

When the user starts the pairing process an SMS message containing a URL is sent to his or her mobile phone, which guarantees the binding between the mobile phone and its owner. This URL contains a randomly generated activation code as parameter. Clicking this URL opens the default browser where the user is prompted to enter his or her user name and password. This ensures that only the legitimate user can change the authentication method. After that, the *ServerBKU* and *TanApp* use the Diffie-Hellman key exchange protocol to negotiate an AES key, the pairing key ssk. For performance reasons, especially in the context of our JavaScript implementation, we use EC-Diffie-Hellman [1]. On the server side, the created AES key is securely stored. On the smartphone side, the key is stored in the HTML5 local storage.

During the pairing process, *ServerBKU* and *TanApp* also exchange the initial value of the AES initialization vector. In the final step of the pairing process, the *ServerBKU* uses this initialization vector to compute the unique identifier ($tanId$) of the current transaction state as the encrypted concatenation of the initialization vector (IV), the eID alias ($mccAlias$) and the mobile-phone number ($mobileNumber$):

$$tanId = \text{encrypt}(iv \| mccAlias \| mobileNumber; iv, ssk) \tag{3}$$

The *ServerBKU* stores the $tanId$. The pairing process is finished by switching the default user-authentication scheme for the respective eID from SMS-OTP mode to *TanApp* mode.

Signature Creation: Once an eID, i.e. an MCC, has been paired, the *TanApp* can be used to authorize signature-creation processes. The required processing steps are shown in Fig. 2. The *TanApp*-based user authentication of a typical signature-creation process consists of the following steps:

1. The *ServerBKU* receives a signature creation request and prompts the user to enter her user name and password (see Fig. 3(a)).
2. After the user has entered the required data (i.e. user name and password) in the browser, the *ServerBKU* identifies the corresponding eID and retrieves the associated pairing key (ssk).
3. The *ServerBKU* creates a new OTP (t) and the initialization vector for the next round (iv_{new}) and stores both in the card database.

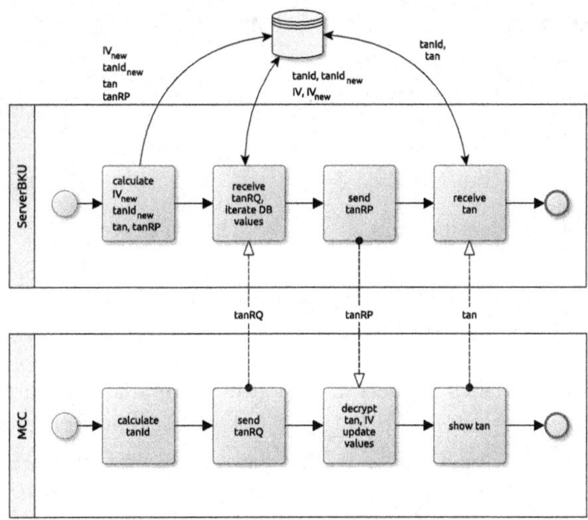

Fig. 2. Tanapp protocol.

4. The *ServerBKU* computes the unique identifier used for transaction binding (cf. Requirement R2) of the next round ($tanId_{\mathsf{new}}$) and stores it as well:

$$tanId_{\mathsf{new}} = \text{encrypt}(iv_{\mathsf{new}} \| mccAlias \| mobilNumber; iv_{\mathsf{new}}, ssk) \quad (4)$$

5. The *ServerBKU* computes the OTP response ($tanRP$) for the expected OTP request ($tanRQ$) and stores it. Note that this is the OTP response for the current signature request and, hence, the IV used for encryption is the also the current one:

$$tanRP = \text{encrypt}(iv_{\mathsf{new}} \| t; iv, ssk) \quad (5)$$

   The OTP response represents an encrypted container used for delivering the OTP t (cf. step 3) and the IV for the next round (iv_{new}) from the *ServerBKU* to the *TanApp*.
6. The user's browser window prompts for the OTP, as shown in Fig. 3(b).
7. On the smartphone, the user opens the *TanApp* and selects the eID he or she wants to use for signing. This eID must correspond to the credentials she provided in step 2. Selecting the corresponding icon causes the *TanApp* to compute the value $tanId'$ for the OTP request ($tanRQ$):

$$tanId' = \text{encrypt}(iv' \| mccAlias \| mobileNumber; iv', ssk') \quad (6)$$

   Note that $tanId'$ has the same value as the one that the *ServerBKU* has created and stored in the final step of the pairing process (cf. page 8), or the value $tanId_{\mathsf{new}}$ of a previous signature creation process.
8. The $tanId'$ is embedded in the OTP request and sent to the *ServerBKU*.
9. The *ServerBKU* receives $tanId'$ to identify the corresponding eID. If no match can be found, the *ServerBKU* and the *TanApp* have run out of synchronisation and the corresponding eID has to be reset and paired again.

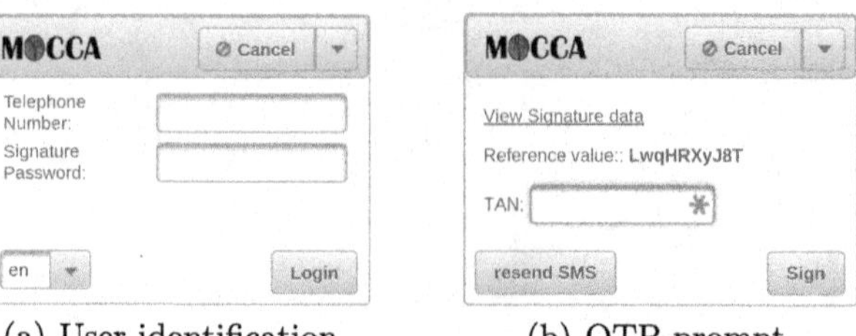

(a) User identification. (b) OTP prompt.

Fig. 3. Web user interface

10. The *ServerBKU* verifies if there is a pending signature request for the eID by checking whether the OTP entry is not `null`. The *ServerBKU* updates the database ($iv = iv_{\mathsf{new}}$, $tanId = tanId_{\mathsf{new}}$, $iv_{\mathsf{new}} = tanId_{new} =$ `null`) and sends the OTP response ($tanRP$), pre-computed in step 5, to the *TanApp*.
11. The *TanApp* receives the OTP response $tanRP$ and decrypts it using the pairing key (ssk) for extracting the OTP t and the IV for the next round iv_{new}.

$$iv'_{\mathsf{new}} \| t' = \text{decrypt}(tanRP; iv', ssk') \tag{7}$$

12. The *TanApp* updates the initialization vector ($iv' = iv'_{\mathsf{new}}$) and displays the OTP t' to the user as shown in Fig. 4.
13. The user enters the OTP t' in the browser window shown in Fig. 3(b), which has been displayed in step 6.
14. The *ServerBKU* checks the OTP, and if $t' = t$ the authentication is successful. It cleans up the database ($tan = tanRP =$ `null`), issues the signature and returns the signed document.

Synchronisation. As already mentioned, the *ServerBKU* and *TanApp* may become unsynchronized. Especially, this can happen if the connection drops during the OTP response delivery. In that case, the *TanApp* will not update the

Fig. 4. OTP displayed on smartphone

AES IV and, hence, the next OTP request will use the same *tanId* as the interrupted request. However, since the *ServerBKU* has performed the IV update before sending the OTP response, no matching record would be found and, thus, the signature creation fail. Once *ServerBKU* and *TanApp* are asynchronous, they must be reset and paired again. If the user is still able to log on to the *ServerBKU*, e.g., by means of an additional eID, he can perform this re-pairing himself. Otherwise, a *ServerBKU* administrator must perform this step. For reasons of usability, efficiency and operational costs this is an undesirable situation. To mitigate this effect, the *ServerBKU* keeps the previous value $tanId_{\mathsf{old}}$. If the *TanApp* for some reason has not updated the IV and, hence, uses the same *tanId* as in the previous OTP request, the *ServerBKU* will be able to identify the corresponding eID by checking the values of *tanId* and $tanId_{\mathsf{old}}$. Once a signature creation request succeeds the *ServerBKU* deletes $tanId_{\mathsf{old}}$ and keeps only the value for the next round ($tanId = tanId_{\mathsf{new}}$), because in that case it is guaranteed, that the *TanApp* has updated the IV. Obviously, if the same OTP request can be sent twice, we must ask if this could bring the potential for a replay attack. However, we could show that yields no advantage for an adversary.

5.2 *QR TanApp*

The pairing process for the *QR TanApp* is akin to the paring process for the *TanApp* described in Subsect. 5.1.

Signing on the other hand differs in some aspects albeit maintaining the same level of security (R3). After the *ServerBKU* receives a signature request, the user is prompted to enter her phone number of an already paired smartphone and signature password to access her eID. Similar to other approaches, the eID is locked for some time if repeatedly wrong login credentials are provided to avoid brute-force attacks (R3). After successful identification, the parameters necessary for the signature creation process are calculated and temporarily stored in the database. Finally a QR code is generated and presented to the user as shown in Fig. 5.

Fig. 5. Second authentication factor QR code prompt

This code contains an URL to the *ServerBKU* signature servlet. Subsequently, the user has to take a photo of this code using a QR reader and continue the signature creation process by opening the contained URL. Since QR code readers are available on all major platforms the platform independence requirement R1 is fulfilled. To complete the signature creation the user has to click a sign button, as shown in Fig. 6(a). Although not strictly necessary, the button was integrated to improve the user experience (R4). Finally, a message indicating the success status is shown on the smartphone, as in Fig. 6(b) and the signature gets issued on the server side.

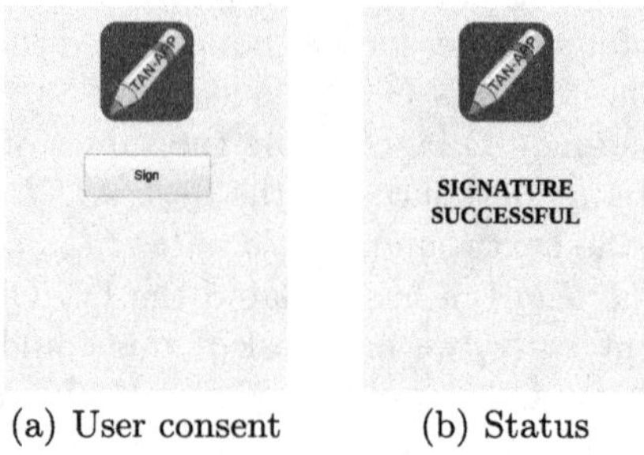

(a) User consent (b) Status

Fig. 6. *QR TanApp* application

Implementation and Protocol Details. The *QR TanApp* was implemented as native smartphone app for Android. This improves the usability (R4) since we could directly access the camera and include a QR reader library. Furthermore, the security could be increased by making use of the smartphone's system key store (R3). To fulfil the platform independence requirement R1, it would be necessary to implement this native app for all major mobile operating systems. A simplified sequence of a signature creation process using the *QR TanApp* can be seen in Fig. 7.

After the successful identification, several parameters have to be pre-computed and stored in the database. As mentioned before, the pairing key ssk is only accessible in the HTTP session where the user has entered her credentials. Therefore, all parameters that require this key have to be pre-computed now. These parameters are:

- iv_{new}: A random initial vector for the next signature.
- $mccTag$: A user can potentially hold multiple eIDs. To distinguish them each eID has an alias $mccAlias$.

$$mccTag = \text{hash}(mccAlias \| phoneNumber) \tag{8}$$

- $tanId$: The $tanId$ is the reference value to verify the possession of the paired mobile device. It contains a random OTP t.

$$tanId = \text{encrypt}(mccTag \| t \| iv; iv_{\mathsf{new}}, ssk) \tag{9}$$

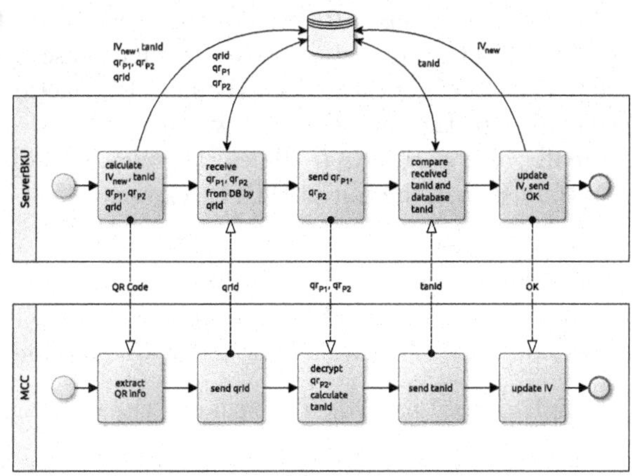

Fig. 7. *QR TanApp* protocol

- qr_{P1}: The encryption result of $mccTag$ concatenated by iv_{new}.

$$qr_{\mathsf{P1}} = \text{encrypt}(mccTag \| iv_{\mathsf{new}}; iv, ssk) \tag{10}$$

- qr_{P2}: The hash value of the $mccAlias$.

$$qr_{\mathsf{P2}} = \text{hash}(mccAlias) \tag{11}$$

- $qrId$: A random value for the identification of the current transaction. This is a reference value to fulfil the transaction binding requirement R2.

These values are stored in the database, except $mccTag$, which is only an intermediate value.

A QR code is generated that contains the URL to the *ServerBKU* servlet processing the signature, including the parameter $qrId$ and the OTP t. This code is shown to the user, as in Fig. 5, who has to take a photo of the code using the *QR TanApp* on her paired mobile device. By decoding the QR code and dereferencing the URL, $qrId$ is transmitted to the *ServerBKU* and the OTP t is stored for later use. Note that we now have a second, independent HTTP session. Using the $qrId$ the *ServerBKU* is able to match the two sessions and returns the parameters qr_{P1} and qr_{P2}.

Using qr_{P2} the *QR TanApp* is able to identify the active eID. Now, qr_{P1} can be decrypted using the corresponding pairing key ssk' and the IV currently stored on the smartphone.

$$mccTag' \| iv'_{\mathsf{new}} = \text{decrypt}(qr_{\mathsf{P1}}; iv', ssk') \tag{12}$$

With these values it is possible to calculate the $tanId'$ similar to the $tanId$ calculated by the *ServerBKU* beforehand.

$$tanId' = \text{encrypt}(mccTag' \| t \| iv'; iv'_{\mathsf{new}}, ssk') \tag{13}$$

This value is transmitted to the *ServerBKU* once the user presses the sign button. The *ServerBKU* verifies that $tanId = tanId'$, in which case the authentication was successful. The new IV gets stored for the next transaction ($iv = iv_{\mathsf{new}}$) and the status is returned to the *QR TanApp*, which in turn also updates the IV ($iv' = iv'_{\mathsf{new}}$). Finally, the *ServerBKU* issues the signature and returns the signed document to the user via the initial HTTP session.

Additional Protocol Features. As with the *TanApp*, the protocol has some additional features to make the application more robust and flexible but which are not of significance for the authentication or signature creation itself:

- A mechanism is implemented to allow to exchange the cryptographic primitives.
- There is support to use multiple eIDs on a single device.
- If the IV synchronization gets lost due to failed transactions the protocol has limited possibilities for self recovery. If this recovery fails a new pairing process is necessary.
- It is not possible to issue multiple signatures in parallel. This is a desired behavior and only the latest request is completed in this case.

6 Conclusion

Due to recent technological advances in the mobile sector, authentication schemes based on SMS-delivered OTPs must be regarded as outdated and inappropriate. This raises challenges for server-based signature solutions that still heavily rely on this approach. To overcome this challenge, we have proposed a novel two-factor based authentication scheme that completely avoids SMS technology. The proposed authentication scheme has three basic advantages. First, it provides a higher level of security, by using strong cryptographic algorithms and hardware key stores on the mobile devices. In particular, it prevents Android-specific attacks that employ techniques to intercept incoming SMS messages. Second, it meets all relevant requirements of server-based signature solutions. Third, it provides enhanced usability by integrating QR codes. Concretely, it prevents users from manually copying unintelligible OTPs from received SMS message messages to the browser.

We have successfully evaluated the proposed authentications scheme by means of two different prototype implementations. The applicability of both implementations has been shown by integrating them into and using them together with an existing mobile eID and e-signature solution. This has proven that the two implementations and the underlying concept are feasible. Practical tests of the two prototype implementations have also revealed their strengths and weaknesses. In particular, it turned out that the QR-based implementation is advantageous in terms of usability. Future work, which will mainly focus on a further consolidation of the current prototypes and their integration into productive solutions, will hence mainly focus on the QR-based approach.

The proposed authentication scheme, its prototypical implementation, and the conducted evaluation presented in this paper show that there are secure and usable alternatives for authentication schemes based on SMS-delivered OTPs. This way, this paper contributes to the further improvement of mobile eID and e-signature solutions and paves the way for their for a successful future e-government.

Acknowledgements. The authors have been supported by the European Commission Seventh Framework Programme through project *FutureID*, grant agreement number 318424.

References

1. Recommendation for Pair-Wise Key-Establishment Schemes Using Discrete Logarithm Cryptography (2007). http://csrc.nist.gov/publications/nistpubs/800-56A/SP800-56A_Revision1_Mar08-2007.pdf. Accessed March 2015
2. Check Point Software Technologies Ltd.: Media Alert: Check Point and Versafe Uncover New Eurograbber Attack (2012). http://www.checkpoint.com/press/2012/120512-media-alert-cp-versafe-eurograbber-attack.html
3. Diffie, W., Hellman, M.: New directions in cryptography. IEEE Trans. Inf. Theory **22**(6), 644–654 (1976). http://dx.doi.org/10.1109/TIT.1976.1055638
4. Fairchild, A., de Vuyst, B.: The Evolution of the e-ID card in Belgium: Data Privacy and Multi-Application Usage. In: The Sixth International Conference on Digital Society, pp. 13–16. Valencia (2012)
5. Leitold, H., Hollosi, A., Posch, R.: Security Architecture of the Austrian Citizen Card Concept. In: 18th Annual Computer Security Applications Conference, 2002, Proceedings, pp. 391–400 (2002)
6. Mulliner, C., Borgaonkar, R., Stewin, P., Seifert, J.-P.: SMS-based one-time passwords: attacks and defense (short paper). In: Rieck, K., Stewin, P., Seifert, J.-P. (eds.) DIMVA 2013. LNCS, vol. 7967, pp. 150–159. Springer, Heidelberg (2013)
7. National Institute of Standards and Technology: Advanced Encryption Standard (AES) (2001). http://csrc.nist.gov/publications/fips/fips197/fips-197.pdf
8. Orthacker, C., Centner, M., Kittl, C.: Qualified mobile server signature. In: Rannenberg, K., Varadharajan, V., Weber, C. (eds.) SEC 2010. IFIP AICT, vol. 330, pp. 103–111. Springer, Heidelberg (2010)
9. Rath, C., Roth, S., Schallar, M., Zefferer, T.: A secure and flexible server-based mobile eID and e-signature solution. In: Proceedings of the 8th International Conference on Digital Society, ICDS 2014, Barcelona, Spain. pp. 7–12. IARIA (2014)
10. The European Parliament and the Council of the European Union: DIRECTIVE 1999/93/EC OF THE EUROPEAN PARLIAMENT AND OF THE COUNCIL of 13 December 1999 on a Community framework for electronic signatures (1999). http://eur-lex.europa.eu/LexUriServ/LexUriServ.do?uri=OJ:L:2000:013:0012:0020:EN:PDF
11. Zefferer, T., Krnjic, V.: Usability evaluation of electronic signature based E-Government solutions. In: Proceedings of the IADIS International Conference WWW/INTERNET 2012, pp. 227–234 (2012)

Leveraging the Adoption of Mobile eID and e-Signature Solutions in Europe

Thomas Zefferer(✉) and Peter Teufl

Institute for Applied Information Processing and Communications,
Graz University of Technology, Inffeldgasse 16a, 8010 Graz, Austria
{thomas.zefferer,peter.teufl}@iaik.tugraz.at
http://www.iaik.tugraz.at

Abstract. The concepts of electronic identities (eID) and legally binding electronic signatures (e-signature) are crucial for transactional e-government services in Europe. Mobile technologies facilitate secure and usable implementations of these fundamental concepts. Various European countries already rely on such implementations and have deployed mobile eID and e-signature solutions on a large scale. These deployments are used by applications from both the public and the private sector. Available deployments differ in various technical and organizational aspects yielding a heterogeneous ecosystem of European mobile eID and e-signature solutions. This makes it difficult for those in charge of developing and deploying such solutions to identify relevant trends, to follow best practices, and to make the right decisions. In order to facilitate these tasks, this paper surveys and assesses existing mobile eID and e-signature solutions that are currently available in Europe. From obtained assessment results and findings, concrete recommendations are derived that facilitate an effective and efficient adoption of mobile eID and e-signature solutions.

Keywords: e-government · Electronic identity · Electronic signatures · Mobility · Mobile government · Mobile eID · Mobile signatures

1 Introduction

Driven by the need to reliably and securely authenticate remote users and to obtain their written consent in electronic form, the concepts of electronic identities (eID) and electronic signatures (e-signature) have gained relevance during the past years. This applies to electronic services from both the private and the public sector. The private sector applies eID and e-signature concepts e.g. in e-commerce or e-banking solutions to authenticate users and to authorize financial transactions. The public sector employs similar concepts in e-government solutions e.g. for the implementation of transactional administrative procedures. Concepts and solutions related to eID and e-signature are of special relevance in Europe, where these concepts are based on respective legal frameworks [1,2]. These frameworks define the concept of qualified electronic signatures (QES)

© Springer International Publishing Switzerland 2015
A. Kő and E. Francesconi (Eds.): EGOVIS 2015, LNCS 9265, pp. 86–100, 2015.
DOI: 10.1007/978-3-319-22389-6_7

representing a subset of electronic signatures that need to satisfy several requirements and that are legally equivalent to handwritten signatures. Concretely, QES must be created using a Secure Signature Creation Device (SSCD) and must be based on qualified electronic certificates.

To meet the requirements of QES as defined by European law [1,2] and to achieve a sufficient level of security, eID and e-signature solutions, i.e. solutions that implement eID and e-signature functionality, have been based on smart-card technology for several years. Smart card based solutions have been deployed in various European countries including Austria [3], Belgium [4], Estonia [8], Portugal [10], and Spain [9]. Unfortunately, smart card based solutions have turned out to lack usability and user acceptance in many cases. Conducted assessments have revealed that the need for additional hardware (card-reading devices) and software (modules for smart-card access) are the main factors that reduce usability. To overcome drawbacks of smart card based approaches, mobile eID and e-signature solutions have emerged early. The general idea behind these solutions is to replace smart cards with mobile phones in order to avoid the need for additional hardware and software on the user's client system. Popular examples for mobile eID and e-signature solutions are the Austrian Mobile Phone Signature [11] or the Estonian Mobiil-ID [12].

During the past decade, numerous mobile eID and e-signature solutions have been proposed, tested, and deployed in various European countries. While some of these solutions are still in productive operation, others have already been abandoned or replaced. Today, Europe faces a heterogeneous ecosystem of mobile eID and e-signature solutions, comprising a steadily growing number of different technological concepts and deployments. This heterogeneity and the strong dynamic of mobile markets make it difficult for responsible decision makers to keep track of emerging trends, ongoing developments, and the current state of the art. This complicates effective decisions related to the adoption and deployment of mobile eID and e-signature solutions. To address this issue, this paper surveys and assesses existing European mobile eID and e-signature solutions. From the findings obtained from the conducted assessments, recommendations are derived that assist decision makers in choosing appropriate concepts and solutions for different use cases. This way, this paper contributes to further successful adoptions and deployments of mobile eID and e-signature solutions in Europe.

2 Methodology

The survey of existing mobile eID and e-signature solutions and the conducted assessments have been based on a thorough methodology, which is also reflected by the structure of this paper. In general, the concept of mobile eID is rather generic and covers a broad spectrum of different approaches and solutions. To define and limit the scope of the conducted survey to those solutions being relevant for legally binding electronic procedures, a set of selection criteria have been defined first. Concretely, only those solutions that comply with the following criteria are considered in this paper:

- **Selection Criterion 1:** Focus is put on European mobile eID and e-signature solutions. This is reasonable, as EU laws ensure a common legal basis for eID and e-signature solutions. This facilitates a meaningful comparison of surveyed solutions.
- **Selection Criterion 2:** Focus is put on solutions that can be used together with public-sector services. Pure private-sector solutions that are not compatible with existing public-sector infrastructures and e-government solutions are not considered.
- **Selection Criterion 3:** Focus is put on solutions that provide at least eID or e-signature functionality. However, support for both features is no mandatory requirement for consideration by this survey.
- **Selection Criterion 4:** Only those solutions are considered that rely on a hardware-based security token to store critical data and to create electronic signatures. This is reasonable, as a secure hardware token is a mandatory requirement for legally binding electronic signatures, i.e. QES, in Europe [1,2]. Hence, pure software-based solutions are not considered.
- **Selection Criterion 5:** Focus is put on mobile eID and e-signature solutions that are currently available or in productive operation. Abandoned solutions are briefly mentioned where useful, but are not assessed in detail.

Solutions complying with these selection criteria are surveyed in Sect. 3. Compiled information on surveyed solutions has mainly been obtained from a literature and Internet research, whereas respective scientific publications such as [5,6], white papers such as [13,16], and case studies such as [14,15] have served as most relevant sources of information.

In a subsequent step, all solutions surveyed in Sect. 3 are systematically assessed in Sect. 4. To follow a systematic approach, all solutions are assessed by means of the same set of assessment criteria. These criteria have been selected such that strengths and weaknesses of assessed mobile eID and e-signature solutions are revealed. Concretely, conducted assessments are based on the following technical (T) and organizational (O) assessment criteria.

- **Assessment Criterion T-1 - Architecture:** This criterion refers to the location of the hardware-based security token that is used to provide eID and e-signature functionality. Depending on the respective solution, this token is implemented either locally on the user's mobile device or remotely in the form of a server component. The architecture, i.e. the location of the hardware-based security token, determines possible implementation alternatives, influences the feasibility of concrete implementations, and has an impact on employed user-authentication schemes.
- **Assessment Criterion T-2 - Security Token:** While Assessment Criterion T-1 covers the location of the used hardware-based security token, this criterion refers to this token's realization. The token can be realized e.g. by means of a Hardware Security Module (HSM), a Subscriber Identity Module (SIM), or a Secure Element (SE). Its concrete implementation has an influence on the security token's provided level of security, on potential attack vectors, and on necessary user-authentication schemes.

- **Assessment Criterion T-3 - Client Requirements:** Depending on the set of functionality implemented locally, the user's mobile end-user device needs to meet several technical requirements. If the user's client device does not comply with these requirements, feasibility and applicability of the respective mobile eID and e-signature solution are reduced.
- **Assessment Criterion T-4 - Roaming Support:** Reliance on special technologies or dependence on involved stakeholders can reduce the applicability of mobile eID and e-signature solutions in roaming scenarios, i.e. in scenarios, in which the user's mobile device is logged-in to a foreign mobile network.
- **Assessment Criterion T-5 - Features:** This criterion refers to the set of functionality provided by the respective solution. According to the defined selection criteria, all surveyed solutions support at least eID or e-signature functionality. The concrete set of provided functionality, which has an impact on the respective solution's potential use cases, is covered by this assessment criterion.
- **Assessment Criterion T-6 - User Authentication:** All eID and e-signature solutions implement a user-authentication scheme, in order to restrict access to personal data and functionality to legitimate users. The implemented user-authentication scheme defines required user interactions and hence influences the respective solution's perceived efficiency and usability.
- **Assessment Criterion O-1 - Stakeholders:** Deployed eID and e-signature solutions usually depend on various stakeholders, including e.g. Certification Authorities (CAs) and Mobile Network Operators (MNOs). The set of involved stakeholders depends on the respective solution's architecture and on the deployment scenario. An increasing number of stakeholders potentially also increases complexity and raises the risk of conflicts of interest.
- **Assessment Criterion O-2 - Free of Charge for Users:** Depending on involved stakeholders, their interests, and their business models, the use of mobile eID and e-signature solutions can cause costs. This, in turn, can reduce user acceptance.
- **Assessment Criterion O-3 - In Operation Since:** The number of years, for which a mobile eID and e-signature solution has been available, is an indicator for its success. As unsuccessful solutions are typically abandoned after some time, solutions that have been in productive operation for several years can be assumed to be successful. Hence, their start of productive operation is a relevant assessment criterion for deployed solutions.
- **Assessment Criterion O-4 - Roaming Support:** Compliance with roaming scenarios has already been identified as relevant technical assessment criterion. However, roaming support is not only a matter of technical capabilities, it must also be supported by involved stakeholders. Hence, roaming support is regarded as relevant organizational assessment criterion as well.
- **Assessment Criterion O-5 - Application Domains:** From a user's perspective, the number of services that support a mobile eID and e-signature solution is of importance. A higher number of application domains supporting the respective eID and e-signature solution is hence advantageous, as it

increases the number of potential use cases and hence the user's incentive to use the provided service.
- **Assessment Criterion O-6 - Legally Binding Signatures:** The capability to create legally binding electronic signatures is another relevant assessment criterion. Only those mobile eID and e-signature solutions supporting this feature can be employed in transactional online procedures to provide legally binding written consent.

Listed assessment criteria are used to systematically assess surveyed eID and e-signature solutions. From obtained assessment results, relevant findings and recommendations are derived in Sect. 5. Finally, conclusions are drawn in Sect. 6.

3 Mobile eID and e-Signature Solutions in Europe

In Europe, the relevance and usefulness of electronic identities and legally binding electronic signatures have been recognized early. While a legal foundation for these concepts had been established already in 1999 by the EU Signature Directive [1], many EU member states initially had problems to find and provide successful technical solutions. Early approaches to provide eID and e-signature functionality with the help of smart cards quickly turned out to be disadvantageous in terms of usability. This has for instance been discussed in detail by Zefferer et al. [5].

In order to overcome limitations of smart card based solutions, mobile approaches have emerged early. Although these approaches follow different strategies, they all have in common that they aim to replace smart cards by mobile phones. From a historic perspective, Austria, the Baltic countries, and countries from Scandinavia can be regarded as pioneers with regard to mobile eID and electronic signatures. These countries were among the first ones to deploy respective solutions on a national level. In Finland, first experiences with mobile eID and e-signature solutions have already been gained in the early noughties. Approximately at the same time, Austria introduced a first national mobile eID and e-signature solution called A1-Signatur.

Even though most of these pioneering solutions have been abandoned and replaced in the meantime, experiences gained have been incorporated in successor solutions and products. In particular, basic design decisions have been maintained by early-adopting countries over the years. Baltic and Scandinavian countries have relied from the beginning on client-based architectures that employ the SIM as local security token. In contrast, Austria has always followed a server-based architecture and has relied on a central HSM as security token. These basic design decisions have already been taken for the countries' first solutions and are still maintained for current deployments.

In Austria, the Austrian Mobile Phone Signature [11] is the national mobile eID and e-signature solution that enables citizens to authenticate at services from public-sector agencies and from private-sector companies. Furthermore, the Austrian Mobile Phone Signature enables citizens to create legally binding electronic signatures in online procedures. Relying on the theoretic concept proposed by Orthacker et al. [6], the Austrian Mobile Phone Signature makes use of a central service and HSM to securely store eID data and to carry out cryptographic operations. The user's mobile phone is solely used to authenticate the user at the central service in order to authorize the provision of eID data and the creation of electronic signatures. The Austrian Mobile Phone Signature is operated by the Austrian CA A-Trust [17] and has been in productive operation for more than five years.

Baltic and Scandinavian countries have relied on SIM-based approaches from the beginning. Still, this approach is followed by current mobile eID and e-signature solutions in these countries. In Estonia, the national mobile eID and e-signature solution is called Mobiil-ID [12]. It requires users to acquire enhanced SIMs that are capable to store eID data and to create electronic signatures. Estonian MNOs act as gateway to these SIMs and enable online services to include mobile eID and e-signature functionality. A solution following a similar approach is provided in Norway. This solution is called BankID [18]. Its name already indicates that the banking sector has been the main driver behind this solution. Solutions following the SIM-based approach have also been rolled out in Finland [19] and Lithuania [20]. This shows that Scandinavian and Baltic states are—beside Austria—still among the leading countries in terms of mobile eID and e-signature adoption.

Apart from these states, other European countries have also deployed mobile eID and e-signature solutions during the past years. Already in 2007, Turkey deployed a respective solution called MobilImza [21]. This solution is mainly driven by the Turkish MNOs Turkcell and Avea, and allows users to authenticate at e-services and to create legally binding electronic signatures. Similar to Scandinavian and Baltic countries, also the Turkish solution MobilIzma relies on a client-based architecture and makes use of enhanced SIMs.

Recently, SIM-based mobile eID and e-signature solutions have also been introduced in Moldova and Switzerland. In Moldova, a respective solution has been deployed in 2012 [22]. Involved stakeholders include the Moldovan Government acting as CA and several Moldovan MNOs. In Switzerland, the mobile eID and e-signature solution Swiss Mobile ID [15] has been set into productive operation in 2013. In contrast to most other solutions surveyed, Swiss Mobile ID has focused on the provision of eID functionality first. Electronic-signature functionality has only been added recently by means of a cloud-based service.

Due to the growing popularity of mobile eID and e-signature solutions, their implementation and provision has become an attractive business opportunity. During the past years, several companies have emerged as technology providers for mobile eID and e-signature solutions. These companies provide ready-to-deploy products that facilitate a fast roll-out of eID and e-signature solutions. Examples for such technology providers are Valimo Wireless Ltd. [23] and Methics Ltd. [24], which offer SIM-based solutions. Recently, two technology providers for server-based eID and e-signature solutions have emerged as well. The two server-based solutions ServerBKU [7] and PkBox [25] both rely on a central HSM and are hence especially useful in scenarios, in which enhanced SIMs are not available or desirable.

In summary, it can be concluded that a heterogeneous ecosystem of mobile eID and e-signature solutions has evolved during the past years in Europe. This heterogeneity is mainly caused by different employed architectures, which are typically chosen such that requirements of the respective application scenarios and the intended use cases are met. To identify strengths and weaknesses of the various mobile eID and e-signature solutions that are currently in productive operation in Europe, we systematically assess them with the help of the defined assessment criteria in the next section.

4 Assessment

The conducted survey shows that mobile eID and e-signature solutions currently available in Europe can be classified into two categories. First, there are several solutions representing products offered by technology providers. These solutions implement core eID and e-signature functionality and can be deployed in arbitrary application scenarios. An example for this category is Valimo Mobile-ID. Solutions assigned to the first category can hence be regarded as ready-to-deploy products. In contrast, the second category covers mobile eID and e-signature solutions that are already deployed and ready for use. An example is the Austrian Mobile Phone Signature, which has been in productive operation in Austria since 2010.

Depending on their assigned category, different assessment aspects must be considered for mobile eID and e-signature solutions. For ready-to-deploy products, the six technical assessment criteria defined in Sect. 2 must be considered. For deployed solutions, defined organizational assessment criteria must be taken into account as well. In the following subsections, all surveyed solutions are assessed by means of their relevant assessment criteria.

4.1 Ready-to-Deploy Products

Assessment results of surveyed ready-to-deploy products are summarized in Fig. 1. In total, four products have been surveyed including two server-based and two client-based solutions. The two server-based solutions PkBox and Server-BKU differ from each other in a few aspects only. Concretely, PkBox shows a higher degree of flexibility regarding supported features and user-authentication schemes. The same applies to the two client-based solutions, i.e. Valimo Wireless's Mobile ID and Methics Oy's Kiuru MSSP. These two solutions resemble each other in most relevant aspects and mainly differ in the set of supported security tokens.

Main differences between the two server-based solutions and the two client-based products are mainly imposed by their varying architectures. Depending on the underlying architecture, different types of security tokens must be employed. Server-based solutions rely on HSMs for this purpose, whereas client-based solutions usually make use of local SIMs. Accordingly, client-based solutions define

Technology Provider	Vendor	Architecture	Security Token	Client Requirements	Roaming Support	Features	User Authentication
PkBox	Intesi	Server	HSM	Depends on chosen user-authentication method	Yes	Encryption and decryption, authentication, electronic signatures	PIN and OTP
ServerBKU	IAIK	Server	HSM	SMS reception	Yes	Electronic ID, electronic signature	Password and OTP
Mobile ID	Valimo Wireless	Client	SIM, SE	Enhanced SIM or secure element	Yes	Electronic ID, electronic signature	PIN
Kiuru MSSP	Methics Oy	Client	SIM	Enhanced SIM	Yes	Electronic ID, electronic signature	PIN

Fig. 1. Technical aspects of available ready-to-deploy products.

higher client requirements, as mobile end-user devices need to be equipped with enhanced SIMs. The varying implementation of the used security token has also an impact on implemented user-authentication schemes. While client-based solutions require the user to enter a secret Personal Identification Number (PIN) only, server-based solutions typically rely on more complex authentication schemes, which require users to enter a static password and to receive and enter a dynamically created one-time password (OTP).

A detailed assessment of the four surveyed ready-to-deploy products according to the six technical assessment criteria is provided in Fig. 1. In summary, it can be concluded that available products can be classified into client-based and server-based solutions. Products assigned to the same category resemble each other to a large extent. Differences can mainly be identified between solutions of different categories.

4.2 Deployed Solutions

Beside ready-to-deploy products, deployed solutions represent the second category of mobile eID and e-signature solutions surveyed in Sect. 3. These solutions are already in productive operation in Europe. For deployed solutions, the same technical assessment criteria must be considered as for ready-to-deploy products. A mapping between deployed solutions and relevant technical assessment criteria is provided in Fig. 2.

In addition, the six organizational assessment criteria listed in Sect. 2 need to be taken into account as well. Organizational criteria target the assessed solutions' application context and focus on different operation-related details. Figure 3 shows a mapping between deployed solutions and relevant organizational assessment criteria.

Assessment by means of technical criteria (Fig. 2) shows analogies to the assessment of ready-to-deploy products. Again, surveyed solutions can be classified into server-based and client-based solutions, whereas client-based solutions currently represent the majority. Surveyed client-based solutions resemble each other in most technical criteria. This becomes apparent from Fig. 2, which shows that most surveyed solutions share the same technical characteristics. The Austrian Mobile Phone Signature is the only deployed solution following a server-based approach.

Solution	Architecture	Security Token	Client Requirements	Roaming Support	Features	User Authentication
Austrian Mobile Phone Signature	Server	HSM	SMS reception	Yes	Electronic ID, electronic signature	Password + OTP
Estonian Mobiil-ID	Client	SIM	Enhanced SIM	Yes	Electronic ID, electronic signature	PIN
Turkish MobilImza	Client	SIM	Enhanced SIM	Yes	Electronic ID, electronic signature	PIN
Finnish Mobiilivarmenne	Client	SIM	Enhanced SIM	Yes	Electronic ID, electronic signature	PIN
Norwegian Bank-ID	Client	SIM	Enhanced SIM	Yes	Electronic ID, electronic signature	PIN
Swiss Mobile ID	Client	SIM	Enhanced SIM	Yes	Electronic ID	PIN
Moldovan Mobile e-ID	Client	SIM	Enhanced SIM	Yes	Electronic ID, electronic signature	PIN
Lithuanian Electronic Signature	Client	SIM	Enhanced SIM	Yes	Electronic ID, electronic signature	PIN

Fig. 2. Technical aspects of available deployed solutions.

Solution	Involved Stakeholders	Free of Charge for User	Start of Operation	Roaming Support	Application Domains	Support for Legally Binding Electronic Signatures
Austrian Mobile Phone Signature	A-Trust (CA, Operator)	Yes	2010	Yes	Public sector, private sector	Yes
Estonian Mobiil-ID	AS Sertifitseerimiskeskus (CA) EMT/Elion, Elisa, Tele2 (MNOs, Operators)	No	2007	Yes	Public sector, private sector	Yes
Turkish MobilImza	Turkcell, Avea (MNOs, Operators) eGuven (CA)	No	2007	Yes	Public sector, private sector	Yes
Finnish Mobiilivarmenne	Elisa, Sonera, DNA (MNOs, Operators, CA)	No	2010	Yes	Public sector, private sector	Yes
Norwegian Bank-ID	Several banks (CA), Telenor, Tele2, NetCom, TDC (MNOs, Operators)	No	2009/ 2013	Yes	Public sector, private sector	Yes
Swiss Mobile ID	Swisscom (MNO, Operator)	Yes	2013	Yes	Public sector, private sector	No, signature as cloud service which uses Mobile ID for authentication
Moldovan Mobile e-ID	Orange, Moldcell/TeliaSonera (MNOs, operators), Moldovan Government (CA)	No	2012	Yes	Public sector, private sector	Yes
Lithuanian Electronic Signature	Omnitel, BITĖ, Tele2 (MNO, Operator), AS Sertifitseerimiskeskus (CA)	Depends on MNO	2007	Yes	Public sector, private sector	Yes

Fig. 3. Organizational aspects of available deployed solutions.

Accordingly, it is the only solution with significant technical differences to other surveyed solutions. Concretely, the Austrian Mobile Phone Signature differs from client-based solutions in terms of the used security token, imposed client requirements, and the implemented user-authentication scheme.

More diverging assessment results for deployed solutions are obtained with regard to organizational criteria (Fig. 3). Surveyed solutions differ considerably in terms of involved stakeholders. This is comprehensible, as all assessed solutions are deployed in national contexts with different requirements and circumstances. Thus, involved stakeholders mainly include country-specific companies and institutions such as MNOs, service operators, and CAs. Differences between deployed solutions can also be identified with regard to their start of operation and costs they cause for the user. Surveyed solutions have been set into productive operation between 2007 and 2013. Only two of them are completely free of charge for the user. All other solutions either charge the user a monthly fee or implement a pay-per-use scheme.

Detailed assessment results of all surveyed solutions are provided in Figs. 2 and 3. In summary, it can be concluded that deployed solutions mainly differ in organizational aspects due to different application scenarios and business models of involved stakeholders. From a technical perspective, considerable difference can mainly be identified between the two categories of server-based and client-based solutions.

5 Findings and Recommendations

From the obtained assessment results summarized in Figs. 1, 2 and 3, several findings can be derived. These findings will serve as input for the identification of recommendations, which aim to facilitate the selection of appropriate approaches and solutions for the adoption of mobile eID and e-signature functionality in different use cases and application scenarios. Derived findings are discussed in the following subsection.

5.1 Findings

Derived findings cover technological trends, service provision and adoption, as well as the identification of drivers and barriers. These aspects are discussed in the following in more detail.

Technological Trends: Assessment of available products and deployed solutions show that there are currently two predominating architectures, i.e. client-based and server-based architectures. Solutions following a client-based architecture typically rely on the user's local SIM as hardware-based security token. This is reasonable, as SIMs are available on virtually all mobile phones. In theory, client-based solutions could also rely on other local security tokens such as secure elements. However, the availability of such tokens is restricted to modern smartphones. Furthermore, current smartphone platforms such as Android, iOS, or Windows Phone show several differences with regard to support of local security tokens, which complicates their integration into mobile eID and e-signature solutions. The SIM appears to be the common denominator available on and compatible to all current mobile phones. Reliance on the SIM for client-based solutions hence seems appropriate.

In contrast to client-based solutions, server-based solutions make use of a central security token. In most cases, this security token is implemented by a HSM. For server-based solutions, the implementation of the central security token is completely independent from capabilities of the mobile end-user device. Hence, arbitrary realizations that meet relevant security requirements are conceivable. However, HSMs have turned out to be an appropriate technological choice for server-based mobile eID and e-signature solutions.

Another interesting finding is the fact that the underlying architecture influences implemented user-authentication schemes. Concretely, solutions following a client-based approach require the user to enter a PIN in order to authenticate and to grant access to critical data such as cryptographic signing keys. By entering the PIN, the user completes a two-factor authentication process. The local security token covers the authentication factor *possession*. In addition, the entered PIN covers the authentication factor *knowledge*.

Solutions following a server-based architecture typically implement a more complex user authentication scheme in order to cover two different authentication factors. This can be explained by the fact that the server-based architecture imposes a central security token. In this case, the security token is not under physical control of the user and hence cannot cover the authentication factor *possession*. Therefore, this authentication factor must be covered by other means. Current solutions usually rely on OTPs for this purpose. For instance, the Austrian Mobile Phone Signature sends OTPs to users via SMS. By proving reception of the OTP, the user proves possession of his or her mobile phone. This way, the authentication factor possession can be covered, even though the mobile eID and e-signature solution uses a central security token.

The conducted assessments have also revealed that all available products and deployed solutions support roaming. This means that the user can access provided mobile eID and e-signature functionality, even if his or her mobile phone is logged in to a foreign mobile network. Roaming support is achieved by relying on SMS technology. This applies to server-based solutions, which often make use of SMS to deliver OTPs. Furthermore, this also applies to client-based solutions, which use special SMS messages to communicate with the local SIM during eID-related and e-signature-related processes. This way, roaming is supported, as long as the user is able to receive SMS messages.

Finally, another interesting finding derived from the conducted assessments pertains to the supported set of functionality. Most surveyed solutions provide both eID and e-signature functionality. This is comprehensible, as the concepts of electronic identities and electronic signatures are closely related and often used together in practice. From all surveyed solutions, the Swiss Mobile ID is the only solution that has focused solely on eID functionality first. However, its basic functionality has recently been complemented by a cloud-based signature service. Other cryptographic functionality that goes beyond eID and e-signature features can hardly be found for current solutions.

Service Provision and Adoption: Assessment of organizational aspects have revealed several interesting findings with regard to service provision and adoption. Concretely, it has turned out that the way, in which mobile eID and e-signature services are provided, heavily depends on specific national circumstances and requirements. This especially affects the set of stakeholders that are involved in the provision and operation of mobile eID and e-signature solutions. In Scandinavian countries, where the banking sector has been the main driver behind the development of eID and e-signature solutions, banks are still relevant stakeholders. The set of involved stakeholders is also influenced by the respective solution's underlying architecture. As client-based solutions typically require SIM access, MNOs are relevant stakeholders for most of these solutions. From the user's point of view, a high number of involved stakeholders can be disadvantageous, as it increases the probability that the consumption of mobile eID and e-signature services is charged, in order to satisfy the interests of all stakeholders. This is also underpinned by obtained assessment results. The only two deployed solutions that are totally free for the user involve one stakeholder only. Concretely, this applies to the Austrian Mobile Phone Signature and to the Swiss Mobile ID.

With regard to service adoption, the conducted assessments have revealed that all deployed solutions are used by both the private and the public sector. For the public sector, e-government is the main use case. From the private sector, especially e-banking solutions benefit from available mobile eID and e-signature solutions. As all surveyed and assessed solutions have been in productive operation for several years, electronic services from both the private and the public sector can benefit from time-tested technologies.

Drivers and Obstacles: From the conducted survey and obtained assessment results, drivers and obstacles of mobile eID and e-signature solutions can be identified. Considering the evolution of mobile eID and e-signature solutions, the need for secure and usable alternatives to smart card based solutions can be identified as one of the main drivers. Powered by the emergence of mobile information and communication technologies, especially banking institutions and governments have aimed to develop mobile eID and e-signature solutions. This has finally led to the current—still growing—ecosystem of national solutions in Europe.

Although most available solutions are experiencing a growth in usage and user acceptance, the conducted assessments have revealed several obstacles that threaten to hinder the success of deployed solutions. First and foremost, client requirements imposed by deployed solutions represent a potential barrier. This especially applies to client-based solutions, which implement the mandatory security token locally on the user's mobile device. Currently deployed solutions typically rely on the SIM for this purpose. As enhanced SIMs are needed to implement required cryptographic functionality, SIM-based solutions often require users to replace existing SIMs. This causes additional effort for the user and represents a potential obstacle, especially if the required SIM replacement comes with additional costs for the user.

Additional costs are in general a potential obstacle and threat for the success of mobile eID and e-signature solutions. Except for the Austrian Mobile Phone Signature and the Swiss Mobile ID, all surveyed and assessed solutions charge users, who want to use provided eID and e-signature services. This can reduce user acceptance and in turn the success of provided solutions.

Finally, reduced usability caused by complex user interactions can also represent a potential obstacle for successful mobile eID and e-signature solutions. In this regard, especially server-based solutions are affected, as they need to implement more complex user-authentication schemes to assure a sufficient level of security by means of two-factor authentication.

5.2 Recommendations

From the derived findings, a set of recommendations can be derived. These recommendations facilitate the provision and adoption of mobile eID and e-signature solutions by taking into account experiences gained during implementation and operation of respective solutions in different European countries. Concretely, the following actions are recommended:

- **Use synergies between public and private sector:** Conducted assessments have shown that all successful mobile eID and e-signature solutions can be used for both public-sector and private-sector applications. Employing synergies between the private and the public sector is reasonable, as it saves operational costs for both sectors. Furthermore, it raises the number of applications for users, which in turn increases the incentive for the user to make use of provided mobile eID and e-signature solutions.
- **Select appropriate architecture:** The first step in designing and developing a mobile eID and e-signature solution is the selection of an appropriate architecture. Current solutions either follow a client-based or a server-based architecture. Both approaches come with several advantages and disadvantages. Strengths and weaknesses of different architectures should be understood and considered with regard to the special requirements of the environment, in which the solution to be developed shall be deployed.
- **Assure cross-platform applicability:** Mobile eID and e-signature solutions should consider the heterogeneity of current mobile platforms, devices, and operating systems. Mobile eID and e-signature solutions should be designed and developed such that they are compatible to all major mobile platforms. This way, exclusion of certain user groups can be prevented.
- **Consider stakeholder interests:** Existing solutions show that development and operation of mobile eID and e-signature solutions typically involves multiple stakeholders including MNOs, CAs, and service operators. With a growing number of stakeholders, the probability of conflicts of interest increases. Consideration of potentially diverging stakeholder interests is hence crucial to assure sustainable success.
- **Consider factors influencing user-acceptance:** On the strength of past experience, lack of user acceptance is one of the main threats for mobile eID

and e-signature solutions. Considering factors that influence user acceptance is hence important for the success of mobile eID and e-signature solutions. These factors must already be taken into account during design and development, as several aspects influencing user acceptance depend on the solution's architecture and implementation.

6 Conclusions

Electronic identities and legally binding electronic signatures are key concepts for transactional e-government services in Europe. Mobile technologies enable a secure and usable implementation of these concepts. Today, several European countries already rely on mobile eID and e-signature solutions that are employed by services from both the public and the private sector.

Due to historic reasons and because of diverging national circumstances and requirements, a heterogeneous ecosystem of mobile eID and e-signature solutions has evolved during the past years. We have surveyed existing deployments and assessed them with the help of technical and organizational assessment criteria. From conducted assessments, several useful findings have been obtained. These findings cover the identification of drivers and obstacles, insights in service provision and adoption, and the identification of technological trends. From the obtained findings, five concrete recommendations have been derived that facilitate the successful adoption of mobile eID and e-signature solutions.

The provided overview, results from conducted assessments, and derived recommendations support those in charge with the development and deployment of mobile eID and e-signature solutions. This way, this paper contributes to an effective adoption and use of electronic identities and electronic signatures and helps to pave the way for successful transactional e-government services.

References

1. The European Parliament and the Council of the European Union: DIRECTIVE 1999/93/EC OF THE EUROPEAN PARLIAMENT AND OF THE COUNCIL of 13 December 1999 on a Community framework for electronic signatures. http://eur-lex.europa.eu/LexUriServ/LexUriServ.do?uri=OJ:L:2000:013:0012:0020:EN:PDF
2. The European Parliament and the Council of the European Union: REGULATION (EU) No 910/2014 OF THE EUROPEAN PARLIAMENT AND OF THE COUNCIL of 23 July 2014 on electronic identification and trust services for electronic transactions in the internal market and repealing Directive 1999/93/EC. http://eur-lex.europa.eu/legal-content/EN/TXT/HTML/?uri=CELEX:32014R0910&from=EN
3. Leitold, H., Hollosi, A., Posch, R.: Security architecture of the austrian citizen card concept. In: 18th Annual Computer Security Applications Conference, pp. 391–400 (2002)
4. Fairchild, A., de Vuyst, B.: The Evolution of the e-ID card in Belgium: data privacy and multi-application usage. In: The Sixth International Conference on Digital Society, pp. 13–16 (2002)

5. Zefferer, T., Krnjic, V.: Usability evaluation of electronic signature based e-government solutions. In: Proceedings of the IADIS International Conference WWW/INTERNET 2012, pp. 227–234 (2012)
6. Orthacker, C., Centner, M., Kittl, C.: Qualified mobile server signature. In: Rannenberg, K., Varadharajan, V., Weber, C. (eds.) SEC 2010. IFIP AICT, vol. 330, pp. 103–111. Springer, Heidelberg (2010)
7. Rath, C., Roth, S., Schallar, M, Zefferer, T.: A secure and flexible server-based mobile eID and e-signature solution. In: The Eighth International Conference on Digital Society (2014)
8. ID.ee. http://id.ee
9. DNI Electrnica. http://www.dnielectronico.es
10. Carto de Cidado. https://www.cartaodecidadao.pt
11. Handy-Signatur. https://www.handy-signatur.at
12. Mobiil-ID. http://id.ee/index.php?id=36881
13. Mobi Solutions Ltd.: Mobile Government: 2010 and Beyond (2010)
14. GSMA: Finnish Mobile ID: A Lesson in Interoperability. http://www.gsma.com/personaldata/wp-content/uploads/2013/07/SC_GSM_288_Finland-Mobile-ID-executive-summary-100713-v4.pdf
15. GSMA: Swisscom Mobile ID. https://www.swisscom.ch/content/dam/swisscom/de/biz/mobile-id/join-and-follow-us/pdf/case-study-on-digital-identity-swisscom-mobile-id_en.pdf
16. GSMA and SIA: Mobile Identity - Unlocking the Potential of the Digital Economy. http://www.gsma.com/personaldata/wp-content/uploads/2014/10/14-10-10-GSMA-SIA-Joint-Paper-Mobile-Identity_October-2014.pdf
17. A-Trust. http://atrust.at/
18. BankID. http://www.bankid.no/
19. Mobiilivarmenne Mobile ID. http://www.mobiilivarmenne.fi/
20. Omnitel: E. paraas. http://www.omnitel.lt/privatiems/planai-ir-paslaugos/paslaugos/ismaniosios-paslaugos/e-parasas/59787
21. GSMA: Mobile Signature in Turkey. http://www.gsma.com/personaldata/wp-content/uploads/2012/09/MI_TurkcellReport_print_FINAL.pdf
22. Moldova Mobile e-ID Solution. http://egov.md/images/pdf/flyer%20CASE\%20STUDY.pdf
23. Valimo. http://www.valimo.com
24. Methics. http://www.methics.fi
25. Intesi Group: PkBox. http://www.pksuite.it/eng/pr_pkbox.php

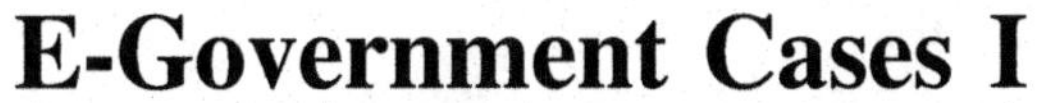

E-Government Cases I

Biometric Identification in eHealthcare: Learning from the Cases of Russia and Italy

Polina Kachurina[1], Francesco Buccafurri[2], Lyudmila Bershadskaya (Vidiasova)[1(✉)], Elena Bershadskaya[3], and Dmitrii Trutnev[1]

[1] ITMO University, St. Petersburg, Russia
{polina.kachurina, bershadskaya.lyudmila}@gmail.com, trutnev@egov-center.ru

[2] DIIES Department, University of Reggio Calabria, Reggio Calabria, Italy
bucca@unirc.it

[3] Penza State Technological University, Penza, Russia
bereg@pgta.ru

Abstract. Biometric identification technologies have become very popular in the last ten years. Applications that use biometrics are multiple and can be used for a variety of purposes: from physical access control, to authentication and access to information, recognition of people, etc. E-government is certainly a context where biometrics has a crucial role, because high level of assurance about the identity of citizens is required, whenever they interact by means of digital procedures with the Public Sector. Advanced technologies of digital identity may be seen as a factor influencing the quality improvement and raising the availability of services that require trusted environment.

This paper is aimed to find promising methods and models of building infrastructure of public and commercial services in the field of biometrics identification. Two practical cases (Russian and Italian) have been taken for the analysis in this regards. The authors are focused on modern technological trends in ICT- distribution of biometric technologies and mobile applications in the field of e-government and prepared conclusions on its best implementation not just in two studied countries but worldwide as well.

Keywords: Biometric identification · eHealthcare · Multiply identification · Healthcare applications · Voice identification

1 Introduction

The term biometrics derives from the Greek words "bios" (life) and "meters" (measure) to indicate that it is related to measurement of physiological and behavioral components of living organisms. As a consequence, biometric data are directly, uniquely, and stably linked to an individual thus denoting the strong relationship between behavior, body, physical features, and identity of a person. Basically the process of biometric authentication, within the meaning of computer science, refers to the automatic identification or verification of identity of the examined person, according to their physical or behavioral characteristics. Despite the need of using biometric data for those cases in

© Springer International Publishing Switzerland 2015
A. Kő and E. Francesconi (Eds.): EGOVIS 2015, LNCS 9265, pp. 103–116, 2015.
DOI: 10.1007/978-3-319-22389-6_8

which high levels of assurance about the identity of the author of a digital action is required, the above characteristics enforce special precautions to adopt whenever these data are managed. In other words, the adoption of biometric systems may result in specific threats to the fundamental rights of dignity and freedom of people.

Biometrics is divided into two parts:

- Physics biometrics, based on analysis of data derived from measurements made on the physical parameters of a human being (conformation of the retina or iris, fingerprint analysis of the geometry of the face or hands, etc.);
- Behavioral biometrics, based on analysis of data derived from measurements of behavioral parameters (timbre and tone of voice, type of gait, signature analysis).

In recent years, scientists have focused their efforts on how to make an identification of individuals with a negligible error. Due to the difficulty of the alteration of the physiological characteristics of a human being, it is believed that the biometrics can be the only true turning point for positive identification of human identity.

Applications that use biometrics are multiple and can be used for a variety of purposes: from physical access control, to authentication and access to information, recognition of people, etc. E-government is certainly a context where biometrics has a crucial role, because high levels of assurance about the identity of citizens id required, whenever they interact by means of digital procedures with the Public Sector.

Advanced technologies of digital identity may be seen as a factor influencing the quality improvement and raising the availability of services that require trusted environment. Understanding of the latest technological developments helps to form a vision of a promising methods and models of building infrastructure of public and commercial services. In this article, we focus on modern technological trends in ICT- distribution of biometric technologies and mobile applications in the field of e-government. It is also remarkable that, usually, voice biometrics has been used for security, however the concept of its use in e-government services is not broadly implemented.

This paper is aimed to find promising methods and models of building infra-structure of public and commercial services in the field of biometrics identification. Two practical cases (Russian and Italian) have been taken for the analysis in this regards. The authors prepared conclusions on its best implementation not just in two studied countries but worldwide as well.

The structure of the paper is the following: Sect. 2 gives a brief state of the art description based on scientific researches. Section 3 provides an overview of the contemporary trends in eHealth technologies. In Sect. 4, the necessity of focus on voice biometrics in applications and services provision is highlighted. Section 5 describes the developed system of biometrics identification underlining advantages and barriers of its implementation. Section 6, through a portrait of biometric identification systems in Italy including legislative and applied aspects, focuses on privacy issues related to the adoption of biometric solutions. In Sect. 7, the conclusion is drawn, it implies a perspective view of biometric-based services, moreover embracing not only the studied domain (i.e., Russia and Italy), but wider range of countries all over the world.

2 Literature Review

In the recent scientific literature various studies about biometric authentication have been proposed. We provide a brief review about the most relevant recent proposals in this field.

In Bailadors et al. work [1], a biometric feature based on accelerations of in-air signature has been proposed. HMM, DTW and Bayesian classifiers have been tested to deal with this problem. This biometric feature has shown to be robust against spoofing attacks. DTW with an algorithm to extract an average template has yielded the best results.

Bastys and colleagues [2] present a novel iris representations based on binary features from the multi-scale Taylor expansion. Enhancement of the local extrema-based approach with efficient matching. Combination of the above two performs with highest recognition rates. Evaluation results are provided using Casia 2.0, ICE-1 and MBGC-3l.

The authors of [3] present a survey covering the historical development and current state of the art in image understanding for iris biometrics. Contributions are categorized into: image acquisition, iris segmentation, texture analysis and matching of texture representations. Other important research described in the survey includes experimental evaluations, image databases, applications and systems, and medical conditions that may affect the iris.

In Tan, Zhang and Sun research [4], an effective method is proposed for visible light iris image matching by using multiple characteristics of iris and eye images. The method consists of image preprocessing, iris data matching, eye data matching, and multi-modal fusion. Ordinal measures and color analysis are adopted for iris data matching, and texton representation and semantic information are used for eye data matching.

Che and Veldhuis [5] focus on extracting binary biometric strings for a key binding verification scheme. In particular, the paper deals with the secure bit extraction module by quantizing and coding every feature individually. To extract bits from every feature involves two tasks: designing the quantization intervals and determining the number of quantization bits. The final binary string is then the concatenation of the output bits from all the features.

Another research team [6] primarily focuses on multi-biometric template protection method that encompasses biometric feature level fusion, feature transformation and bit-extraction. In the proposed solution, two different biometric modalities, i.e. fingerprint and palmprint are initially fused at the feature level. Subsequently, a revocable feature extraction method is proposed which is known as Random Tiling and a reliable bit extraction method that makes use of the fused features for the purpose of template protection.

Biometrics is also used for continuous authentication. In Crawford et al. paper [7], a framework for transparent, continuous authentication on mobile devices is presented. The framework uses behavioral biometrics to uniquely identify the device owner. The biometrics are supplemented with an explicit authentication method for backup. The owner explicitly authenticated 67 % less often than with explicit methods alone.

An emergent approach is also keystroke dynamics, which is a behavioral measurement utilizing the manner and rhythm in which each individual types. The paper of

Karnan et al. [8] summarize the well-known approaches used in keystroke dynamics in the last two decades.

In [9] a bio-cryptographic system based on offline signature images is presented. To do this, the concept of dissimilarity representation is employed to produce signature representations with low IPS and IPV. The dissimilarity approach is mainly introduced to differentiate between classes with modeling the proximity between class objects, instead of modeling the objects themselves.

McDuff and colleagues [10] presented an automated method for classifying "liking" and "desire to view again" of online video ads based on 3268 facial responses to media collected over the Internet. The results demonstrate the possibility for an ecologically valid, unobtrusive, evaluation of commercial "liking" and "desire to view again", strong predictors of marketing success, based only on facial responses.

Finally, adaptive Bloom filter-based transforms are applied in order to mix binary iris biometric templates at feature level, where iris-codes are obtained from both eyes of a single subject [11]. The irreversible mixing transform, which generates alignment-free templates, obscures information present in different iris-codes. In addition, the transform is parameterized in order to achieve unlinkability, implementing cancelable multi-biometrics.

Literature review emphasizes the versatility of biometrics application: decisions based on it are used in access systems, access to the personal account in the web, personal information and mobile terminals.

Biometric access systems have been used in various fields: customs, government, military, financial, travel.

This paper aims to analyze real case studies in two countries (Russia and Italy) with focus on positive trends and shortcomings of biometrics trying to provide best solutions for biometrics usage.

3 eHealthcare and Its Applications

According to Frust & Sullivan [12], healthcare in Europe is facing major challenges in both structural reform and unavailability of resources as the region working population is far lower in comparison to those of 'non-working' age, who are usually referred to as economic dependants. This calls for the introduction of new schemes in healthcare that would support Europe to deal with ageing issues. The involvement of Information and Communication Technology (ICT) in healthcare is evident from the fact that, in recent years, the number of Internet users for health purposes has considerably increased. This is basically in the form of purchasing health products and services, and also for communicating with peers and healthcare professionals.

E-Healthcare is the term given to the application of ICT in the healthcare sector to organize available healthcare information in order to improve the efficiency of the ecosystem. Various applications such as Electronic Health Records (EHRs), Picture Archiving and Communication System (PACS), ePrescription, Computerized Physician Order Entry (CPOE) and Electronic Health Cards (EHCs) are being developed to make the healthcare system more efficient. These applications, in turn, are adding value to various services such as Telemedicine and Telecare, that have made healthcare information ubiquitous by removing the geographical boundaries, supporting social mobility and initiating the stakeholders of different European Union (EU) member states to work together.

In the EU, governments have spent more than €500.0 million of research funding to the development of eHealthcare tools and systems over the past two decades [13]. The European Parliament Resolution of May 2007 addressed the necessity for sharing patient data across Europe. The Seventh Framework (FP7) and Horizon 2020 programs fund numerous healthcare IT-related researches.

Mobile Health is the sub-sector of eHealthcare that refers to the use of mobile devices such as mobile phones, patient monitoring devices, Personal Digital Assistants (PDA) and other wireless devices.

Though most of the devices used are operated using Wi-Fi (Wireless Fidelity) and Bluetooth, there are several limitations in the use of these technologies. Consequently, this has created a window of opportunity for the cellular operators to play a pivotal role in the healthcare sector. Research projects such as AWARENESS, U-care and MyoTel by MobiHealth have helped mobile operators to understand the various opportunities in the healthcare sector. However, these opportunities have to be clearly defined and understood by both cellular operators and healthcare providers so that a sustainable business model can enable them to realize the synergies that can be attained by venturing into this new integration.

According to the official EU reports and market research, there are several key findings connected to the healthcare services in the EU. As for the European Commission, every year, approximately 8.0 percent to 12.0 percent of patients admitted to hospitals in EU suffers from healthcare associated infections, much of which are preventable [14]. The most common adverse events in the EU healthcare sector are medication-related errors such as patients receiving the wrong dose or wrong medicine, surgical errors, medical device and equipment-related failures and errors in diagnosis or the failure to act on the results of tests.

Due to the increase in the ageing population in Europe, the cost of healthcare is also rising significantly, with the tax base at a huge stake. Given the current economic downturn, hospitals in Europe are in a challenging position to receive huge funding from the government in their annual budgets for E-Healthcare– especially when they are not able to justify the return on investment in using the new services.

Though many applications like EHR, PACS, EPS, CPOE and DSS have been developed to support the healthcare sector, they are still in their pilot stages in several parts across Europe.

Nevertheless, the integration of various eHealthcare applications has been achieved with the advent of several wireless technologies. Various client devices such as mobile phones and personal digital assistants (PDAs) enabled with cellular, Wi-Fi, Bluetooth technology have been adding value to healthcare applications by enabling smooth transfer of clinical information.

The EU and its European eHealth Action Plan has launched initiatives such as Netc@rds that aims to replace the existing systems with smart cards that would facilitate cross-border healthcare for all European citizens. Major mobile operators, such as Orange, Vodafone, Telefonica, TeliaSonera, Telecom Italia, Telenor, Portugal

Telecom, Telekom Austria and Swisscom, have already started small-scale implementations of Mobile Healthcare in several parts of Western Europe.

With the implementation of eHealthcare services such as telemedicine and telecare, the use of wireless technologies has increased considerably, as most of the remote monitoring devices are wirelessly enabled. There is a concentrated shift towards patient-centric care in Europe; hence, the use of wireless devices has enabled successful communication between the various stakeholders of healthcare.

Moreover, it must be realized that no hospital will use a single wireless technology for all eHealthcare services and applications, but will, instead, adopt several wireless alternatives depending on capacity, range, throughput, regulatory issues, interference levels, multi-applications support, economies of scale and ease of use of certified client devices based on a ratified standard.

It has been estimated that the number of chronic patients in Europe during the next decade will be more than 100 million. Hence, even if one out of ten people uses mobile health services, the economic benefits are wide spread, ranging from service providers, application developers, insurance companies, hospitals to patients.

Regarding biometrics, Global Industry Analysts (GIA) estimate that by 2017 market size biometrics will be 16,47 billion dollars. At the same time, Frost & Sullivan writes that the international market of military and civil biometrics was 4 493,7 million dollars in 2010 and by 2019, this market will reach 14 684,9 million dollars. (Global Civil and Military Biometrics Market Assessment, Frost & Sullivan, 2012).

A growing need for quick payback biometric systems, e.g. biometric system of attendance time, becomes a new trend of the market of biometric technologies. The largest geographical markets will be the USA, at the same time in the first place by the pace of development will be the Asia-Pacific region (APR): the annual average growth rate of the biometric market in these states, calculated at compound interest CAGR, will be up to 23.8 % [15].

It is important to mention that many specific modules in healthcare systems are a part of confidential data and it is quite impossible to get information on them and their features.

In a system with biometric identification it is possible to build a system of database management connected to the healthcare sector and unifying basic services and disease history database within a network of healthcare organizations. As a matter of fact, there is no standardized system of medical records management in the EU states. The same differentiation is found in Russian regions.

Special attention should be paid on unified database of patients' disease history data, with a high security level for the information protection based on biometric characteristics and providing differentiated access control for different groups of users.

4 Experience and Potential of Voice Biometrics in eHealthcare

Biometric authentication can provide increased user convenience, and, when used as an alternative to passwords, can reduce authentication-related help desk to a great extent. However, usability problems remain, and Tier 2 and Tier 3 (Tier 1-3 – technical support managers gradation, where Tier 1 specialists solve primitive problems, while Tier 2 and Tier 3 focus on specific and more complicated issues) support costs will typically be higher than for passwords (as with other authentication methods).

Biometric authentication can provide higher levels of accountability than any other kind of authentication method, since it cannot be shared by coworkers as it happens for passwords and tokens.

Any biometric system involves the following scheme of work: the system stores a biometric sample (this is called the registration process or record of a biometric sample) and makes a few samples in order to make the most accurate biometric image; the information is processed and converted into a mathematical code. In addition, the system assumes the so-called multi-factor authentication, which can produce actions in order to associate the biometric sample with a specific person. For example, a personal identification number (PIN) is attached to a certain pattern, or a smart card containing the sample, which is applied to the reader. In this case, a sample of biometric characteristics is compared with the submitted sample.

Identification of any biometric characteristic goes through four stages:

- Registration or recording of a biometric sample - the physical or behavioral pattern memorized system;
- Isolation - the unique information is removed from the sample and compiled with a biometric sample;
- Comparison - compared with the stored sample submitted;
- Match/mismatch - the system determines whether the biometric samples are the same, and renders a decision.

Voice biometrics is one of the most accurate technologies therefore.

The procedure of speaker search (identification) is an automatic pairwise comparison by "voice models" in which the encoded individual (biometric) characteristics of voice and speech of speakers. As a result of the comparison shows a ranked list of soundtracks that contain a specified probability of matches.

The search is performed by three methods of biometric identification by voice with the adoption of a generalized solution.

Logical types of searches are the following:

1. "Famous among the famous": verification of registration is already available in the database speaker (with the exception of registration of the speaker under an assumed name);
2. "Unknown among the renowned" and vice versa: an identity of interest to the speaker;
3. "Unknown among unknowns".

ITMO University international laboratory of multimodal biometric and speech systems has developed multimodal approach to biometric identification, which helps to raise the accuracy of the system.

Universal common health care is a broad concept that has been implemented in several ways. The common denominator for all such programs is some form of government action aimed at extending access to health care as widely as possible and setting minimum standards.

Most implement universal health care through legislation, regulation and taxation. Legislation and regulation direct what care must be provided, to whom, and on what basis. Usually, some costs are borne by the patient at the time of consumption but the bulk of costs come from a combination of compulsory insurance and tax revenues. Some programs are paid for entirely out of tax revenues. In others tax revenues are used either to fund insurance for the very poor or for those needing long term chronic care. Many countries use mixed public-private systems to deliver universal health care.

As ICT practical use in the social sector is rather low, development of this area should focus on two main aspects in the scope of standardization: legal feasibility and standardization.

Legal feasibility implies creation of legal frames for storage and voluntary (for the patient) share of private healthcare data and disease history with the other healthcare services of the same kind (network) or insurance companies; software components standardization which implies acceptance of standards for the system's quality management. This standards should correspond to the ISO standards in the field and new standardization scheme should be accepted if required.

Contribution to standards includes the demand for special standards to be issued. Universal health care is a term referring to organized healthcare systems built around the principle of universal coverage for all members of society, combining mechanisms for health financing, technical support and service provision.

By the extent of government involvement in providing care and/or health insurance, universal health care systems diverse much. In some EU states, such as Spain, Italy and the Nordic countries, the government has a high degree of involvement in the commissioning or delivery of health care services and access is based on residence rights not on the purchase of insurance. Others have a much more pluralistic delivery system based on obligatory health with contributory insurance rates related to salaries or income, and usually funded by employers and beneficiaries jointly. Sometimes the health funds are derived from a mixture of insurance premiums, salary related mandatory contributions by employees and/or employers to regulated sickness funds, and by government taxes. These insurance based systems tend to reimburse private or public medical providers, often at heavily regulated rates, through mutual or publicly owned medical insurers. A few countries such as the Netherlands and Switzerland operate via privately owned but heavily regulated private insurers that are not allowed to make a profit from the mandatory element of insurance but can profit by selling supplemental insurance.

In Russia such standards are also have been started to be developed recently. However, there is no unified federal standard and even the database management differs from one region to another.

ITMO University specialists are active in the process of standardizations development. Annual world competitions or software show high results and accuracy of systems developed in ITMO University. The concept described in this article is also based on these high standards of software.

5 Voice Biometrics Identification: Case of eHealth Project in Russia

Regardless of the scenario and specific case, it is important that we understand the technological core of such a system – an out-of-the-box solution, which may be used in several fields.

Analyzing the regulatory framework it is possible to conclude that the legislation is not yet developed, however the frames based on the primacy of the international law is used. By the article 1 of the federal law 113 (On the biometric data protection) "Information on physiological and biological characteristics of a person on the basis of which one can establish his identity (biometric personal data) and which are used by operator to determine the identity of the subject of personal data may be processed only with the consent in a written form of the subject of personal data" [16], the same policy is implemented in the healthcare sector.

Biometric authentication methods use biometric characteristics or traits to verify users' claimed identities when accessing devices, networks, networked applications or Web applications. Across a wide range of use cases, any biometric authentication method may be used in one of two modes: one-to-one comparison (when the user enters a user ID) or one-to-many search mode (when the user simply presents his or her biometric, with no explicit claim of identity, and the system determines his or her user ID from a range of candidates).

Some devices embed biometric authentication, which impacts usage and business value. This is as a special case — "device-embedded biometric authentication".

The Russian market is characterized by the presence of three large segments that are experiencing growth implementations of biometric systems:

- system monitoring and access control (ACS),
- control of working time and access to a PC,
- biometric systems for law enforcement agencies and intelligence services.
- Other segments that should be said, are:
- voice authentication in call centers (in banking, telecommunications companies);
- intelligent video surveillance system and video analysis with the possibility of biometric authentication;
- biometric authentication in mobile applications, for example, for banks (http://www.biometrics.ru/).

Biometric authentication methods embrace a variety of discrete technologies differentiated by the biometric characteristic used and, in some cases, further differentiated by sensor types. In addition, biometric authentication is used in a wide range of use cases, such as for workforce local access (such as login to Windows PCs and networks or downstream applications), external users (such as login to Web applications) and, less often, workforce remote access (such as login to virtual private networks [VPNs]), each of which makes different demands. The position and time to plateau of this technology represent the optimal cases; individual technologies in particular use cases may be less advanced and may never reach the plateau.

Biometric authentication can provide medium to high levels of assurance, but established, non-biometric alternatives are available at a similar price point. Enterprises should evaluate biometric authentication as the sole method if user convenience is a primary consideration. However, although this can free users from the need to remember passwords or carry some kind of token, established fingerprint technologies cannot be used reliably by every user, necessitating the provision of an alternative at a higher per-user cost. Biometric authentication can, however, provide a higher level of accountability than alternatives [17].

Enterprises should also consider alternative approaches. The comparison score generated by a biometric technology can be used as a variable input to dynamic risk assessment in adaptive access control, rather than as the basis for a clear-cut, binary authentication decision (see "Adaptive Access Control Emerges"). Biometric technologies, such as face topography and typing rhythm, can also be used as a postlogin preventive or detective control to verify that only the legitimate user is or has been using the PC.

6 Privacy Issues: The Biometric Experience in Italy

In this section, through a portrait of biometric identification systems in Italy including legislative and applied aspects, we focus on privacy issues related to the adoption of biometric solutions.

The regulation of the usage of biometric data in Italy is quite recent. Indeed, with the General measure prescriptive regarding biometrics Act, issued by the Privacy Guarantor in November 2014, finally it ends a long period of attempts to give rules to this very critical field [18] The Act premise is that the use of devices and technologies for the collection and processing of biometric data is rapidly proliferating, in particular for the assessment of personal identity in the delivery of information society services and access to digital information. Biometric data can be used also for access control in local areas, for the activation of electromechanical and electronic devices, and to subscribe electronic documents. The diffusion of these potential application has attracted the attention of the Italian data protection authority, according to the direction indicated in the Article 29 of the Working Party (WP29) [19], which is an outstanding reference for the study of the phenomenon. The biometric data are in fact personal data, since they can always be regarded as "information relating to an identified or identifiable natural person" taking into account "all the means likely reasonably to be used either by the controller or by other to identify a person." Therefore fall within the scope of the Italian Privacy Act (D.lgs 196/2003 art. 4, paragraph 1, letter b), as a specific case of electronic data treatment. According to WP29, biometric data are biometric samples, biometric templates, biometric references and any other data obtained by computer from biometric characteristics and which can be traced, even through interconnection to other databases, to an identified or identifiable individual. By this Act, the Guarantor intended to provide a framework to orientate technological choices, and to indicate when the treatments on biometric data are conform to the principles of privacy and compliant with security standards. The guidelines also introduce the right terminology to use for the description of the technological aspects. The peculiar characteristics of biometric data enforce the adoption of high levels of security, according to the provisions of the European Regulation eIDAS [20] in terms of identification, authentication and electronic signature. The Act introduces also the obligation of reporting to the Guarantor all security incidents and data breaches involving biometric data. Moreover, who intend to provide processing of biometric data, must submit a request to the Guarantor to obtain authorization. There are a number of exceptions to the above obligation, in all the cases where the level of risk is low. In case of the required level of assurance is required to guarantee National security and safety, biometric data can be used to authenticate individuals without their authorization. No preliminary verification of the biometric system is required in the following cases:

(a) The biometric features consist in the fingerprint or vocal recognition.
(b) In the case of use of fingerprint, the acquisition device has the ability to detect the liveness of the individual.
(c) In the case of use of vocal emission, this feature is used only in combination with other authentication factors and precautions to exclude the risk of fraudulent use of any voice recordings
(d) The deletion of biometric data is done immediately after their transformation into samples or biometric templates.
(e) The devices used for the initial acquisition and those used for the acquisition during ordinary operations are directly connected or integrated into computer systems.
(f) Data transmissions between acquisition devices and computer systems is made secure by using cryptographic techniques characterized by the adoption of encryption keys of appropriate length, according to the size and to the life cycle of data.
(g) Biometric data are stored in secure portable devices (smart cards or similar secure devices) with appropriate cryptographic capabilities and certificates complying with technical standard ISO/IEC 15408 or FIPS 140-2 at least level 3. Thus: (i) the support is released in a single copy and destroyed at the end of the procedure with a recorder procedure; (ii) the memory area in which data are stored is accessible only to authorized readers and protected from unauthorized accesses; (iii) samples or references are encrypted by biometric- cryptographic techniques with key lengths appropriate to the size and life-cycle data.
(h) Storage is done in systems protected with biometric authentication with proper logs, strict control about software and malware installation, ensuring adequate encryption of biometric data, and they are kept separately from identifying data.

The implementation of biometric centralized archives has been always denied, but now technology and lifestyle demands meet each other perfectly [21].

Biometric data can be also used for controlling physical access to "sensitive" areas of personnel employed and use of dangerous machinery and equipment. The adoption of biometric systems based on the development of the fingerprint or the topography of the hand may be allowed to restrict access to areas and premises deemed "sensitive" where you need to ensure high and specific levels of security, or to allow the use of dangerous machinery and equipment only to qualified persons and specifically engaged in the activities. Also in this case, no authorization is required. Again, as for authentication, no preliminary verification is required if security measures similar to those listed earlier are adopted. The biometric techniques may also used to enable, adjust and simplify physical access of users to physical areas in the public domain (e.g. Libraries) or private (e.g. Airport areas reserved) or services. In these cases a consent is required. Finally, biometric data are used for subscription of electronic documents. In this case, the processing of biometric data consists of the dynamic information associated with the handwritten signature using specific hardware devices. Storing these data is locally permitted without preliminary verification and this is the base of solutions of advanced electronic signature, as defined by the Legislative Decree of March 7, 2005, n. 82, containing the "Digital Administration Code" that do not provide the centralized storage of biometric data.

7 Conclusion and Discussion

The results of our study allow summarizing the promising technological trends in biometric authentification systems:

- distribution of biometric identification systems: emergence of cheap and reliable devices. The presence of domestic research and manufacturing base for the implementation of such systems on local levels (national maintenance);
- development of infrastructure of non-financial services that requires identification/ authentication. The development of a secure infrastructure financial services capable of ensuring secure use of non-financial services;
- sharp increase in the use of mobile devices for the purposes of identification: ratification, informatization, financial and non-financial services and payments;
- development of national scientific and production base, capable of ensuring the implementation of systems using microprocessor cards and mobile devices.
- privacy issues assumes a specific importance in the field of biometric authentication; however the Italian experience show that a good balance between security and privacy requirements can be found in such a way that usability and invasiveness are suitably controlled and the risk of misuse of biometric data is minimized.

Applications of best practices based on international comparative analysis could bring special value for quality of life and healthcare system [22]. According to international trends and state legislation in Italy and Russia the following potential applications for prospective technological infrastructure of digital identity should be advised:

- Authorization and authentication in information systems, including state portals of Federal and regional importance
- Campus projects - access control on the territory of educational institutions and related infrastructure (student residences, sports centers etc.)
- Social services - implementation of the civil rights to receive social support, and organization of individualized services.

- Public transport - the use of biometric characteristics-key person, as an identifier in ticketing systems in public transportation services;
- Commercial services - the use of biometric data as a primary or secondary factor for authentication/authorization to conduct transactions with your Bank account. It supposes the possibility of confirmation of non-cash payment method in obtaining various products and services.

The system has no limitations of the amount of users – it just needs some data mining and store systematization for etalons. The authors believe that proposed biometrics applications could bring public value and increase the efficiency of healthcare system.

Acknowledgments. This work was partially financially supported by research work No.415825 "Development of opinion-mining tool for getting citizens'assessment on government activities".

References

1. Bailador, G., Sanchez-Avila, C., Guerra-Casanova, J., Sierra, A.: Analysis of pattern recognition techniques for in-air signature biometrics. Pattern Recogn. **44**(10–11), 2468–2478 (2011)
2. Bastys, A., Kranauskas, J., Krüger, V.: Iris recognition by fusing different representations of multi-scale Taylor expansion. Comput. Vis. Image Underst. **115**(6), 804–816 (2011)
3. Bowyer, K.W., Hollingsworth, K., Flynn, P.J.: Image understanding for iris biometrics: a survey. Comput. Vis. Image Underst. **110**(2), 281–307 (2008)
4. Tan, T., Zhang, X., Sun, Z., Zhang, H.: Noisy iris image matching by using multiple cues. Pattern Recogn. Lett. **33**(8), 970–977 (2012)
5. Chen, C., Veldhuis, R.: Extracting biometric binary strings with minimal area under the FRR curve for the hamming distance classifier. Sig. Process. **91**(4), 906–918 (2011)
6. Chin, Y.J., Ong, T.S., Teoh, A.B.J., Goh, K.O.M.: Integrated biometrics template protection technique based on fingerprint and palmprint feature-level fusion. Inf. Fusion **18**, 161–174 (2014)
7. Crawford, H., Renaud, K., Storer, T.: A framework for continuous transparent mobile device authentication. Comput. Secur. **39**(B), 127–136 (2013)
8. Karnan, M., Akila, M., Krishnaraj, N.: Biometric personal authentication using keystroke dynamics: a review. Appl. Soft Comput. **11**(2), 1565–1573 (2011)
9. Eskander, G.S., Sabourin, R., Granger, E.: A bio-cryptographic system based on offline signature images. Inf. Sci. **259**, 170–191 (2014)
10. McDuff, D., El Kaliouby, L., Senechal, T., Demirdjian, D., Picard, R.: Automatic measurement of ad preferences from facial responses gathered over the Internet. Image Vis. Comput. **32**(10), 630–640 (2014)
11. Rathgeb, C., Busch, C.: Cancelable multi-biometrics: Mixing iris-codes based on adaptive bloom filters. Comput. Secur. **42**, 1–12 (2014)
12. Economic 360 for Egypt: Growth Prospects and Emerging Opportunities in the Healthcare Industry (2011). https://frost.com/prod/servlet/report-brochure.pag?id=4721-01-00-00-00
13. Public Health: Improving health for all EU citizens (2013). http://ec.europa.eu/health/health_policies/docs/improving_health_for_all_eu_citizens_en.pdf

14. Patient Safety and Quality of Care. Special Euro barometer 411 (2013). http://ec.europa.eu/public_opinion/archives/ebs/ebs_411_en.pdf
15. Market Statistics 2012. Biometric Technology Today, 16(6), 12 (2008). doi:10.1016/S0969-4765(08)70168-1
16. Federal Law of the Russian Federation "On personal data №152 from 21.07.2014, art.11, p. 2 (2014)
17. Gamassi, M., Lazzaroni, M., Misino, M., Piuri, V., Sana, D., Scotti, F.: Acccuracy and performance of biometric systems. In: Proceedings of MTC 2004 – Instrumentation and Measurement Technology Conference (2014). http://crema.di.unimi.it/~fscotti/ita/pdf/Scotti14.pdf
18. Privacy Guarantor General Act about Biometry November, 2014. Published in "Gazzetta Ufficiale" n. 280, 2 December 2014
19. Article 29 Working Party, European Commission, Directive 95/46/EC of the European Parliament and of the Council of 24 October 1995 (1995)
20. Electronic identification and trust services (eIDAS): regulatory environment and beyond. Digital Agenda for Europe. European Commission Directorate General (2015). http://ec.europa.eu/dgs/connect/en/content/electronic-identification-and-trust-services-eidas-regulatory-environment-and-beyond
21. Matveev, Y.N.: Biometric technologies of person identification by voice and other modalities, Vestnik MGTU. Priborostroenie. Biometric Technol. Special Issue **3**(3), 46–61 (2012)
22. Gorelik, S., Lyaper, V., Bershadskaya, L., Buccafurri, F.: Breaking the barriers of e-participation: the experience of russian digital office development. In: Kö, A., Francesconi, E. (eds.) EGOVIS 2014. LNCS, vol. 8650, pp. 173–186. Springer, Heidelberg (2014)

Towards a Model of Client-Driven Access to Public e-Services

József Károly Kiss(✉), Peter József Kiss, and Gábor Klimkó

MTA IT Foundation, Budapest, Hungary
mtaita@t-online.hu

Abstract. The take-up of the usage of public e-services in Hungary is slow, though a lot of efforts were exerted in order to accelerate the process. The paper points out barriers rooted in the traditional logic of access to public e-services in which clients are required to use the same e-authentication technique and way of electronic document exchange. We present a client-driven model that gives the freedom of choice to the client with respect to the e-authentication technique as well as the document exchange to be used, thereby eliminating these barriers. A simplified form of the model was enacted by the law and is now being implemented in Hungary.

Keywords: e-government enterprise architectures · Electronic identity · Identity management · Electronic document exchange

1 Introduction

In order to enable usage of electronic government services (public e-services for short) in Hungary, a single and unified electronic authentication method and contact channel called "Client Gate" was introduced in 2005 [1]. Under the "Client Gate" brand the Hungarian state offers a free electronic authentication service that uses username/password pairs. Citizens are required to register for the "Client Gate" service in person. The service includes the registration of one e-mail address of a client as well as a limited but free storage capacity where clients can upload and download their electronic documents to be used during exchanges of documents with public authorities. Uploaded documents are certified by digital time stamps; all files are handled via the Government Portal https://magyarorszag.hu/. Later certain public administration organisations also got their own similar electronic service, called the "Office Gate". The Office Gate uses username/password authentication, too [2].

Though politicians envisioned a widespread usage of the Client Gate, at the beginning there was a low level of interest in using it [3]. Having experienced this situation, the Hungarian Government made the usage of "Client Gate" services compulsory for certain taxation-related activities in a wide circle of enterprises and entrepreneurs. Consequently the number of registered "Client Gate" users increased steadily and significantly.

© Springer International Publishing Switzerland 2015
A. Kő and E. Francesconi (Eds.): EGOVIS 2015, LNCS 9265, pp. 117–131, 2015.
DOI: 10.1007/978-3-319-22389-6_9

There are more than 1.86 million registered Client Gate users today, but the seemingly continuous development is mainly due to the fact that the usage of the Client Gate service became mandatory by law for a new group of users from time to time.

At the end of 2013 there were 718,792 companies, 380,794 individual entrepreneurs and 684,064 private individuals (with tax number) performing independent activities, that is, all together 1,783,650 taxpayers with tax numbers. Those who have a tax number are obliged to use Client Gate services. However, there are 3.6 million employees among Hungarian taxpayers, who are not obliged by law to use Client Gate services [4]. It is now clear that this group does not use Client Gate services heavily; that is, it is not within their obvious natural needs.

We do not know exactly what percentage of the registered Client Gate users conduct personal (i.e., for his/her own purposes) electronic business with the government. In order to estimate this data, let us consider the number of visitors to the Hungarian Government Portal, https://magyarorszag.hu/.

The number of visitors is usually in the range of 450.000-500.000 per month. If we consider the 5.4 million Hungarian taxpayers (this figure does not include students and pensioners), the current rate of e-government service users is at most 20 % of the potential beneficiaries.

The primary driver of using e-government services is their availability, but in our case it is not a real issue. Although in principle, everybody of the 5.4 million Hungarian tax-paying population could use the electronic tax form service in 2013 there were 2.4 million personal client contacts in the tax customer offices [4].

One may assume that potential users are afraid of using electronic services in general. In contrast, however, when the Hungarian Tax Office offered a comfortable remote (phone) service, the number of users showed a very dynamic increase. When employment relationship between private persons for the performance of housework was introduced, employers were let to notify the Tax Office by phone as well as through the Client Gate. Almost 64 % of the employers chose the phone and only 36 % used the Client Gate [4].

As Internet penetration in Hungary is high enough there must be other barriers that block the usage of e-services. The relatively low usage of e-government services might not be attributed to a limited service portfolio, either [5]. This statement was confirmed in the e-Government Benchmark Report in 2014, where the recommended action for Hungary was to invest to enable more people to actually use services [6]. We believe though that if we understand and serve the real needs of citizens better, a higher usage rate could be achieved. This is the reason why we looked for a more attractive model of accessing electronic public services.

2 Goal and Method of the Study

The starting point of our study is that there are a reasonable number of clients who posses Client Gate access and there are also working public e-services in

Hungary that are useful and valuable for the clients, but still take-up of public e-services is relatively low.

We wanted first to identify certain barriers that hinder the widespread usage of public e-services. We looked for possible usability, privacy and security concerns that could be removed by organisational and technical solutions. Usability and privacy/security are in correlation; the higher the privacy/security level of an e-service, the more uncomfortable is its usage. We did not study human (psychological and sociological) aspects as we were not interested in studying the whole population but only those who are digitally literate. (Note that 'digitally literate' does not equal to being an information technology professional.) We are talking about such potential clients of whom a lot have Internet access anyway. As Client Gate services are free in the sense that clients do not have to pay for them, therefore the cost of public e-services is not a potential barrier.

In order to understand the real security needs of the citizen we used data acquired during the process of setting up new one-stop-shop customer service centers called "Government Windows" in Hungary [7]. Citizens will be able to conduct about 2,300 different types of public administration cases in a Government Window in the near future. These facilities are introduced as part of the structural reform of the Hungarian public administration [8]. We interviewed some officers who participate and direct the reform.

Having identified three barriers we propose a new model that is based on the principle that the client and not the authority should be allowed to choose from separate e-authentication techniques and document exchange methods during the course of doing business with public authorities. The model is based on certain registers and systems; their role will be described in separate subsections. Communication among these systems will be presented with sequence diagrams.

A simplified version of the model was already enacted in Hungarian law and is now being implemented. For the sake of brevity we shall focus on and present the logical model omitting implementation details.

3 Barriers of Widespread Usage of Public e-Services

We are going to point out three barriers that are rooted in the traditional logic in the access to public e-services. Salvodelli at al. gave a comprehensive literature overview on the paradox of the still low adoption of e-government after more than two decades of policy efforts and public investments for the deployment of online public services. They identified 16 different types of barriers among which the lack of digital skills is the most often cited one between 2005 and 2009. The second most important type of barrier is user participation, which is in our focus [9].

When a client uses public e-services there is a need for authentication and often for some form of formal exchange of electronic documents. Issues associated with authentication and the exchange of documents can discourage the usage of e-services. If a client does not intend to use a public e-service in person then s/he should nominate a trustee. Unfortunately, this nomination process also leads to challenges.

Note that it is an evident usability requirement that clients want access to public e-services via devices they are using for other purposes, too. As the use of tablets and smartphones is increasing fast we took this phenomenon as a constraint in our study.

3.1 The Barrier Attributable to a Prearranged e-Authentication Technique

There are a number of electronic authentication techniques available that differ in their strengths. The strength of an electronic authentication technique is usually characterised by the number of applied independent factors (knowledge, ownership, inherence) used as well as the communication channel (Internet, GSM etc.).

In Hungary currently the only form of electronic authentication for public e-services is the Client Gate where citizens use a username/password pair. It is well known that this authentication technique has a relatively low security and this weakness might lead to the limited usage of public e-services.

Austria, Belgium, Estonia and Portugal use smart card technology to support public e-services [10–13]. /Note that there are other European examples, too, see Kubicek's comparative study [14]/. The idea of using such strong two-factor authentication technique seems to be appealing at first glimpse and it was proposed to be used in Hungary, too. Smart card-based electronic authentication, however, was not successful at all in the private sector. For example, in home banking the usage of a bank card that requires a card reader device is practically non-existent in Hungary; other forms of two-factor authentication as one time passwords sent by SMS or tokens are preferred instead.

If we categorise electronic authentication techniques according to whether authentication is done in a controlled environment and with a controlled device or not, the inherent problem of the smart card based e-authentication becomes clear (see Table 1). The typical usage of public e-services happens in an uncontrolled environment with an uncontrolled device. The strength of the same authentication technique in a controlled environment is very different from that of at home (i.e. uncontrolled) environment.

We can conclude that a single e-authentication technique that is purely based on the need of the highest level of security can be a barrier to widespread usage of public e-services.

Table 1. Smart-card based e-authentication situations

e-authentication	With controlled device	With uncontrolled device
In controlled environment (person is present)	e.g. border crossing with biometric passport	e.g. using e-service in an Internet cafe, authentication is done by digital signature
In remote (uncontrolled) environment (person is not present)	e.g. usage of an ATM	e.g. usage of a public e-service from home, or home banking

We found another obstacle attributable to the single, unified e-authentication solution. In Hungary, new one-stop-shop customer service centers called "Government Windows" are to be introduced. In a Government Window clients can conduct about 2,300 different types of public administration cases in the near future.

We classified the 2,300 types according to the security needs of the citizen into three categories. We rank as "high security" needs those cases where the citizen need to provide sensitive, personal data such as health data, social status or penalty data). Cases, where there is no need for sensitive, personal data, were ranked as of low security needs. In these cases the citizen usually notifies or declares something or requests not sensitive data. The remaining cases were ranked as of medium security needs. We found that 74 % of the cases are categorized as low security needs, 11 % as medium and 15 % as high security needs. Therefore it is unnecessary to pose high security requirements on a significant portion of the cases. There are, however, cases where using a low security solution would result in a high risk. One can get the idea that it could be worth linking the required strength (level) of authentication to the type of the case. That is, there should be different authentication techniques available for the citizens. There are countries that have taken steps in this direction (e.g. Estonia, see below). In Hungary, the use of mobile phones for Client Gate authentication is being developed, too.

In this approach the client is allowed to select from the authentication techniques but specific types of cases determine the applicable authentication techniques. This, however, still does not explain why the usage of services based on the username/password authentication technique does not reach a higher proportion for cases with low security needs. The underlying reason is that the Client Gate approach as well as other initiatives in the public administration is based on a simplified understanding of the clients. Clients are viewed as a basically homogenous group, however, that is a wrong perception.

In summary, we identified a significant barrier that inhibits the widespread usage of public e-services. Governments typically offer public e-services with an all or nothing logic; that is, if a citizen gets his/her e-authentication credentials, then all available public e-services are allowed to be accessed with these. The client is not allowed to select among different e-authentication techniques, neither can s/he declare his/her wish that certain types of cases should be treated personally.

3.2 The Barrier Attributable to a Prearranged Way of Electronic Document Exchange

An essential element of conducting e-business with public authorities is the exchange of information. Though there are on-line interactive technical solutions for this purpose, the significance of the exchange of electronic documents has just slightly decreased – if a case ends with a resolution issued by the authority concerned, the client (for his/her own sake) should receive an authentic copy of it. In contrast, in the business sector document exchange is often simply based on e-mail systems, parties trust in each other. To support the exchange of electronic documents for public e-services in Hungary, a free central storage facility is available for Client Gate owners. This service is available for each Client Gate user and it is always on – if this service fails, that is legal reason for exemption in case of being late.

A mistrustful client, however, may not be happy with this service. Using a central document storage facility means that all electronic documents of the client can be found at a well-defined place. If we compare the consequences of hacking a transactional e-government system and a central storage facility, the differences are striking. The annual number of cases (i.e. documents) at an average Hungarian public authority is about 2 million. That is, on any working day, roughly thousands of documents are processed within a couple of minutes. The defence against hacking today is often done by on-line surveillance, which means that intrusions are detected within (maximum) a couple of hours and the necessary countermeasures are taken. Therefore in case of hacking into a public administration system, we might expect the illegal access to maximum of a few thousand documents that are being processed.

The risks are very different in the case of a central storage facility that provides a large scale service. Due to the necessary large bandwidth to the central storage facility more documents can be captured by a hacker during the same period of time. At a transactional system a hacker can only get documents related to specific public administration cases, whereas at the central storage facility documents of separate cases might be found that may enable the building of personality profiles.

The ordinary citizen is reluctant to conform if the state wants to observe and control his/her activities and a central storage facility might be a proper tool to achieve this. Thus it is understandable that citizens do not willingly use the central storage facility and they prefer e-mail as a communication channel. We identified therefore a second barrier against the widespread usage of public e-services.

Note that the individual needs of the clients might be different, too. A citizen might prefer to share a document on Facebook or send it by e-mail; or can manage it separately form his/her private mails.

3.3 The Barrier Attributable to the Assignment to the Client

We found a third barrier that might be the toughest. When using public e-services, the main focus is usually on the secure and precise authentication (assignment) of the client. In practice this approach is not appropriate when

1. there is no need to present the personal data of the client asking for a service at all;
2. it is not the client him/herself but his/her trustee who is going to do the business.

The current Hungarian legislation handles the first issue – in accordance with the personal data protection rules – by introducing four types of electronic authentication.

The second issue, the case of a trustee who can act on behalf of the client in e-services, however, is not handled in Hungarian law. Currently, a Client Gate owner is legally entitled to use public e-services only on their own behalf. The only exception is the Tax and Customs Office where there is a dedicated, paper-based system in which those Client Gate owners who are entitled to act in cases on behalf of a company can be named [15]. A wide-spread use of such a paper-based solution would result in a confusing situation for the clients as they were expected to follow to whom, for what purpose and what period of time a mandate for being trustee was given.

A certain number of citizens do not use Client Gate as they would prefer to have a trustee to act in their cases. The only way to do this would be to disclose their personal Client Gate credentials to their trustee. There is a need for a proper way of authorising trustees, in other words the hiatus of such a mechanism is a barrier.

4 A Client-Driven Model of Access to Public e-Services

According to the traditional logic of e-government, public authorities specified how to run the office work and which e-authentication techniques are allowed. Having identified the aforementioned three barriers as consequences of the traditional logic, we present a model in which rules (precepts) are to be defined by the client and authorities should adapt to those and not vice versa. This is a breakaway from the traditional approach, the client is not enforced to use any authentication technique claimed to be the superior one (e.g. PKI based approaches [16]).

In this model the clients are allowed to give their precepts for specific types of cases, where they declare that

- with which authorities what type of authentication technique should be used (among the available ones), as well as
- who is allowed to act as their trustee.

For example, if the client declares that s/he is willing to authenticate him-/herself only with username/password in a certain type of case, then the proper authority is not allowed to accept smart card based authentication even if the client happens to have a valid smart card. Note that the Indian Aardhaar Authentication Service is similar to this model in the sense that it allows for using different e-authentication techniques. In the Aardhaar system, however, there is a Central Identities Data Repository that contains all the credentials of a client [17]. In the model to be shown there is no need for such a central repository as Identity assertion Providers (IdPs) can store the client's credentials.

The client can also declare that in certain types of cases s/he wants to act personally (i.e., the use of e-services are excluded) only because of possible abuse (note that in principle this should decrease the number of abuses).

The implementation of this model is based on the Central Register of the Clients Precepts (CRCP) where the precepts are stored. In principle it would be possible to have separate registers for precepts, e.g. by branches of government; however such a requirement has not been raised even in the strict Hungarian data protection environment. The reason for having one central register is that storing the client's precepts separately at different authorities would cause a burden for both for the authorities and for the client. Authorities would have to bear the development costs; clients would have to continuously monitor where and what kind of precepts they made. Having separate registers would also lead to the requirement of some form of federation that would increase complexity, too. The solution is to have a central register of the client's precepts.

Let us note the providers of public e-services with $SP_1 \ldots SP_n$ identity assertion providers for these e-services with $IdP_1 \ldots IdP_m$ and the Document Exchange Providers for these e-services with $DEP_1 \ldots DEP_l$. Note that we shall use the expressions "service provider" and "public authority" interchangeably, that is, "public authority" refers to the authority that is responsible to provide the e-service. Having introduced the concept of CRCP the model of operations shown on Fig. 1. could be envisaged (lines represent flow of data between the nodes).

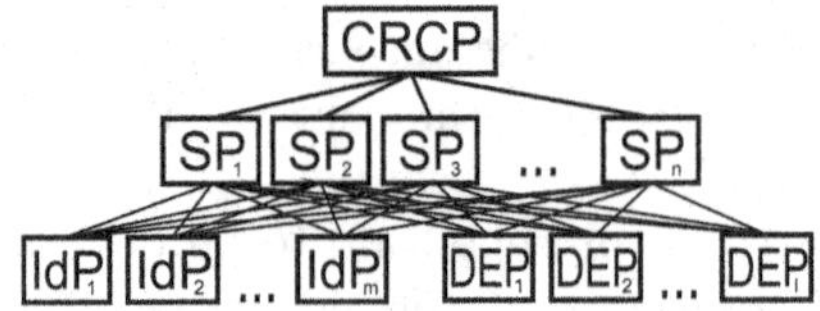

Fig. 1. First-cut architecture of the model

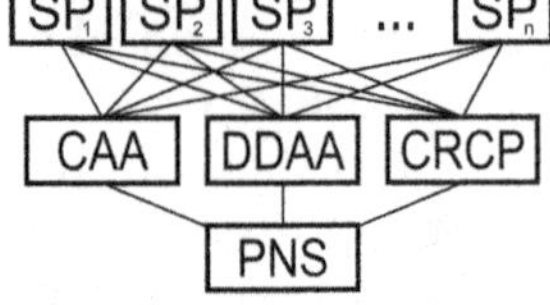

Fig. 2. Architecture of the model

Each service provider is required to use the data stored in the CRCP, that is, precepts for both authentication and document exchange. These precepts specify then which IdP and which DEP should be contacted.

A straightforward implementation of the above model is not appropriate for two reasons:

- each service provider should communicate with each IdP and with each DEP;
- in order to query a client's precepts in the CRCP, a prior authentication of that client should happen, i.e. there would be need for multiple authentications.

These problems can be resolved by using the concept of the 'agent', that is, an intermediary party that manages centrally the flow of data. On that basis we introduce the following agents:

1. The Central Authentication Agent (CAA) offers the services of the available IdPs to the client requesting of an e-service. The e-service providers communicate with the separate IdPs via the CAA.
2. The Document Delivery and Arrival Agent (DDAA) offers the services of the available DEPs to the requesting service provider, and it manages document

exchange between the client and the e-service providers. The DDAA handles incoming and outgoing electronic messages sent by and received from various DEPs. The DDAA also incorporates basic document management functionality; it logs the sending event as well as the event of receiving of a return receipt into the filing register of a service provider.

We introduce one more element in the model, the Periodical Notice Service (PNS). The client's freedom of choice amongst different authentication techniques might lead to the usage of solutions with lower security level. The increase in risk should be compensated with the introduction of some forms of guarantial items. The PNS is such a guarantial item. Electronic events related to a client (e.g. s/he logged in a system, his/her precepts were retrieved from the CRCP; s/he was sent official messages etc.) are to be logged and a summary will be regularly sent to the client by the PNS (if the client asked for it). Thereby the client can check whether somebody cheated him/her and s/he can take the necessary actions (including criminal complaints). The PNS is analogue to the practice of banks that send an immediate SMS notice when somebody logs in the home bank. The PNS, similarly, sends a certified official message that contains the log of related events in a predefined period of time. Note that in order to strengthen confidence in the model other guarantial items might be also needed.

Using CRCP, CAA, DDAA and PNS, the model of operations shown in Fig. 2. can be proposed which is better suited for implementation.

In the next sections we will discuss the functionality of CRCP, CAA, DDAA and PNS in more detail.

4.1 The Central Register of Client's Precepts

The CRCP should contain certified public records. Certified public records should be accepted by the law unless one disputes the content of that record in court in Hungary.

A precept of a client can be generic or specific and it can belong to the following types

- precepts for permitted ways of contact with authorities (personal, by phone, electronic)
- precepts for authentication techniques to be used
- precepts for delivery channels and
- precepts for trustees

A precept can concern a natural person as well as a legal entity. In that way the CRCP manages all variations for nominating trustees. Samples for the possible scenarios are presented in Table 2.

The legal requirements of personal data protection should also be taken into consideration at the implementation of CRCP. In Hungary it is forbidden by law to use a single, universal personal identifier and, as a consequence, the primary key of CRCP that identifies a person should only be known within the CRCP. The CRCP should therefore communicate with other systems with their

Table 2. Scenarios for nominating trustees

	Trustee		
Authorizing entity		Person	Legal entity
	Person	A husband sends his wife to act on behalf of him	A person authorises a law firm to act on behalf of him
	Legal entity	somebody (who is not an official representative) has the mandate to act on behalf of a company	A company authorises an accounting firm to act on behalf of that company

corresponding own primary keys. The CRCP should not store the document containing a precept but only its data content. When a service provider (system) requests a person‘s precept, the CRCP sends and certifies its data content only. The problem due to the prohibition of using universal personal identifiers can be circumvented by the introduction of the "linking register" (LR). The service based on the LR provides a method of secure interconnection of registers containing personal data. The LR contains encrypted anonymous linking codes that are generated and encrypted separately by the operators of the registers. The detailed discussion of LR is not in the scope of this paper, for our purposes it is enough to know that personal identifiers can be legally obtained.

There should be a service provider for the CRCP, too. A client can enter (store) a precept into the CRCP as the sequence diagram in Fig. 3. shows.

If the public e-service provider SP_1 requests for a certified precept of a person from CRCP, it is provided with the help of the LR as shown in Fig. 4.

Each precept can be specific to a certain type of case and to a certain authority. To enable this feature the CRCP uses taxonomy of concepts as well as that of the authorities concerned.

The CRCP is a critical element from the point of security as the client is allowed to specify low security authentication techniques and communication channels. As a guarantial element the very first so-called "base precept" of a client differs from the other ones. The base precept contains a precept about who and how is allowed to change precepts of the client. The base precept can be created only by a secure way, e.g. personally or such a way where stealing of personality can be excluded. For example, the client can prescribe in the base precept that his/her precepts can only be modified with personal appearance; or s/he can allow it remotely, using a secure authentication technique. The client is also allowed to use precepts for communication via phone. For example, having been authenticated via phone, s/he might give a precept for a trustee.

4.2 The Central Authentication Agent

The task of the CAA is to hide away the complexity of using several IdPs for the systems requesting a client's authentication. The CAA should use a common communication protocol with its requesting parties (service providers), e.g.

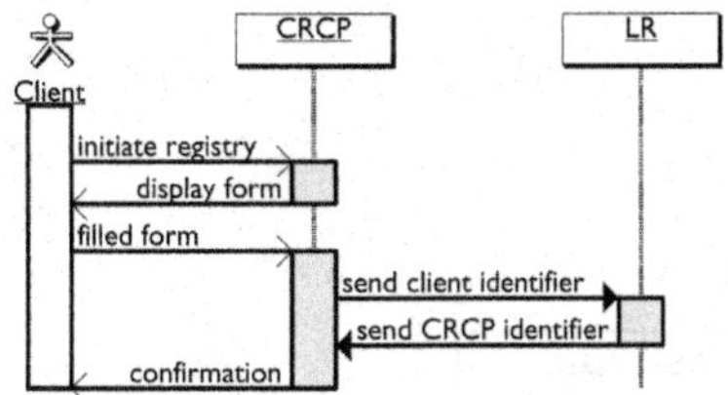

Fig. 3. Entering a precept in the CRCP

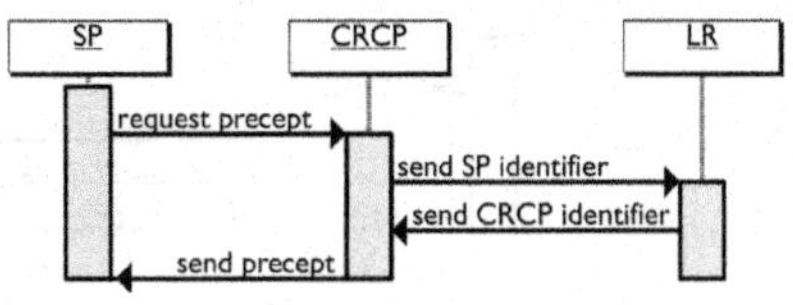

Fig. 4. Retrieving a precept from the CRCP

Security Assertion Markup Language (SAML) that is widely used in EU countries [18]. The CAA, however, might use other protocols in communicating with the IdPs.

The CAA offers the client different authentication possibilities, and, on the basis of the client's choice, it passes the control to the selected IdP. The main steps in the (basic) authentication process are shown in Fig. 5. (note that for the sake of simplicity error handling is not included).

The CAA might offer third party IdPs, too. Third party IdPs sometimes verify such credentials that are not suitable for authentication of the client in the public sector. Google, for example, can verify an e-mail address and this data is not enough to conduct business with the public administration. The CRCP solves this problem as the client is able to specify a third party IdP as well as its credential holder, this data then authenticates him for public e-services. If the client wishes to use a third party IdP, then the CAA can match the acquired data with a query from the CRCP to establish whether there is a corresponding precept. The simplified process is shown in Fig. 6. (from the point when the IdP sends the result to the CAA).

4.3 The Document Delivery and Arrival Agent

It is advantageous to give the user of the public e-services the freedom of choice among contact channels, too. In Hungary the following electronic communication channels are available for document exchange in general:

- storage provided for the owners of a Client Gate
- the secure electronic mail service operated by the Hungarian Post
- e-mail (provided by an arbitrary service provider)
- the official conversion service between paper based document and its authentic electronic document version; including conversion from paper to electronic document and the other way round.

Note that fax services might be still in use in exceptional cases; this can also be integrated in the model if it is necessary. If an e-service allows for using SMS based communication, this can also be managed.

The rationale behind having the DDAA is that the Hungarian public administration still heavily relies on using documents; therefore document management has a distinctive role. Delivery and dispense/distribution of documents (especially with structured data) can be automated with the DDAA services. The

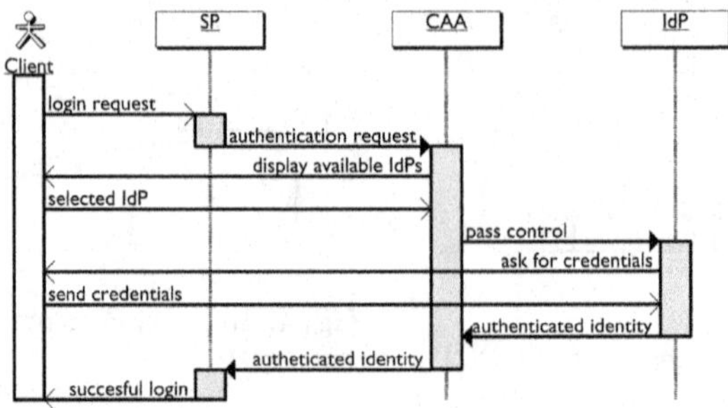

Fig. 5. Authentication via the CAA

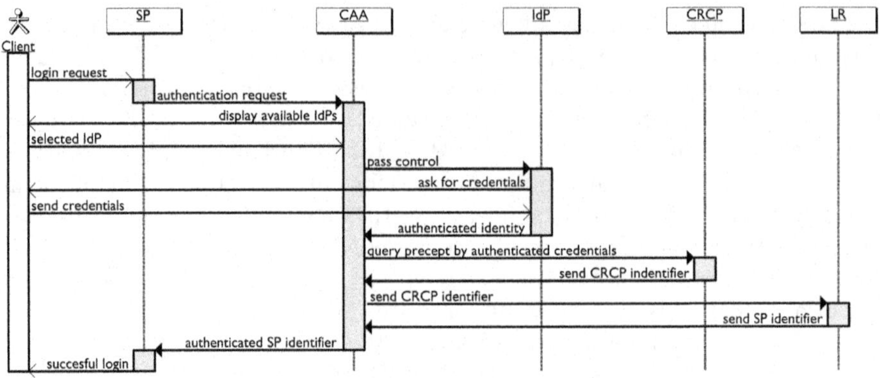

Fig. 6. Authentication by third-party IdP via the CAA

DDAA is able to receive documents sent by the client via different communication channels. According to the precepts of the addressed public authority, the DDAA can virus check and register the arrival of the sent document and upon request of the client, it can create and return a receipt note. The DDAA converts the officially certified (signed) document into the format expected by the selected communication channel; then it sends for delivery and records the delivery event into the filing register of the issuing authority (that is, the authority of which electronic system passes to the document to the DDAA).

The DDAA provides for the return receipt, and it can also check if the return receipt was sent in time and if not, it notifies the sending party (system) of the document. The main steps of this process are shown in Fig. 7. (without error processing).

4.4 The Periodical Notice Service

The client's freedom of choice allows solutions with lower level security to be used but the overall security should not be compromised. This need justifies the introduction of the PNS.

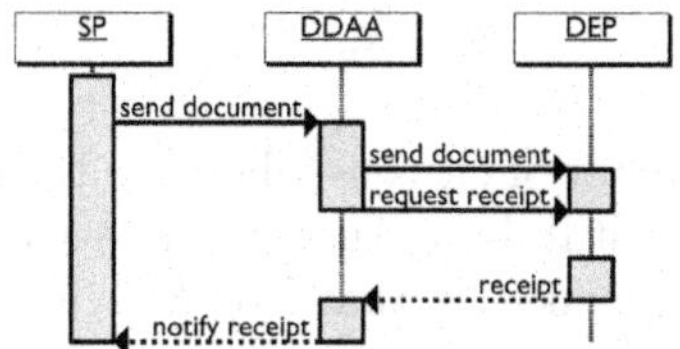

Fig. 7. Document exchange via the DDAA

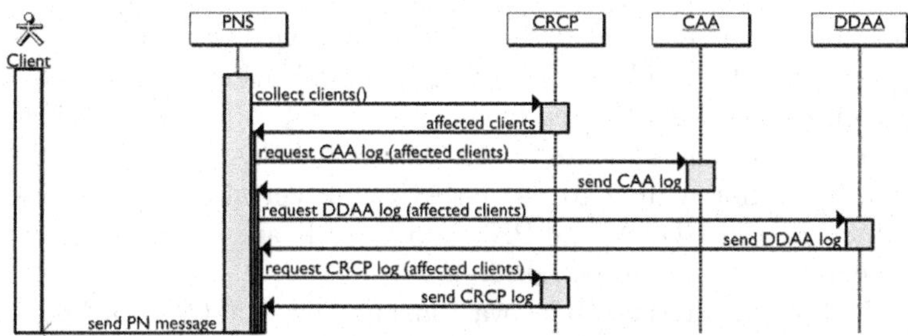

Fig. 8. Processing logic of the PNS

Generally, the necessary level of security can be achieved by two approaches. According to the current prevailing approach the possibility of any abuse should be – in principle – completely excluded. The effectiveness of this approach, however, is questionable. One constraint is the available authentication technique. Security can be comprehended only for the whole system which includes the client; and it is often the client who the weakest point is – for example, he writes his password on a paper and puts it into his drawer.

The other approach to achieve the necessary level of security is to provide feedback to the affected parties; a number of systems work that way. Similarly, the PNS provides feedback to the user of public e-services. It assembles periodical reports containing logs of events for the client that concern him – if he asked for it – over a certain period of time. Such an event may be when the client was authenticated (CAA has the data); a document was sent to him or he sent a document to public authorities (DDAA has the data); or his precepts were used (CRCP has the data). The report assembled by the PNS is typically a digitally signed (certified) document. The main steps of the PNS process are shown in Fig. 8.

The PNS queries in blocks from the LR on a daily basis, and then it batches reports from other registers on the basis of the blocks. The order of the answers is random; this part is asynchronous. On the basis of the batch report the PNS assembles individual reports and it sends them to the clients.

In summary, whatever authentication and communication method the client uses during accessing public e-services, he could detect abuses on the basis of the reports sent by the PNS and therefore he can act upon them. Resolutions of public authorities can be legally challenged; previous status can be restored; in case of personality theft, criminal proceedings can be initiated.

5 Conclusion

In Hungary there are a number of citizens who have the necessary infrastructure to use public e-services but still do not use public e-services extensively. A possible reason for this phenomenon is that the individual comfort and security requirements of the clients have not been taken into consideration in a proper way. We have identified three barriers that are rooted in the simplified picture of the clients which led to an imposed way of e-authentication and document exchange.

We showed a model of client-driven access to public e-services. In this model the client is entitled to decide what kind of communication channel and authentication technique is to be accepted by which authorities; he can decide in which type of case and who is allowed to act on his behalf. The client might also declare that he is not willing to use e-services in certain types of cases. The CRCP, the CAA, the CDAA, the PNS and the LR are the building blocks of the implementation of the proposed model.

A simplified form of the model was enacted by Act CXL of 2004 on the General Rules of Administrative Proceedings and Services and by Government Decree 83/2012.(IV.21) on the regulated electronic administration services and services to be provided by the state. The model is now being implemented in Hungary. The project that built the CRCP and CAA was finished at the beginning of 2015 (Generic Client Authentication Project, EKOP-2.3.8-2012-2012-0001).

References

1. European Commission, eGovernment in Hungary, Edition 16.0. https://joinup.ec.europa.eu/elibrary/factsheet/egovernment-hungary-april-2014-v160 (2014)
2. OECD e-Government Studies: Hungary 2007, OECD Publishing, Paris (2007). doi:10.1787/9789264030527-en
3. Harindranath, G.: ICT in a transition economy: the case of hungary. J. Global Inf. Technol. Manag. **11**(4), 33–55 (2008). http://dx.doi.org/10.1080/1097198X.2008.10856478
4. Nemzeti Adó- és Vámhatóság. 2013 Yearbook of the National Tax and Customs Administration (in Hungarian) (2013). http://www.nav.gov.hu/nav/kiadvanyok/nav_vilaga
5. Csüllög, K., Varga, A.: A survey on mass perception of e-government services in Hungary, Information Society (1/2007) (2007)
6. Directorate General for Communications Networks, Content and Technology Delivering on the European Advantage? eGovernment Benchmark. Final Insight Report: May 2014 (2014). ISBN 978-92-79-38051-8
7. Hajnal, G., Kovács, E.: Government Windows: One Stop Shops For Administrative Services In Hungary (2014). http://www.cocops.eu/wp-content/uploads/2013/10/Hungary-CGov-Government-Windows.pdf
8. OECD, Public Governance Reviews. Hungary: Towards a Strategic State Approach (2015). http://www.oecd.org/publications/hungary-towards-a-strategic-state-approach-9789264213555-en.htm

9. Salvodelli, A., et al.: Understanding the e-government paradox: Learning from literature and practice on barriers to adoption. Gov. Inf. Q. **31**, 63–71 (2014)
10. Aichholzer, G., Strauss, S.: Electronic identity management in e-Government 2.0: Exploring a system innovation exemplified by Austria. Inf. Polity **15**(1–2), 139–152 (2010)
11. Marin, I., Audenhove, L.: The Belgian e-ID and its complex path to implementation and innovational change. Identity. Inf. Soc. **3**(1), 27–41 (2010)
12. Vasconcelos, A., The Portuguese Interoperability Framework applied to the Portuguese Citizen Card Project. OECD Workshop on Digital Identity Management (IDM), May 9, 2007 (2007). http://www.oecd.org/dataoecd/36/9/38573902.pdf
13. Martens, T.: Electronic identity management in Estonia between market and state governance. Identity Inf. Soc. **3**(1), 213–233 (2010)
14. Tejchman, J., Kozicki, J.: Introduction: conceptual framework and research design for a comparative analysis of national eID Management Systems in selected European countries. Identity Inf. Soc. **3**, 1–2 (2010)
15. Nemzeti Adó- és Vámhatóság, Tájékoztató az adóügyek elektronikus úton történő intézéséhez. 32. számú információs füzet (2013). http://nav.gov.hu/nav/regiok/kiemeltadozok/aktualis/adougyek_32.html
16. Molnár, B., et al.: Identity-background checking: a solution, which Meets the requirements of privacy and personal data protection at identity management domain. SEFBIS Journal No.1, 22–32 (2006)
17. Shrivastava, S., Saquib, Z., P., G., Chomal, P.: Unique identity enabled service delivery through NSDG. In: Kő, A., Leitner, C., Leitold, H., Prosser, A. (eds.) EDEM 2012 and EGOVIS 2012. LNCS, vol. 7452, pp. 103–111. Springer, Heidelberg (2012)
18. Zwattendorfer, B., Zefferer, T., Tauber, A.: The prevalence of SAML within the european union. In: 8th International Conference on Web Information Systems and Technologies (WEBIST), pp. 571–576 (2012)

Collaborative Innovation in the Public Sector a Case of the Brazilian Federal Government

Herman Resende Santos[1(✉)], Kawaljeet Kapoor[2], Dany Flávio Tonelli[1], Vishanth Weerakkody[2], Dalton Sousa[3], and Paulo Henrique de Souza Bermejo[1]

[1] Universidade Federal de Lavras, Lavras, Brazil
herman.r.santos@gmail.com, danytonelli@dae.ufla.br, bermejo@dcc.ufla.br

[2] Brunel University London, Uxbridge, UK
{kawaljeet.kapoor, vishanth.weerakkody}@brunel.ac.uk

[3] Universidade Federal do Mato Grosso do Sul, Campo Grande, Brazil
dalton.sousa@gmail.com

Abstract. The purpose of this study is to verify the statistical validity of a *collaborative public sector innovation* model in the Brazilian Federal Government context. This model essentially addresses aspects of co-creation, public sector innovation, and innovation ecosystem. Structural Equation Modeling results show a good model fit. It is concluded that the creative collaborative processes (co-creation) may generate new public values and foster public sector innovation. This stimulates the development of an innovation ecosystem supported by new public values and co-creative dynamics.

Keywords: Co-creation · Innovation ecosystem · Public sector innovation · Public value · Public governance

1 Introduction

The capacity to generate collaborative innovation in the public sector is being gradually perceived as a strategic asset associated with competitive advantage from a government perspective. This is related to the optimization of the processes that generate public value. According to Szkuta, Pizzicannella and Osimo [1] (p. 560), the collaborative relationships between government and society have been "defined in several overlapping ways and terms" such as: government 2.0 [2], open government, public services 2.0 [3], government as a platform [4], wiki government [5], networked government [6], etc. These initiatives converge on the essentiality of dialogical relations between state (public) and non-state (private) actors, which compose the "Government Information Networks" [7]. They refer to the perception of emerging patterns of interaction and action in non-linear and unpredictable environments.

These emergent governance models agree that the extraction and use of collective competencies and intelligence forms a potential source of strategic knowledge and advantage, which can be effectively employed in overall management and democratic improvement. The capacity to explore collective intelligence relates to the concept of

© Springer International Publishing Switzerland 2015
A. Kő and E. Francesconi (Eds.): EGOVIS 2015, LNCS 9265, pp. 132–145, 2015.
DOI: 10.1007/978-3-319-22389-6_10

"smart governance" and "smart government", which according to Gil-Garcia, Helbig and Ojo [8] (p. 11) refers to "activities that creatively invest in emergent technologies coupled with innovative strategies to achieve more agile and resilient government structures and governance infrastructures". According to the European Commission [9] (p. 5), public sector innovations are capable of "unlocking radical productivity improvements and efficiency gains, to foster the creation of more public value and a better response to societal challenges". However, at the same time, it is also highlighted that the factors that prevent more and better innovations in the public sector have "limited knowledge and application of innovation processes and methods" [9] (p. 5).

Sørensen and Torfing [10] (p. 17) observe that there is no "commonly accepted theoretical framework for analyzing collaborative innovation in the public sector". According to Chathoth et al. [11] (p. 19), "research should explore the process of co-production and co-creation from a strategic perspective". In reviewing the literature, it was observed that there is a lack of theoretical models empirically validating collaborative innovation in the public sector. To fill this research gap, this study will verify the theoretical validity of a descriptive model for public sector collaborative innovation in a Brazilian federal government context. The model evaluates three constructs: Co-creation, Public sector innovation and Innovation ecosystem. The development of this paper was in line with the following guiding question: Which theoretical model can explain the process of collaborative public sector innovations? The following objectives were thus established:

(a) Propose a theoretical model that describes the elements of public sector collaborative innovations.
(b) Statistically verify the validity of the proposed model using structural equation modeling (SEM).

The structure of this paper is as follows: Sect. 2 introduces the theoretical background, which presents the operational definitions of the constructs, the hypotheses development, and the conceptual model; Sect. 3 presents the methodology, while Sect. 4 shows the results from SEM and offers discussions on the same; Sect. 5 then highlights the conclusions from this study.

2 Theoretical Background

The processes of interaction, sharing and collaboration intrinsic to the concept of web 2.0 guide the design of new participatory architectures [1]. Given the complex social, cultural, political and economic challenges inherent to the public governance processes, it is observed that the emergence of networks and relationships are reiterated by concepts like network society, network state [12], governance networks [10], government information networks [7], etc. The generation of public sector innovations through collaborative processes is being perceived as a strategic tool for the promotion of governmental competitive advantage, capable of increasing citizen trust on democracy and on the government itself.

One example of such innovative public policies is the Presidential Innovation Fellows (PIF) Program, which is a partnered initiative of the White House Office of

Science and Technology Policy (OSTP) and the U.S. General Services Administration (GSA). The program intends to accelerate the achievement of results for the American people; bringing "the principles, values, and practices of the innovation economy into government" [13]. As stated in White House website: "*This highly-competitive program recruits talented, diverse individuals from the innovation community and pairs them with top civil servants to tackle many of our Nation's biggest challenges, and to achieve a profound and lasting social impact*". Programs such as PIF represent the amalgamation of public policies with collaborative public sector innovations.

2.1 Constructs, Hypotheses and Conceptual Model

The theme of this study concerns an emergent vision related to the citizens, which, according to Nambisan and Nambisan [14] (p. 6) is associated with the "shift from that of a passive service beneficiary to that of an active, informed partner or co-creator in public service innovation and problem-solving". New democratic institutional designs, capable of integrating these models of citizenship and their relationships with government activities are supported by two fundamental aspects: the innovation ecosystem and the innovation platform (Nambisan and Nambisan [14] (p. 7). The operational definitions of the three constructs: Co-creation, Public sector innovations and Innovation Ecosystem explored in this study have been presented in Table 1.

Table 1. Operational definitions of constructs

Constructs	Operational definitions	Sources
Co-creation	**CC 1**. Access and openness of transparent public information	Prahalad and Ramaswamy **(2C04)**; Santos, Tonelli e Bermejo **(2014)**
	CC 2. Continuous analogical communication	Prahalad and Ramaswamy **(2004)**; Santos, Tonelli e Bermejo **(2014)**
	CC 3. Collaborative creation	Bason **(2010)**; Santos, Tonelli e Bermejo **(2014]**
	CC 4. Engagement experience	Ramaswamy e Gouillart **(2010)**
Public Sector Innovation	**PSI 1**. New ideas/designs implementation	Koch e Hauknes **(2005)**; Mulgan **(2007)**; Windrum **(2008)**; Bason **(2010)**
	PSI 2. Public Value Generation	Vargo, Lusch e Morgan **(2006)**; Mulgan **(2007)**; Eason **(2010)**
	PSI 3. Social distribution and appropriation of value	Gault **(2012)**
Innovation ecosystem	**IE 1**. Communities for new co-creation experiences	Nambisan **(2013)**; Estrin **(2003)**
	IE 2. Shared worldview	Nambisan **(2013)**
	IE 3. Architecture of participation	Nambisan **(2013)**

Source: adaptated from Chen, Tsou, and Ching [15].

2.1.1 Co-creation

In 1996, co-creation was first defined by Kambil, Ginsberg and Bloch [16]. Studies about open innovation [17], user-led innovation and customer-active paradigm [18], and the participatory and convergence culture established co-creation approaches [19], originated from private sector investigations about co-production, which considered them as external source of efficiency gains [20–22]. A possible comprehension of co-creation, from a strategic perspective, could be the one of collective intelligence and/or competence capture and use in creative processes. Zwass [23] points out at the "intellectual space of co-creation research" that comprises of: Virtual communities and social capital; Commons, Open access, Open source; Collective Intelligence; and Open Innovation.

In response to the question "what is co-creation?" Prahalad and Ramaswamy [24] (p. 8) argue that: *"Co-creation is about joint creation of value by the company and the customer. Joint problem definition and problem solving. Creating an experience environment in which consumers can have active dialogue and co-construct personalized experiences; Continuous dialogue. Co-constructing personalized experiences. Innovating experience environments for new co-creation experiences".*

As principal outcomes of the co-creative process, Nambisan and Nambisan [14] (p. 6) point out: *Problem identification, discovery and definition. Solution conceptualization. Solution design and development. Support/facilitation of public innovations adoption and diffusion.* In the public sector context, co-creation refers to the idea of democratic participation, which may involve a process of politicization of society. According to Santos, Tonelli and Bermejo [25], co-creation is found in the most complex level of Sociopolitical Digital Interactions (SDI), and the background of co-creation refers to informational and communicative processes.

The observable variables for the *co-creation* construct were defined as follows:

CC.1. Access and Openness of Transparent Public Information

"Transparency of information is required to create the trust between institutions and individuals" [26].

CC.2. Continuous Dialogical Communication

Prahalad and Ramaswamy [26] (p. 10) observe that "dialogue involves more than listening and reacting. It requires deep engagement, lively interactivity, empathetic understanding, and a willingness by both parties to act, especially when they're at odds". According to Theunissen [27] (p. 613), "Co-creational thinking emphasizes communication and dialogue. Meaning is not static; it is created together and dependent on the continually evolving (or devolving) social environment".

CC.3. Collaborative Creation

Bason [28] observes that co-creation consists of a model of innovative design through which solutions are conceived and built with people.

CC.4. Engagement Experience

According to Ramaswamy and Gouillart [29] (p. 35), "engaging people to create valuable experiences together" is the "core principle" for transforming organizations to incorporate co-creation. The co-creational activity is based on an engagement experience.

2.1.2 Public Sector Innovation

One of the pioneering studies in public sector innovation was 'Incentives to innovate in public and private organizations' by Roessner [30]. According to Windrum [31], innovations can be produced from new designs and concepts related not only to the final production/provision of services and policies, but also related to the interaction with stakeholders. Sørensen and Torfing [32] suggest that public innovation is based on a nonlinear and open-ended process of collaborative innovation. According to Mulgan [33] (p. 6), "*The simplest definition is that public sector innovation is about new ideas that work at creating public value. The ideas have to be at least in part new (rather than improvements); they have to be taken up (rather than just being good ideas); and they have to be useful. Public sector innovation may be understood as creating new public values.*"

The observable variables for the *Public Sector Innovation* construct were defined as follows:

PSI.1. New Ideas/Designs Implementation

The generation of tangible or intangible results, as well as the new ways of interaction with stakeholders may be related to the following typology of public innovations, as proposed by Windrum [31], which draws from Koch and Hauknes [34] and comprises of: service innovation; service delivery innovation; administrative and organizational innovation; conceptual innovation; policy innovation and systemic innovation.

PSI.2. Public Value Generation

The main approaches to the concept of public value are characterized by two distinct views, the one of societal consensus [35] and the other related to concrete government policies that "*create the conditions for economic prosperity, civility in social relationships, and the advancement of justice*" [36] (p. 257). These imply increasing trust on government and public interest.

PSI.3. Social Distribution and Appropriation of the Generated Public Value.

Regardless of the nature of approaches to the concept of public value, it is appropriate to consider that "there is no value until an offering is used […] experience and perception are essential to value determination" [37] (p. 44). Gault [38] suggests that the understanding of implementation could be improved by verifying if it is made available to the potential users.

2.1.3 Innovation Ecosystem

Innovation ecosystem may be considered as a hybrid and complex arrangement of actors and networks; the initial research about Innovation ecosystem focused its role on private sector. Mercan and Göktas [39] (p. 102) observed that "innovation ecosystem consists of economic agents and economic relations as well as the non-economic parts such as technology, institutions, sociological interactions and the culture". According to Nambisan and Nambisan [14] (p. 7), "Innovation ecosystem relates to the organizing structure for an ensemble of actors (e.g., citizens, government agency employees, nonprofits) to collaborate, to come together and co-create" and comprises of a "foundational element of the support infrastructure needed for hosting citizen co-creation activities".

The observable variables for the *Innovation ecosystems* construct were defined as follows:

IE.1. Communities for New Co-creation Experiences

Nambisan and Nambisan (2013; [14] (p. 10) note that it is necessary to "Build and sustain the community of innovators". According to Estrin [40] (p. 37), "innovation ecosystems are made up of communities of people with different types of expertise and skill sets".

IE.2. Shared Worldview

Promoting "a shared worldview among citizens and government employees" [14] (p. 10) is based on a cultural dimension of innovation ecosystem that tends to create a common understanding and willingness (social capital) related to collaborative innovation experiences.

IE.3. Architecture of Participation

Nambisan and Nambisan [14] (p. 10) point out that defining the "architecture of participation to coordinate collaboration activities" is an essential part of the innovation ecosystem infrastructure, making it the innovation platform; these aspects are related to the regulation of collaborative activities, and the establishment of a "physical or virtual venue for citizen co-creation".

2.2 Hypotheses Development

Several studies have observed positive effects of collaboration on innovation practices [41–45]. However, empirical research related to the verification of the extent of co-creative effects on public sector innovation, and on the innovation ecosystem, as well as the public sector innovation effects on innovation ecosystem, is scarce. It was thereby proposed that co-creation enhances public sector innovation processes, as citizen inputs foster co-creation practices. Thus, public Sector and society will work together to generate new public values (Fig. 1).

H1. Co-creation has a positive effect on Public sector innovation

Considering that public sector innovation can enhance the design quality of innovative collective arrangements (Innovation ecosystem), the following hypothesis was proposed,

H2. Public sector innovation has a positive effect on Innovation ecosystem

It is assumed that citizens' collaboration will contribute in enhancing the synergy of collective arrangements (Innovation ecosystem), and drive the innovative potential to higher levels. The following hypothesis was thus proposed,

H3. Co-creation has a positive effect on Innovation ecosystem

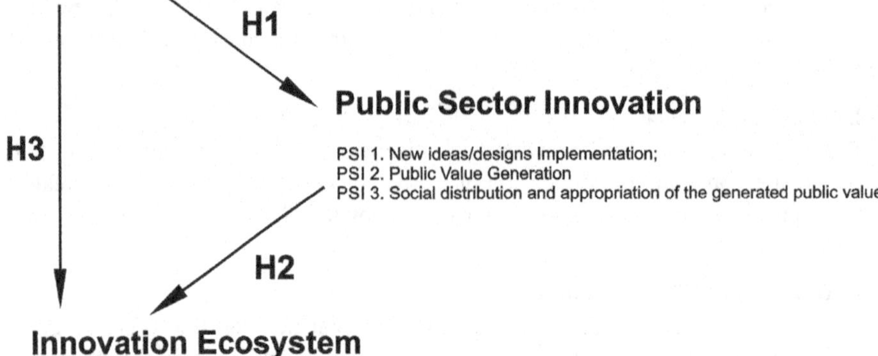

Fig. 1. Conceptual model

2.3 Conceptual Model

3 Methodology

In examining the relationships among co-creation, public sector innovation, and innovation ecosystem in a Brazilian context, a quantitative study was undertaken that was analyzed using Structural Equations Model (SEM). The SEM analysis was run using AMOS 22.0 (statistical tool).

According to Debata et al. [46] (p. 27), "SEM depicts a diagram or a pictorial representation of a model that is transformed into a set of equations. The set of equations are solved simultaneously to test model fit and estimate parameters".

SEM is based on multivariate analysis that combines factor analysis [47] and path analysis [48]. This allows the verification of the statistical validity of theoretical models that support descriptive theories (explanations about mechanisms of occurrence of events) and/or normative theories that "define what causes the outcomes of interest" [49] (p. 6).

3.1 Samples, Questionnaire and Data Collection

For this research, a non-probabilistic and convenience sampling approach was adopted based on the availability of the respondents for filling out the survey. This sample included representatives from the Brazilian federal government. Questionnaires were uploaded on Survey Monkey (web platform) and e-mailed to relevant addresses found in the Executive, Legislative and Judiciary websites; a total of 3582 emails were sent out. The questionnaires were first sent on 22nd December 2014, and the data collection process ended on 20th January 2015. A total of 231 responses came in, of which, 170 questionnaires were complete, 57 had missing answers (24 with one missing answer, and 33 with two missing answers), and four questionnaires had repetitive patterns. It was thereby decided that the 170 complete questionnaires, plus the 24 questionnaires with one missing answer would be considered for emprical evaluations, making up a total of 194 valid responses for this study. One missing value in the 24 questionnaries was substituted with the simple average of other responses.

Based on the operational definitions of the constructs, the survey questionnaire had 10 questions, in alignment with the made propositions. Each question was related to the established observed variables for the three constructs of this study. The questionnaire did not target respondents' demographic and ethnic characteristics. A cover letter describing the research purpose, its objectives, and a statement of confidentiality was sent to the respondents. Based on Chen, Ching, and Tsou's [15] suggestion on offering an incentive, a declaration was made on the questionnaire that read: "the study's findings would be made available to the respondents if they returned a completed questionnaire" (p. 1336). All questions had to be answered across a 5-point Likert scale (1 = strongly disagree to 5 = strongly agree).

4 Results and Discussion

According to Hair et al. [50], a minimum of 100 to 150 responses are necessary when using the maximum likelihood estimation technique (which has been adopted in this study). With the fit indices showing acceptable values (Table 2), the model was declared to be of an adequate fit.

Table 2. Fit indices

Adjustment measures	Referential values	Results
Chi-squoreon degrees of freedom (**$\chi 2$/GL**)	$2 < \chi 2 < 3$	(29,606/21) = 1,409
Root Mean Square Error of Approximation (**RMSEA**)	0,05 ≤ RMSEA ≤ 0,08	0,035
Tucker-Lewis Index (**TLI**)	≥0,9	0,988
Comparative Fit Index (**CFI**)	≥0,9	0,992
Goodness-of-Fit Index (**GFI**)	≥0,9	0,967
Normed Fit Index(NFI)	≥0,9	0,961

The reliability of the factors (see Table 3) was confirmed using Cronbach's Alpha, with all three factors having an alpha value greater than 0.7 [51]. Co-creation was initially composed of four items, but was later reduced to three, as eliminating variable cc1 in the reliability test resulted in a higher Cronbach's alpha value.

As shown in Table 3, the loadings for the three observed variables were set at 1 for the identification of the model. All other variables significantly loaded onto the

Table 3. Reliability test

Factor	Cronbach's Alpha (CC)	Items
Co-creation	0,772	3
Innovation Ecosystem	0,813	3
Public sector innovation	0,816	3

Table 4. Regression weights

			Estimate	β[1]	S.E.	C.R.	P	Hypotheses
Innovation	<---	Cocreation	,588	**,534**	,105	5,598	***	Supported
Ecosystem	<---	Innovation	,512	**,497**	,094	5,470	***	Supported
Ecosystem	<---	Cocreation	,521	**,459**	,103	5,039	***	Supported
cc4	<---	Cocreation	1,000	**,776**				
cc3	<---	Cocreation	1,033	**,760**	,113	9,132	***	
cc2	<---	Cocreation	,872	**,641**	,109	8,010	***	
ie3	<---	Ecosystem	,896	**,680**	,097	9,272	***	
ie2	<---	Ecosystem	1,031	**,855**	,089	11,524	***	
ie1	<---	Ecosystem	1,000	**,776**				
psi1	<---	Innovation	1,000	**,757**				
psi2	<---	Innovation	1,034	**,788**	,104	9,972	***	
psi3	<---	Innovation	,991	**,767**	,101	9,778	***	

1. Standardized Regression Weights

constructs. To verify the hypotheses validities (Table 4), the statistical significances and the magnitude of the estimated parameters were analyzed, based on t-values (or Critical Ratios), Factorial Loadings and Standardized Regression Coefficients (β). According to Hair et al. [50], the t-values reflect the significance of an estimated parameter. The factor loadings indicate the strength of each of the established relationships. A significant factor loading implies that the relationship between two variables is empirically proved [50]. Co-creation presented a highly significant factor loading of 0.534 (at 99.9 %) on Innovation in the Public Sector.

As shown in the research model (Fig. 2), the following three hypotheses were confirmed:

H1. Co-creation has a positive effect on Public sector innovation
H2. Public sector innovation has a positive effect on Innovation ecosystem
H3. Co-creation has a positive effect on Innovation ecosystem

SEM thus confirmed the statistical validity of the Collaborative Public Sector Innovation model. The results from this study showed that co-creation has a significant effect on Public Sector Innovation, and that Public Sector Innovation and Co-creation have positive effects on Innovation Ecosystem.

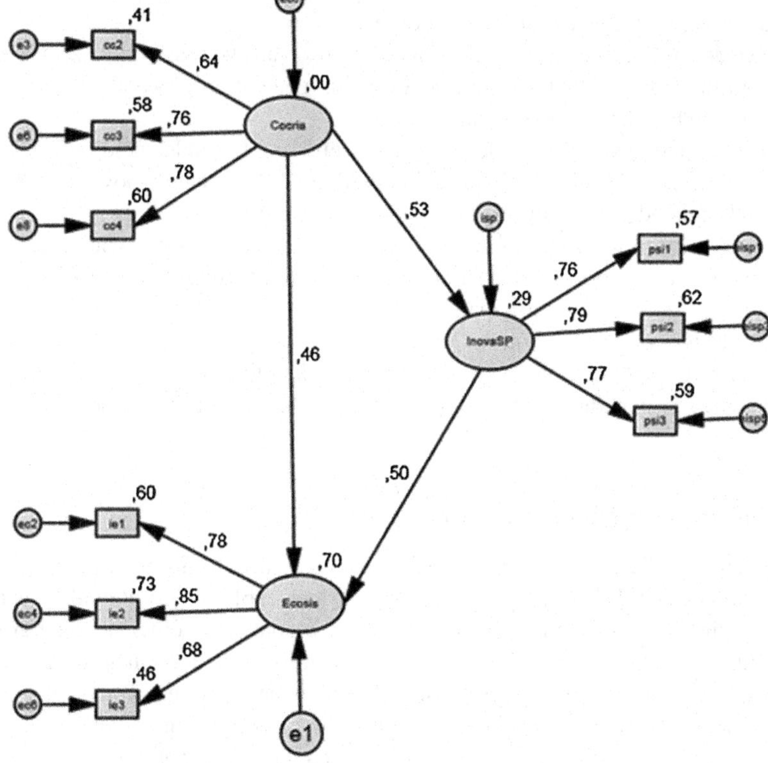

Fig. 2. Research model

5 Conclusions

In an attempt to fill in the research gap that pointed at the absence of a theoretical framework for collaborative public sector innovations [32], this paper evaluated, through a triangular model, the mutual effects of Co-creation, Public Sector Innovation and Innovation Ecosystem in a context of the Brazilian Federal Government. The study statistically validated the main idea, that is: *creative collaborative processes (co-creation) may generate new public values and foster of public sector innovation. This stimulates the development of an innovation ecosystem that is supported by new public values and co-creative dynamics.* This study was based on the assumption that synergy among the three constructs may represent a strategic asset related to competitive advantage (from the government perspective) concerning the optimization of public value generation.

The key conclusions from this study are:

(a) Brazilian Federal Government representatives perceive co-creation as a process capable of generating public sector innovation, which leads to the development of innovation ecosystem. Analysis of survey responses confirmed that co-creation has a positive influence on innovation ecosystem.

(b) Co-creation is a key asset to the formulation of answers to complex challenges and to the improvement of new public value generation processes in non-linear and unpredictable environments.

(c) The validated theoretical model may be a useful tool for understanding, analysing, improving and designing digital collaborative public sector innovations that are directly related to the innovation ecosystem development.

(d) The capacity to generate public sector innovations through co-creative processes showcases the importance of policy planning by combining government intelligence and democratic participation.

(e) This design of public policies that incorporates government intelligence and democratic participation may offer a key directive for achieveing strategic advantage in generating new public values and social politicization.

5.1 Limitations and Future Research

The theoretical validity of this model has been verified only in the Brazilian federal government context. Future research should consider exploring additional constructs, whilst applying the proposed research model in the context of other national governments. Future research could design smart organizational models integrating collaborative innovation in governance processes. Probabilistic sampling would be used for further statistical validation. Positive relations among innovation ecosystem, co-creation and innovation could be also verified in the private sector and social innovation context.

Acknowledgments. to Minas Gerais State Foundation for Research Development (FAPEMIG) – Brazil.

Appendix

Questionnaire

CO-CREATION (CC)

Through the digital environment...

CC 1. Citizens have access to relevant, transparent and open public information.
CC 2. Citizens communicate and discuss their needs openly.
CC 3. Citizens work collaboratively with our organization.
CC 4. Citizens actively participate in collaborative government practice improvement processes.

INNOVATION ECOSYSTEM (IE)

Through the digital environment...

IE 1. Our organization fosters citizen's voluntary mobilization around themes that demands innovative solutions.
IE 2. Our organization encourages citizens to share knowledge and propose new ideas or new solutions to solve problems.
IE 3. Our organization designs and implements regulation (rules, criteria, specifications) and platforms related to co-creative practices among state and non-state actors.

PUBLIC SECTOR INNOVATION (PSI)

In recent years, our organization has...

PSI 1. Implemented brand new practices related to services; policies; stakeholders interactions.
PSI 2. Generated new public values (new problem solutions, best results to community, increased trust).
PSI 3. Has facilitated citizen's access to generated new public values (new problem solutions, best results to community).

References

1. Szkuta, K., Pizzicannella, R., Osimo, D.: Collaborative approaches to public sector innovation: a scoping study. Telecommunications Policy (2014). ISSN 0308-5961
2. Eggers, W.D.: Government 2.0: using technology to improve education, cut red tape, reduce gridlock, and enhance democracy. Rowman & Littlefield (2007). ISBN 0742541762
3. Huijboom, N., et al.: Public Services 2.0: the impact of social computing on public services. Institute for Prospective Technological Studies, Joint Research Centre, European Commission. Luxembourg: Office for Official Publications of the European Communities (2009)
4. O'Reilly, T.: What is web 2.0. O'Reilly Media, Inc. (2009). ISBN 1449391079
5. Noveck, B.S.S.: Wiki government: how technology can make government better, democracy stronger, and citizens more powerful. Brookings Institution Press (2009). ISBN 0815703465
6. Goldsmith, S., Eggers, W.D.: Governing by network: the new shape of the public sector. Brookings Institution Press (2004). ISBN 0815797524
7. Janowski, T., Pardo, T.A., Davies, J.: Government information networks-mapping electronic governance cases through public administration concepts. Gov. Inf. Q. **29**, S1–S10 (2012). ISSN 0740-624X
8. Gil-Garcia, J.R., Helbig, N., Ojo, A.: Being smart: emerging technologies and innovation in the public sector. Gov. Inf. Q. **31**, I1–I8 (2014). ISSN 0740-624X
9. Europeann Commission, E. Powering European Public Sector Innovation: Towards A New Architecture (2013)
10. Sørensen, E., Torfing, J.: Theories of democratic network governance. Palgrave Macmillan (2007). ISBN 1403995281
11. Chathoth, P., et al.: Co-production versus co-creation: a process based continuum in the hotel service context. Int. J. Hosp. Manag. **32**, 11–20 (2013). ISSN 0278-4319

12. Castells, M., Majer, R.V., Gerhardt, K.B.: A sociedade em rede. Paz e Terra, São Paulo (2000)
13. White House. Presidential Innovation Fellows. http://www.whitehouse.gov/innovationfellows/
14. Nambisan, S., Nambisan, P.: IBM. Engaging Citizens in Co-Creation in Public Services (2013)
15. Chen, J.-S., Tsou, H.-T., Ching, R.K.: Co-production and its effects on service innovation. Ind. Mark. Manag. **40**(8), 1331–1346 (2011). ISSN 0019-8501
16. Kambil, A., Ginsberg, A., Bloch, M.: Re-inventing value propositions. Information Systems Working Papers Series (1996)
17. Chesbrough, H.W.: Open innovation: the new imperative for creating and profiting from technology. Harvard Business Press, (2003). ISBN 1578518377
18. Von Hippel, E.: Democratizing innovation: the evolving phenomenon of user innovation. J. für Betriebswirtschaft **55**(1), 63–78 (2005). ISSN 0344-9327
19. Jenkins, H.: Convergence culture: where new and old media collide. New York University Press, New York (2006)
20. Prahalad, C.K., Ramaswamy, V.: Co-opting customer competence. Harvard Bus. Rev. **78**(1), 79–90 (2000). ISSN 0017-8012
21. Lusch, R.F., et al.: The Service-Dominant Logic of Marketing: Dialog, Debate, and Directions. ME Sharpe, Armonk (2006). ISBN 0765614901
22. Von Hippel, E.: Horizontal innovation networks—by and for users. Ind. Corporate Change **16**(2), 293–315 (2007). ISSN 0960-6491
23. Zwass, V.: Co-creation: Toward a taxonomy and an integrated research perspective. Int. J. Electron. Commer. **15**(1), 11–48 (2010). ISSN 1086-4415
24. Prahalad, C.K., Ramaswamy, V.: Co-creation experiences: the next practice in value creation. J. Interact. Marketing **18**(3), 5–14 (2004). ISSN 1520-6653
25. Santos, H.R., Tonelli, D.F., Bermejo, P.H.: Sociopolitical digital interactions' maturity: analyzing the brazilian states. Int. J. Electr. Gov. Res. (IJEGR) **10**(4), 76–93 (2014). doi:10.4018/ijegr.2014100104
26. Prahalad, C.K., Ramaswamy, V.: The co-creation connection. Strategy and Business, pp. 50–61 (2002). ISSN 1083-706X
27. Theunissen, P.: Co-creating corporate identity through dialogue: a pilot study. Public Relations Review (2014). ISSN 0363-8111
28. Bason, C.: Leading public sector innovation: co-creating for a better society. Policy Press (2010). ISBN 1847426336
29. Ramaswamy, V., Gouillart, F.J.: The power of co-creation: build it with them to boost growth, productivity, and profits. Simon and Schuster (2010). ISBN 1439181063
30. Roessner, J.D.: Incentives to innovate in public and private organizations. Adm. Soc. **9**(3), 341–365 (1977). ISSN 0095-3997
31. Windrum, P.: Innovation and entrepreneurship in public services. In: Windrum, P., Koch, P. (eds.) Innovation in Public Sector Services: Entrepreneurship, Creativity and Management, pp. 3–22. Edward Elgar, Cheltenham (2008)
32. Sørensen, E., Torfing, J.: Enhancing collaborative innovation in the public sector. Administration & Society, p. 0095399711418768 (2011). ISSN 0095-3997
33. Mulgan, G.: Ready or Not?: Taking Innovation in the Public Sector Seriously. Nesta (2007). ISBN 184875017X
34. Koch, P., Hauknes, J.: On Innovation in the Public Sector. Citeseer (2005)
35. Bozeman, B.: Public Values Concepts and Criteria: The Case for "Progressive Opportunity" as a Criterion. Creating Public Value in a Multi-Sector, Shared-Power World, Minneapolis (2012)

36. Moore, M.H., Benington, J.: Conclusions: looking ahead. In: Benington, J., Moore, M.H. (eds.) Public Value: Theory and Practice, pp. 256–274. Palgrave Macmillan, London (2011)
37. Vargo, S.L., Lusch, R.F.: Service-dominant logic: What It Is, What It Is Not, What It Might Be, The Service-Dominant Logic of Marketing: Dialog, Debate and Directions, pp. 43–56. M.E. Sharpe Inc., Armonk (2006)
38. Gault, F.: User innovation and the market. Science and Public Policy **39**(1), 118–128 (2012). ISSN 0302-3427
39. Mercan, B., Göktaş, D.: Components of innovation ecosystems: a cross-country study. Int. Res. J. Finan. Econ. Iss. **76**, 102–112 (2011)
40. Estrin, J.: Closing the Innovation Gap: Reigniting the Spark of Creativity in a Global Economy. McGrew Hill, New York (2009)
41. Deeds, D.L., Rothaermel, F.T.: Honeymoons and liabilities: the relationship between age and performance in research and development alliances. J. Prod. Innov. Manage. **20**(6), 468–485 (2003)
42. Dodgson, M.: Technological Collaboration in Industry: Strategy, Policy, and Internationalization in Innovation. Routledge, London (1993)
43. Faems, D., Van Looy, B., Debackere, K.: Interorganizational collaboration and innovation: toward a portfolio approach. J. Prod. Innov. Manage **22**(3), 238–250 (2005)
44. Hagedoorn, J.: Inter-firm R&D partnerships: an overview of major trends and patterns since 1960. Res. Policy **31**(4), 477–492 (2002)
45. Schilling, M.A., Phelps, C.C.: Interfirm collaboration networks: the impact of large-scale network structure on firm innovation. Manage. Sci. **53**(7), 1113–1126 (2007)
46. Debata, B.R., et al.: Interrelations of service quality and service loyalty dimensions in medical tourism: a structural equation modelling approach. Benchmarking Int. J. **22**(1) (2015). ISSN 1463-5771
47. Spearman, C.: General intelligence, objectively determined and measured. Am. J. Psychol. **15**, 201–293 (1904)
48. Wright, S.: Correlation and causation. J. Agric. Res. **20**, 557–585 (1921)
49. Carlile, P.R., Christensen, C.M.: The cycles of theory building in management research (2004)
50. Hair, J., Anderson, R., Tatham, R., Black, W.: Multivariate Data Analysis with Readings, 4th edn. Prentice Hall, New Jersey (1995)
51. Hair Jr., J.F., Anderson, R.E., Tatham, R.L., Black, W.C.: Análise multivariada de dados, 5th edn. Bookman, Porto Alegre (2005)

Open Innovation and G-Cloud

Concept of Estonian Government Cloud and Data Embassies

Taavi Kotka and Innar Liiv(✉)

Department of Informatics, Tallinn University of Technology,
10133 Tallinn, Estonia
taavi.kotka@gmail.com, innar.liiv@ttu.ee

Abstract. Cloud Computing and e-Government are increasingly important topics in state ICT development plans, including that of Estonia. In the course of developing the Estonian Government Cloud concept, it became clear that Estonia's requirements for Cloud Computing are not identical to those of other European states, and that due to its highly developed information society, Estonia needs to expand the previously accepted scope of government clouds. Therefore, the goals of this paper are: to describe and justify Estonia's peculiarities, which define the additional requirements for the development of the Government Cloud and separate us from other states; to offer solutions for how these additional requirements can be resolved in the Government Cloud, and to present the Data Embassy concept; and to present the core implementation plan for constructing the first phase of the Government Cloud concept.

1 Introduction

Public sectors all over the world are facing increasing pressure on budgets and expectations to provide a greater number of public services with better quality. Many of these issues can be solved by cloud computing. It has advantages for the public and as well as the private sector, such as cost effectiveness, flexibility, faster development and testing of new solutions, enabling innovation, etc. Several countries, such as the US, the UK, the Netherlands, Spain, France, India, China, and the Nordic countries, have an agenda for developing cloud computing in the public sector and are actively taking steps towards implementing it (see [6] for a great comparison of eight European countries and [12] addressing adoption). In the public sector it is recognized that cloud computing provides better services with fewer resources.

The European Union is also taking up cloud computing - in September 2012, the European Commission adopted a strategy for "Unleashing the Potential of Cloud Computing in Europe" [1]. The strategy outlines actions to deliver "a net gain of 2.5 million new European jobs, and an annual boost of €160 billion to the European Union GDP (around 1 %), by 2020" [1]. The strategy is designed to speed up and increase the use of cloud computing across all economic sectors in a safe and trusted environment [2].

Although it is too early to evaluate the accuracy of those numbers, given the cost savings and increase in efficiency, scalability and high availability achievable with virtualization, it is clear that governments have a huge potential to benefit by using

© Springer International Publishing Switzerland 2015
A. Kő and E. Francesconi (Eds.): EGOVIS 2015, LNCS 9265, pp. 149–162, 2015.
DOI: 10.1007/978-3-319-22389-6_11

cloud computing. Public data on the uptake of cloud computing shows that in a few years, around 80 % of organizations will be dependent on cloud computing [3].

Therefore cloud computing [4] and e-Government are increasingly important topics in Estonia's ICT development plans. In the course of developing the Estonian Government Cloud concept, it became clear that Estonia's requirements for cloud computing are not identical to those of other European states. Because it already has a highly developed information society, Estonia needs to expand the scope of the Government Cloud. In fact, the Estonian government has been using cloud services offered by large multinational corporations since 2009, when the national tourism website visitEstonia.com was placed in the Amazon cloud. The main reason for cloud hosting was the need for flexible server resource management and the availability of sufficient performance capacity (the application must be fast regardless of where a query is sent from). Also, some Estonian municipalities have been using cloud services, for instance for email services.

Estonia's public sector conducted an analysis of the usage of server resources in 2013 [7], which concluded that the server rooms which are currently spread out among various ministries and buildings need to be consolidated into more efficient datacenters which meet established security standards [8].

The idiosyncrasies of Estonia's information society mandate the innovation of the new Government Cloud. This paper presents the concept of the Estonian Government Cloud with its peculiarities and main principles. The concept includes an action plan for implementing the Estonian Government Cloud.

2 Current Situation and Peculiarities of the Estonian Government Cloud

For at least a decade, researchers have been intrigued by the possibility of moving state infrastructure to the cloud (e.g. [5, 11, 13–15]), presenting interesting results from variety of perspectives: requirements, goals, focus (core business vs technological challenges), adoption, and legal and technical aspects of implementation. Though, Estonia can learn from other states' experiences with government clouds, its unique context, goals, and new ambitions necessitate the innovation of novel and context-specific cloud computing solutions.

In 2013, the Ministry of Finance commissioned analyses of the necessity and opportunities for consolidating the ICT resources of the Estonian state. The study's goal was to determine the optimal infrastructure for the state based on the following assumptions [9]:

- The state's distributed IT architecture must remain – e.g. each ministry/agency must retain the role of customer and budget holder;
- The possibility of free competition must remain;
- The quality of ICT services provided to ministries/agencies must improve.

Analyses [9] emphasized the need for a consolidated networking and datacenter layer to develop high quality cost-effective services. Research and interviews conducted by ministries with experts called attention to various reasons why the Estonian state needs to develop its own Government Cloud, and what nuances must be considered when developing it. The main reasons for building the Government Cloud are:

1. Server farm fragmentation must be eliminated and high-quality cost-effective services must be ensured.
2. There is a need to ensure the cyber defence of "digital monuments" (websites with symbolic status such as president.ee, website of the Ministry of Defence, etc.). Though these websites contain only public information, their symbolic significance means that it is nonetheless important to protect them from cyber-attacks.
3. There is a need to ensure Estonia's digital continuity and the functioning of the state in any situation or emergency.
4. There is a need to ensure the reliability and quality of cross-border services, because Estonia is starting to issue digital IDs to non-residents and building up "a state without borders."
5. Flexible cost-effective solutions for local municipalities must be developed.

All these topics are described in the following sections in more detail. The need for the Estonian Government Cloud is motivated by the desire to improve service quality, not to save costs. The people responsible for Estonia's public sector ICT spending understand that it is increasingly hard to find major opportunities for cost optimization within Estonia. Their focus is now on maintaining service quality levels in an ever-developing ICT world without a massive jump in expenditures.

2.1 Fragmentation and Service Quality Issues

The IT architecture in the Estonian state information system is distributed. State IT is managed separately by various institutions, usually across the governance areas of ministries, whose functions do not overlap. On a national level, there is a data communication service (ASO) and channel layer (eesti.ee), but there is no significant server hosting offering, and the quality of the services is fragmented between various agencies, because not all agencies have access to the necessary funding and competent human resources [7]. Currently Estonia's public sector does not have the ability to host its information systems in datacenters that guarantee high availability and security. Information systems are mostly located in spaces constructed and maintained by the agencies themselves, and these do not satisfy modern requirements for security, energy and cost efficiency. The only one to maintain larger server rooms of proper quality in the public sector is the State Infocommunication Foundation (RIKS), which hosts servers across 900 m2 of floor space. The main tasks of RIKS are providing operational radio and maritime communication, and telephone services. Additionally RIKS has installed high quality secure server spaces for institutions and companies related to the state.

In the ministerial areas of governance ICT services are managed by each agency individually. As a rule, the agency will have created an ICT unit for this purpose. Based on the needs of the agency's main area of activity, the necessary competences are either developed entirely or partially by the in-house ICT unit, or they are procured from external service providers. Such units usually have small staffs, with one employee serving multiple roles, and personnel risks are high. Agencies within one area of governance do not have close cooperation with each other. Because of this, there is significant duplication, and resource usage is not as efficient as it could be.

Due to this fragmentation, there is a need for the state to procure secure datacenters that comply with agreed-upon service levels (server rooms including electricity, connectivity, cooling, and security; virtual machines including servers down to the operating system; storage devices; zoning and management) and to create a proper Government Data Cloud.

2.2 Protection of "Digital Monuments"

On several occasions, Estonia has experienced a wide range of cyber-attacks. These attacks have targeted primarily public websites which are not part of the state's critical infrastructure. As a result, the physical damage caused by these attacks has been relatively small and they have not endangered human lives or the functioning of the Estonian state. However, the website of the Ministry of Defence or the President's website have a symbolic status. They are "digital monuments", which must be protected from damage or defacement by any state that finds cyber defence important. Each successful attack produces damage to the reputation of the state and decreases the trustworthiness of its ICT cyberspace in the eyes of both its population and its external partners.

Though the fragmentation of Estonian state infrastructure is a boon for state security in that it makes it harder to stage a mass assault, it also complicates the prospect of protecting Estonia's "digital monuments." The variation in technical expertise and human resources across state agencies leaves some "digital monuments" without the requisite levels of protection. Although "monumental websites" contain only public information and nothing sensitive it is still important to protect them from cyber-attacks to maintain international reputation and keep "monuments" available for the population.

2.3 Digital Continuity

Active implementation of the "paperless governance" policy has brought Estonia to a situation in which some essential registries, e.g. Land Register (contains information on land ownership) exist only digitally and only have evidential value in digital form. The threat of cyber-attacks or a situation, in which Estonia would be occupied and would lose its independence for an indefinite length of time, have led to an additional requirement for the Data Cloud solution of the Estonian state: ensuring digital continuity regardless of the prevalent conditions in the territory of Estonia.

Furthermore, digital continuity requires more than just the preservation of critical data sets and IT solutions on Estonian territory; a solution must also be found for a situation in which the Estonian state does not have control over the datacenters located within its own territory. The need may also arise for operating some services outside the borders of Estonia. The challenge here is to develop a solution whereby the Estonian state would endure even despite an occupation of its territory.

2.4 A Country Without Borders

Estonian society is highly dependent on ICT. Estonian citizens are able to perform nearly every public and private sector transaction in digital form, including signing any document. Now Estonia has an ambitious plan to start issuing Estonian e-identities to non-residents. This might significantly alter the country's visibility and functioning. This in turn requires the country to reach beyond its own borders, closer to potential and existing "customers", and to realize the dream of a "state without borders".

So far, the Estonian electronic identity has not been extended to foreigners who are permanent residents of countries other than Estonia. Recently the Estonian government has approved the concept of issuing digital IDs to non-residents. Since the end of 2014, foreigners have been able to receive a secure Estonian e-identity. This creates a unique opportunity to create a new set of remotely usable global services [10]. E-residence provides a globally innovative suite of public and private services that are usable irrespective of location: convenient business services, bank transactions, tax reporting, medical counselling, etc. E-residence can be based on existing Estonian e-services, developing them further and adding new ones.

The state intends to create a solid foundation for new business opportunities in this area. However, the development of the necessary infrastructure and range of services requires the coordination and joint effort of the public and private sectors. To support the spread and success of e-residency, digital continuity must be ensured, and the risk that an e-resident might lose their land, money or stocks as a result of a security breach must be ruled out. Therefore certain guarantees for e-residency continuity are required, especially from the perspective of proving ownership (primarily the Commercial Register and Land Register).

E-residency is pushing Estonia closer to potential customers with its public and private services, which entails additional cloud computing development needs both inside and outside of Estonian borders.

2.5 Cost-Savings Need for Local Municipalities

The pressure to save costs drives municipal governments to optimize processes, to look for flexible solutions, and to seek out more economical licensing policies for the use of everyday tools (such as email, file management, productivity software, etc.). Automation and the use of IT solutions are an excellent method to achieve this. An increasing number of companies, such as Google, Microsoft, Apple, etc. are offering cloud-based solutions, allowing state and municipal agencies to use resources and software based on their changing needs. In addition, agencies no longer need to purchase separate licenses for each workstation: pricing is based on actual usage. This flexibility is very attractive to municipal governments as well.

A typical municipality runs over 100 different systems for local government administration (area planning, kindergartens, social services, schools, roads, cemeteries, clinics, care for the elderly etc.). Estonia has over 200 municipalities, therefore, it is extremely difficult to find solutions for cost-effective digital services. This is true with respect to everything from office productivity software to horizontally cross-penetrating software categories, such as ERP, document management, open governance, etc. Though the exchange of sensitive data between municipalities is uncommon, the existence of this practice forces us to consider data security and protection issues.

3 Concept of the Estonian Government Cloud and Data Embassies

This concept has been developed based on the peculiarities of the Estonian Government Cloud. It describes three main principles:

1. Cloud solution located within Estonia's national borders
2. Opportunities and dangers of using international public clouds
3. Necessity of Data Embassies.

3.1 Government Cloud on Estonian Territory

The core of the Estonian Government Cloud concept is a classic datacenter solution, which differs very little from models used elsewhere in the world. The main difference stems from Estonia's small size, which makes it difficult to achieve competition and save costs through large-scale procurement. Estonia currently has plans for at least two datacenters with combined heat and power plants. The public sector, excluding municipal authorities, requires around 2000 m^2 of datacenter space in total. Considering that Estonia needs a primary and a secondary site, the total requirement is on the order of 4000 m^2.

Additionally, the management of cloud computing resources must be sufficiently flexible. Even a small country like Estonia has peak times (e.g. periods of e-elections, the period of electronic tax return filing, etc.). Therefore, it is necessary to involve resources provided by the private sector in the Government Cloud solution that is located on Estonian territory. This may account for as much as a third of the total capacity used by the state.

A separate issue is the mutual network-level separation and firewalling of the resources of different agencies. It is needed to create a set of security classes which define the parts of the Government Cloud which exist in a public IP space or in a special network zone.

Figure 1 illustrates the components of the Government Cloud: a primary datacenter, a secondary datacenter, a private-sector-provided resource. In the drawing there is depiction of X-Road which is a technical and organizational environment for enabling secure Internet-based data exchange between the public and private sector enterprises and institutions.

3.2 Use of International Public Clouds

The Estonian government has been using cloud services offered by large multinational corporations since 2009, when the national tourism website visit visitEstonia.com was

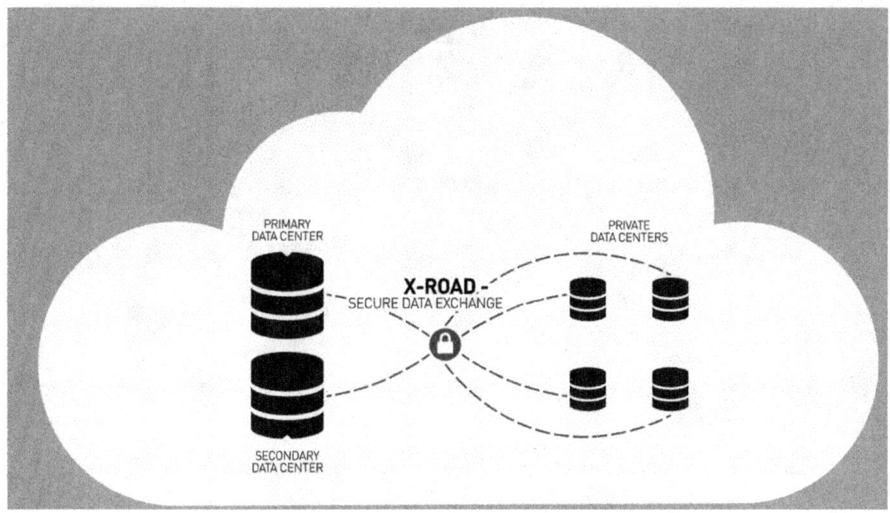

Fig. 1. The government Cloud inside Estonian territory

placed in the Amazon Cloud. The main reason for cloud hosting was the need for flexible server resource management. In addition to load tolerance, the customer (Enterprise Estonia) primarily required the availability of sufficient performance capacity (the application must be fast regardless of where the query has been sent from), which necessitated that the portal be "moved closer" to its primary target audiences, and the solutions offered by the international public cloud enabled this.

Additionally, international public clouds reduce the issue of licensing and software costs. Therefore it is logical that IaaS, PaaS and SaaS service models offered by large multinational corporations must be considered in the architecture of the Government Cloud.

In Estonia it is possible to use Cloud software for email, team collaboration, file management, etc., even if the Cloud is outside of Estonian territory. Estonia's Data Protection Inspectorate does not see an inherent problem in using cloud services and moving the information outside of the state's borders. According to Estonian legislation it does not matter if the service is offered from inside Estonia or from outside, as long as the data is protected. The limited sensitive information on the municipal level mainly includes personal data and procurement-related information.

The price and quality of services offered by international cloud providers are also tempting from the perspective of protecting so-called "digital monuments". To reduce the likelihood of a successful attack on websites with national symbolic significance, it is pragmatic to outsource their defence, and host President.ee, Valitsus.ee (Government Office), the Ministry of Defence website, etc., in an international public cloud. The information on these websites is not sensitive, and the server farms and information distribution will make attacks on them unreasonably costly. This distribution can be done using the services offered by Amazon, Microsoft or Google, for example. The use of these public clouds does not entirely eliminate risk, and their availability is not

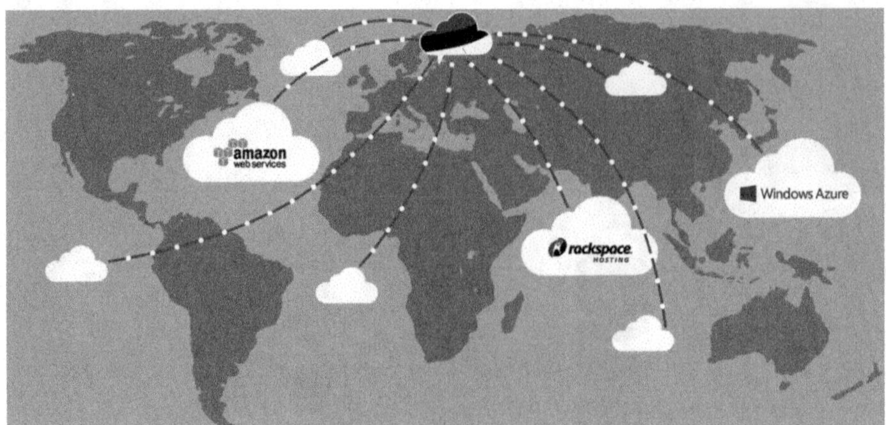

Fig. 2. The Estonian Government Cloud includes international public clouds

100 % guaranteed, but their capacity to deal with the most widespread attacks is greater than that currently existing in many ministries and agencies. Therefore, the Estonian-soil-based Government Cloud must be augmented to include companies that offer international cloud computing services. The augmented service is illustrated on Fig. 2. Certain reservations need to be maintained about holding sensitive information in international public clouds, even if that information is encrypted. Storing sensitive information in international public cloud is not acceptable due to substantial damages and reputation risks associated with data leaks, especially regarding to recent cases (PRISM, Snowden case, etc.).

On the other hand, the use of international public cloud services for backing up sensitive information is possible in a crisis and war-time situation, where the necessity to maintain digital continuity outweighs the risks of possible leaks of sensitive data. It is also acceptable that in an emergency situation, critical services such as parliamentary or Government tools could be operated from public clouds located outside of Estonian territory. In addition to protecting the information provided by these applications, it is also possible to use the encryption capability provided by the core infrastructure of the Estonian state.

Estonia already uses various international public cloud SaaS, PaaS and IaaS services. Therefore it is important to involve these international public cloud providers in the Estonian Government Cloud concept. However, it must be considered that as the state does not have full control of the storage and location of this data, there is a chance that the data may leak.

3.3 Use of Data Embassies

Estonia's need for digital continuity and its desire to provide additional guarantees to e-residents are two of the biggest factors that differentiate its cloud computing needs from those of other countries. Estonia needs to have a server resource that is 100 %

under the control of the Estonian government, but is located outside of Estonian territory. Currently there are specific procedures which are followed to backup necessary data and applications, so the service availability can be restored using the backup copy if necessary. However, in order to ensure digital continuity, some registers (such as the State Gazette, the online depository of all legislation in Estonia) should have an active copy that can be used in real time and updated according to the law, even if the Estonian state no longer has control over datacenters located in Estonian territory, or there is another crisis or emergency that makes the operation of the State Gazette application from within Estonia impossible.

Therefore, the Estonian state must own server resources outside of its own territory, those resources must be 100 % under Estonian state control, and must be usable not only for data backup, but also to operate services if necessary. To ensure this, there are two solutions proposed:

(1) Using Estonian embassies which are already established outside of Estonian territory. By ensuring the necessary technological resources, embassies could house backups for registers. With limited construction work, larger embassies can establish special environments for regular data and application backups, mirroring and service operations. Even transitioning to this model and a weekly backup schedule would give the Estonian state a significant benefit compared to the current model, as the current quarterly or twice-annual backups do not maintain the information sufficiently up to date, and digital continuity is not entirely ensured.

However, the use of Estonia's physical embassies presents certain problems. These embassies do not have sufficient technical competence to offer the level of technical support that is necessary to maintain the infrastructure and react in a crisis. In a situation where an enemy is making a cyber-attack on Estonian IT solutions located both on Estonian territory and in our embassies, the embassies generally will not have sufficient capability to protect themselves.

Additionally, embassies do not have control over the telecommunications service they are offered. It is possible that as part of an assault, an embassy's internet connection would be disabled by a telecoms operator that is controlled by the adversary; or the network segment that is being attacked would simply be disabled in order to save other resources on the same network from overload.

In summary, we cannot rely on Estonia's embassies alone, because in addition to the problems outlined above, embassies are also not physically constructed according to proper standards in order to meet the data security requirements.

(2) An improved solution is the Data Embassy concept. The goal is to procure resources under bilateral agreements from the Government Clouds of states that are friendly to Estonia. The Estonian state would sign a bilateral treaty, under which Estonia will rent special floor space or an enclosed room in an existing datacenter that has been constructed and operates according to necessary standards. The corresponding perimeter would be physically separated, equipped with security devices in order to ensure that the Estonian state maintains complete control over the servers within that agreed-upon perimeter. Similarly to a physical embassy, Estonian jurisdiction would be

applicable within that established perimeter, and it would have all the same provisions (including immunity) as a physical embassy or an ambassadorial residence.

A Data Embassy solution of this kind (Fig. 3) would be significantly better than server rooms constructed on the premises of Estonia's physical embassies. The datacenter of a state that is friendly to Estonia, would have been constructed as a dedicated data storage facility, with the possibilities of various risks (overheating, power outages, network overload, cable damage, etc.) having been minimized. Dedicated datacenters have their own requirements for service quality assurance, and they can employ professional staff, trained to maintain service availability in an emergency and to repel cyber-attacks. The advantages of Estonian Data Embassies are shown in the illustration below.

Furthermore, the Data Embassy concept is in line with 1963 Vienna Convention on Consular Relations.

Fig. 3. The Estonian Government Cloud includes international public clouds

Server rooms in physical embassies and dedicated Data Embassies would together create a network that would ensure Estonian digital continuity and be extremely costly for an enemy to damage or take down.

Such a network is illustrated in Fig. 4, but of course one must bear in mind that all Data Embassies are connected to all other embassies over the internet, using encryption to exchange data. The illustration is also not completely accurate because Estonia needs more server resources nearby.

In conclusion the conceptual model of the Estonia's Government Cloud contains three interdependent layers:

1. Cloud solutions on Estonian territory, requiring the construction of primary and secondary datacenters, and involving private sector resources for at least a third of the entire required capacity.
2. Public Cloud services provided by major multinational corporations and used with an awareness of the risk that information hosted there may leak to third parties.
3. A Data Embassy network, comprised of server rooms physically constructed in Estonia's foreign embassies and server resources hosted in datacenters of states friendly to Estonia.

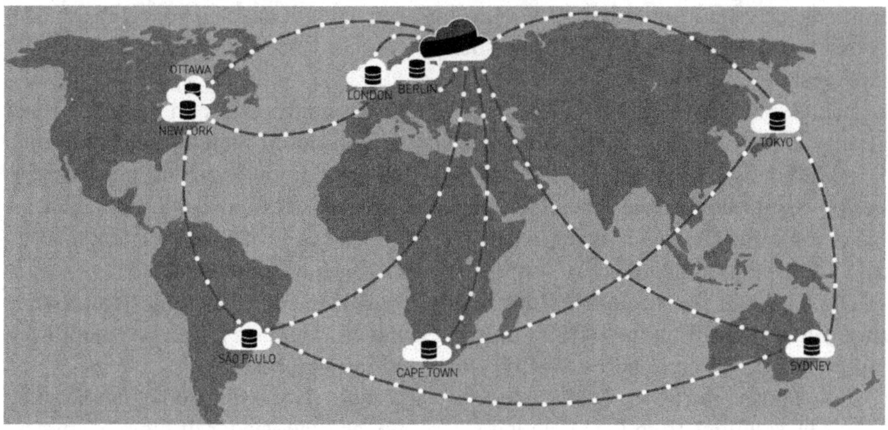

Fig. 4. The proposed network of Estonian Data Embassies

These layers working together will meet the currently identified requirements for an Estonian Government Cloud, including the challenges stemming from Estonia's particular situation: the need to reduce fragmentation, provide an increase in service quality, find cost-effective solutions for municipalities and ensure digital continuity and reliable e-services for e-residents.

4 Implementation Plan of the Estonian Government Cloud

To implement the Estonian Government Cloud, a number of activities have to be completed. The following sections provide a brief overview of the main activities necessary for implementing the three aspects of the Estonian Cloud concept.

4.1 Building the Government Cloud on Estonian Territory

In-country server resource consolidation must be finalized, and the **business model for server resource administration** and development must be implemented. Ministries and agencies must present their server resource requirements to RIKS, who will then deliver the resources out of its available supply, or arrange a further capacity procurement from the private sector, if necessary. According to RIKS action plan for 2014, RIKS will complete the development of server hosting facilities using existing facilities. The resource that will be created will be appropriate, among other things, for acting as a buffer during the consolidation of the server parks of state agencies.

RIKS has also developed an **implementation plan for new datacenters** (primary and secondary), including budget calculations, the execution of which is currently dependent on a decision by the Estonian Government. It is also necessary to begin negotiations with **private sector** enterprises which currently possess datacenters and server resources on Estonian territory that match the standards established by the

Information System Authority (RIA). This engagement will enable to develop a model for the flexible involvement of these resources in accordance with public procurement principles.

Due to the inconsistent service quality that currently exists in ministries and agencies, there have been discussions of adopting **additional regulation** to accelerate the consolidation of a single Government Cloud. Additionally, it is necessary to develop **regulation for the special circumstances** under which ministries and agencies may possess their own server resources. In all other cases, the services provided by RIKS must be used and thereby server resource consolidation is enforced.

The extent of the **responsibilities of the Cloud service's Customer (ministries and agencies) and Vendor (RIKS) must be clarified**. To make transition smooth and convenient for the customer, it will be conducted in two phases.

In first phase each Cloud service user is responsible for the functioning and backup of their IT solutions from the operating system up, and the vendor of the Government Cloud has responsibility purely for the infrastructure service. The first phase must be treated as an introduction and pilot phase on the road to a more service-oriented model.

In the second phase a comprehensive service portfolio must be implemented for the Government Cloud. This leads to the creation of opportunities for the state's IT centers and the private sector to work together to offer more complex and intricate solutions to agencies who use the Government Cloud (for example, database management, mass OS deployment, monitoring services, log collection and processing, managing specific application servers and information systems as a whole). Preparation for this phase must substantively begin in parallel with the implementation of the first phase.

4.2 Principles for Using International Private Clouds

Clear guidelines or role-played usage scenarios are required for Estonia's local municipalities, on how to technologically construct their agencies' IT solutions. Constant budgetary pressure and the more flexible licensing conditions offered by major vendors make it necessary to assess the possibility that, for example, MS Office productivity software is no longer installed on every workstation, but Office 365 is used from the cloud instead.

Estonia offers a state infrastructure for data encryption, any information generated by a private person, company or government entity can be securely encrypted, if necessary. In terms of data protection, clear instructions are needed on how to handle information (including sensitive information) produced in municipalities.

All this requires **specific guidance** from the Ministry of Economic Affairs and Communications (MKM) for the **conditions under which it is reasonable to purchase server resources or cloud applications from the private sector**, and which factors must be considered. Also, the Data Protection Inspectorate has to **develop guidelines for ministries, municipalities and agencies** to consult in order to ensure data integrity and protection.

4.3 Constructing the Data Embassy Network

The Data Embassy Network is a long-term project and therefore constructing the network has to be carried out in several phases.

The first phase includes the **deployment of three locations from the Data Embassy network**, two of which are within Europe and one is outside Europe. Two of these locations will involve the development of additional server rooms on the premises of Estonia's existing embassies, and one will involve the procurement of space by Estonia in the Government Cloud of a friendly state.

The technical requirements have already been prepared along with procedural rules for the backup and operation of registers and applications. The legal aspects of the agreements between Estonia and the friendly state, including guarantees for Estonian servers located in the datacenter of another state, are in process. The first phase involves only a physical room that the Estonian state will be using. The broader concept envisions Estonia hosting a Data Embassy in a friendly state's Cloud.

The extent of the second phase of Data Embassy development depends on the results of the first phase and the expenses.

As some registries exist only in digital form, it is essential to ensure the digital continuity of the Estonian state. Furthermore, to succeed in the plan to issue foreigners Estonian e-identities, certain guarantees for e-residents are needed, such as proving ownership of land, company or other assets. Therefore **the government has to develop principles for how registries are backed up and how frequently**. A list of registers and services, which are available even if Estonia's datacenters are not available in-country, must be created. Necessary services have to be designated for ensuring digital continuity as essential services. Action plans for risk scenarios and crisis situations need to be developed.

5 Summary

The Estonian state has built the foundation of a highly developed information society, and the population depends on the functioning of information and communication technologies in its everyday life. IT development has taken Estonia to a stage where many registers and services only exist in digital form. Scenarios where, for example, digital signatures do not work for days at a time, or the data in the Land Register is corrupted, are not acceptable to Estonian society.

This environment requires a flexible Government Cloud solution, whose growth, requirements and future capacity cannot be fully predicted today. Therefore, sufficient flexibility has to be planned in advance. The consolidation of domestic server rooms into standards-compliant datacenters, the flexible involvement of private sector resources both inside and outside the state's borders, and the construction of the Data Embassy network, will create a strong foundation for a working Government Cloud that provides a higher quality of service without increasing hosting costs.

References

1. European Commission: European Cloud Computing Strategy. http://ec.europa.eu/digital-agenda/en/european-cloud-computing-strategy
2. European Commission: Trusted Cloud Europe. http://ec.europa.eu/digital-agenda/en/news/trusted-cloud-europe
3. ENISA: Good Practice Guide for securely deploying Governmental Clouds. http://www.enisa.europa.eu/activities/Resilience-and-CIIP/cloud-computing/good-practice-guide-for-securely-deploying-governmental-clouds
4. Mell, P., Grance, T.: The NIST definition of Cloud Computing, National Institute of Standards and Technology, Special Publication 800-145 (2011)
5. Wyld, D.: Moving to the cloud: an introduction to cloud computing in Government (2009)
6. Zwattendorfer, B., Stranacher, K., Tauber, A., Reichstädter, P.: Cloud computing in egovernment across europe: a comparison. In: Kő, A., Leitner, C., Leitold, H., Prosser, A. (eds.) EDEM 2013 and EGOVIS 2013. LNCS, vol. 8061, pp. 181–195. Springer, Heidelberg (2013)
7. Estonian Information System Authority: Riiklike andmekeskuste konsolideerimine ja ehitamine (in Estonian), Tallinn (2014)
8. IT Department of Ministry of Finance: Riigi info- ja kommunikatsioonitehnoloogia korralduse analüüs (in Estonian), Tallinn (2013)
9. Noormaa, M.: Riigi IKT analüüsi tulemused (in Estonian). Ministry of Finance, IT Department, Tallinn (2013)
10. Estonian Ministry of The Interior: Uus digilahendus annab välismaalastele võimaluse e-Eestis tegutseda (in Estonian), Tallinn (2014)
11. Gongolidis, E., Kalloniatis, C., Kavakli, E.: Requirements identification for migrating eGovernment applications to the cloud. In: Linawati, Mahendra, M.S., Neuhold, E.J., Tjoa, A.M., You, I. (eds.) ICT-EurAsia 2014. LNCS, vol. 8407, pp. 150–158. Springer, Heidelberg (2014)
12. Williams, M.D.: E-government adoption in Europe at regional level. Transf. Gov. People Process Policy **2**(1), 47–59 (2008)
13. Gashamia, J.P., Chang, Y., Park, M.-C.: Cross-national study on factors affecting cloud computing adoption in the public sector: Focus on perceived risk. In: Proceedings of Pacific Asia Conference on Information Systems (2013)
14. Bhiskar, A.: G-Cloud: new paradigm shift for online public services. Int. J. Comput. Appl. **22**(8), 24–29 (2011)
15. Khan, F., Zhang, B., Khan, S., Chen, S.: Technological leap frogging e-government through cloud computing. In: 4th IEEE International Conference on Broadband Network and Multimedia Technology (IC-BNMT), pp. 201–206 (2011)

Open Innovation and Social Participation: A Case Study in Public Security in Brazil

Antonio Claret dos Santos, André Luiz Zambalde, Ricardo Braga Veroneze(✉), Giancarla Aparecida Botelho, and Paulo Henrique de Souza Bermejo

Federal University of Lavras, Lavras, Minas Gerais, Brazil
{kktecnologic, rbveroneze, giancarla.ufla}@gmail.com, {zamba, bermejo}@dcc.ufla.br

Abstract. In Brazil the predominant culture is not the appreciation of community participation in solving local problems. However the solutions presented by authorities are not the most efficient, and do not solve the problems. Nowadays, however, with the use of information and communication technologies associated with open innovation and gamification, citizens began to actively participate in decision-making processes of government. In this context, this study aims to describe the project of the 8th State Police Battalion of Minas Gerais, in Brazil, entitled Prêmio Ideia Cidade Segura (Safe City Idea Prize). Through a qualitative and quantitative research, in which we used the case study method, it was found that the project allowed the Police to evaluate new strategies applied to public safety (crowdstorming), to know local and regional needs, to reward the best ideas, encouraged the production of collective knowledge, and also the networking collaboration. Considering the potential contributions of crowdstorming to promote innovations and improvements in the public sector and its potential to engage citizens, it is suggested that the project idea should be replicated in other parts of Brazil.

Keywords: Open innovation · Social participation · Public securiy · Gamification

1 Introduction

Crowdsourcing is the act of taking a job traditionally performed by a designated agent (usually an employee) and outsourcing it to an undefined, generally large group of people in the form of an open call [1].

In the context of public organizations, crowdsourcing involves an association between open innovation and social participation supported by information and communication technologies. The use of these technologies has enabled citizens to participate more actively in decision-making processes of governments all over the world [2].

In Brazil it is not different, the prevailing culture of non-appreciation of citizen participation in solving local problems is being changed by this practice of collective intelligence (crowdsourcing), associated not only to information and communication technologies, but also to the gamification and the use of social networks [3].

© Springer International Publishing Switzerland 2015
A. Kő and E. Francesconi (Eds.): EGOVIS 2015, LNCS 9265, pp. 163–176, 2015.
DOI: 10.1007/978-3-319-22389-6_12

In Minas Gerais State, a projet stands out among the projects based on open innovation, gamification and social networks in the public sector, and the reason for this highlight is given because it is an iniciative of a military organization.

It is common for state police institutions in Brazil to maintain a restrictive posture and away from the community. They are usually closed institutions, extremely based on hierarchy and discipline, and do not accept external participation in planning their actions. However, at a certain moment in history, a commander said, “we are not the owners of the truth”, and promoted challenges in social networks encouraging the community to participate with ideas and suggestions to improve the safety of cities. In just one year there were more than a thousand ideas, and some of them were put into practice, becoming a reference for other battalions and even for other polices in Brazil.

This paper aims to describe the project of the 8th Battalion of the State Police of Minas Gerais, Brazil, located in the South and Midwest region of the state, titled as Safe City Idea Prize. What this innovative project from the 8th Battalion searched did exactly opening a channel of direct communication with the online community, providing the same opportunity to participate directly in the public security in their city, through social networks applications with challenges to propose new ideas and strategies.

2 Theoretical Framework

The crowdsourcing technique has become common in businesses and governments. This is the process of obtaining necessary services, ideas or content soliciting contributions from a diverse group of people and especially from an online community, rather than using traditional suppliers as a team of hired employees [4].

According to Noveck [5], there are numerous reasons for organizations to use crowdsourcing method to find solutions to their problems. This process generates cheaper costs and better results, because access a wide range of talents that may be present inside the organization, or even outside.

The problems to be solved with the adoption of a crowndsourcing technique are as diverse as possible. However, it is noticed that in the literature the crowdsourcing typology is very well defined according to the areas of problems [6]:

1. Knowledge Discovery and Management - for information management problems, where an organization mobilizes a crowd to find and gather information. Ideal for creating collective resources.
2. Human Intelligence Distributed in Multitasks - to information management problems, where an organization has a set of information in hand and involves a crowd to process or analyze the information. Ideal for processing large sets of data that computer scan not easily do.
3. Broadcast Research - for problems of ideas, where an organization mobilizes a crowd to find a solution to a problem that has a correct and objective response. Ideal for solving scientific problems.
4. Point-barred of Creative Production - to problems of ideas, where an organization mobilizes a crowd to find a solution to a problem that has an answer that is

subjective or dependent on public support. Ideal for aesthetic or mapping projects of political problems.

But what does drive people to contribute with ideas for products and services that often have no direct relationship to what they do? Researchers argue that there are two intrinsic and extrinsic motivations that lead people to contribute to the crowdsourcing tasks and that these factors influence on different types of taxpayers [7, 8]. Intrinsic motivations are divided into two categories [7, 8]:

- Basic motivations: refer to motivations related to fun and enjoyment that the experiences of taxpayers through their participation allow them feel. These reasons include: range of skills, task identity, task autonomy, direct feedback from work and hobby.
- Community Motivations: refer to the motivations related to community participation, and includes the identification of the community and social contact.

Extrinsic motivations are divided into three categories [7, 8]:

- Immediate payments, through cash payment: are the compensations received immediately for those who complete the tasks.
- Late payments: are the benefits that can be used to generate future benefits such as training skills and be noticed by potential employers.
- Social motivations: are the rewards of prosocial behavior, such as altruistic motivations.

However, despite being used since the 19th century, the crowdsourcing gained force with the advent of the Internet, social networks and computer games, the so-called gamification, and with the overvaluation of the concept of open innovation.

According to Dauscha [9], Information Technology director of Siemens, the best way to understand the origin of open innovation, is to understand that before it, something should exist, like a Closed Innovation in companies. And it really was, because for a few decades ago, large companies had their own research and development centers, with stratospheric funds destined to create and develop technologies and products not necessarily aligned with the immediate needs of the market and without the worry of talking to other areas of companies, and much less with other actors outside the organization's walls (customers, suppliers and other partners).

Before arriving in the current model of Open Innovation adopted by several companies, there was a process of maturation, where they first opened their closed departments of research and development to listen to their partners inside the company. Following, they began to involve its suppliers in the chain of innovation, as well as the own clients. The Innovation Network that appeared soon after already involved other agents, such as universities and research institutes and even other competing companies, in pre-competitive moments [9].

According Chesbrough [10], researches go far beyond, large companies seek knowledge and innovations also between the consumers of their products, taking advantage of the growing acceptance of consumers and organizations connected to the world network. The open innovation is coined term for industries and organizations that promote ideas, thoughts, processes and open researches, in order to improve the development of its products, provide better services to its customers, increase efficiency and enhance the added value.

Today, open innovation is linked to social networks and gamification [11]. The gamification can be understood as the use of thought and game engines in contexts unrelated to games, to engage users to solve problems. The term was first used in 2003 by Nick Pelling, which established a consultancy with the objective to redefine standards and operating rules of companies and industry, with the use of gamification. Navarro [9] states that, despite Pelling has not succeeded, in 2005, it was founded the company Bunchball, the first gamification platform that applied elements, mechanisms, dynamics and game techniques in companies in order to achieve greater engagement of employees and better results.

On the other hand, in the public sector, listen to the citizen is becoming a requirement among the various agencies. According to Souza et al. [3] the inclusion of citizens in public problem solutions encouraging democracy and are "a fundamental aspect of open government initiatives to: seek transparency; allow citizens access to government documents and procedures; encourage participation in order to allow people to opine about government procedures; and promote collaboration and co-production of solutions to manage the common wealth".

We have the "social participation", with consists of interactions between the government and the population, redistributing power and allowing citizens to influence decision-making process in public sector [13]. The inclusion of more individuals in the decision-making increases the flexibility of formulated policies, directing government efforts to the real needs of society.

Vigoda [12] supports the importance of listening to the public, "the views of service receivers should be considered good outcome indicators of public policy. This information can help us to: understand and establish public needs; develop, communicate and distribute public services; and assess the degree of satisfaction with the service". That is, a public company must also worry about satisfying its customer.

The crowdstorm is an open innovation technique that associated with social networks and gamification can improve participation social actions in the public sector. Related papers, such as Souza et al. [3]; Linders [2]; Seltzer and Mahmoudi [14]; and Nam [15] highlight the viability of using these techniques in order to stimulate the participation of citizens. Martins and Bermejo [16]; Netzley and Rath [17] and Lathrop and Ruma [18] present platforms examples of how crowdstorm can increase citizen participation in decision-making process, manage ideias and promote innovation in public sector.

Brabham [6] presents a practical example: The Pilot Program of Participation in the American Public Transportation. In this experiment it was used the crowdsourcing in a project to test the public participation process in traffic planning in Salt Lake City, conducted from 2008 to 2009, funded by a donation of US Federal Transit Administration.

Another example, according Souza et al. [3] "used since 2009 by the United states government, the "Open Government Initiative" aims to advance transparency, participation and collaboration with society in government affair though the use of open innovation to capture ideas that enable the development of projects in various public institutions".

3 Methodology

The present work is a qualitative and quantitative research that used the case study method, in which we attempted to describe a practical case in detail and depth [19].

The universe researched was the 8th Battalion of State Police of Minas Gerais (PMMG), located in southern Minas Gerais - Brazil, and that has an operating range of 25 cities and 03 Districts, directly affecting 405.820 citizens. This is the first unit of a state police in Brazil to use open innovation, social network and gamification, seeking to solve problems related to public safety.

The 8th Battalion created in 2012 the Prêmio Ideia Cidade Segura (Safe City Idea Prize), and started to launch challenges to the online community, aiming to find problems solutions that affect the public safety, and began to reward the best scorer participants in these challenges.

Basically, the process, to be described in details in Sect. 4 (Results and Discussion), consisted on launching challenges related to solving problems of public safety in the Premio Ideia Software Platform (www.premioideia.com.br), so the citizens could make suggestions to solve them. This platform is integrated into the Facebook social network and to a gamification and ranking module which makes that, through sharing, the challenge moves across the network. Citizens enter the network and present their ideas for the solution of one or more challenges. These ideas are "posts" on Facebook and can be liked (voted), shared and commented on. It creates then a ranking of the best ideas that are rewarded at the end of the challenge (2 to 3 months).

For this research, it was sought to conduct a synthetic descriptive study of actions implemented by the 8th Battalion, from the beginning to the end of a set of 4 (four) challenges. It was basically used document analysis involving data from each challenge (ideas - posts, polls, comments and shares) analysis of memos, reports, spreadsheets, newspaper reports and other internal documents.

Therefore, the technique used to describe the actions throughout the investigation was the documentary research. A valuable technique of qualitative and quantitative data approach, as complementing the information obtained by other techniques, as revealing new aspects of a topic or problem [19].

4 Results and Discussion

The project Prêmio Ideia Cidade Segura of the 8th State Police of Minas Gerais (8th BPM), was born from a partnership between the police and the ProGolden company, in the end of 2013.

The ProGolden has an application connected to social networks that allows doing consultations to the internal and external employees of a company, seeking to improve services, products or processes, or even create new ones. The application allows a score of the ideas, which generates the prize to the highest scoring participant. Ideas are analyzed by company managers and the most viable may become projects, managed by the application itself.

Analyzing the application used by 8th BPM, it appears that it is composed of three platforms:

- PrêmioIdeiaWeb Portal (Web Portal Idea Prize): is the site where it will be all project information, how it works, press page, project status, realization, etc.
- PrêmioIdeiaWeb Application (Web Application Idea Prize): is the own PrêmioIdeiaplatform, where people will post ideas, like and comment.
- PrêmioIdeiaMobile Application (App): is the Prêmio Ideia platform where people will post ideas, like and comment, but in the version for mobile devices (smartphones).

Through this partnership, the 8th BPM created the Prêmio Ideia Cidade Segura, where the main objective is to promote participation and collaboration of the community in large quantity, seeking innovation and pursuit of solutions to public safety problems. The project has also as specific objectives, evaluate new strategies applied to public safety, know local needs, reward the best ideas, encourage the production of collective knowledge, and encourage collaborative networking.

The target population of this project covers the population of the 25 cities and 03 districts under the responsibility of the 8th Battalion, directly affecting 405,820 citizens living in these cities. However, as the participation in the challenges occurs through access to internet, people from anywhere in the world can participate.

The implementation and realization of the Prêmio Ideia Cidade Segura was done by 5 distinct phases (Fig. 1).

The first phase was conducted to identify the needs of the State Police and settled the project objectives. The second phase consists of the gathering of information on the internet. In a third moment, a manager committee does the moderation of the ideas and approves only those that are actually related to the challenge. In the fourth phase, the State Police start to implement projects based on the posted ideas, and that were of interest of the institution. Finally, the fifth stage is made an analysis of the benefits and improvements are executed to the new challenge.

Community participation also occurs in 5 distinct phases. In the first phase, the citizen, properly connected to a social network, post these ideas (Fig. 2).

In the second phase a Manager Committee of the State Police, analyzes the ideas, check which ideas are related to the topic and does not homologate those that do not fit in the proposed challenge (Fig. 3).

After the approval of the idea by the Manager Committee, the community begins to give opinions about the posted idea (Fig. 4).

Every posted idea, commented or liked, makes the participant accumulate points. Figure 5 describes how the scoring system works.

So, the more you participate higher is the possibility of score. The participant that, at the end of the challenge, has more points is the winner (Fig. 6). In the case of 8th BPM, the Unit always rewards the two better scorers. The application displays the score in real time, which encourages participation both of whom gave the idea, as its friends in social network.

Finally, a team of 8th BPM advisors analyzes the ideas and writes new projects to be put in practice (Fig. 7).

The first challenge of the Prêmio Ideia Cidade Segura occurred on November 20th, 2013, under the theme: “Strategies and Actions to Combat Crimes Against Heritage” (Fig. 8).

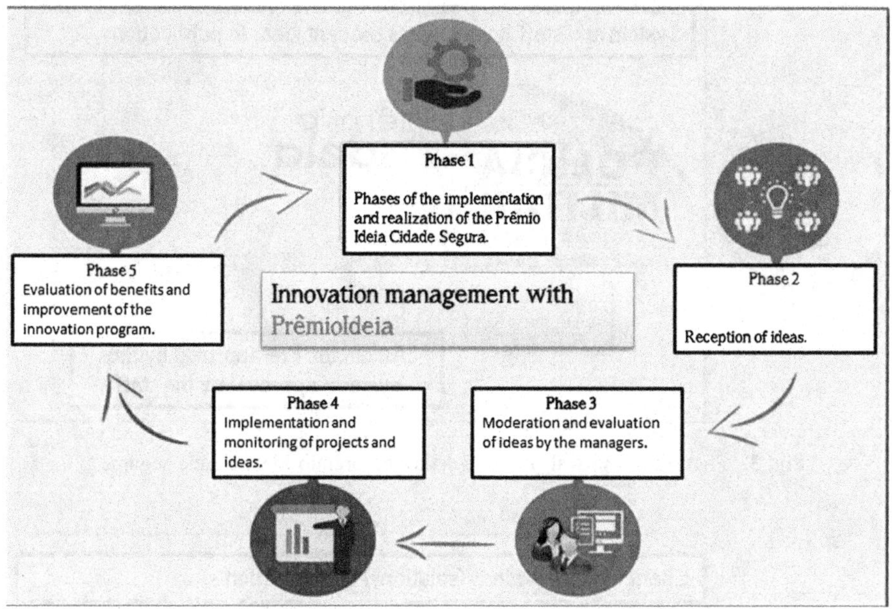

Fig. 1. Phase's from innovation management with Prêmio Idea

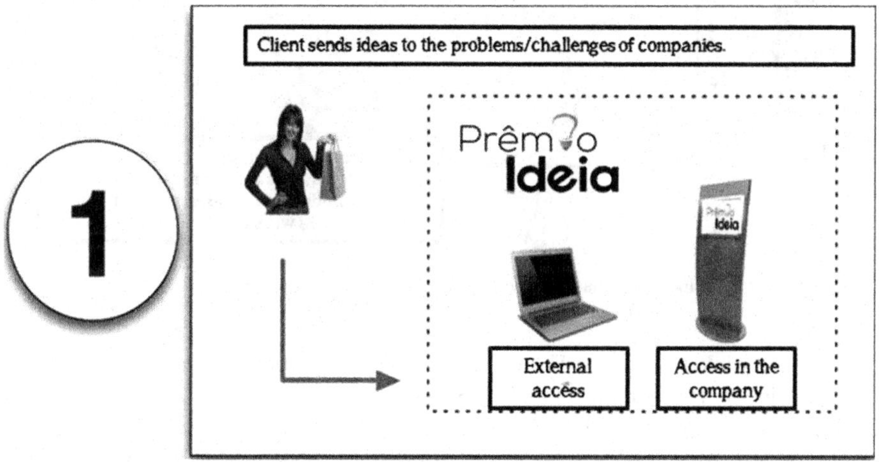

Fig. 2. Phase 1 - citizen participation in Prêmio Ideia Cidade Segura.

The challenge had 336 ideas, 1,243 comments, 19,738 likes, with the participation of 883 people. The two participants who scored higher received a TV and a smartphone, respectively.

The second challenge began on February 15th, 2014, soon after the end of the first, and the theme was "Actions and strategies to Lei Seca" (Lei Seca is a law of Brazil that

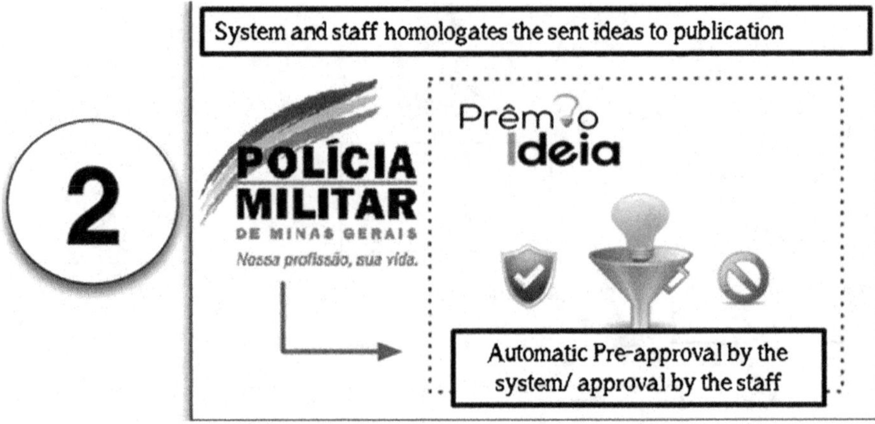

Fig. 3. Phase 2 - approval of the ideas to the prêmio ideia cidade segura.

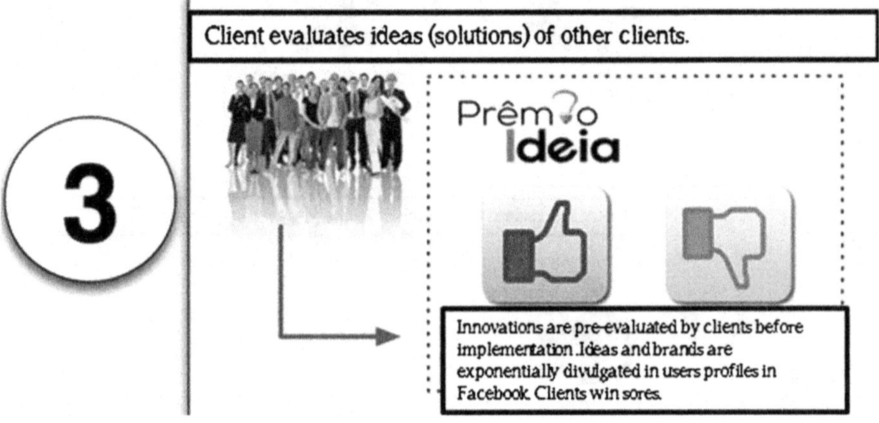

Fig. 4. Phase 3 - interaction with online community

combats the drunken drivers). The challenge had 545 participants, who together produced 171 ideas, 109 comments and 7,435 likes.

"Ideas and strategies to increase the action of Police in protection networks or creation of new networks" was the theme of the third challenge, which had 420 ideas, produced by 164 participants, with 3,067 comments and 15,252 likes.

The fourth challenge was titled, "What can I do as a citizen to not fall victim to crimes". The objective was to reverse a logical process, where is always seen the Police giving safety tips to community. This time the community produced self-protection actions to the community itself. The challenge produced 550 actions of self-protection, which had 2,600 comments, 14,221 likes, with the participation of 180 people.

The best suggestions were placed on a primer produced by the Police and distributed to the community (Figs. 9 and 10).

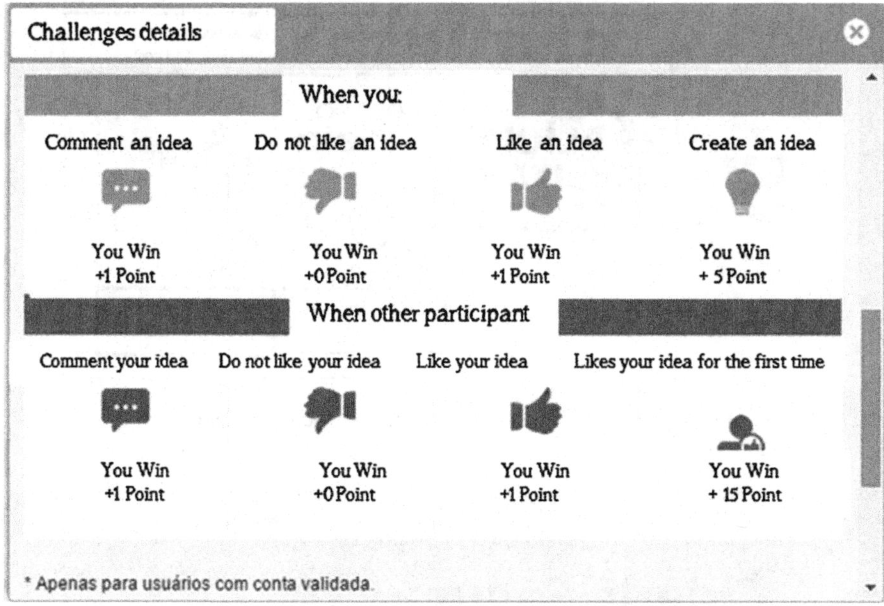

Fig. 5. Score of the Prêmio Ideia Cidade Segura participants

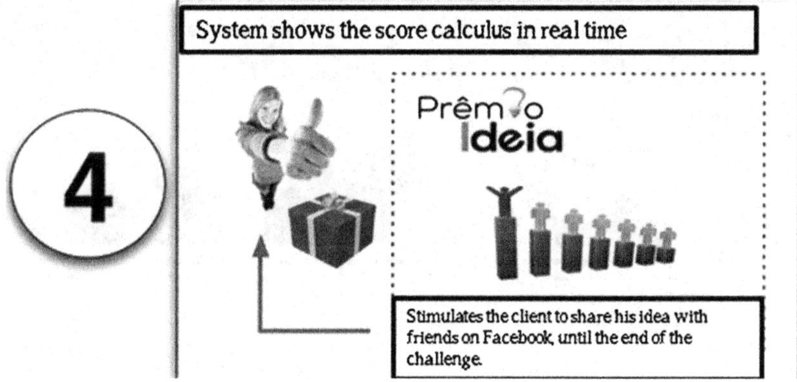

Fig. 6. phase 4 – award of thePrêmio Ideia Cidade Segura

A citizen, concerned about the health of the police officers, has proposed a joint work of different health professionals, conducting activities to improve the quality of life and health of police officers.

Based on this idea, the 8th BPM command created a project to reduce the rate of absenteeism in the Unit, entitled "Your absence Does Fault". The project was developed by the health professionals form the own Police, together with professionals from two universities. In general, the project consists of:

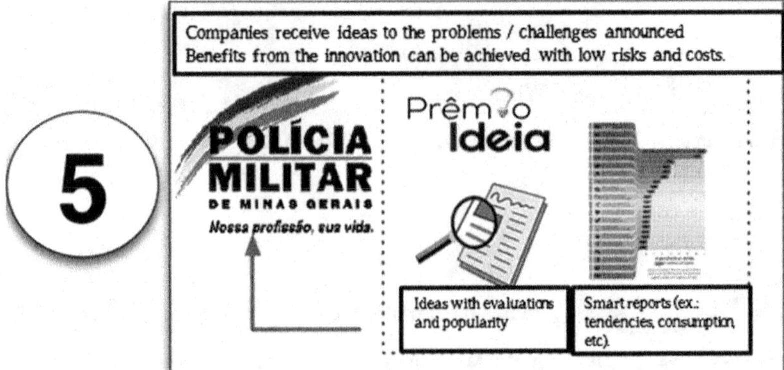

Fig. 7. Phase 5 - development of new projects and reports.

Fig. 8. Page Screen of the Prêmio Ideia Cidade Segura.

- Initially, the psychologist team applied a questionnaire to police officers, assessing the degree of motivation and satisfaction at work;
- At the same time, a team of physical therapists and physical educators performed strength, flexibility and coordination tests, to assess the physical capability of the police officers, and conducted a research to assess what were the more frequent musculoskeletal injuries among police officers;
- In the physical part, professionals conducted series of lectures, showing the main detected lesions, procedures to prevent them, as well as an incentive work to sports practice and loss weight.

Fig. 9. Side A of the Primer with the self-protection actions

Fig. 10. Side B of the primer with self-protection actions.

- Given that the project is still in progress, it was not possible to measure whether or not there was a reduction of absenteeism. However, the project was very well accepted by the troops and command.

In the Prêmio Ideia Cidade Segura page (http://premioideia.com/casos.php), we can find two examples of successful stories produced based on posted ideas in the challenges.

One of them had national repercussion. It is the creation of the first Network of Student's Houses Protected of Brazil. The idea collected and put into practice by the 8th Battalion works like this:

- The Police does a mobilization work of university residents of student's houses and promotes a meeting with them;
- At this meeting are passed on preventive actions for people and property;
- The student's houses which decide to join the network sign a term of participation, and so they post an identification sign, saying it is part of the network;
- During the holiday period the Police of Lavras gives special attention to this student's houses, passing from time to time in the place and leaving a card called Legal Visit, where the police officer makes observations about the property;
- The student who is traveling, can also pass a message to the service officer through a private group of WhatsApp, and request information about this house. In a first opportunity the vehicle passes through the place and the officer reports to the student the property situation.

This great innovation pleased a lot the university students, promoted greater interaction between the Police and the student community, reduced burglaries in student's houses, according to the Police data, and got media attention. Report age about the project can be viewed in https://www.youtube.com/watch?v=znuNwoPSf-c.

Another successful story that was reported internationally was patrolling with Unmanned Aerial Vehicle (UAV), popularly known as Drone. On June 10th, 2014, a young man from the city of Juiz de Fora - MG, around 22:01 h, posted a suggestion to conduct pat ols with drones. The next day, when the commandant of the 8th Battalion viewed the idea, immediately wrote a project to the city mayor, who assent the idea and submitted the project to approval of the City Council.

In six months the resource was released by the city hall, and the State Police acquired its first Drone. Less than a month after the date of purchase, the 8th Battalion was news in Brazil and abroad, with the identification, by the Drone, of a marijuana plantation in the backyard of a residence in the city of Lavras - MG.

Many TV stations reported the news, making the 8th Battalion a reference in air patrols with Drones (http://g1.globo.com/mg/sul-de-minas/jornal-da-eptv/videos/t/edicoes/v/com-ajuda-de-drone-policia-encontra-plantacao-de-maconha-em-lavras/3904777/).

Exactly two days after the 8th Battalion successful case have caused an uproar in the national pubic security, taking advantage of the good idea, the State Secretary for Social Defense of Minas Gerais announced in the newspapers, that the State Police of Minas Gerais would go on in the use of Drones in policing the cities (http://www.hojeemdia.com.br/horizontes/pm-de-minas-usara-drones-e-ganhara-reforco-de-450-militares-1.294877).

5 Conclusions and Suggestions

The Open Innovation combined with gamification and the crowdsourcing technique are gaining more space in private and public companies and also governments.

On the other hand, the need to listen to the customer/citizen argued by Vigoda [10] is becoming an obligation for public organizations. The innovative project of the 8th State Police Battalion (8th BPM) of the State Police of Minas Gerais is a proof that even in institutions historically closed, and with a rigid system of hierarchy, social participation is possible in the strategic planning of public safety.

Unlike the American examples cited in this article, the 8th Battalion model is much more participatory, because in the American models, citizen gives ideas, but there is not the discussion, the contribution, the evolution of the idea from these contributions, and not even the dispute caused by gamification, as in the case Premio Ideia Cidade Segura.

In just over 12 months, the 8th BPM managed to collect nearly 1,200 ideas, and most importantly, managed to turn some ideas in innovative projects in Brazil, becoming reference to other battalions and for the State Department of Social Protection.

Among the ideas posted by the community and transformed into successful stories, this work highlighted the Primer of Self-protection actions, the program to reduce absenteeism, "Your absence Do Fault", the unprecedented Network of Protected Student's Houses and the innovative Patrol with Drones.

We can see that with this innovative action of the 8th Battalion command the state police got, promoting the participation and community collaboration in large number for innovation and pursuit of solution for public safety problems, because nearly 2,000 citizens participated with ideas.

The project also allowed the PM to evaluate new strategies applied to public safety, to know local needs, prize the best ideas, encouraged the production of collective knowledge, as well as collaborative networking.

From the achieved success of the 8th BPM, it is suggested that the idea can be replicated in other State Units, and even that, the State Police of Minas Gerais can hear his client, the citizen, when preparing its new strategic planning.

Acknowledgement. The authors thank the Minas Gerais State Foundation for Research Development (FAPEMIG), the Brazilian Council for Scientific, Technological Development (CNPq) and Federal University of Lavras for their financial support.

References

1. Howe, J.: O Poder das Multidões - Por que a força da coletividade está remodelando. Campus/Elsevier, Rio de Janeiro (2008)
2. Linders, D.: From e-government to we-government: Defining a typology for citizen coproduction in the age of social media. Gov. Inf. Quart. **29**(4), 446–454 (2012)
3. Souza, W.V.B., et al.: Planning the use of crowdstorming for public management: a case in the ministry of education of brazil. In: 2014 European, Mediterranean & Middle Eastern Conference on Information Systems, Doha Quatar, 27–28 October 2014
4. Merriam-Webster: Crowdsourcing - Definition and More, 31 August 2012. http://www.merriam-webster.com/dictionary/crowdsourcing. Accessed 3 February 2014

5. Noveck, B.S.: Wiki Government: How Technology Can Make Government Better, Democracy Stronger, and Citizens More Powerful. Brookings Institution Press, Washington (2009)
6. Brabham, D.: Crowdsourcing as a Model for Problem Solving: An Introduction and Cases. Convergence: Int. J. Res. New Media Technol. **14**(1), 75–90 (2008)
7. Ipeirots, P.: Wang Quality Management on Amazon Mechanical Turk (2010). http://www.ipeirotis.com/wpcontent/uploads/2012/01/hcomp2010.pdf
8. Lakhani, et al.: The Value of Openness in Scientific Problem Solving (2007). http://www.hbs.edu/faculty/Publication%20Files/07-050.pdf
9. Dausha, R.: O que é esta tal de Inovação Aberta? (2012). http://www.endeavor.org.br/artigos/estrategia-crescimento/inovacao-implementacao-decultura-de-inovacao/o-que-e-esta-tal-de-inovacaoaberta#sthash.bkWtpab6.LOoin0oR.dpuf
10. Chessbrough, H.W.: Open Innovation: The New Imperative for Creating and Profiting from Technology. Harvard Business Press, Boston (2006)
11. Navarro, G.: Gamificação: a transformação do conceito do termo jogo no contexto da pós-modernidade. In: CELACC/ECA – USP (2013)
12. Vigoda, E.: From responsiveness to collaboration: governance, citizens, and the next generation of public administration. Public Adm. Rev. **62**, 527–540 (2002)
13. Arnstein, S.R.: A ladder of citizen participation. J. Am. Inst. Planners **35**(4), 216–224 (1969)
14. Seltzer, E., Mahmoudi, D.: Citizen participation. open innovation, and crowdsourcing: challenges and opportunities for planning. J. Plan. Lit. **28**(1), 3–18 (2013)
15. Nam, T.: Suggesting frameworks of citizen-sourcing via Government 2.0. Gov. Inf. Quart. **29**(1), 12–20 (2012)
16. Martins, T.C.M., Bermejo, P.H.S.: Open social innovation. In: Dolicanin, C., Kajan, E., Randjelovic, D., Stojanovic, B. (eds.) Handbook of Research on Democratic Strategies and Citizen-Centered E-Government Services. IGI Global, Hershey, PA (2015)
17. Netzley, M.A., Rath, A.: Social networks and the desire to safe face: a case from Singapore. Bus. Commun. Quart. **75**(1), 96–107 (2012)
18. Lathrop, D., Ruma, L.: Open Government: Collaboration, Transparency and Participation in Practice. O'Reilly Media, Inc., Sebastopol (2010)
19. Flick, U.: Introdução à pesquisa qualitativa. Artmed, Porto Alegre (2009)

Open Innovation for Citizen Coproduction

Teresa Cristina Monteiro Martins[1(✉)],
Paulo Henrique de Souza Bermejo[1],
and Wagner Villas Boas de Souza[2]

[1] Federal University of Lavras, Lavras, Minas Gerais, Brazil
teresacristina@prg.ufla.br, bermejo@dcc.ufla.br
[2] Ministry of Education of Brazil, Brasília, Brazil
wagnersouza@mec.gov.br

Abstract. Open innovation has become an emergent topic in public innovation. Governments and public institutions have used the crowdsourcing, one of the Open Innovation practices, for the development of projects with the citizen participation and open government. These actions are socially relevant and deserve further studies that contribute to the improvement and verification of citizens' participation and government innovation. This review aims at identifying how ideas crowdsourcing collaborate with coproduction of innovations in the public sector. This paper showed the main ideas of crowdsourcing that is been used for open government and the citizen coproduction. Considering the literature review and the platforms found, the paper concludes that the crowdsourcing of ideas has the potential to contribute to the innovations of coproduction and for solving social problems, providing a space for interaction among different audiences.

Keywords: Open innovation · Crowdsourcing · Crowdstorm · Ideas challenge

1 Introduction

In the global context, the Open Innovation concept has gained much attention, becoming one emergent topic in public innovation. More specifically, the interest in crowdsourcing is growing. Companies use the ideas crowdsourcing to improve its innovation process and public institutions use the ideas crowdsourcing for solving social problems, using the internet [1]. The citizen participation can help governments to improve the public policy and to face economic and social crises [2]. Some practices of Open Innovation, originally created for the private sector, have been used in the public sector and have involved more citizens in the search for solutions to their demands. This paper presents cases of ideas crowdsourcing used for solving social problems.

This theme is relevant in the current context and covers emerging concepts such as localism [3], social management and expansion of the public sphere [4]; the search for more open and transparent government institutions (Open Government Partnership) and strategies to enable the active participation of citizens for solving public problems [5].

© Springer International Publishing Switzerland 2015
A. Kő and E. Francesconi (Eds.): EGOVIS 2015, LNCS 9265, pp. 177–188, 2015.
DOI: 10.1007/978-3-319-22389-6_13

Therefore, this paper fulfill the gaps in the studies on the applicability of Open Innovation to the public context [6], regarding greater citizen participation and government openness [5]. This work was developed in order to identify how ideas crowdsourcing collaborate with coproduction of innovations in the public sector. For this purpose, we conducted an exploratory qualitative study and a review of the literature [7] on ideas crowdsourcing aimed at the coproduction innovations by governments and citizens. Platforms were researched with these characteristics in scientific papers and on the Internet. This research resulted in the development of a table in which the ideas crowdsourcing were listed, and these platforms were compared to platforms crowdsourcing used in the private sector.

Based on the literature review, this paper proposed hypothesis related to ideas crowdsourcing, that creates the innovation process using citizens' ideas, adding efficiency to the products and services in the Public Sector, as it is been done by the private sector. The ideas crowdsourcing provides a collaborative space for interaction between various stakeholders in supporting innovation in the Public Sector.

The remainder of this paper was organized as follows: Sect. 2 presents a literature review, which was divided into two parts; the first on Open Innovation and Ideas crowdsourcing and the second on the application of Open Innovation in the Public Sector and the types of coproduction. Then, Sect. 3 deals with methodological considerations, and Sect. 4 presents the ideas crowdsourcing and the citizen coproduction in which one. Next, in Sect. 5, a discussion highlights the hypotheses proposed in this paper and finally, Sect. 6 concludes and proposes future work.

2 Background

2.1 Open Innovation and Ideas Crowdsourcing

Chesbrough's definition of Open Innovation is the most commonly used in the literature [8]. Open innovation means that innovative ideas for an organization can come from inside or outside and the reverse is also true: ideas generated within an organization can be put on the market by itself or by another organization [9]. Thus, the Open Innovation can occur in processes "inside-out", "outside-in"; or both outside-in and inside-out process [10], proving that an organization does not innovate in isolation, but rather through engagement with different types of partners, acquiring ideas and resources from the external environment [9].

Innovations should not be categorized only as open or closed, but rather as a part of a continuum, ranging from fully closed to fully open [8]. Open Innovations is categorized in four stages of this continuum that can be demonstrated in the following matrix (Table 1) [8].

The Open Innovation embraces, connects and integrates several innovation strategies (Hopkins, 2011). Some of these strategies are cited by Loren [11]: "Paid program" (selling ideas); the "Campus program" (partnership between universities and companies); "Costumer partner program" (partnership with consumers) "Supply chain partner program" (partnership with members of the supply chain). Among these Open Innovation strategies is Crowdsourcing: a practice that has emerged as a result of the

Table 1. Open innovation stages

	Pecuniary	Non pecuniary
Outbound innovation	Companies commercialize their inventions and technologies through selling or licensing out resources developed in other organizations. "*Selling*"	Companies reveal internal resources without immediate financial rewards, seeking indirect benefits to the focal firm. "*Revealing*"
Inbound innovation	Companies acquire input to the innovation process through the market place. "*Acquiring*"	Companies scan the external environment prior to initiating internal R&D work. If there are ideas and technologies available, the companies use them. "*Sourcing*"

expansion of the concept "crowd", which occurred with the advance of Internet between the late 90th and early 2000 s [12].

Created by Howe [13], the term "crowdsourcing" was based on the word outsourcing. Crowdsourcing is different from outsourcing because there is no formal hiring of a number of outsourced people, but rather a collaboration of the crowd without a formal relationship. Crowdsourcing is the use of collective intelligence presented on the Internet as an Open Innovation Tool [14].

There are some subdivisions to crowdsourcing as crowdfunding, to designate the financing of innovations at an early stage by a multitude of small investors [15–17] and the crowdstorm, to designate a "brainstorming" and discussions on the same issue [18]. Thus, although some ideas crowdsourcing as the InnoCentive, date from the 1990 s, the term crowdstorm is a recent definition for describing what had been called Ideas Challenge or even brainstorm on the Internet [12].

Although it was proposed to explain a practice of business strategy and literature innovation [19], Open Innovation, especially crowdsourcing, have been used in the field of public administration as a way to integrate governments and society. The following section presents how the crowdsourcing has been used in the public context and in Sect. 4, crowdsourcing examples of ideas in the Public Sector is described.

2.2 Ideas Crowdsourcing for the Coproduction of Innovations on Public Sector

The concept of coproduction in Ostrom [20] is similar to Open Innovation. For the author, coproduction is a process in which the inputs for processing the products and services are acquired through the individuals who are not in the same organization. The author states that the term originated in a Theory Workshop Politics and Policy Analysis that happened in 1970 and was associated with proposals in which public officials encouraged the participation of citizens in the debate on urban infrastructure. Ostrom [20] presents as benefits of coproduction: the reduction of corruption, the growth of horizontal relationships and increased capital and the improved quality of products and services.

The social media collaborated with the evolution of citizen coproduction. The author categorizes citizen coproduction into three categories: "Citizen to Government," in which the audience helps the government to be more effective; "Government to Citizen," in which the government publishes online data to increase citizen knowledge; and "Citizen to Citizen" in which citizens organize themselves to produce innovations that address their demands [5]. These relationships between government and citizens can occur in three phases: in public planning; on the day by day of the organization to maintain a constant consultation with citizens and in monitoring so citizens constantly assess what has been accomplished.

The ideas crowdsourcing are Open Innovation initiatives that allow one to send ideas of discussions on how to solve public problems. Through these crowdsourcing, there are coproduction solutions to public problems and the flow of information from the "Citizen to Government (C2G)" is favored [5].

In the private field, the coproduction of innovations occurs with the emotional involvement of customers related to the objectives of the company; by approaching customers to the company's work; when there is a selection of clients to solve a particular problem of the company or when they are invited to develop products with the company [21]. Thus, customers are agents liabilities to assets and generate benefits that impact on costs [22]; the efficiency and effectiveness of innovations [22–24]; and closer relations between customers and companies [25].

Ideas crowdsourcing exemplify the coproduction of "Citizen to Government" regarding planning (IdeaScale [26]), implementation of the activities of the Government (challenge.gov [27]) and monitoring (FixMyStreet [28]). Other examples of crowdsourcing for sending ideas will be presented in the next section, as well as its operation and the type of coproduction aimed [5].

3 Research Methodology

This paper brings a literature review and presents the theme "ideas crowdsourcing" (openly), in order to explore the subject without a strict protocol for the preparation of the paper [29]. For data collection, we initially preceded a literature review, by searching for scientific papers from the last three years in renowned journals in the area that can be found in indexed databases such as Science Direct, Scopus, SAGE and SciELO. The searches took place from September 2014 to January 2015, using the following search terms in Portuguese and English: "ideas platform" and "ideas crowdsourcing." In order to verify these approaches in the public context, these terms were combined with "government", "public sector" and "social participation".

Among the papers collected in the study, we used only those that addressed the topic ideas crowdsourcing. Other types of crowd approaches were not considered. Based on the papers, we have found various ideas delivering platforms that exist around the world. In addition to a research of these platforms through papers, we also conducted research over the Internet with the same search terms, in order to find news that could lead to some crowdsourcing platforms of ideas.

Twelve national and international ideas crowdsourcing platforms were selected, which meet two requirements: be a plataform of ideas crowdsourcing and have served as a platform for the purpose of generating innovations in the public sector.

The Ushahidi [30] platform is a relevant example of crowdsourcing for the development of democracy in vulnerable regions. However, it was not included in this research because it is not a platform to delivery ideas, but rather for the sharing and mapping of local problems. For similar reason, other large range of platforms such as Fix my street [28] and MySociety [31] program were not included. We also did not considered delivering ideas platforms for generating innovation for private companies or social purpose, as the precursor of crowdsourcing: Threadless [32] and iStock [33].

The twelve selected platforms were accessed to obtain information on the institution that created the platform as well as the people allowed to propose challenges and ideas and the purpose, results and types of coproduction expected of each platform. These data are shown in a frame and were used as a basis for creating a scheme on the operation of these platforms aiming at coproduction innovations to public problems.

4 Ideas Crowdsourcing

Considering the research described above, it was possible to list twelve social crowdsourcing ideas, which was listed in Table 2. All described ideas crowdsourcing have national or international scope (InnoCentive, OpenIdeo, IdeaScale, UserVoice, Mindmixer, DigitalSkiills). Most of the identified platforms was created by private institutions that work with platform offer for public and private institutions in order to propose ideas crowdsourcing to solve problems and coproduction innovations. Usually, in these platforms the crowdsourcing promoter pays a fee for the creation and management of crowdsourcing and offers a prize to the winner of the challenge. Thus, citizens do not usually propose crowdsourcing, but their participation is extremely important, as well as the participation of public officials involved with the problem.

The challenges from these platforms are very similar to those that aim the innovation in the private sector. As companies seek the involvement of consumers for increased innovation, public institutions or political agents propose ideas crowdsourcing in order to capture the knowledge and participation of citizens who, in turn, can receive an award for his ideas [11].

In such cases, the platforms are spaces in which occurs the joint participation from citizens to Government (C2G). The government is funding the challenge and hopes that citizens collaborate with ideas that provide clear knowledge of the situation in question and thus allow the government to be more responsive and effective in its actions [5]. In this case, citizens participate encouraging challenge proponents with their knowledge and innovative ideas.

Two of the platforms presented are references in papers that deal with the application of ideas crowdsourcing in the public context: challenge.gov and eCitizenIdeas! [5, 34, 35]. They have been developinging by the Government of the United States and Singapore, respectively, aiming at hearing the views of citizens. In this case, the goal is not only to capture the perception of society around certain topics, but also look for

Table 2. Ideas crowdsourcing platforms

Crowdsourcing platforms	Developer	Stakeholder	Aim
PremioIdeia [36] * C2G	Private company Brazil	Public and private institutions.	Solving public problems.
Democratic City [37] C2C C2G	Seva Institute – NGO Brazil	Citizens, public agents, public institutions, NGO, politics, organized religion.	Providing a free space for the development of solutions on issues of collective interest.
eCitizen Ideas! [38] C2G	Private company (*Ideascale*) USA	Singapore Government.	Solving public problems in Singapore.
Open Ideo [39] * C2G	Private company USA	Public and private institutions and NGO.	Generate ideas on major global issues.
Digital Skills [40] C2G C2C	NGO UK	Citizens and institutions	Find solutions and people willing to share their skills.
HunchBuzz [41] * C2G	Private company New Zealand	Public and private institutions and NGO.	Capture and encourage innovation.
Mindmixer [42] * C2G	Private company USA and Canada	Government, and Educational institutions.	Creation of public meetings.
Innocentive [43] * C2G	Private company USA	Public and private institutions, and NGO.	Complex problem solving on the theme.
Betterific [44] * C2G	*Crowdsourcing.* org NGO	Public and private institutions and citizens.	Being an open suggestion box for the contribution.
IdeaScale [26] * C2G G2C	Private company USA	Public and private institutions, governments, NGO.	Identify great ideas and put them into practice.
Chalenge.gov C2G G2C	U.S. General Services Administration USA	USA Government.	Establish a partnership between government and citizens to address major challenges.

(*Continued*)

Table 2. (*Continued*)

Crowdsourcing platforms	Developer	Stakeholder	Aim
UserVoice [45] *	Private company USA	Public and private institutions, governments, NGO.	Find innovative ideas.
C2G			

* Platforms used for innovation in the private and public sector.
C2C: Citizen to Citizen; C2G: Citizen to Government; G2C: Government to Citizen.
Note: In some cases, the information presented overlap, for example, who participates in the MindMIxer are Citizens and Students, who are also citizens. These overlays have been maintained as shown on each platform.

innovative projects and ideas for Government Institutions and gather data for the formation of databases with relevant information.

NASA, for example, is part of the challenge.gov initiative proposing crowdsourcing on scientific problems that can be solved by researchers from outside the Government. Furthermore, the main coproduction identified in the platforms created by the Government is also from the Citizens to Government (C2G). However, it was identified that the idea of partnership between Government and Society and collaboration for the public good is evident in messages with discourses of citizenship and social participation published in the platforms pages.

The flow of information from Government to the citizens is also identified in eCitizenIdeas! platform, which features a section of ads on successful projects as well as guidance on funding social entrepreneurs. Moreover, the challenge.gov platform also publishes government data, showing to the citizen the governments quantitative view regarding the problem. Thus, this information help the citizens to propose more consistent ideas with the government situation [5]. This type of coproduction is found when accessing the crowdsourcing, verifying that in some web pages of public institutions the proponents of the crowdsourcing provide useful information and databases that allow the participant of the challenge a better understanding about the problem proposed so he can suggest ideas thereafter.

The platforms created by non-governmental institutions (Democratic City and Digital Skills) also offer room for Governments to propose crowdsourcing of improvement or innovation in any Public Institution. However, these platforms also are open to anyone who wants to publish a challenge without the need of payment or award, which facilitates the Citizens to describe a problem asking for help in the resolution.

In this case, besides the interaction C2G, there is also the Citizens self-organization around the research of problems and solutions. This self-organization features the Citizen-to-Citizen coproduction (C2C). In this sense, the open platform for sending ideas also act as a structure in which the citizens can interact, benefiting from the resources of the Internet to organize themselves regarding the problems solution. They can also mobilize to highlight a specific problem or innovative ideas until it reaches the authorities with expertise and resources to implement them.

Table 3. Comparison of crowdsourcing in the public sector and the private sector.

	Public Sector	Private Sector
Audience	Citizens, public institutions and private and their agents, non-governmental organizations.	Private companies interested in opening their process of innovation or sell their innovations [6], consumers, developers employed innovation and members of the supply chain [11].
Aims	Troubleshooting of public interest and the Government through the opening for social participation.	Products, services, systems and models geared to consumer demand [46].
Expected results	Learning, mobilization, sensitization, awareness and engagement around a problem. Formation of an online collaborative framework and development of innovations. Data dissemination Government for encouraging participation. Promotion of self-organization of citizens around the community problem solving.	Consumer producer of goods and services [25]; identification of latent needs of consumers [25]; consumers engaged in learning and experimentation of the company's products [25]; consumer satisfaction guarantee [23]; cost reduction, information on how good the product and improvement needs [22]; effectiveness and efficiency in strategic planning. [24]

Despite being created by an NGO, the Betterific is an online suggestion box in which any person may bring any idea for any public or private institution. For this, the participant must only complete the sentence "Wouldn't it be better if…", proposing a suggestion that can be commented by other participants and yet acquiring the visibility of private companies and public institutions.

Expected results with the use of these platforms are given in Table 3, and involve benefits linked to the participant's challenge, such as: learning, mobilization, sensitization, awareness and the commitment of citizens around a problem.

Results about the formation of an online collaborative structure are also expected: the formation of online collaborative communities and interactive space, mainly in relation to the expectation of an innovation in government transparency, in research innovation and solving social problems.

Table 3 was created based on the results found in the analysis of ideas crowdsourcing mentioned above, which shows the characteristics of ideas crowdsourcing in the public sector compared to the literature on the crowdsourcing in the private sector.

The presentation of the audience, goals and expected results in Table 3 shows that the ideas crowdsourcing contributes to the inclusion of stakeholders in solving a certain demand. In the private sector, companies insert consumers in their innovation processes to give greater effectiveness to its products and services, generating more profit.

The legitimacy of products and services tends to increase customer satisfaction in the public sector, being sought by governments seeking the Citizen welfare and also political interests, such as the re-election [19]. Citizens themselves also seek for the legitimacy of products and services in order to meet their demands, getting a space for self organizing [2].

Aiming either at innovation in the public or private sector, the institutions launch the crowdsourcing and promote discussions in an online collaborative environment where it is possible to achieve innovation coproduction. This is the innovation promoted by crowdsourcing: an online framework for discussion of problems shared by a group of people.

It is in this structure that happen the flow of knowledge between citizens and governments, in favor of the generation of government and social innovations that meet the common interest.

5 Discussion

The analysis of the literature reveals the peculiarities of an online space for the formation of communities and the interaction among the various audiences, who are interested in innovation as the main contribution of ideas crowdsourcing for innovation coproduction in the Public Sector.

Besides its main objective, which is the generation of innovations, the ideas crowdsourcing is itself an innovation. It is considered a social media that drives the re-emergence of citizen coproduction and which aims at transforming passive consumers to active citizens, solving social problems [5].

This paper points crowdsourcing as an example of new social media in the service of Governments, complementing Linders [5], showing more examples where crowdsourcing is used for the interaction of the Government to Citizens and Citizens to Citizens.

This paper also highlights the emergence of the wisdom of the crowd theory of Lévy and Bonomo [47] in the context of social media, showing several cases on how to use the practice of crowdsourcing with social and governmental purposes.

The delimitation of the subject of this paper excluded several widely known crowdfunding platforms, choosing only the research of crowdsourcing platforms that aim at proposing ideas with activities directed to the public sector. Examples of crowdfunding platforms are: Crowdrise, which aims to generate collective financing of social enterprises; and OpenStreetMap and Ushahidi platforms that allow the detection and mapping of local diseases and conflicts.

Despite the delimitation of the subject, we avoided to assign new nomenclature to ideas crowdsourcing in order to avoid being counterproductive. However, this procedure was productive once it highlighted one of the crowdsourcing applications that is sending ideas to solve public problems and the opening of public institutions [6].

Thus, to specifically explore the literature on the ideas crowdsourcing and their applications in the public context, the bibliographic search contributed to the literature of Open Innovation, showing its valuable application in the Public Sector and related crowdsourcing to the types of coproduction showing that it is possible to the governments to receive valuable information about the realities and perceptions of the citizens. Furthermore, there is an interaction among citizens, who can facilitate self-organization to the problems in question. In addition, the paper describes several examples of ideas crowdsourcing, used by governments and citizens in order to facilitate further research to investigate the various ideas crowdsourcing delivery platforms available.

The analyzes showed relevant practical implication of ideas crowdsourcing in the current context, in which governments are realizing the importance of increasing its openness and transparency and have recognized the potential that Information and Communication Technologies (ICT) have to create a significant change in initiatives that aim at greater transparency and effectiveness in government policies [48].

6 Conclusion

In this paper Open Innovation concepts were presented and, more specifically, the crowdsourcing of ideas; and how this practice of Open Innovation has been used in order to co-produce innovations in the Public Sector. Based on the literature, we selected twelve ideas crowdsourcing platforms aiming to find innovative ideas to solve social and listed its characteristics problems. These characteristics showed that the ideas crowdsourcing has the potential to contribute to the innovations of coproduction in the public sector as it provides a space that facilitates the interaction between different audiences, who are able to propose ideas for solving social problems.

Considering the theory of collective intelligence, the sum of the collaboration of several audiences with their theoretical skills, practices and financial resources have greater potential for co-produce innovations, which makes the crowdsourcing platform an innovation coproduction instrument in the Public Sector.

The coproduction, through crowdsourcing ideas, can occur in three ways. The first is the cooperation of the Government towards the citizens, as in challenge.gov platform. The second, by the cooperation of citizens to the government, which is what happen in almost all platforms, with the exception of Digital Skills platform on which the Government's participation is not mentioned. Considering that the ideas crowdsourcing originally aimed at fomenting innovation in the private sector, where the crowdsourcing is proposed by the Citizen interested in innovation, it is expected that most platforms have as main proponents Public Institutions and the coproduction Citizen to Citizen is more scarce. However, the type of coproduction has also been found, which signals the emergence of organizations interested in financing such platform, aiming not just the collaboration between governments and citizens, but also the self-organization, solving problems of their communities.

It is important to emphasize that this literature review does not guarantee that all ideas crowdsourcing used to solve social problems were cited. However, it can be improved with a systematic review of these platforms. The limitations of this work are related to not performing a more in-depth study of some of the platforms and also the fact that the information described have been raised only through the documentation for each platform and by the observation of the platforms' operation by the researcher.

Future work may use the research presented in this paper to select platforms to carry more in-depth case studies to test the actual relevance of these platforms for innovation coproduction. Case studies on the application of these platforms will allow the formation of an empirical research framework that will help the understanding on how new social media can be used by governments. Furthermore, it will be possible to verify what are the benefits and limitations of using open innovation practices for the opening of the governments and encouraging citizen participationchange in initiatives that aim at greater transparency and effectiveness in government policies [48].

References

1. Brabham, D.C.: Moving the Crowd at Threadless. Inform. Commun. Soc. **13**(8), 1122–1145 (2010)
2. Murray, R., Caulier-Grice, J., Mulgan, G.: The open book of social innovation. National Endowment for Science, Technology and the Art (2010)
3. Schaffers, H., Komninos, N., Pallot, M., Trousse, B., Nilsson, M., Oliveira, A.: Smart cities and the future internet: towards cooperation frameworks for open innovation. In: Domingue, J. (ed.) The Future Internet 2011. LNCS, vol. 6656, pp. 431–446. Springer, Heidelberg (2011)
4. Tenório, F.G.: Gestão social: uma perspectiva conceitual. Revista de administração pública 32(5), 7–23 (2013)
5. Linders, D.: From e-government to we-government: Defining a typology for citizen coproduction in the age of social media. Gov. Information Q. **29**(4), 446–454 (2012)
6. Huizingh, E.K.: Open innovation: state of the art and future perspectives. Technovation **31** (1), 2–9 (2011)
7. Soares, L., et al.: Literature review: particularities of each type of study/Revisão de literatura: particularidades de cada tipo de estudo. Revista de Enfermagem da UFPI **2**(5), 14–18 (2014)
8. Dahlander, L., Gann, D.M.: How open is innovation? Res. Policy **39**(6), 699–709 (2010)
9. Chesbrough, H.W.: Open innovation: The new imperative for creating and profiting from technology. Harvard Business Press, Boston (2003)
10. Enkel, E., Gassmann, O., Chesbrough, H.: Open R&D and open innovation: exploring the phenomenon. R&d Manage. **39**(4), 311–316 (2009)
11. Loren, J.D.: What is Open Innovation? In: A guide to Open Innovation and Crowdsourcing. KoganPage, Editor. United States (2011)
12. Hopkins, R.: What is Crowdsourcing? In: A guide to Open Innovation and Crowdsourcing. S. Paul, Editor, London (2011)
13. Howe, J.: The rise of crowdsourcing. Wired Mag. **14**(6), 1–4 (2006)
14. Nascimento, A., Heber, F., Luft, M.C.: O uso do crowdsourcing como ferramenta de inovação aberta: uma categorização à luz da teoria de redes interorganizacionais. Revista Gestão Organizacional 6(2) (2014)
15. Mollick, E.R.: The dynamics of crowdfunding: Determinants of success and failure (2013)
16. Belleflamme, P., Lambert, T., Schwienbacher, A.: Crowdfunding: Tapping the right crowd. J. Bus. Ventur. (2013)
17. Schwienbacher, A., Larralde, B.: Crowdfunding of small entrepreneurial ventures. SSRN Electronic Journal (2010)
18. Abrahamson, S., Ryder, P., Unterberg, B.: Crowdstorm: The Future of Innovation, Ideas, and Problem Solving. Wiley, Hoboken (2013)
19. Seltzer, E., Mahmoudi, D.: Citizen participation, open innovation, and crowdsourcing: challenges and opportunities for planning. J. Plan. Lit. **28**(1), 3–18 (2013)
20. Ostrom, E.: Crossing the great divide: coproduction, synergy, and development. World Devel. **24**(6), 1073–1087 (1996)

21. Payne, A.F., Storbacka, K., Frow, P.: Managing the co-creation of value. J. Acad. Mark. Sci. **36**(1), 83–96 (2008)
22. Etgar, M.: Co-production of services. The Service-Dominant Logic of Marketing, pp. 128–138 (2006)
23. Oliver, R.L.: Co-producers and co-particpants in the satisfaction process. In: The Service-Dominant Logic of Marketing: Dialog, Debate, and Directions, pp. 118–27 (2006)
24. Kalaignanam, K., Varadarajan, R.: Customers as co-producers. In: The Service-Dominant Logic of Marketing: Dialog, Debate, and Directions, pp. 166–179 (2006)
25. Jaworski, B., Kohli, A.K.: Co-creating the voice of the customer. In: The Service–Dominant Logic of Marketing: Dialog, Debate and Directions, pp. 109–117 (2006)
26. IdeaScale. http://ideascale.com/(10 October 2014)
27. Desouza, K.C.: Challenge. gov: Using Competitions and Awards to Spur Innovation. IBM Center for the Business of Government, Washington, DC (2012). http://www.businessofgovernment.org/report/challengegov-using-competitions-and-awards-spur-innovation. Accessed 23 September 2013
28. FIXMYSTREET, 10 October 2014. http://www.fixmystreet.com/
29. Cordeiro, A.M., et al.: Systematic review: a narrative review. Revista do Colégio Brasileiro de Cirurgiões **34**(6), 428–431 (2007)
30. USHAHIDI, 10 October 2014. http://www.ushahidi.com/
31. MYSOCIETY, 10 October 2014. http://www.mysociety.org/
32. THREADLESS, 10 October 2014. https://www.threadless.com/
33. ISTOCKPHOTO, 10 October 2014. http://www.istockphoto.com/
34. Leitmann, J.: Integrating the environment in urban development: good practice in Singapore. Odtü Mimarlik Fakültesi Dergisi = Metu journal of Faculty of Architecture **18**(1–2), 37–61 (1998)
35. Parvanta, C., Roth, Y., Keller, H.: Crowdsourcing 101: A Few Basics to Make You the Leader of the Pack. Health Promot. Pract. **14**(2), 163–167 (2013)
36. PRÊMIOIDEIA, 10 October 2014. http://www.premioideia.com
37. CIDADEDEMOCRÁTICA, 10 October 2014. http://www.cidadedemocratica.org.br
38. ECITIZENIDEAS, 10 October 2014. https://ideas.ecitizen.gov.sg
39. OPENIDEO, 10 October 2014. https://openideo.com
40. DIGITALSKILLS, 10 October 2014. http://www.digitalskills.com
41. HunchBuzz, 10 October 2014. http://hunchbuzz.com/
42. MINDMIXER, 10 October 2014. http://mindmixer.com/
43. INNOCENTIVE, 10 October 2014. https://www.innocentive.com
44. BETTERIFIC, 10 October 2014. https://betterific.com/
45. VOICE, U., 10 October 2014. https://www.uservoice.com/
46. Baldwin, C., Von Hippel, E.: Modeling a paradigm shift: From producer innovation to user and open collaborative innovation. Harvard Business School Finance Working Paper, pp. 4764–4809 (2010)(10-038)
47. Lévy, P., Bonomo, R.: Collective intelligence: Mankind's emerging world in cyberspace. Perseus Publishing, New York (1999)
48. Bertot, J.C., Jaeger, P.T., Grimes, J.M.: Using ICTs to create a culture of transparency: E-government and social media as openness and anti-corruption tools for societies. Gov. Infor. Q. **27**(3), 264–271 (2010)

Intelligent Systems in E-Government I

Analyzing Suspicious Medical Visit Claims from Individual Healthcare Service Providers Using K-Means Clustering

Tiago P. Hillerman[1(✉)], Rommel N. Carvalho[2], and Ana Carla B. Reis[1]

[1] University of Brasília – UnB, Campus Universitário Darcy Ribeiro, Brasília, DF 70910-900, Brazil
t_hillerman@yahoo.com.br, anacarlabr@unb.br
[2] Department of Research and Strategic Information (DIE), Brazilian Office of the Comptroller General (CGU), Brasília, Brazil
rommel.carvalho@gmail.com

Abstract. This study has as its main objective the analysis of healthcare claims data from individual providers, such as independent doctors and allied health professionals, with the purpose of finding excessive billing of medical visitation procedures. We present a discussion of the main difficulties in preventing against abusive claims, and with the use of the CRISP-DM method and the k-means clustering algorithm, propose a model for assessing the behavior of providers engaged in this sort of practice. We conclude that the clustering algorithm was able to provide a more efficient, objective, and reproducible framework for identifying outliers, which could be used for future investigations in similar datasets.

Keywords: Healthcare · Claims · Cluster analysis · K-means

1 Introduction

Healthcare insurers, both in the private sector and as government-funded systems, often find it difficult to identify suspicious behavior in claims data. This is in large part due to the massive volume of processed records, the multitude of business rules and regulations, and of course the complex nature of medical procedures themselves. Analysts and auditors are sometimes overwhelmed with the extensive amount of information that is processed, and lack the resources and technology required for the rapid detection of inconsistencies, abuses, and errors that result in wasteful spending. There is an unfortunate shortage of automated features aimed at tracking the performance and behavior of medical service providers, which would permit timely identification of anomalous and suspicious activities. Some estimates have been made regarding the yearly cost of healthcare expenses that are linked to abusive and inconsistent claims. In the United States, it has been suggested [1] that 30 % of healthcare costs (which is predicted to reach almost 20 % of that country's GDP in 2016 [14]) is linked to wasteful practices.

© Springer International Publishing Switzerland 2015
A. Kő and E. Francesconi (Eds.): EGOVIS 2015, LNCS 9265, pp. 191–205, 2015.
DOI: 10.1007/978-3-319-22389-6_14

In South America, the largest[1] healthcare market is in Brazil, a country which in 2012 saw healthcare costs account for 8 % of its' GDP. Though it is unclear how much of that amount is wasted, as of 2013 the country was unfortunately ranked last[2] in terms of healthcare efficiency in a study by Bloomberg, which evaluated among 48 countries with a per capita GDP of over $5.000.

This paper aims at identifying suspicious behavior related to medical claims data processed by one such Brazilian health insurance provider, with its main focus being the investigation of one specific type of abuse, known as the "impossible day" scenario [17]. We have studied unsupervised datasets which contained records from medical visitation claims, and attempted to pinpoint inconsistent behavior linked to abnormally high visitation quantities submitted by individual providers. Using statistical and cluster analysis, our goal was to isolate specific behaviors from the dataset, constructing a model which could be used to improve the efficiency of auditing efforts, which usually face various limitations in terms of manpower and time available for investigating suspicious claims. Results showed that clustering the claims datasets made it possible for us to identify, with greater confidence, the incidences of this kind of activity, considering factors such as amount charged per day, patient visits per month, and frequency of services provided. We have structured our work by means of first presenting an overview of the organization which provided the data in Sect. 2. We then followed by discussing a few of the growing trends and main types of abusive practices found in the healthcare sector (Sect. 3), by way of introducing other related works which have also addressed, through data mining and knowledge discovery, a few of these issues (Sect. 4). In Sects. 5 and 6, we begin the second part of this paper by explaining our methodology, which was based mainly on a simplified version of the CRISP-DM method and the concepts of anomaly detection in large datasets. In Sect. 7 we describe the nature of the evaluated data, the steps taken in manipulating and selecting meaningful variables for analysis, and the development and evaluation of our model. We finish by explaining our conclusions and knowledge gained through the entire process in Sect. 8, along with the next steps which have been planned for both improving our model and expanding our analysis into other types of healthcare data.

2 Healthcare Claims Processing

The organization in question is one of the largest self-funded[3] health insurance operators in Brazil, overseeing approximately 1 million beneficiaries, with total yearly expenses in the order of R$ 3 billion (about US$1 billion as of 2014). As with most other healthcare insurers, the organization's payment process involves receiving, analyzing, and approving claims submitted by its providers for services rendered to its beneficiaries. Providers are classified as institutions (such as hospitals, laboratories, or

---

[1] http://www.pwc.com.br/pt/publicacoes/setores-atividade/assets/saude/healthcare-tsp-13.pdf. Accessed 11-Dec-2014.

[2] http://veja.abril.com.br/blog/impavido-colosso/em-ranking-sobre-a-eficiencia-dos-servicos-de-saude-brasil-fica-em-ultimo-lugar/. Accessed 11-Dec-2014.

[3] See http://healthinsurance.about.com/od/faqs/f/selffund.htm.

clinics) or individual persons (independent doctors and allied health professionals). The electronically submitted claims are first reviewed by an automated payment system. If a specific predefined inconsistency is detected (for example, incompatibility between the procedure and patient gender), the system itself generates an automatic denial, which is then sent for manual validation depending on the aggregate procedure cost. The flagged inconsistencies can then be reversed or sustained, generating a partial or total denial of the amount charged by the service provider.

3 Healthcare Waste and Abuse

The occurrence of waste in the healthcare market has been studied extensively by foreign entities. In 2012 the former chief of the United States' Centers for Medicare and Medicaid Services (CMS), estimated[4] that healthcare waste accounted for roughly $98 billion of that country's Medicare and Medicaid spending, which represented about 10 % of the total expenses. Also in the U.S., the National Health Care Anti-Fraud Association (NHCAA) has projected[5] that abuse in the system could reach tens of billions of dollars yearly. Such is the magnitude of abuse in the American healthcare system that its Department of Health and Human Services (HHS) has made some significant efforts [13] in using advanced technology, such as predictive data analytics, to combat and prevent wasteful activities.

Along with governmental measurers, the academic and private sectors have also offered promising studies aimed at identifying the types of waste and abuse which result in the figures cited above. Though, as of the writing of this paper, no other research has been located concerning anomalous billing detection in the Brazilian healthcare sector specifically, the following section presents a few previous examples of this type of research conducted abroad.

4 Related Works

In [2], the authors focused on external fraud detection through multivariate latent class clustering. In that case, the analysis focused on the procurement process of a European financial institution. The researchers grouped their data into three clusters and determined the risk profile for each one through descriptive analysis. A detection system based on a committee of multilayer perceptron neural networks (MLP) for suspect entities was constructed in [3], achieving a marked improvement in detection rate. Musal [4] presented two models based on geographical data to detect possible fraud in the Medicare system, both using unsupervised databases. The first model used clustering algorithms in order to group zip codes according to socioeconomic characteristics. The second evaluated the distance travelled by patients in order to obtain medical

[4] http://www.economist.com/news/united-states/21603078-why-thieves-love-americas-health-care-system-272-billion-swindle.

[5] http://www.nhcaa.org/resources/health-care-anti-fraud-resources/the-challenge-of-health-care-fraud.aspx.

services, with the objective of identifying risk metrics linked to "impractical" distances. A similar method is presented in [12], which oversaw a discussion over the different types of proposed approaches related to healthcare anomaly detection, such as the supervised approach with labeled data, unsupervised approach using unlabeled data, and a hybrid method, where the former is used in order to improve the latter's performance. In [5], social network analysis was used to identify suspicious entities in the automobile insurance sector. Chandola et al. [6] proposed three models for studying the behavior of known fraudulent versus unidentified entities. In this case, the authors applied large scale text analytics, social network analysis, and temporal analysis of claims sequences in order to study the data. Becker, Kessler, and McClellan [7] evaluated the impact of increased law enforcement on the billing habits and types of care provided.

The most pervasive types of healthcare abuse have been detailed and grouped by various publications [7, 8, 12], and include billing for services not rendered or equipment not provided, charging for each item in a procedure as if they were used separately (i.e. "Unbundling"), performing medically unnecessary procedures, among many others.

Among these is the so-called "impossible day" scenario [15–17], where a provider may submit claims which, when analyzed, show a greater quantity of services rendered than would otherwise be possible on a single day. This specific type of inconsistency was the one chosen for evaluation in this paper. Though the previous examples demonstrate that the study of anomalous billing is a matter of some concern to healthcare organizations, preliminary research[6] found no other works with the specific use of cluster analytics for detecting anomalies related to excessive medical visit claims.

5 The CRISP-DM Methodology

In this study we chose the CRISP-DM methodology as a guide for each step of this work's data mining and discovery process. The Cross Industry Standard Process for Data Mining is a data mining model that sets a framework for solving data mining-related problems [11]. This methodology consists of several levels of abstraction, going from generalized to specific tasks. Its main phases are:

Business Understanding: In the first phase, one aims to understand the business objectives and the project's success conditions. The idea is to gather some sense of the end-user's goals and what kind of prior understanding is required, in order to define what the specific problem is that needs to be solved.

[6] Research focused on the IEEE Xplore Digital Library (ieeexplore.ieee.org), ScienceDirect (www.sciencedirect.com) Google Scholar (scholar.google.com), SpringerLink (http://link.springer.com) and Elsevier (http://www.elsevier.com/about/open-access/sponsored-articles). Keywords included *impossible day, healthcare billing, excessive medical claims, healthcare fraud and abuse, cluster analysis* etc.

Data Understanding: The next step is to select and analyze the data set, in order to gain initial insights through descriptive analysis. The data's structure, relationships, and any underlying issues are described in this phase.

Data Preparation: "Preparation", in this context, involves "pruning" the data, through attribute selection, formatting, construction, and integration with the tools which will be used. Irrelevant, incorrect, and missing values are also eliminated in this stage.

Modeling: This stage involves the definition of the models, parameters, and testing plans. The chosen models are then used to define the training, testing, and validation subsets.

Evaluation: In this step, through the use of classifiers, we have the prediction of classes for each instance, and a success rate is calculated and validated among all instances. Model quality and selection criteria are defined in an attempt to achieve the intended business objectives.

Deployment: The selected model is incorporated into the organization's decision-making process. A maintenance and monitoring plan are developed to oversee the continued (and correct) use of the model's results over time.

6 Anomaly Detection

Anomaly detection, as outlined in [9], consists of trying to detect a set of data points, which are considerably different from all others. This is usually done by establishing a "normal" behavior profile, defining thresholds, and scoring data points in order to detect deviations from the norm. One very common approach in anomaly detection is clustering, which has as one of its main advantages the ability to consider many variables which share the same characteristics, grouping them by similarity. Classes are created from the data itself, which is useful in the context of this study as there were no initial labels that could be used to classify the different data points. In this sense, the classification done in this work would fall into the category of unsupervised classification (Tan et al., 2005), seeing as there was no initial "ground truth" variable that could be used to classify data as suspicious or normal. Clustering, in particular, was chosen since there is a need to analyze the relationship between data and to group it together if, and when, it represents a high degree of association.

7 Applied CRISP-DM Methodology

7.1 Business Understanding

On the one hand, medical providers classified as institutions, such as hospitals and affiliates, typically possess the staff needed to service many patients on a single day. On the other hand, individuals such as doctors or other specialists would, in theory, possess inherent limitations in receiving large numbers of patients in a 24-hour period.

Normally, an organization might possess various automatic system checks for excessive procedure claims related to a single beneficiary on the same date (for instance, multiple services rendered for a single individual on the same date). However, it is likely that no automatic control that would assess the amount of different patients seen by a provider on a certain date exists. This is due to the fact that institutions (which are most likely to attract attention due to their proportionally greater expenses) are assumed to be able to service many patients per day. Less emphasis is often given to low-volume individual providers. The possible existence of this gap was one of the factors that motivated this study.

Over the course of evaluating the company's claims processing through risk assessment methodologies, it was hypothesized that one possible type of existing abuse could be the overcharging of medical procedures by individual providers, considering the number of visits from distinct patients on the same day. Therefore, the ultimate goal of this study was to evaluate the billing practices of registered individual providers in a 12-month period.

7.2 Data Understanding and Preparation

In the initial data extraction phase, we chose claims records for providers flagged as "individuals". We also selected providers who submitted their claims through the organization's external electronic authorization system. This tool is used to approve the simplest medical care procedures, with a transaction log that allowed us to verify the exact date and time of the authorization request for a particular procedure.

The extracted data consisted of approximately 1 million payment records from over 13,000 individual providers and 350,000 distinct patients who, between January and December 2013, generated medical visitation claims in excess of R$ 65 million. This total represented, in that period, about half of all expenses related to individual providers. The expenses from this type of procedure alone were over three times higher than the next largest events combined (psychotherapy, speech therapy, and acupuncture, respectively). Besides the costs involved, we chose this procedure type due to its relative simplicity and the ease in terms of approximating, if needed, the typical duration for each visit.

The records were extracted via SQL queries, and loaded into RStudio[7] for initial manipulation. Of 23 initial attributes, six were chosen for analysis: Patient and Provider ID, Claim number, Service Date, Paid amount, and quantity. Table 1 presents an overview of the evaluated and discarded attributes.

At first, all claims records were grouped by provider and service dates, totaling the service quantity and amount paid for each group. The payment amount was disregarded after this point, since the visitation charge rate was contractually standardized and showed little deviation. Subsequently, the records were grouped by provider, procedure, and service dates, with totals for the service quantities in each date. This result contained about 620,000 records.

[7] RStudio is a widely used development environment for R, available at http://www.rstudio.com/products/RStudio/.

Table 1. Attributes considered for analysis

Attribute Description	*Chosen (Y/N)*	*Reason for selection / removal*
Patient ID	**Y**	**Necessary for patient identification**
Patient Name	**N**	**Patient can be located by Patient ID**
Provider ID	**Y**	**Necessary for provider identification**
Provider Name	**N**	**Can be located by Provider ID**
Authorization Code	**N**	**Can be located through Claim #**
Claim Batch #	**N**	
Claim Group #	**N**	
Claim #	**Y**	**Necessary for claim identification**
Prvdr. Specialty #	**N**	**Provider types and specialties were filtered in extraction phase**
Provider Type	**N**	
Service Date	**Y**	**Used for calculating service qty. / day**
Received Date	**N**	**Outside the scope of analysis**
Payment Date	**N**	
Procedure Code	**N**	**Visitation codes were filtered in extraction phase**
Procedure Desc.	**N**	
Cost Item Code	**N**	**Cost items are usually standardized by procedure type**
Cost Item Desc.	**N**	
Amt. Submitted	**N**	**Evaluation focused on amount and quantity paid.**
Qty. Submitted	**N**	
Denied Billing Amt.	**N**	
Denied Billing Qty.	**N**	
Paid Amount	**Y**	**Necessary for calculating total involved**
Paid Quantity	**Y**	

Preliminary statistical analysis revealed a relatively skewed distribution, with some visit quantities in excess of 50 per day for some providers (with a maximum of 93 visits per day), a somewhat surprising upper limit given the obvious minimum time needed for each visit.

At this point, a logical assumption would be that the higher the number of visits on a single day, the greater the risk for abuse. In this case, it would be possible to define a preliminary threshold for further investigation. Consultation with medical experts yielded a few simple standards, such as an 8-h workday and 15-min interval between visits, which resulted in a maximum of 32 visits per day. Evidently, this estimate would not account for breaks or the simple fact that medical professionals typically allocate less than 8 h per day for medical visits. Nonetheless, samples were taken of the evaluated data, and the electronic authorization logs linked to some of the highest service-per-day claims were analyzed. Indeed, as Fig. 1 shows, there is strong evidence to suspect the existence of abusive practices. As recorded by the system log for one of the providers, on one specific date, 55 procedure claims were submitted between 10:33 and 11:29 AM. In this instance, the average interval between claims is approximately 30 s.

Initial Date 13/12/2013 **End Date** 13/12/2013

Date	13/12/2013	13/12/2013	13/12/2013
Time	11:28:38	11:29:00	11:29:25

Fig. 1. Example log of suspicious billing.

Initially, 18 providers exceeded this "32-visit-per-day" limit, and their records were separated for further investigation. This involved verifying all physical claims documentation for the existence of patient signatures and the presence of erasures in the form fields. The supposed visitation motives were also verified, as well as those occurring on holidays or weekends. Finally, a sample of patients from each provider was selected for a short phone interview, using a standard questionnaire, which included queries over service frequency, provider availability, average visit duration, and degree of satisfaction with services rendered. After evaluation, 11 of the 18 providers were found to have submitted erroneous claims. The claim amounts in their records corresponded to approximately 70 % of the total amount initially sent for investigation. The results of the initial analysis are summarized in Table 2:

Table 2. Results of initial analysis

	Providers	*# Records*	*Amt. Paid*
Initial Dataset	**~13,000**	**~1,000,000**	**~65,000,000.00**
Above 32/day limit	**18**	**39 (above limit)** **1,289 (provider total)**	**~100,000.00 (records above limit)** **~600,000.00 (provider total)**
Confirmed suspects	**11**	**903 (provider total)**	**~300,000.00 (provider total)**

However, analyzing all such incidences of above-average payments proved to be very time-consuming and inefficient. Additionally, the somewhat subjective nature used in defining the maximum daily interval meant that any providers who presented payment-per-day quantities below the initial threshold of 32 per day were being left out of the analysis.

Initial evaluation showed a number of possible justifications for billing such high amounts of procedures per day. For example, due to clerical error or simple convenience, a month's or week's visitations could be billed on one specific date at the end of each period, with every procedure's "service date" field being filled in with that day's date. While technically incorrect, this practice would not be considered abusive, as the services would still have been rendered.

Another alternative was the existence of specific programs (such as company-wide periodic exams mandated by law) where a provider would indeed be hired to consult with many patients in a single day. In both of these scenarios, one would expect to view, in a given period, "normal" stretches of visitation quantities punctuated by "spikes" of abnormal billing rates. Table 3 shows such a scenario, in which a provider, which normally sees few patients on a monthly basis, suddenly charges for many times the usual billing amount, only to return to a "normal" behavior in subsequent months. Alternatively, having a particular high-volume day be just another in a series of similar high-volume days or months would raise more suspicion. If (aside from the outliers) we consider the frequency and volume displayed in Table 3 as normal, the billing behavior shown in Table 4 would stand out as worthy of investigation.

Therefore, we made the decision to add new variables to the previous dataset, in order to build a multivariate model capable of automatically and objectively defining the analysis threshold, reducing incidences of false-positives and false-negatives.

Table 3. Potentially justifiable billing activity

	May	*Jun*	*Jul*	*Aug*	*Sep*	*Oct*
Patients seen in month	01	03	94	50	04	02
# of service dates in month	01	02	02	04	03	01

Table 4. Habitually suspicious billing activity

	Jan	*Feb*	*Mar*	*Apr*	*May*	*Jun*
Patients seen in month	68	143	48	93	68	51
# of service dates in month	15	14	14	19	15	14

Beside the existing variable of "amount of patients seen on that specific day" (defined as QTY_ON_DAY), we would also consider the variables "number of patients serviced in that record's month" (QTY_PATIENTS_MO), and "amount of billed days in the same month" (DAYS_ON_MO). The new variables would permit the "weighing" of each record, in an attempt to cluster together behaviors which closely matched those seen in Table 4. Ideally, the model would prioritize providers which a combination of three main variables: (a) large amount of visitations on a specific date, (b) greater number of high-volume days in the same month (representing frequency) and (c) high number of different patients seen on a given month (representing volume).

Through quantile analysis, it was possible to verify that most of the initial records contained less than 10 visits per day. They were classified into 10-unit-length sub-intervals with cut, using R's table function to compute the frequency of service quantities in each interval (Table 5). Approximately 99.6 % of records constituted service amounts of 10 or less patients per day for each provider.

Table 5. Intervals for amount charged per day

Interval	*# records*	*Interval*	*# records*
[0,10)	620.975	[50,60)	5
[10,20)	2.642	[60,70)	2
[20,30)	257	[70,80)	1
[30,40)	51	[80,90)	0
[40,50)	7	[90,100)	1

The mean (1.73) and standard deviation (1.48) for the QTY_PER_DAY field was used for calculating the attribute's six-sigma limit of 10.6. This parameter was used in order to establish a cut-off point for our analysis, separating the records most likely related to suspicious claims (as those with more than 10 visits per day would be furthest from the dataset's mean). This also presented an advantage in the reduced computational costs associated with building the clustering model, as the new subset only contained approximately 2.100 records of the initial ~ 630.000. K-means cluster analysis was then chosen for further study.

7.3 Modeling

K-means is a prominent clustering technique first developed by Stuart Lloyd in 1957 and refined by J. Hartigan and A. Wong in 1975 [18]. It is based on a user-specified number of clusters represented by centroids, which are usually the means of groups of points [9]. The chosen number of initial centroids is assigned a single point, with the centroid itself being recalculated after each insertion. This is repeated until the centroids remain unchanged. It is widely chosen for its efficiency, though it sometimes suffers due to the subjective nature in choosing the number of clusters.

In our case, the first method for determining the number of clusters was the sum of squares, or "knee" method, as described in [9, 10]. This consists in evaluating, for a different number of clusters, the sum of the "within cluster" sum of squares. The largest variation in the sum of the "within cluster" sum of squares is chosen.

In our case (Fig. 2, above), the largest "drop" for the standardized dataset is seen at the 4-cluster number, and therefore this was the number of clusters chosen for creation.

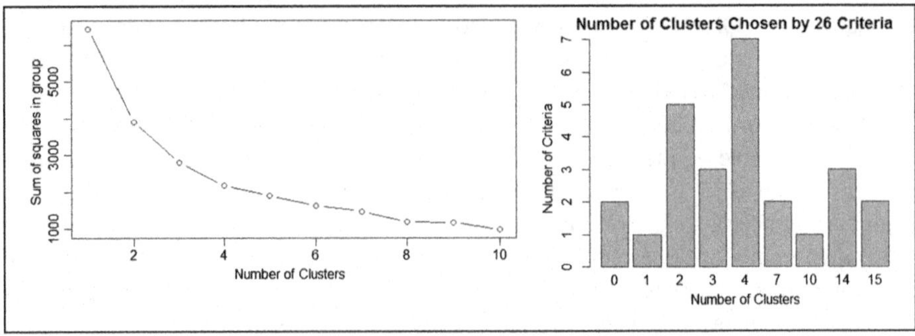

Fig. 2. Number of clusters (4) derived from the elbow method and NbClust function

This result was validated with the use of the NbClust [10] function, which also pointed to a 4-cluster model as having the optimal results (also seen in Fig. 2).

Cluster analysis resulted in four clusters of 741, 944, 178 and 284 records respectively. Figure 3 presents the scatterplots matrix of the record distributions and their each cluster results, considering the three target variables QTY_ON_DAY, QTY_PATIENTS_MO, and DAYS_ON_MO.

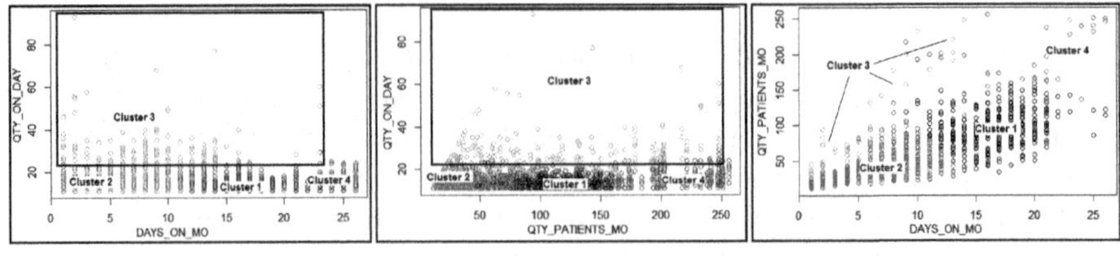

Fig. 3. Results of cluster analysis.

The relationship between the variables in the unclustered set and in both clusters is discussed in detail in the Evaluation phase.

8 Evaluation – Cluster Validation

The first step in our validation procedure was to check the cluster algorithm's performance in terms of its ability to correctly group the records which were initially identified as suspect (previously shown in Table 2). Table 6 shows that the algorithm was able to assign all 39 initially suspect records to Cluster 03, corresponding to the initial 18 suspect providers (along with 36 other providers who were not evaluated in the first model, since their records did not exceed the 32 visitations/day threshold). Since the analysis was done at the record level, some of the providers might be present in more than one cluster, though none of the 18 suspect providers were found in any other cluster besides Cluster 03.

Table 6. Number of Records and Providers in each cluster

Cluster #	# of Records	Initial Class	# of Records /Class	# Providers
Cluster 1	741	Below 32/day limit	741	121
Cluster 2	944		944	273
Cluster 3	178	Above 32/day limit	39	18 (all initial suspects)
		Below 32/day limit	139	36
Cluster 4	284		284	18

For each cluster, the standard deviation was chosen as a metric for defining the degree of variable closeness. This was calculated for each variable in each cluster, along with their means, as a way of measuring both point dispersion and number of risk factors, as applied by Jans, Lybaert, and Vanhoof [2].

As highlighted on Table 7, results revealed that Cluster 03 contained the highest risk factor (mean value) for the QTY_ON_DAY variable (30.12). In the same cluster, the comparatively high standard deviation (9.64) suggest a greater number of outliers. Also of note is that Cluster 04, with the second-highest average in the QTY_ON_DAY variable, also exhibits the highest averages in the other two risk variables. Based on these preliminary results, one could suggest an investigative approach that focused first on the providers whose records were present in the clusters with the highest outlier factors (specifically in this case, Clusters 03 and 04).

We also considered the correlation between each variable in both the unclustered group and in each individual cluster, as seen on Table 8.

In all cases, there was a stronger correlation between the DAYS_ON_MO and QTY_PATIENTS_MO variables, which makes sense, as more patients tend to correspond to a greater number of visitation dates. In this case, Cluster 03 has presents the highest score among all others. The negative correlation between the QTY_ON_DAY

Table 7. Results of multivariate clustering: means and sd

	QTY_ON_DAY		DAYS_ON_MO		QTY_PATS_MO	
	mean	*sd*	*mean*	*sd*	*mean*	*sd*
Unclustered	15.14	6.07	11.77	6.23	98.02	61.53
Cluster 1	12.81	2.16	16.05	3.08	108.37	27.06
Cluster 2	13.81	3.06	6.64	3.10	50.93	25.81
Cluster 3	30.12	9.64	8.86	4.27	127.37	65.87
Cluster 4	16.27	3.90	19.48	5.00	209.18	35.31

Table 8. Correlation matrix for clustered variables

		QTY_ON_DAY	DAYS_ON_MO
Unclustered	**QTY_ON_DAY**	1.0	-0.12
	DAYS_ON_MO	**-0.12**	1.0
	QTY_PATIENTS_MO	**0.21**	**0.71**
Cluster 1	**QTY_ON_DAY**	1.0	-0.16
	DAYS_ON_MO	**-0.16**	1.0
	QTY_PATIENTS_MO	**0.01**	**0.15**
Cluster 2	**QTY_ON_DAY**	1.0	-0.08
	DAYS_ON_MO	**-0.08**	1.0
	QTY_PATIENTS_MO	**0.03**	**0.44**
Cluster 3	**QTY_ON_DAY**	1.0	-0.09
	DAYS_ON_MO	**-0.09**	1.0
	QTY_PATIENTS_MO	**0.04**	**0.65**
Cluster 4	**QTY_ON_DAY**	1.0	-0.20
	DAYS_ON_MO	**-0.20**	1.0
	QTY_PATIENTS_MO	**0.11**	**0.35**

and DAYS_ON_MO variables suggests that the highest visitation-per-day quantities are distributed among fewer days in each month. In all cases there is a weak correlation between the QTY_ON_DAY and QTY_PATIENTS_MO variables.

Finally, the pnorm command as used in R for building a cumulative distribution function, in order to discover the probability that a mean value for a variable in Cluster 03 (with the highest QTY_ON_DAY values) could belong to (have similar parameters as those in) the other Clusters.

As seen in the above Table 9, with a mean of 30.12 visits per day, Cluster 3's QTY_ON_DAY values are very unlikely to be found in the distributions of the other clusters (whose mean and standard deviation values were listed in Table 7). However, its DAYS_ON_MO and QTY_PATIENTS_MO fit closely with Cluster 04's distribution.

Table 9. Probability matrix for clustered variables

		For each factor, probability of mean being in:	
Cluster 3	QTY_ON_DAY	~0.00%	Cluster 1
	DAYS_ON_MO	99.01%	
	QTY_PATIENTS_MO	24.12%	
	QTY_ON_DAY	~0.00%	Cluster 2
	DAYS_ON_MO	23.64%	
	QTY_PATIENTS_MO	0.15%	
	QTY_ON_DAY	~0.00%	Cluster 4
	DAYS_ON_MO	98.31%	
	QTY_PATIENTS_MO	98.97%	

9 Deployment

After evaluating the results of the cluster model, we were able to conclude that in the future, records belonging to the third and fourth clusters should be prioritized for further analysis, as they showed higher incidences of risk factors and a low probability of being mistaken for "normal" values, when compared to results from the other clusters. Based on this framework, it would be possible to create automatic system controls, which would flag any claims records in which the "quantity-per-day" variable deviated excessively from the peer group's mean values.

10 Further Works and Conclusion

Some promising results were achieved through cluster analysis, which gave us a direction for further study of the claims data, with a presumably lower risk of running into false negatives, and thus enabling a better allocation of scarce human and time resources available for auditing the suspicious claims records.

In terms of performance evaluation, the next steps would be the application of other cluster models, such as mclust[8] and pamk,[9] in order to further evaluate the data's performance with other clustering algorithms.

The model could also be improved by eliminating claims related to contractually-related visitations, where a provider would be specifically hired to service a large number of patients on the same date. This would significantly reduce the chance of false-positives in the dataset.

We also hope to use confirmed cases of abuse as starting points for a supervised approach, expanding the study to other types of procedures, such as acupuncture, speech therapy, psychotherapy, and other serial treatment procedures.

---

[8] http://cran.r-project.org/web/packages/mclust/index.html.

[9] http://cran.r-project.org/web/packages/fpc/fpc.pdf.

Another possible improvement in the model would be to compare the data at the provider level, instead of at the record level. In this case, the analysis would consider the mean values, for each provider, in each of the three variables QTY_ON_DAY, QTY_PATIENTS_MO, and DAYS_ON_MO.

One point to take into account is that not all individual records could be linked to excessive billing, even if their providers are confirmed abusers. Experience shows that it is more likely that each claim is "padded" with additional procedure quantities, instead of being fabricated wholesale. Thus, even a confirmed abusive provider might present a set of records with plausible QTY_ON_DAY values, mixed with other excessive claims records.

The base dataset could also be used for analyzing other kinds of possibly suspect billing practices, such as excessive services rendered in weekends and holidays, providers charging for services rendered to themselves (or while they were demonstrably unable to practice), medications and exams prescribed per visit, and the incidence of abuse per State or region. As we can see, the data itself is rich in possibilities, and we see some promise in building a framework for future investigations.

References

1. "IOM Report: Estimated $750B Wasted Annually In Health Care System | Kaiser Health News" (Accessed 10 Dec 2014)
2. Jans, M., Lybaert, N., Vanhoof, K.: Internal fraud risk reduction: results of a data mining case study. Int. J. Acc. Inf. Syst. **11**(1), 17–41 (2010)
3. Ortega, P.A.: A medical claim fraud/abuse detection system based on data mining: a case study in chile. In: Proceedings of the 2006 International Conference on Data Mining, DMIN 2006, June 26–29, Las Vegas, Nevada, USA (2006)
4. Musal, R.M.: Two models to investigate medicare fraud within unsupervised databases. Expert Syst. Appl. **37**(12), 8628–8633 (2010)
5. Šubelj, L., Furlan, Š., Bajec, M.: An expert system for detecting automobile insurance fraud using social network analysis. Expert Syst. Appl. **38**(1), 1039–1052 (2011)
6. Chandola, V., Sukumar, S.R., Schryver, J.C.: Knowledge discovery from massive healthcare claims data. In: Proceedings of the 19th ACM SIGKDD International Conference on Knowledge Discovery and Data Mining, New York, NY, USA, pp. 1312–1320 (2013)
7. Becker, D.J., Kessler, D.P., McClellan, M.B.: Detecting medicare abuse, Social Science Research Network, Rochester, NY, SSRN Scholarly Paper ID 579820, August 2004
8. Thornton, D., Mueller, R.M., Schoutsen, P., van Hillegersberg, J.: Predicting healthcare fraud in medicaid: a multidimensional data model and analysis techniques for fraud detection. Procedia Technol. **9**, 1252–1264 (2013)
9. Tan, P.-N., Steinbach, M., Kumar, V.: Introduction to Data Mining, 1st edn. Addison-Wesley, Boston (2005)
10. Charrad, M., Ghazzali, N., Boiteau, V., Niknafs, A.: NbClust: an R package for determining the relevant number of clusters in a data set. J. Statist. Software **61(6)**, 1–36 (2014). http://www.jstatsoft.org/v61/i06/
11. Chapman, P., Clinton, J., Kerber, R., Khabaza, T., Reinartz, T., Shearer, C., Wirth, R.: CRISP-DM 1.0 Step-by-step data mining guides (2000)

12. Liu, Q., Vasarhelyi, M.: Healthcare fraud detection: A survey and a clustering model incorporating Geo-location information. In: 29th World Continuous Auditing and Reporting Symposium (29WCARS), Brisbane, Australia (2013)
13. Olmstead, J.: Medicare Fraud and Abuse: Turn Up the HEAT. J. Nurse Pract. **8**(7), 504 (2012)
14. The Not So Short Introduction to Health Care in US", by Nainil C. Chheda, published in February 2007 (Accessed 11 Dec 2014)
15. "Medicare house calls on rise in Michigan – so is fraud. http://www.usatoday.com/story/news/nation/2014/12/01/doctor-house-calls-on-rise/17680939/. (Accessed 10 Dec 2014)
16. Physician Owned Physical Therapy Clinics – Avoiding The Impossible Day | Physicians News. http://www.physiciansnews.com/2010/12/13/physician-owned-physical-therapy-clinics-avoiding-the-impossible-day/. (Accessed 10 Dec 2014)
17. The NC Medicaid Fraud Debacle Costs Taxpayers Millions, Civitas Review. http://civitasreview.com/healthcare/the-nc-medicaid-fraud-debacle-costs-taxpayers-millions/. (Accessed 10 Dec 2014)
18. Hartigan, J.A.: Clustering algorithms. Wiley, New York (1975)

Innovative eHealth Services – PISCES Solution

Andrea Kő[1(✉)], András Gábor[2], and Zoltán Szabó[1]

[1] Corvinus University of Budapest, Budapest, Hungary
{ko, szabo}@informatika.uni-corvinus.hu
[2] Corvinno Technology Transfer Center Ltd., Budapest, Hungary
agabor@corvinno.hu

Abstract. Healthcare sector, especially in Central and Eastern European countries has to face with several challenges, like "brain drain", financing problems and fast aging population. There is a growing demand for more economic way for prevention and monitoring. At the same time Future Internet solutions offer personalized high-quality health services, this can be utilized to move far beyond traditional care. New, innovative solutions are provided, like remote health monitoring, which provide cost effective services in a relative low cost infrastructure. This paper presents PISCES, a responsive health monitoring mobile information system, which enables remote monitoring of the patients' health-status and physical performances. The goal of the PISCES solution is not only to monitor the health status of the participants, but react in any case of deficiency, as well as giving the opportunity to increase the level of the physical activities. The paper discusses PISCES pilot, which run in Hungary in 2014, as well as social, economic, security, privacy and legal perspectives of mHealth solutions.

Keywords: eHealth · mHealth · Responsive health monitoring · Future internet

1 Introduction

Total health expenditure as a share of GDP has seriously risen from 4.7 % in 1970 to about 9 % in 2014 in 28 EU countries.[1] Additionally European population is aging fast, as it is projected by UN. Europe is now and will be in 2060 the oldest continent in the world. Old-age dependency ratio (the ratio of over 65 years old to the working age population), is estimated about 49 % [26], which means that one inactive elderly will eventually be supported by 2 active people from 2060 [1].

There some areas in healthcare, which are in the focus of investigation, like cardiovascular disease. This disease is the leading global cause of death, responsible for 17.3 million deaths per year, and they estimate much higher 23.6 million deaths per year by 2030 [27].

In Europe, the leading cause of hospitalization in the elderly is chronic heart failure, which represents 1–2 % of all hospitalization. The average hospital visit in Europe due

[1] Source: OECD Health Data 2014; Eurostat Statistics Database; WHO Global Health Expenditure Database.

© Springer International Publishing Switzerland 2015
A. Kő and E. Francesconi (Eds.): EGOVIS 2015, LNCS 9265, pp. 206–219, 2015.
DOI: 10.1007/978-3-319-22389-6_15

to Congestive Heart Failure costs 10,000 Euros, based on Bundkirchen [4] report. In addition, 24 % of patients must be readmitted to the hospital within 12 weeks of discharge.

Hungarian healthcare sector has to face with similar, in some cases more serious problems. The most important ones are "brain drain" or "doctor exodus", financing problems, high rate of chronic cardiovascular diseases [31], and fast aging population. Smoking, alcohol addicts and unhealthy way of life are additional major health issues.

Central and Eastern European countries face with a challenge how to keep their highly trained health workers. As János Bélteczki, head of the Hungarian Doctors' Association told in the Guardian's interview: "every day, for six years, three doctors and two nurses have left Hungary" [28].

The share of older workers (aged 55 to 64) in the labour force (aged 20 to 64) is projected to rise by more than 50 % in Hungary compared with the 18.3 % in EU countries. It was 12,7 % in 2013 and expected to be 21,1 % in 2060.

Hungary was and still is it is in the top five countries with the highest rates of heart disease deaths in the world [29]. 49.4 % of all death in Hungary was caused by cardiovascular disease in 2013[2].

Because of the reasons above, eHealth solutions are more and more important nowadays. They simplify administrative procedures in a secure way and raise availability, reliability, accessibility and quality of health services. Studies show that due to having health history and access to this medical data, citizens can save cost and time [7, 19]. Doctors and caretakers have also access to this data which makes the treatment process faster and provide better care to patients [16].

There is a growing demand for more economical way for prevention and monitoring in healthcare, therefore new solutions are required, like remote health monitoring solutions or using smartphones and portable devices. They are providing cost effective services in a relative low cost infrastructure. Number of smart phones and other portable devices are increasing; the estimated number of them is 2 billion in 2016 [30]. These new platforms offer new and unique opportunities for healthcare services and applications and at the same time raise additional new questions, related to security, regulatory and economic environment.

This paper discusses a responsive health monitoring mobile information system called PISCES that enables remote monitoring of the patients' health-status and physical performances. The goal of the PISCES solution is not only to monitor the health status of the participants, but react in any case of deficiency, as well as providing the opportunity to increase the level of the physical activities. We deal with issues related to health monitoring like privacy, security, legal, economic and social issues. PISCES pilot run in Hungary in 2014. We discuss and analyze experiences collected during the pilot.

This paper will be structured as follows:

First, some decisive problems and challenges in the healthcare sector are discussed; then, telemonitoring related theoretical background is detailed. The following part deals

[2] Hungarian Statistical Office http://www.ksh.hu/docs/hun/xstadat/xstadat_hosszu/h_wdsd001a.html, retrieved 2015 March 22.

with social, economic, security, privacy and legal perspectives of mHealth solutions. Next we presents PISCES responsive health monitoring system. We discuss PISCES pilot, and present experiences collected. Finally, conclusion part summarizes strengths and weaknesses of PISCES with further improvement directions.[3]

2 From eHealth to mHealth – Related Work

2.1 The Concept and History of mHealth

The concept of eHealth has a relatively long history, IT supported healthcare is a common practice in many countries. The first eHealth applications concentrated on administration (storing and processing medical data in hospitals - computerized physician order entry, healthcare information systems, etc.), later clinical decision support and telemedicine solutions emerged. Recently electronic health records (countrywide patient records) facilitate the share of patient data between health service provider units. Today IT is an integrated part of health services enabling efficient procedures, improved quality, efficiency; and extending availability [3] (Fig. 1).

As a result of the technology evolution, especially the emergence of mobile technologies, eHealth solutions are being extended into mHealth applications. The widespread use of communication and online technologies provide new potential by integrating the mobile communication with eHealth services. mHealth can be defined as “the application of mobile computing, wireless communications and network technologies to deliver or enhance diverse healthcare services and functions in which the patient has a freedom to be mobile, perhaps within a limited area” [2, 23].

A key domain of mHealth services is mobile remote patient monitoring, that is based on mobile devices and wireless communication technologies, in order to measure vital signs, bio-signals of patients outside hospital environments. The widespread use of monitoring, data gathering and analyzing services becomes the part of standard health services as more and more user-friendly and effective applications are developed. According to the specific requirements monitoring and collection of data can be based on a continuous or periodic measurement method. Various bio-signals can be measured: ElectroEncephaloGram (EEG), MagnetoEncephaloGram (MEG), Galvanic Skin Response (GSR), ElectroCardioGram (ECG). Other parameters like Heart Rate Variability (HRV) can be also calculated. This approach can improve data accuracy (reduced administration errors), and improve access to health data [24].

While remote patient monitoring services are often provided by fixed communication network that can be used in home environments; mobile solutions provide much more flexibility and freedom outside home, that is closer to real-life situations (e.g. walking, commuting, etc.). There are new emerging opportunities for more data-intensive monitoring applications based on the continuous increase of bandwidth.

---

[3] PISCES – Promoting Future Internet Solutions in Health Environment (Celtic Plus CPP2011/1-3) The project is supported by the Hungarian Research and Technology Innovation Fund, (New Széchenyi Plan EUREKA_20_12-1-2012-0007).

Mobile health is typically based on smartphones interacting with various devices through Bluetooth, Wi-Fi, or through direct plug-in. Using the collected data from the sensors mHelath applications facilitate remote monitoring, or even provide analytics or suggestions. mHealth connects individuals to the backbone eHealth applications, provides healthcare access by the use of mobile devices to collect, aggregate real-time individual patient level health data, to monitor real-time the patients, and to provide direct and personalized services to the end users [23, 24].

Numerous emerging technologies, peripheral and sensor devices are integrated into mHealth applications, future internet technologies and big data based approaches can leverage the approach. Based on the Internet of Things (IoT) concept mHealth can be even more powerful and facilitate several new services. Many external information sources can be integrated to the remote monitoring data, extending the potential for analysis. The traditional reactive (symptoms-based) health care models are challenged by the new, preventive healthcare approaches. Besides improving quality of care, these online models are much cheaper than the well-known healthcare institution-based service models, and offer a switch-over from hospital-centered healthcare to a citizen-centered personalized health system. There are potential benefits resulted from time savings at the level of patients and physicians, and analyzing sector level aggregation of individual data to recognize health patterns can be a powerful tool for decision makers.

As West [23] categorized the mHealth services, there are 5 major application categories:

- Public Health Research (collection of health data via mobile networks)
- Primary Care by bridging the gap between health resources and location
- Emergency care based on personal emergency response system
- Management of Long-Term Conditions by facilitating routine diagnostics and check-ups
- Information and self-help (applications promoting wellness).

Applications are ranging from mobile-enhanced appointment booking/reminder system, drug authentication and tracking, remote diagnosis and well-being applications, to mobile telecare. Our paper is focusing on the fourth category, typically remote diagnostic tools, enhanced by sensors.

The study of Seto et al. [6] analyzed why patients and clinicians are willing to use a mobile phone-based remote monitoring system. Both groups perceived benefits, e.g. timely alerts and immediate feedback at the earliest sign of deteriorating health, and encourage the patients' self-care. The study identified also several caveats [6]:

- appropriate training of the users is necessary
- ergonomic design, the application should have to be easy to use
- it's not appropriate and usable tool for everyone (patients with poor manual dexterity or vision, patients predisposed to high anxiety)
- it must enhance and not replace relationship between patients and clinicians
- it should not results in a significant increase in workload for the physicians
- implementation costs should be low

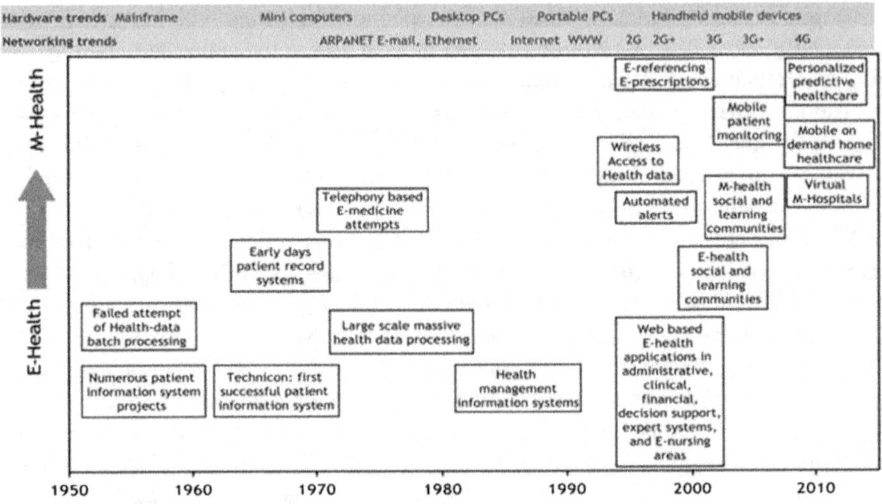

Fig. 1. Evolution from eHealth to mHealth [3]

- risks should be carefully managed, e.g. alerting algorithm would generate inappropriate alerts and instructions to the patient
- security of patient information is a key issue
- incomplete regulative/legal environment.

2.2 Social Issues and Socio Cultural Impact

From the aspect of the society mHealth offers very attractive opportunities: it helps to cut the costs of providing healthcare, it can maintain and improve the quality of care, and it can extend the scope of high quality health services to patients in underdeveloped or remote locations. On the other hand several issues and concerns can be induced by mHealth applications. Al Ameen and his colleagues discussed various aspects of mHealth like privacy, security, legal, economical psychological and political issues [8]. As a key component of mHealth applications sensor network is used for communication. This vulnerable media can cause several security threats. Many researchers [11–15] addressed this issue in their work.

Widespread use of smartphones and the growing popularity of health-related applications are major factors of the social acceptance of mHealth. In contrast with these trends there are concerns about the diagnostic inaccuracy of smartphone applications [25] that can have a negative impact on social acceptance.

The demographic trends show indeterminate growth in the proportion of people aged over 65, their number is expected to double by 2050. This trend will result in a growing need for medical care, and, in parallel the increasing demand of aged people for self sufficient life and active participation in the maintenance of their own health.

Remote patient monitoring enables patients with chronic diseases living self-sufficient life by monitoring various set of vital signs (blood pressure, heart rate, blood glucose, weight, oxygen contents, ECG), predicting aggravations of their chronic condition" [1].

One of the most important impacts is the socio cultural impact of eHealth [19]. eHealth has both positive and negative impacts of on people and on society and its cultural norms. One study [19] showed that eHealth and especially mHealth solutions can be an adequate answer to the challenges in health services of third world countries, while it may have a negative impact by eroding traditional knowledge of the society about remedies and methods.

2.3 Economic and Legal Perspective

Considering economic perspectives of any eHealth system one should explore potential benefits and compare them to the necessary huge investments. More complex mHealth applications require expensive infrastructure, and the integration with existing (core) systems will be also a costly challenge. Calculating tangible and intangible benefits of mHealth initiatives the two common signs of increased efficiency are time savings and cost avoidance. Authors of [20] compared conventional methods to remote monitoring and analyzed potential cost savings. Studies show that due to the availability of health history and access to this medical data, citizens have no need to waste money on tests again and again [7]. Patients save time spend travelling to health care centers and this allow more time for work or family [19]. Physicians and caretakers have also access to this data at the point and time of care so they can save time and provide better care to patients [16]. This study [16] also showed that it leads to amounting to 37 % of the direct benefits. In this perspective, third party payers, including insurance funds can also be saved by avoiding duplicate test and good treatment and this has been estimated as 53 % of the economic benefits.

Financial aspects of mHealth initiatives also require consideration. The cost of such systems may put an extra financial burden on the end-user patient and the operating organization. Investments and the long term operation of such systems require additional resources. Patients should buy relatively expensive smartphones that can create equity issues between different social classes and psychological problems in poor patients. Another psychological problem can be created by placing such devices in the human body and patients can feel an unwanted burden on their privacy.

Legal aspects of mHealth applications raise several questions: who guaranties the correctness of the diagnosis or recommendations, who covers the malpractice liability, who is responsible for any failures or the protection of consumer safety? Especially the privacy concerns over health data transfer on mobile networks are very challenging. Van Doornik in [25] mentioned issues related to the accuracy and unregulated status of health applications. There are thousands of health-related mobile applications with little external control. The usability of such applications also depends on the intended use and reliability of the technology. Health service providers should carefully determine the validity and limitations of the data generated with these tools.

2.4 Data Security and Privacy

Communication intensive mHealth applications involve critical information exchange that requires a number of security services to ensure reliability, confidentiality, availability and trustworthiness. In [8] authors classified the potential attacks against wireless sensor network into four major approaches: data modification, impersonation attack, eavesdropping and replaying. Security attacks are categorized into two main types; active and passive attacks. In passive attacks, the attacker can steal health data and use this data for the wrong purpose. Such attackers can also reroute the data which results change destination. An active attacker can be more harmful. Active attackers can find the location of the patient by eavesdropping and can harm the patient. Physical tempering can be made by active attackers because sensors have fewer external security features. Some attacks that can be possible in eHealth monitoring systems are mentioned in [11]; these are eavesdropping forging of alarms on medical data, location tracking, and modification in the data and jamming attacks in which attackers jam the network traffic and data of patient can't be transferred.

Meingast et al. [9] also discusses some social impact on health monitoring with respect to key challenges of data access, storage and integrity. The authors raised some questions about security of data like who owns the data is still unsettled. Many security issues are attached to this question because if just physician owns the data and insurance provider don't, then it can refuse to pay for expenses associated with collection and storage of data. Another main question arises in which circumstances data would be transferred to the third party. And if this medical data are transferred to the third party then how much risk is involved in it.

One major social unrest is patient's privacy especially in case when a patient has embarrassing disease. And due to such privacy threats, people feel hesitation to take full benefits of eHealth monitoring system. There is a fear in people that such devices may be used for monitoring and tracking people by government or private agencies [10]. The author of [10] defines social implications into three major types that are security, privacy and legal issues. In [9] author raised many questions about privacy of patients who are using eHealth monitoring systems. The question is where the medical record of the patient would be stored and without the patient's consent that should allowed to disclose this information. The author emphasized that it is necessary to answer such questions before implementing such systems. Author of [11] argued that patient's record is a private thing and usually not available to next of kin but due to lack of security the data may go into public domain straight away. Consequences of lack of privacy of such systems are also discussed. Leakage of disease record not only embarrasses the patient rather he/she can lose his/her job. The patient can also loose insurance protection [17]. Patients' privacy can be breached by any attacker and that attacker can post this information on any social site like Facebook or twitter. Especially elder persons threaten to jeopardize the use of such systems and they argue strongly against such systems on ground of privacy [18].

3 PISCES - Responsive Health Monitoring Solution

PISCES responsive health monitoring system represents a mobile information system that enables remote monitoring of the physical performances (activity recognition) and health-status of a person under given environmental condition, like air pressure, humidity, temperature, air pollution. The goal of the PISCES solution is not only to monitor the health status of the participants, but react in any case of irregularity, as well as providing the opportunity to increase the level of the physical activities.

Figure 2 shows "big interaction picture" of the PISCES system. There are three main functional areas of the system: data acquisition via mobile device and special sensors, data storage in a structured way; data processing and visualization the obtained information from the medical point of view. The main components of the system are the mobile sensing component and the server part.

The mobile sensing part includes smartphone and wearable sensors. It is collecting data about the current (level of) physical activity, vital health parameters (physiological data) and environment information. The server is responsible for data collection and integration from external sources, such as social media (e.g. Facebook and twitter), medical records of participating persons and environmental open data (e.g. weather information from the weather stations). The serves connects to the domain knowledge bases too (e.g. pattern and sensor model, context information). The PISCES system uses two CEP (Complex Event Processing) engines. One CEP engine is for the mobile device that is applied for preprocessing of the mobile sensing. The other is a distributed CEP engine that runs on the server is based on cloud computing technologies and detects more complex event patterns involving different types of events coming from environmental sensors or social web. These CEP engines are operating in a collaborative way.

Users get a direct feedback on the mobile device about the result of monitoring their health status. The main components of the PISCES system are the front end, the server side and the middleware layer. On the front end there are mobile MCA (My-CardioAdvisor, detailed in [22]) apps as mobile sensing devices and the MCA User Portal as the web-based interface to the data (real-time, past). Figure 3 shows the screenshots of the Android APP.

3.1 PISCES Pilot

PISCES solution was tested by two pilot scenes: Kelen Hospital and the Military Hospital, both in Budapest. Trial was organized between 2nd of April in 2014 and 23 of September in 2014. The Kelen Hospital is a private hospital where the majority of patients are outpatients. The patients who were selected for the pilots have chronic cardiovascular diseases, arrhythmia, and hypertensions are characteristic for them. The Military Hospital (serving both military and civil patients) is specialized on heart failure; the pilot addressed patients having heart failures. Number of trial participants was 40.

Following **participants' selection**, their customized data, like age, gender, profession, lifestyle, anamnesis, medication history and personalized alert conditions were

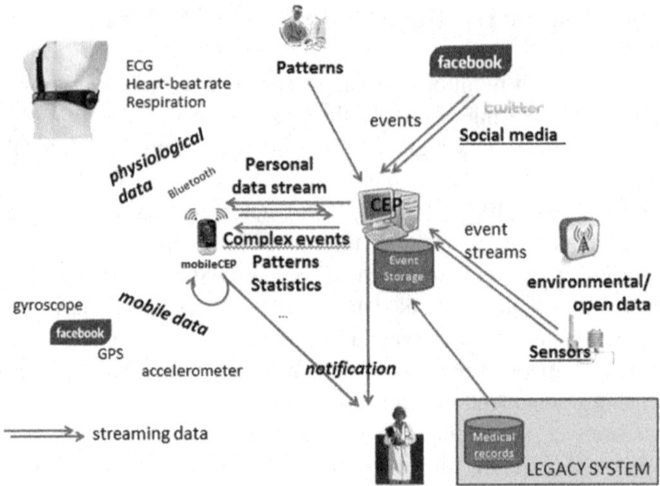

Fig. 2. Overview of the PISCES scenario (Source: [21])

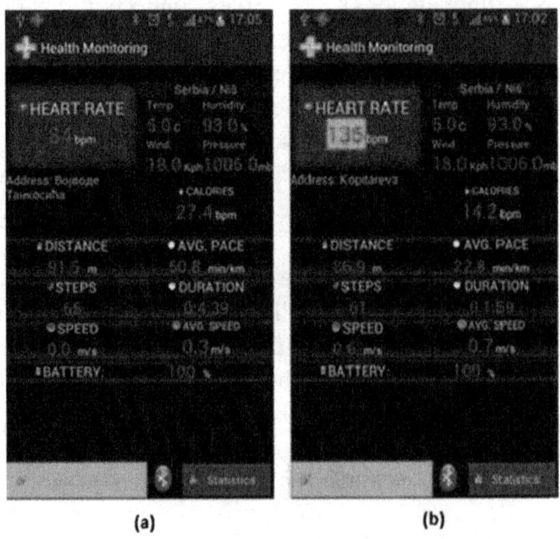

Fig. 3. The screenshots of the Android APP

recorded on PISCES portal and the mobile (Figs. 3 and 4). Two types of alerts were distinguished, intermediate and red alert. The built-in process in case of intermediate (yellow) alert give feedback to the patient in terms of therapeutic advice, in case of red alert notifies the health professionals.

Sample rule for intermediate alert is the following:

If the (blood pressure is higher than 80 Hgmm AND lower 140 Hgmm) AND activity is lowering less than 25 %, THEN Intermediate ALERT.

Sample rule for red alert is the following:

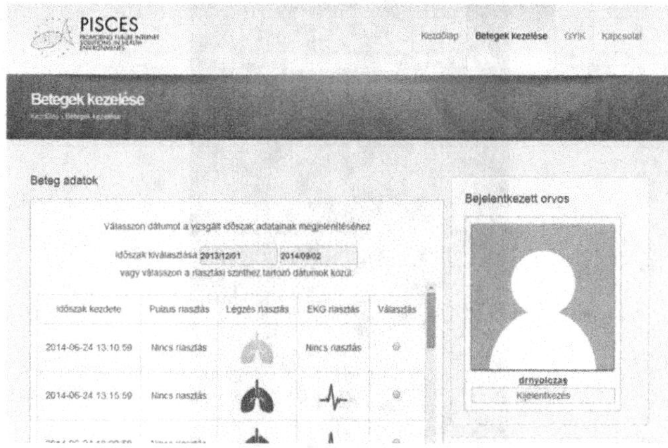

Fig. 4. PISCES portal

If the (blood pressure is higher than 80 Hgmm AND lower 140 Hgmm) AND activity is lowering more than 25 % AND the Patient's temperature is higher than 37,5° C, THEN Red ALERT (Fig. 5).

In the next phase of the trial**, patients got the sensors and mobile phones** and they were trained how to use them. The mobile application and the background service provided unique opportunity for the complex telemonitoring cardiac patients.

The following step of the trial was **data collection** (data were collected all day in every activity during the trial period). Trial participants wore sensors without interruption through one week. The upload of the data is done automatically every 8 h or when the user presses the stop button.

Data collected during the trial can be grouped as follows:

1. data measured by the sensors: ECG, respiratory and heart beat,
2. activity and localization-related data recorded by the smart phones;
3. weather condition: temperature, humidity, air pressure, wind strength
4. participants' customized data: blood pressure, weight, alcohol consumption, smoking.

Patients' mobile was sending continuously data to the PISCES server, so the doctor can monitor the patients' health status real-time. He has additional possibility for the retrospective analysis, especially in case of hardly detectable symptoms, like arrhythmia. One of the key challenges at this point is the volume of the data which has to process. Huge amount of data collected on a smart phone (15 MB data per person for 8 h of remote monitoring) is transferred to the cloud by preserving privacy and by ensuring efficiency (8 MB in 20 s).

The next phase of the trial was **data analysis and assessment.** In a case of personalized conditions are fulfilled in the rules, the mobile sends alert (intermediate or red) to the patient and/or to the doctor. One of the key features of PISCES solution is the real-time information processing in case of red alarms. In data analysis we identified, that the weather conditions and the physical activities have a significant influence

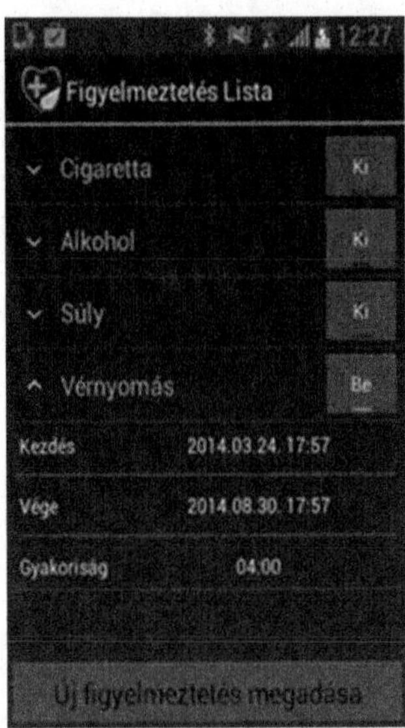

Fig. 5. Alert conditions definition in mobile

on the speed and regularity of the R-R interval (RR). We have identified a few extreme weather conditions as high or low temperature, high or low humidity and high or low pressure and reference points where the weather conditions were average. Weather factors (variables) have statistically significant impact on heart rate at 95 % confidence level. Because of the variety of data types and sources, like physiological parameters (ECG, respiratory and heart beat) environmental, off-line measured (weight, blood pressure, temperature) parameter values, there is a good opportunity for associations identifications in order to help the patients in a customized way. Patients can get feedback about their personal environmental sensitivity in terms of their health situation. When **PISCES solution is used in a day-to-day mode**, the following process phases are distinguished (Fig. 6):

In **data collection phase** sensors are continuously recording physiological parameters (ECG, respiratory and heart beat) and environmental, off-line measured (weight, blood pressure, temperature) data. In **data analysis** phase the previously mentioned data are investigated and assessed real-time. In **feedback/alert phase** according to the customized condition set reports/alerts are sent back to the patients and/or to the doctors. One of the most important added value of PISCES solution are the self-reporting functionality, the real-time information processing in case of red alarms, the widget provided for the users feedback and the automatic detection of the patient patterns. In **monitoring phase** reassessment of alert conditions are done. All parameters have to rechecked, because of the possible changes in the conditions and requirements. Pilots clearly showed that the PISCES concept is possible, practical, and viable both from technical and economic standpoint.

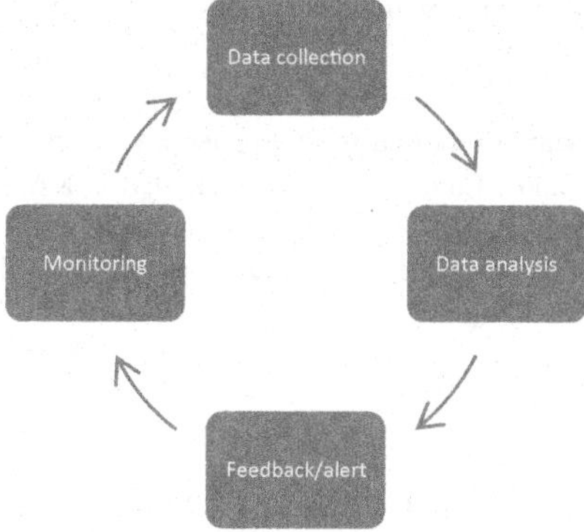

Fig. 6. PISCES in a day-to-day mode

4 Conclusion

Pilot partners from the hospital concluded that data collection and transfer by PISCES components (mobile device, sensors and the server) was done efficiently and in a reliable way. Data quality problems occurred only in a situation, when sensor was not properly put on the person's body and it moved away. During the pilot these cases were identified and filtered out. Users' experiences, feedback were analyzed as well. Some of them were not satisfied with the sensors' accumulator lifetime, which was between 4-6 h. Using smart phones for elderly people is challenging, based on their feedback the user interface was redesigned. Wearing the sensors didn't cause any difficulties for the users; even they felt themselves safer, than without the devices. One conclusion from IT aspect is that users prefer the simplified user interface. Doctors remarked that they need more complex search capability in the portal. PISCES solution can have added value in a case of patient, who has seldom cardiac arrhythmia, because users could identify those intervals when they didn't feel well themselves. PISCES solution follows a service approach using functionalities already built in the devices. It is flexible to extend the platform to other sensors and applications. The added value of the solution comes from the self-reporting functionality, the real-time information processing in case of red alarms, the widget that provides for the users feedback in case of yellow alert, and the automatic detection of the patient patterns. PISCES is also about extending the processing power by using semantics and giving meaning to the data, crossing it also with big data that bring contextual information. The pilot proved that PISCES solution provides effective and efficient technical support to collect real-time physiological data in connection data regarding the environment. It evaluates the data on-the-fly and sends alerts (yellow or red) to the patient and/or to the doctor. This experiment helps to utilize PISCES solution in operational telemonitoring, can reduce patients' physical examinations, it can increase quality of life and can decrease the cost of these patients' treatment. Future work includes additional pilots to improve PISCES capabilities. A possible future research direction is to investigate the application of formal frameworks and methods [32, 33] to analyze PISCES architecture in order to make it more efficient. PISCES system justified how the Future Internet and semantics can be used to provide customized health services, improving prevention and management in healthcare services.

Acknowledgement. The research reported in this paper was supported by PISCES-Promoting Future Internet Solution Health Environment project (EUREKA_HU_12-1-2012-0007), in cooperation with the Corvinno Technology Transfer Center. Special thanks goes to Dr. Nenad Stojanovic for guiding and mentoring the system development and pilot.

References

1. Abadie, F., Codagnone, C., van Lieshout, M., Pascu, C., Baum, P., Hoikkanen, A., Valverde, J.A., Maghiros, I.: Strategic Intelligence Monitor on Personal Health Systems (SIMPHS) Market Structure and Innovation Dynamics. European Commission Joint Research Centre, Institute for Prospective Technological Studies (2011). http://ipts.jrc.ec.europa.eu. (ISBN 978-92-79-18947-0)
2. Pawar, P., Jones, V., Van Beijnum, B.J.F., Hermens, H.: A framework for the comparison of mobile patient monitoring systems. J. Biomed. Inform. **45**(3), 544–556 (2012)
3. Tan, J. (ed.): E-health care information systems: an introduction for students and professionals. Wiley, Chichester (2005)
4. Bundkirchen, A., Schwinger, R.H.: Epidemiology and economic burden of chronic heart failure. Eur. Heart J. Suppl. 6(suppl. D), D57–D60 (2004)
5. Patel, S., Park, H., Bonato, P., Chan, L., Rodgers, M.: A review of wearable sensors and systems with application in rehabilitation. J. Neuroeng. Rehabil. **9**(1), 21 (2012)
6. Seto, E., Leonard, K.J., Masino, C., Cafazzo, J.A., Barnsley, J., Ross, H.J.: Attitudes of heart failure patients and health care providers towards mobile phone-based remote monitoring. J. Med. Internet Res. 12(4), e55 (2010)
7. Klersy, C., De Silvestri, A., Gabutti, G., Raisaro, A., Curti, M., Regoli, F., Auricchio, A.: Economic impact of remote patient monitoring: an integrated economic model derived from a meta-analysis of randomized controlled trials in heart failure. Eur. J. Heart Fail. **13**(4), 450–459 (2011)
8. Al Ameen, M., Kwak, K.S.: Social issues in wireless sensor networks with healthcare perspective. Int. Arab J. Inf. Technol. **8**(1), 52–58 (2011)
9. Meingast, M., Roosta, T., Sastry, S.: Security and privacy issues with health care information technology. In: 28th Annual International Conference of the IEEE Engineering in Medicine and Biology Society, EMBS 2006, August 30–September 3, pp. 5453–5458 (2006)
10. Hanna, L., Hailes, S.: Privacy and Wireless Sensor networks. University College, London (2010)
11. Kargl, F., Lawrence, E., Fischer, M., Lim, Y.Y.: Security, privacy and legal issues in pervasive ehealth monitoring systems. In: 7th International Conference on Mobile Business, ICMB 2008, pp. 296–304. IEEE (2008)
12. Meingast, M., Roosta, T., Sastry, S.: Security and privacy issues with health care information technology. In: 28th Annual International Conference of the IEEE Engineering in Medicine and Biology Society, EMBS 2006, pp. 5453–5458. IEEE (2006)
13. Ng, H.S., Sim, M.L., Tan, C.M.: Security issues of wireless sensor networks in healthcare applications. BT Technol. J. **24**(2), 138–144 (2006)
14. Wang, Y., Attebury, G., Ramamurthy, B.: A survey of security issues in wireless sensor networks. IEEE Commun. Surv. Tutorials **8**(2), 2–23 (2006)

15. Zia, T., Zomaya, A.: Security issues in wireless sensor networks. In: International Conference on Systems and Networks Communications, ICSNC 2006, p. 40. IEEE (2006)
16. Stroetmann, K.A., Jones, T., Dobrev, A., Stroetmann, V.N.: eHealth is Worth it. The economic benefits of implemented eHealth solutions at ten European sites. Published by the European Commission(2006). http://ec.europa.eu/information_society/activities/health/docs/publications/eHealthimpactsept2006.pdf. (last checked on 25 2010)
17. Kumar, P., Lee, H.J.: Security issues in healthcare applications using wireless medical sensor networks: A survey. Sensors **12**(1), 55–91 (2011)
18. Rigby, M.: Applying emergent ubiquitous technologies in health: The need to respond to new challenges of opportunity, expectation, and responsibility. Int. J. Med. Inform. **76**, S349–S352 (2007)
19. Hunter, J., Scott, R.E.: Considering the socio-cultural impact of E-health. In: Global Telehealth: Selected Papers from Global Telehealth 2010 (GT 2010): 15th International Conference of the International Society for Telemedicine and EHealth and 1st National Conference of the Australasian Telehealth Society, vol. 161, p. 77. IOS Press (2010)
20. Lee, S.I., Ghasemzadeh, H., Mortazavi, B., Lan, M., Alshurafa, N., Ong, M., Sarrafzadeh, M.: Remote patient monitoring: what impact can data analytics have on cost? In: Wireless Health, p. 4 (2013)
21. Gábor A.: "PISCES – Responsive Remote eHealth". In: Proceedings of 8th International Conference on Software, Knowledge, Information Management and Applications, Paper id. 199 (2014)
22. Gábor A., Tóth G., Stojanovic N., Megyesi C.S.: "D 4.1 Scenario Architecture and Component Specification", PISCES deliverable (2014)
23. West, K.L.: mHealth: A Comprehensive and Contemporary Look at Emerging Technologies in Mobile Health (2014)
24. mHealth: New horizons for health through mobile technologies: second global survey on eHealth. World Health Organization. http://www.who.int/goe/publications/goe_mhealth_web.pdf (retrieved 22 March 2015) (ISBN 978 92 4 156425 0)
25. Wolf, J.A., Moreau, J.F., Akilov, O., Patton, T., English, J.C., Ho, J., Ferris, L.K.: Diagnostic inaccuracy of smartphone applications for melanoma detection. JAMA Dermatol. **149**(4), 422–426 (2013)
26. European Commission: The 2015 Ageing Report (2015). (ISSN 0379-0991)
27. Go, A.S., Mozaffarian, D., Roger, V.L., Benjamin, E.J., Berry, J.D., Borden, W.B., Turner, M.B.: On behalf of the American Heart Association Statistics Committee and Stroke Statistics Subcommittee. Heart disease and stroke statistics — 2013 update: a report from the American Heart Association. Circulation, 127(1), e1–e240 (2013)
28. Nolan, D.: NHS hiring drive hurts Hungary but India can cope with doctor exodus, in: The Guardian (2015). http://www.theguardian.com/society/2015/jan/28/-sp-hungary-india-doctors-nhs-recruitment-drive-effect
29. Whitbourne, S.K., Martin, J. (eds.): The Wiley-Blackwell handbook of adulthood and aging, vol. 40. Wiley New York (2011)
30. 2 Billion Consumers Worldwide to Get Smart(phones) by 2016. http://www.emarketer.com
31. Maier, R.: Heart Disease Statistics (2014). http://www.healthline.com/health/heart-disease/statistics#1
32. Molnár, B., Benczúr, A.: Facet of modeling web information systems from a document-centric view. Int. J. Web Portals (IJWP) **5(4)**, 57–70 (2013). IGI Global
33. Molnár, B.: Applications of hypergraphs in informatics: a survey and opportunities for research. Annales universitatis scientiarum budapestinensis de rolando eotvos nominatae sectio computatorica **42**, 261–282 (2014)

Predictive Models on Tax Refund Claims - Essays of Data Mining in Brazilian Tax Administration

Leon Sólon da Silva[1,2(✉)], Rommel Novaes Carvalho[1,3], and João Carlos Felix Souza[1]

[1] University of Brasilia - UnB, Brasília DF, Brazil
leon.silva@receita.fazenda.gov.br
[2] Secretariat of Federal Revenue of Brazil-RFB, Brasilia, Brazil
rommel.carvalho@cgu.gov.br
[3] Office of the Comptroller General - CGU, Brasilia, Brazil
jocafs@unb.br

Abstract. One of the main goals of every tax administration is safeguarding tax justice. For that matter, accurate taxpayers' auditing selection plays an important role. Current scenario of economic recession, budget cuts and tax professionals' hiring difficulty combined with growth of both population and number of enterprises presents the necessity of a more efficiently approach from tax administration in order to meet its objectives. The present work intends to show how data mining techniques usage helps better understand the profile of non compliant tax payers who claim for tax refunds. Moreover, we present results on the adoption of predictive models towards selection improvement of those who claims that are more likely to be rejected in Federal Revenue of Brazil (RFB). Preliminary results shows that this approach is an efficient way for selecting tax payers rather than not using it.

Keywords: Tax compliance risk · Tax refund · Data mining · Predictive models

1 Introduction

Before the advent of statistical techniques and information technology tools, tax administrations were likely to dispose random taxpayers selections or even select taxpayers out of those who have never been audited before aiming to reduce tax compliance risk.

The latest 1990 s and early 2000 s brought a significant increase in number of taxpayers and information provided by them to tax authorities (tax returns). In Brazil, since 1991, tax returns for income tax has become electronic. Significant growth of such returns were evident from 1996 on, reaching more than 30 million returns in 2014 [2]. Besides the increment of information gathered from taxpayers, financial crisis and budget constraints pushed the tax administrations

© Springer International Publishing Switzerland 2015
A. Kő and E. Francesconi (Eds.): EGOVIS 2015, LNCS 9265, pp. 220–228, 2015.
DOI: 10.1007/978-3-319-22389-6_16

to make a better and efficient selection of taxpayers and work on those who have higher risk on noncompliance. The Brazilian Tax Administration (and Customs) is the Secretariat of Federal Revenue of Brazil – RFB.

Companies and individuals have different ways of using its credit with the tax administration. It can ask for reimbursement or it can be use to cancel a debit of the same or other federal tax. The former way of using the credit is called compensation and is of more interest of taxpayers since its less bureaucratic than having the credit back (reimbursement). This characteristic leaded to a great amount of compensation claims as the number of companies has grown in recent decades to over 16 million in 2013 [1]. To request the compensation the individual or company must complete an application using a program called PER/DCOMP program (Electronic Order of Restitution/Compensation, Reimbursement and Compensation Statement).

The requests are processed by the Credit Control System (SCC), an application developed by the Data Processing Service (Serpro) - a government information technology enterprise. SCC analyzes tax refund claims (compensation requests) and based on taxpayers characteristics, credit information and tax compliance risks can automatically accept or reject compensation or classifies the compensation claims for manual analysis of tax auditors. With the growth in the number of compensation claims, the queue of processes that are separated for manual analysis also increased. Many offices cannot afford analyzing all processes and may select in ways that are not always the most effective in terms of tax compliance risks. Thus, this study aims to analyze variables and characteristics of taxpayers using statistical tools to define which has a greater impact on the decision to reject tax credit's compensation claims. Knowing taxpayers' characteristics, we came up with predictive models using different techniques of data mining and obtained interesting results that can later be compared to the efficiency of current selection process.

In the following sections we present the related work done by other tax administrations, the methodology used in this work with the phases of the CRISP-DM model, the preliminary results, conclusion and future work.

2 Related Work

Many tax administrations have used data mining tools to reduce the risk of noncompliance with tax obligations (tax compliance risk). Despite being a topic of great interest, it is perceived that many works are not presented at conferences and are restricted to publications of government. One reason may be the difficulty in presenting the results of applying mining techniques in tax matters given that information and results are confidential in most cases.

A great source of such information, case studies, methodologies and best practices are intergovernmental organizations. For tax administrations and customs the World Customs Organization (WCO) and the Organization for Economic Cooperation and Development (OECD) are important sources. In a recent survey that gathered many countries OECD presented a comparative chart that shows the use of data mining to detect tax fraud.

Tax Administration's internal publications also presents many studies that can be applied by other countries and many of them have developed methodologies based on statistical analysis and data mining to create tax compliance risk systems. Most countries use data mining for taxpayers' classification considering its risks of non-compliance.

Our research found work related to fraud accessing tax evasion and tax avoidance, but could not find work with direct correlation to ours, that is, approaching tax refund. This does not mean that the other tax administrations are not using statistical and data mining techniques to help selecting most risky tax refund claims, but we did not find studies that address the problem directly.

The references that are closer to this work are presented as the OECD study results. Tax administration of the United States of America (Internal Revenue Service - IRS) uses data mining for different purposes, according to [3], among which are taxpayer classification due to its non-compliance risk, tax fraud detection, tax refund fraud, criminal activities and money laundering [5]. Thus, the IRS conducts work with data mining to improve the selection of tax refund claims, but OECD cites the work as a result of questionnaires and visits to perform in countries consulted and not as a reference to scientific publications addressing the matter.

Another related reference is Jani Martikainen's master thesis [4]. He presents results of studies conducted by Australian tax administration (Australian Taxation Office - ATO) concerning the usage of models to detect high-risk tax refund claims. Also according to the author, the ATO avoided the payment of refunds of about US$ 665,000,000.00 between 2010 and 2011 based on data mining tools. As we can learn from this work, the methods used by the Australian administration, while addressing the same problems and aiming the same goal, differs from our work. The ATO uses refund models based on social networking discovery algorithms that detects connection between individuals, companies, partnerships or tax returns. The models are updated and refined to enhance detection and increase the recognition of new fraud [4].

3 Methodology

The methodology of this work is based on data mining industry standard as known as the Cross Industry Standard Process for Data Mining (CRISP-DM). The standard sets out steps that must be followed to perform any data mining work, so as not to underestimate any of it and ensure that the possible outcomes are valid and practical. The following sections presents each of these steps and how they were implemented on this project. Particularly, by the use of logistic regression we analyze the most statistically valid and important attributes of taxpayers as well as tax compensation claims' information on whether it is accepted or rejected. From taxpayers' characteristics analysis, some attributes were chosen to create predictive models using different data mining techniques.

4 Business Understanding

The main objective on Secretariat of Federal Revenue of Brazil's business perspective is to reduce the risks of not designate compensation claims with a greater chance of being rejected such as taxpayers' errors or fraud, for a manual analysis. A major advantage of tax administrations is its high concentration of information on taxpayers, due to tax returns sent by them as well as collected from the results of auditors' analysis on previous tax refund claims. Based on both sources of information we try to extract knowledge from databases so we may answer the two main questions derived from the aforementioned objective:

- 1 - What are taxpayers main characteristics and tax refund claims' information in order to determine if the request will be accepted or rejected?
- 2 - For not yet analyzed tax refund claims, how to predict if one will be accepted or rejected?

Many other questions can be answered using data mining techniques, such as detecting taxpayers groups carrying out certain type of fraud, or the analysis of automatic tax refund acceptance claims to check possible fraud that go unnoticed. In this study, however, we focus on questions 1 and 2 as stated. Each question's answer will bring value to Secretariat of Federal Revenue of Brazil since the first may derive new controls and legislation, while the second may help selecting those compensation claims that are more likely to be rejected.

An important feature of business which increased the complexity in understanding and preparing the data as we shall see in the following sections is that a taxpayer may claim many compensations as would like regarding a single credit, and each claim has a response from the tax authorities. For example, it may request credit of an income tax that it was paid above the due value and then use it several times to cancel tax debts on previous value added taxes (VAT). Thus, analysis of the requests can not be made for all claims at once, so, for the present work, we must unite all requests from the same credit in what we call "families". The acceptance or rejection of analyzed claims will therefore be due for families of PER/DCOMP statements.

5 Data Understanding

Taxpayers characteristics, credits and compensation claims information are in databases and systems of different information technology architectures (Sotftware AG Adabas, Oracle, MySQL and many more). Some information though, were easier to recover since they're available through data marts, each of which with a different dimension of taxpayers.

Several credit and compensation claims attributes were gathered from interviews with tax refund experts in order to not leave any important taxpayer characteristics out of the analysis. In addition to the tax credit information we aggregated taxpayers information available from different tax returns. For this initial study, we extracted information from taxpayers' compensation claims under the jurisdiction of the 1st Tax Region of Federal Revenue of Brazil, covering 5 (five) Federal Units (Federal District, Goias, Mato Grosso, Mato Grosso do Sul and Tocantins). The information extraction was performed by Internal Revenue Service of Brazil's available softwares - from systems developed by tax auditors to open source applications (such as R Project).

Certain decisions where made in order to extract only the necessary data to perform the analysis. All manually analyzed compensation claims were selected from 2002 to 2014. The origin of the credit may vary, from paying debits above the due value (taxpayer or bank error) to tax exemption compensatory rights. During our analysis we did not discriminate the compensation claims by its origin. The initial extraction contained about 18,000 compensation claims' families and included both manually analyzed requests as well as Credit Control System's automatically processed claims. The following section describes how we prepared the data for further analysis in order to answer business questions.

6 Data Preparation

After initial extraction we had to clean and select compensation claim and taxpayer characteristics data. All data were treated using the statistical and data mining software R (R Project). Some basic treatments were carried out to allow the usage of data on variables analysis and to create predictive models, including:

- Accents removal
- Little or null information's entries removal
- Data type transformation

As mentioned, the data collected were performed both manually or automatically. Considering that the aim is to improve selection of processes to be worked by tax auditor one by one, we removed those families who had application accepted/rejected automatically, leaving only those that had human intervention. An important decision that led back to the understanding of the business and the data was the cut-off point to determine if a family of compensation was rejected or not.

Given that, we developed a join of all compensation requests from the same credit, some of these may have been deferred (the compensation was accepted) and rejected. The analysis may change for each parameter accepted limit, which leads us to an arbitrary decision to consider over 40.

Of all compensation claim attributes and taxpayer characteristics eight (8) were chosen to start the analysis. First we selected using these attributes to test its statistical significance in order to classify the claim as accepted or rejected. Due to taxpayers' confidentiality characteristics as well as to safeguard exposure, selected data can not be presented.

7 Modeling

During modeling stage we started answering listed questions on the business understanding phase. First, we performed an analysis to determine which of the many attributes of compensation claims and taxpayers' characteristics were statistically important to decide if a request is accepted or rejected. That was done using logistic regression with the dependent variable being accepted/rejected. After the statistics analysis we built predictive models using those variables under logistic regression (this time for prediction), Naive Bayes and Random Forests algorithms.

7.1 Attributes Analysis

After data preparation we worked on the compensation claims and taxpayers' characteristics aiming to understand which are statistically more important to classify a family of compensation as accepted or rejected. This information was extracted from the data which has the families of the eight (8) selected attributes and a ninth one indicating if the family was accepted or rejected (above and below 40.

7.2 Predictive Models

Based upon the analysis of the most important variables, we built predictive models in order to improve the selection of tax compensation claims. The algorithms chosen were logistic regression (not to explain, but to create a predictive model), the Naive Bayes algorithm and Random Forests. The compensation claims families data were separated into two, one for training and other to perform tests in the proportion 80 to 20 %. To ensure a good choice of parameters for each algorithm, and to dispose the need of a validation base, we used the well known technique of cross-validation, which enables the same database for both training and validation. We use a cross-validation of 10 different basic settings (10 fold cross-validation). After each training algorithm, the results were compared to the test base. In all cases confusion matrices were generated and also calculated the sensitivity, specificity, accuracy, f-measure and the ROC curve. The results of the confusion matrices are presented in Tables 1, 2 and 3. The specificity, accuracy, sensitivity and f-measure are shown in Table 4.

Table 1. Confusion matrix - naive bayes

		Reference	
		Accept	Reject
Prediction	Accept	545	234
	Reject	239	541

For the three predictive models we built the ROC curve to help analysis and comparison of the models in the evaluation phase. Figures 1, 2 and 3 present the ROC curve for the Naive Bayes models, logistic regression, random forests, respectively.

Table 2. Confusion matrix - logistic regression

		Reference	
		Accept	Reject
Prediction	Accept	443	171
	Reject	341	604

Table 3. Confusion matrix - random forests

		Reference	
		Accept	Reject
Prediction	Accept	545	234
	Reject	239	541

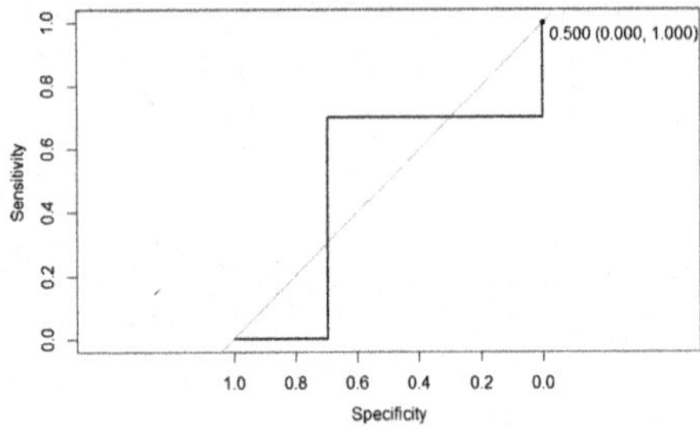

Fig. 1. ROC curve - naive bayes.

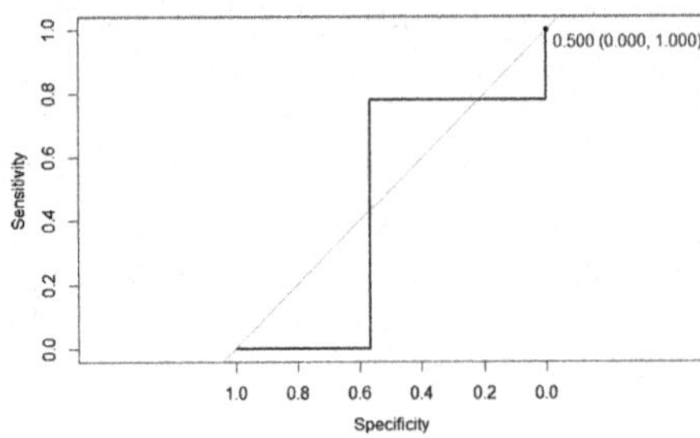

Fig. 2. ROC curve - logistic regression

8 Evaluation

Logistic regression arised as a great tool to understand the most important variables. It can be used to select attributes to build predictive models. We performed some tests with all eight (8) initial variables and the results for the three algorithms of predictive models did not exceed 0.53 of accuracy. With the variables selected with the regression, the best model for accuracy showed 0.69 (Naive Bayes) and the best for f-score (f-measure) of 0.70 (Random Forests). Thus, the

Table 4. Predictive models's results

	Accuracy	Specif	Sensib	F-measure
Naive Bayes	0.6966	0.6981	0.6952	0.6973
Logistic Regression	0.6716	0.7794	0.5651	0.6337
Random Forests	0.6857	0.6194	0.7513	0.7062

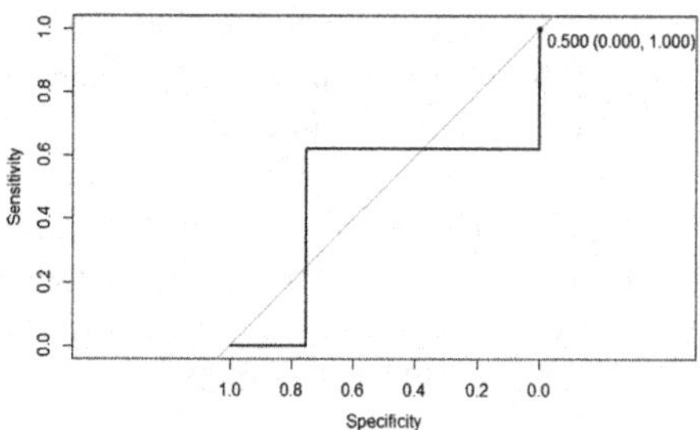

Fig. 3. ROC curve - random forests

choice of selecting the variables before creating predictive models proved to be an important practice in inference rejection of compensation processes.

Predictive models of the three algorithms had a very similar performance with little advantage to Naive Bayes if we consider accuracy. Logistic regression and random forests were better in terms of sensitivity and f-measure. For tax administration business, however, the mistakes in prediction cost differently. It's better to predict a claim will be rejected and turn out to be accepted than the other way around. An actual accepted claim predicted as rejected will cost some time for the tax auditor, but a claim that should be rejected predicted as accepted will not be selected for audit. The former could lead to fraud claims to never be worked by tax auditors. The f-measure aids in this analysis, but gives the same weight to both mistakes, accepted and rejected. In this aspect, the model that uses the Random Forests algorithm is the most appropriate, given that the prediction of negative number is 0.71, up from 0.63 logistic regression and 0.69 of Naive Bayes algorithm.

A prediction of more than 70 % of compensation claims that should be rejected is very promising for business at first sight. Many tax auditors analyze a huge amount of claims manually, and most part of them are accepted, in other words, with the right predictive model, many of those claims could be processed automatically. This work presented thus interesting results that respond well to the understanding of business' issues and should be applied in near future by Secretariat of Federal Revenue of Brazil in the selecting claims for manual analysis.

9 Future Work

The base used in this study was restricted to a tax region, which can skew the results of predictive models, not only by taxpayer's characteristics the region, but also by a small number of tax refund claims. A first step, therefore, would be gathering compensation claims and taxpayer information nationwide, or at least as large as the 8th tax region which includes the federal unit of Sao Paulo - concentrates almost 50 % of non-individuals taxpayers, for example.

One interesting inquiry regards the analysis of variables that influence compensation claims for each type of previous credit. Income tax characteristics are much different than value added taxes. Taking into account the fact that tax characteristics are distinct, there is a good chance that treatment of its attributes are also diverse. Therefore it is feasible that those singularities may affect its acception or rejection. Variables that did not show any significance processing the whole database can be statistically relevant for different types of credit. Given the facility of creating predictive models using different algorithms, we must use other data mining tools in order to achieve better prediction's results. Subsequently to current analysis, and pending on analogous conclusions, in the near future, we intent to select several other offices to verify the selection based on the predictive models.

References

1. Brazilian institute of statistics and geography tax administration and customs website - ferederal revenue of brazil. http://www.ibge.gov.br. Accessed: 09 December 2014
2. Brazilian tax administration and customs website - ferederal revenue of brazil. http://www.receita.fazenda.gov.br. Accessed: 09 December 2014
3. González, P.C., Velásquez, J.D.: Characterization and detection of taxpayers with false invoices using data mining techniques. Expert Syst. Appl. **40**(5), 1427–1436 (2013)
4. Martikainen, J., et al.: Data Mining in Tax Administration-Using Analytics to Enhance Tax Compliance. Department of Information and Service Economy, Aalto University, Espoo (2012)
5. Watkins, R.C., Reynolds, K.M., Demara, R., Georgiopoulos, M., Gonzalez, A., Eaglin, R.: Tracking dirty proceeds: exploring data mining technologies as tools to investigate money laundering. Police Pract. Res. **4**(2), 163–178 (2003)

Intelligent Systems in E-Government II

Dynamic Skill Gap Analysis Using Ontology Matching

Ildikó Szabó[1(✉)] and Gábor Neusch[2]

[1] Department of Information Systems, Corvinus University of Budapest, Fővám Tér 13-15, Budapest 1093, Hungary
iszabo@informatika.uni-corvinus.hu
[2] Corvinno Technology Transfer Center, Közraktár 12/A, Budapest 1093, Hungary
gneusch@corvinno.hu

Abstract. Different sources (best practices, rules and customer requirements) can trigger the need for adapting changes into organizational processes. This paper presents an ontology-based matching process and architecture that can be used to discover discrepancies and similarities between actual and required operation in that the latter is detecting by processing dynamically varying documents. The SMART system was elaborated to investigate the compliance between job market expectations and educational offers. This system is a use case of this architecture.

Keywords: Skill gap · Ontology matching · Education

1 Introduction

Dynamically changing environment should be monitored by flexible organizations. These changes touch different aspects of an organization. If standards, rules are modifying, the enterprise should vary its business processes. Requirements of customers should be monitored permanently to develop new products. These problem areas need to extract required knowledge from relevant documents continually and use them to match the actual status with the required status of organizations. This paper shows a matching architecture and its processes that are capable of processing documents, creating an ontology-based model of required status and actual status and matching these two statuses with each other. The input of this architecture can be domain or process ontologies as well. This paper focuses on domain ontologies.

The system using this matching architecture provides two ontologies for representing each status, having tailored a given ontology (domain ontology) in the light of the contents about actual or required status. The same domain ontology is tailored hence it is not needed to investigate semantic similarities between concepts from ontologies, only to execute structural comparison. Based on the input sources, this system can be customized for goals of business process management [11, 19] and for executing skill gap analysis between the demand and supply side of labor market.

© Springer International Publishing Switzerland 2015
A. Kő and E. Francesconi (Eds.): EGOVIS 2015, LNCS 9265, pp. 231–242, 2015.
DOI: 10.1007/978-3-319-22389-6_17

The relationship between supply and demand of labor market is changing dynamically. The economic growth, among other things, is influenced by investments. A country can attract investments if it ensures a well-qualified workforce, well-built infrastructure, legal certainty etc. The education has a role to provide the structure of qualification satisfied the needs of labor market. But the needs are changing, because the companies want to gain competitive advantage from technology novelties or economic environment. These influences make the relationship dynamic that the supply side just follows with great lead time, because the students are qualified in three-year or five-year qualification cycles. So this raises a question what competences have to be possessed by graduates for starting works right now or for adapting to a new environment.

Several EU initiatives – including the Key Competence Framework, the European Qualifications Framework, the general policy framework for European cooperation in education and training and the initiative New Skills for New Jobs - was launched with the aim of filling skill gap between the two sides of labor market. The initiative New Skill for New Jobs "is intended to promote an improvement in skills forecasting and matching the supply of skills to the needs of the labor market through better cooperation between the worlds of work and education." [15]

CEDEFOP, the European vocational education development center has elaborated a methodological framework that aims at determining discrepancies between supply and demand sides of labor market regarding practical abilities by employing predictive models [6]

The strategy of *vocational education and training* declared by European Ministers for VET, the European Social Partners and the European Commission contains the main guidelines for bridging the gap between both sides of labor market. It contains the next actions:

- cooperation with the relevant stakeholders – representatives of professional sectors, social partners, relevant civil society organizations, and education and training providers – "to review occupational and education/training standard which define what is to be expected from the holder of a certificate or diploma".
- adjusting VET content, infrastructure and methods regularly to new production technologies and work organization in order to keep pace with them.
- considering green economy as mega trend in affecting skill needs across many different jobs and sectors [2].

The directives of the European Higher Education Area call for the competence-base structuring of contents of education programs, moreover tendencies on the demand-side of the labor market can be observed that aim the description of job offerings similarly, on the basis of competences. Significance of an ontology-based system in this case can be measured most importantly in ensuring a common ground for the different viewpoints as well as tracking changes. The applicability of ontology-based approach on this field was investigated by the SAKE project too [10].

The goal of this paper is to show a system using the above-mentioned matching architecture which is capable of mapping the similarity and discrepancies between the two sides of labor market in regard of qualification. This system was implemented under the aegis of the SMART project.[1]

The SMART project aimed to balance the two sides of the labor market in the Andalusia region that has a high ratio of unemployment while showing signs of over-qualification. It is a good selection for presenting a use case of this architecture.

The first section gives an overview about the ontology matching domain. The second section presents the matching architecture. The third section shows the implemented system during the SMART project [5].

2 Ontology Matching

Ontology mapping defined by Su [18] means that "for each concept (node) in ontology A, try to find a corresponding concept (node), which has same or similar semantics, in ontology B and vice verse." Defining semantic relationships between two concepts and an algorithm needs to reveal these correspondences and related concepts, resulting set of mapping rules.

Kalfoglou and Schorlemmer defined ontology mapping based on logical theories. They considered ontologies as "a pair O = (S,A), where S is the (ontological) signature, and A is a set of (ontological) axioms – specifying the intended interpretation of the vocabulary in some domain of discourse." Ontological signature is a mathematical modeling tool to describe ontologies with a hierarchy of concept or class symbols modelled as a partial ordered set. Morphisms (structure-preserving mappings between mathematical structures) are used to define total ontology mapping from ha O1 = (S1, A1) to O2 = (S2,A2) [13].

We could follow different ways – calculating similarity measure or finding morphism – to formalize ontology mapping. Frameworks, methods, tools and case studies can help to understand this domain, and to elaborate a method to match two ontologies with each other in regard of knowledge as competence element. Kalfoglou and Schorlemmer [13] gave an overview about this domain broadly, but other approaches can be interesting and relevant as well [7–9, 16].

This research concerned on finding structural correspondences between two ontologies in dynamic manner. Main functional requirements for this system were to process documents, create tailored ontologies based on them and matching these ontologies with each other without any human intervention. It had to handle changing mapped into the ontologies dynamically and be integrated with other programs (e.g. download programs), if it was needed. Based on this requirements, the following selection criteria were determined to choose an appropriate ontology matching tool.

- ontology matching is achieved in dynamic manner:
  - automatic, semi-automatic or non-automatic working: the level of human intervention
  - the handling of changes occurred in the ontology

[1] SMART project (Skill MAtching for Regional deyelopment-2012-1-ES1-LEO05-49395) LLP Leonardo da Vinci program. www.smart-project.org.

- reusability:
  - usage of different ontology format in matching process
  - type of matching method
  - support for modularity, integration with other systems

Full examination is written in [1]. Compare Ontologies was chosen because it is a built-in function of Protégé ontology development environment, hence it can handle different ontology formats and changes in the ontologies. Due to its free downloadable source code through SVN, its modification or integration were realizable. Its disadvantage is that it is not capable of discovering same concepts with different names. Hence it was used as engine of matching process in the next architecture.

3 System Architecture

The main component of this system is the Studio system that is a competence-based e-learning environment which "provides support in exploring missing knowledge areas of users in the frames of an ontology driven e-learning environment in order to help them to complement their educational deficiencies" [17]. It contains several domain ontologies shaped as one big ontology, related to different domains (e.g. tourism, managing business, information technology etc.). Educational Ontology as a graph represents the skeleton of these domain ontologies. < Knowledge area > , < Basic concept > , < Theorem > and <Example> classes serve as a basis to map the knowledge used in human thinking. The meta-model reflects the hierarchy of knowledge areas by using relations called "has_part" and "has_subknowledge_area". It orders the knowledge elements into a cognitive sequence too by using relations called "required_knowledge_of", "premise", "conclusion" and "refers_to". The detailed description was presented by Vas [21]. These elements can be grouped into concept groups which are used as abstract concepts reflecting the classifying principles. Concept groups can be considered as tasks if knowledge elements of domain ontologies are grouped from the viewpoint of process management or as competences if the knowledge elements are classified by educational viewpoints. These concept groups are used to split the domain ontology into small parts (Fig. 1).

3.1 Processing Input Contents

This matching architecture can provide different cutting principles, depending on the external documents monitored permanently. Mostly these are unstructured documents, but they can be process models as well.

3.1.1 Process Models

Process models have to be preprocessed before using them to tailor the appropriate domain ontology. A preprocessing algorithm was elaborated during the ProKEX project[2] [16]. XSLT transformation facilitates to create process ontologies from process

[2] ProKEX project: Integrated Platform for Process-based Knowledge Extraction. EUREKA Proj. No.: EUREKA_HU_12-1-2012-0039. http://prokex.netpositive.hu/.

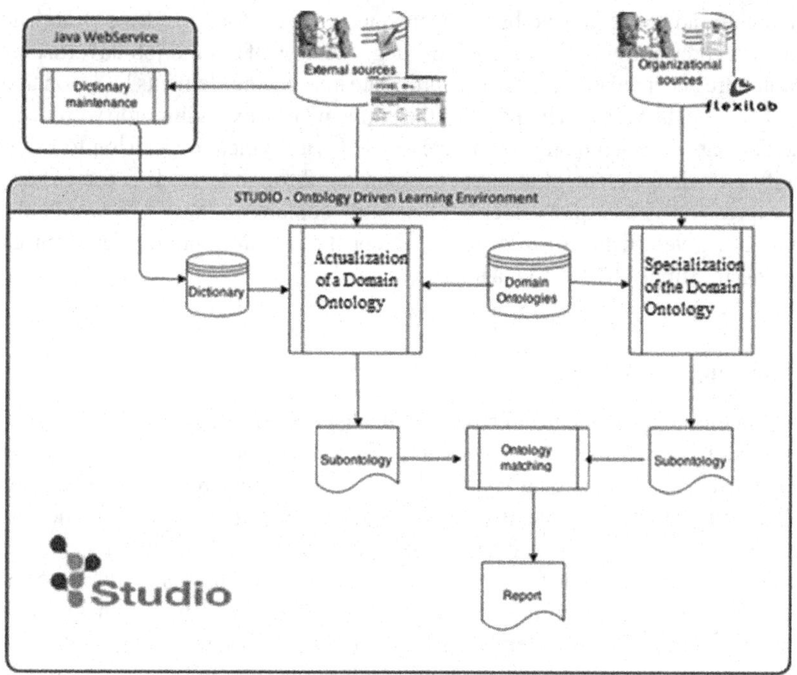

Fig. 1. Matching architecture and its processes

models [14, 20].Text mining component of the Studio is responsible for collecting a list of the task-specific knowledge elements from process descriptions [12].

3.1.2 Unstructured Documents

This list can be generated from unstructured documents as well. If these documents about task descriptions (e.g. published job vacancies), open queries (like queries in Prolog) can be used to recognize knowledge related to a given task [1]. The next table shows an example of open queries in the case of determining task-specific knowledge related to the software developer position Table 1.

Table 1. Open queries

Task	Open query
Collaborating with people	relation with X
Designing software development process	design of X
Creating specification	specify X
Program coding	develop in X
Creating program documentation	document X
Program testing	testing X

Having found the given verbs of open queries (e.g. relation, design) and nouns forming an expression with its preposition (e.g., with or of) in the job advertisements, these nouns are accepted or rejected as appropriate knowledge elements based on that the distance between the verb and noun is less than three words (excluding stop words) or not.

The database of open queries can be extended with typical expression to use them to identify knowledge element in direct manner, not through tasks. E.g. forecast&good typical expression is used for searching text parts containing these two words closely (e.g. within a given distance) in order to accept the domain ontology element called Forecasting in Supply Chain Management.

3.2 Matching Procedure

The domain ontology is actualized based on this list of knowledge areas generated from process models or unstructured documents. Meanwhile the domain ontology is specialized based on organizational sources like actual business process models, organizational documents etc. Hence two subontologies are born, but during these steps attributes will be added to the specialized and actualized domain ontology elements in order to make them different from each other e.g. along spatial-temporal dimensions.

Ontology matching algorithm of Compare Ontologies tool is responsible for discovering the similarity and discrepancies between these two subontologies and creating report from them. The report will include surplus, missing and common knowledge elements, distinguishing these results based on the added attributes e.g. in timely and localized manner.

This architecture was used to investigate compliance between actual and reference nursing process regarding the existence of segregation duties [19] and to examine the compliance between job market expectations (labor market demand through available job postings) and educational offers (learning outcome described by competencies acquired by completing a course) [4]. The next chapter shows the skill gap analysis by the SMART system as the use case of this architecture.

4 Use Case: The SMART System

The need of dynamically matching educational system offer and job market demand represents a relevant challenge to promote and sustain an inclusive and competitive society in Europe. SMART (Skill MAtching for Regional development) gives a response to this need by defining and implementing an innovative learning system which is capable of matching labor market needs with training offers. The Smart system provides regional and temporal comparison, used ontology-based approach to identify competence elements, mostly knowledge elements, which are appeared on each sides of the labor market. The core of this system is the Studio system that is an innovative e-learning and adaptive testing system. The project focused on education and job balance in Andalusia region featured by high rates of unemployment and over-qualification. During the pilot phase, the system tested the compliance of educational offers of following regional institutions - Fundación Universidad Pablo de

Olavide and EUSA - with the job market needs of United Kingdom and Andalusia. The next section presents how the above-mentioned matching architecture was implemented in the SMART system.

4.1 Overall Process of This System

The system consists of four processes:

Setting the Educational Offer process is responsible for creating the specialized version of the Tourism Ontology as domain ontology.

Fetching the Labor Market Needs process creates the actualized version of the Tourism Ontology, having processed job vacancies collected automatically from job portals.

Matching process executes the matching procedure provided by Compare Ontologies tool and provides a technical report about its results. This technical report is structured into blocks that point out surplus, missing and common knowledge elements containing regional information given by the educational institute and the investigated labor market.

Creating report phase transform this technical report into user-friendly report. These steps are detailed in the following sections.

4.1.1 Setting the Educational Offer

In order to use the Smart system the user has to authenticate on the SMART portal (www.smart-project.org) (Fig. 2. Points 1 and 2). The actual matching process is started through the Flexilab portal (www.flexilab.eu) (Fig. 2. Point 3).The Flexilab portal manages and stores a profile of the user, where learning programs and other information are saved. In order to match the supply of the institution with the labor market needs, the educational offer has to be defined by the knowledge elements of a given learning program (Fig. 2. Point 4).

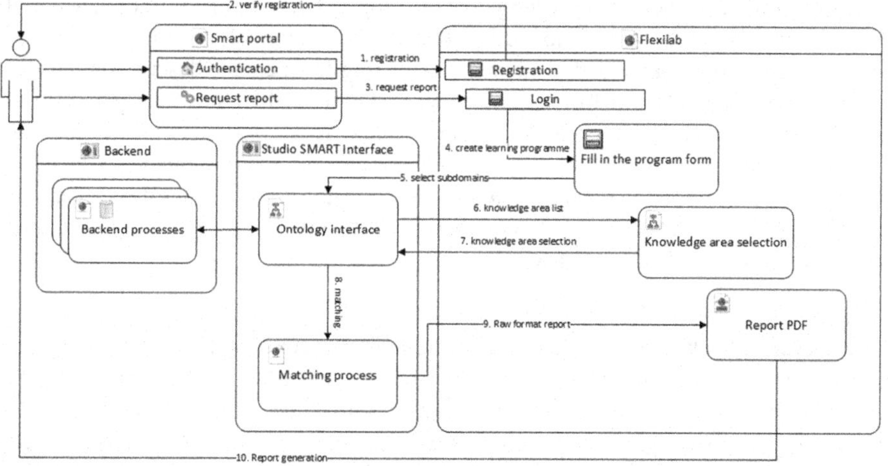

Fig. 2. Overall process

Dear Visitor,

Welcome to the Flexilab portal!

You're about to match your institution's educational output to labour market demand. We recommend that you complete your request on a regular basis as the labour market is dynamically changing. The Smart system collects and updates labour market data periodically. Please note that for the time being, data has only been collected from the UK and Andalusian labour markets.

- To request the report you need to sign in and fill out the form below.
- The fields marked with an asterix are mandatory.
- Mark the knowledge elements related to a given specialization from the list.
- Having pressed the Submit button, you will receive a Smart report to your e-mail address.

Name of Institution*

Specialization*

Region of Institution*

Andalusian labour market

Tourism

Tourism organization

National tourism organizatior

Tour agency

International tourism organiz

Fig. 3. Form for expressing the educational offer

If a learning program has not yet been stored by the institution, than information has to be provided about it by filling 'create program form' on the Flexilab portal (Fig. 3). In this form, basic information (name and region of institution, name of learning program) and knowledge elements extracting from course description have to be given by selecting them from a predefined list provided by the backend systems (Fig. 2. Points 6 and 7). This list of knowledge areas is the backbone of the Tourism Ontology as domain ontology, whose development process was presented by Caballero et al. [3]. Having submitted this information, the backend system creates the specialized version of the domain ontology based on these information provided by the educational institute currently in this manual way.

2. Fetching the Labor Market Needs.

The system tracks the changes of the environment by continually processing the job vacancies representing the Andalusian or the UK labor market needs. In the SMART system the job descriptions are fetched from specified job portals by web crawlers written for this specific purpose. In this version of the SMART system, typical expression are used to identify the required knowledge elements within the Tourism

Ontology (see in 3.1.1). These typical expressions resides in a dictionary. Having identified the required knowledge elements, a substructure of Tourism Ontology – actualized version of this domain ontology - is created based on them (Fig. 2. Point 5).

3. Matching.

Having submitted the form (list of the selected knowledge areas and additional information) to the SMART middleware, the matching process starts (Fig. 2. Point 8). The Compare Ontologies built-in function in Protégé 4.X implemented in JAVA is for examining both subontologies, created based on the learning program was set, and the labor market demand. The main goal of Compare Ontologies function is to compare two versions of the same ontology, so it requires an original and an updated version of the ontology. In our case, the ontology model related to the education offer as an aspect of organizational status is considered as the original model. The updated version is the ontology model related to the job market expectations as demanded status by the environment. This Protégé function creates a technical report which contains the next elements:

Created blocks contain knowledge elements which are required by the labor market but not provided by the educational offer.

Deleted blocks contain knowledge elements that are provided by the educational offer but not required by the labor market.

Modified or Rename and modified blocks contain knowledge elements that are required and provided as well, but within the same or different region (see in Fig. 4.)

4. Creating Report.

A technical report is processed by using a Java algorithm for creating an English and a Spanish PDF report (Fig. 2 Points 9 and 10.). An example output can be seen on the Fig. 5. The report is split into three sections. The first part lists the competencies identified through knowledge elements required by the labor market but not supplied. The second part lists supplied competencies but labor market does not require. The third group shows the matching competencies. The job market expectations are shown in a detailed manner. The report provide detailed information about the competencies:

```
Modified Financial_Planning -> Financial_Planning
-------------------------------------------------
Added:   Financial_Planning region "UK labour market"^^string
Deleted:     Financial_Planning region "Sevilla"^^string
-------------------------------------------------
Modified Financial_accounting -> Financial_accounting
-------------------------------------------------
Added:   Financial_accounting has_sub-knowledge-area Invoice
Added:   Financial_accounting region "UK labour market"^^string
Deleted:     Financial_accounting region "Sevilla"^^string
```

Fig. 4. SMART technical report

SMART	*SMART Matching Report* ***Institute name: Name of Institution*** ***Learning Programme: Name of Specialization*** ***Region: Region of Instituion*** ***Labour market: United Kingdom*** ***Job portal:http://www.jobsite.co.uk/jobs/travelandtourism/*** ***Number of job vacancies: 961*** ***Date: 15-11-2014 02:23*** ***Availability time of job descriptions: 12-11-2014***

Knowledge element	Frequency
Capacity management in SCM	6
Capacity management in SCM was identified in the following job roles: general manager - independent school, regional-hr-business-partner-london-south-east-45k-55k, general manager, banbury - with accommodation, chef manager - catering, area support manager - contract caterer (9 month contract), senior regional operations manager - contract caterer	
Knowledge element	**Frequency**
Planning in SCM	4
Planning in SCM was identified in the following job roles: weekend cook, live-in-cook-housekeeper-central-london, general manager, banbury - with accommodation, chef de partie	
Knowledge element	**Frequency**
Production Planning and Scheduling	3
Production Planning and Scheduling was identified in the following job roles: general manager - independent school, chef manager - catering, head chef - contract caterer	
Knowledge element	**Frequency**
Transport Planning	2
Transport Planning was identified in the following job roles: general manager - fast food retailer, assistant manager - fast food retailer	

Fig. 5. SMART report

- Knowledge element required by the given – Andalusian or United Kingdom – labor market.
- The domain to which the knowledge element reflects.
- Frequency means: how many times a knowledge element appeared in the job advertisements.
- List of job roles appeared in the job advertisements and requires the knowledge element in question.

The knowledge elements, with no frequency, are also part of the domain identified above, however they don't mentioned explicitly in the job advertisements, hence it may be interesting for the educational institution.

This report provides an overview along regional and time dimensions about the balance of actual and required status within a given organization context. It facilitates the planning of future actions to eliminate imbalance between sides.

5 Conclusion

This paper presents an ontology matching architecture that is capable of dynamically processing documents reflecting changing environment, creating ontology models to match actual with required status of organizational working and reporting the discrepancies and similarities for the experts. This architecture can be used for business process management purposes and labor market investigation as well. The latter case was illustrated by the system implemented in the SMART project. This system did not use the whole potential of this architecture, so the processor of unstructured documents will be improved in the next version of this system.

During the ProKEX project [14] this architecture will be used to populate domain ontology with new knowledge elements and facilitate the process improvement by executing semantic ontology matching between actual and reference business processes.

Acknowledgment. The authors wish to express their gratitude to Dr. Andras Gabor, associate professor of the Corvinus University of Budapest, for the great topic and the powerful help provided during the development process.

"This work was conducted using the Protégé resource, which is supported by grant GM10331601 from the National Institute of General Medical Sciences of the United States National Institutes of Health."

References

1. Borbásné Szabó, I.: Design of Higher Education Portfolio, Ph.D. dissertation, Corvinus University of Budapest, Hungary (2012)
2. BrugesCommuniqué: The Bruges Communiqué on enhanced European Cooperation in Vocational Education and Training for the period 2011–2020 (2010). http://ec.europa.eu/education/lifelong-learning-policy/doc/vocational/bruges_en.pdf
3. Caballero, J.G., et al.: Developing and aligning competences in the tourism industry. the smart project experience. In: ICERI 2014 Proceedings, pp. 1013–1022 (2014)
4. Castello, V., et al.: Enhancing competences dynamic alignment between job and education. contributions and evidences from the smart project. In: ICERI 2014 Proceedings, pp. 1131–1139 (2014)
5. Castello, V., et al.: The skill match challenge. evidences from the smart project. In: ICERI 2014 Proceedings, pp. 1182–1189 (2014)
6. Cedefop: Skills supply and demand in Europa Methodological framework (2012). http://www.cedefop.europa.eu/EN/Files/5525_en.pdf
7. Choi, N., et al.: A survey on ontology mapping. SIGMOD Rec. **35**, 34–41 (2006)
8. Ding, Y., Foo, S.: Ontology research and development. part 2 - a review of ontology mapping and evolving. J. Inf. Sci. **28**(5), 375–388 (2002)
9. Ehrig, M., Sure, Y.: Ontology mapping – an integrated approach. In: Bussler, C.J., et al. (eds.) The Semantic Web: Research and Applications, pp. 76–91. Springer, Berlin Heidelberg (2004)

10. Futó, I., Gábor, A., Kovács, B., Kő, A.: Higher Education Portfolio Alignment with World of Labour Needs. In: Enrico, F., Jochen, S., Maria, A.W. (eds.) Electronic Government: 7th International Conference, EGOV 2008; Proceedings of Ongoing Research, Project Contributions and Workshops, pp. 265–272, Turin, 1–4 September 2008. (Schriftenreihe Informatik (Linz, Austria); 27)
11. Gábor, A., Szabó, Z.: Semantic technologies in business process management. In: Fathi, M. (ed.) Integration of Practice-Oriented Knowledge Technology Trends and Prospectives, pp. 17–28. Springer, Heidelberg (2013)
12. Gillani, S.A., Kő, A.: Process-based knowledge extraction in a public authority: a text mining approach. In: Kő, A., Francesconi, E. (eds.) EGOVIS 2014. LNCS, vol. 8650, pp. 91–103. Springer, Heidelberg (2014)
13. Kalfoglou, Y., Schorlemmer, M.: Ontology mapping: the state of the art. Knowl. Eng. Rev. **18**(01), 1–31 (2003)
14. Kő, A., Ternai, K.: A development method for ontology based business processes. In: Cunningham, P., Cunningham, M. (eds.) eChallenges 2011: Conference and Exhibition, pp. 125–131, 26-28 October 2011 (ISBN:978-1-905824-27-4)
15. NeSkNeJo: New Skills for New Jobs. Policy initiatives in the field of education: Short overview of the current situation in Europe. EACEA: Accessed on 09 June 2015. http://eacea.ec.europa.eu/education/eurydice/documents/thematic_reports/125EN.pdf
16. Neusch, G., Gábor, A.: Prokex – integrated platform for process-based knowledge extraction. In: ICERI 2014 Proceedings, pp. 3972–3977 (2014)
17. Studio: Ontology Learning Driven Environment Accessed on 30 March 2015. http://www.corvinno.hu/web.nsf/do?open&lang=en&page=proj-studio
18. Su, X.: A text categorization perspective for ontology mapping: Position paper. 832256 (2002)
19. Szabó, I., Varga, K.: Knowledge-based compliance checking of business processes. In: Meersman, R., et al. (eds.) On the Move to Meaningful Internet Systems: OTM 2014 Conferences, pp. 597–611. Springer, Berlin Heidelberg (2014)
20. Ternai, K., Török, M., Varga, K.: Combining knowledge management and business process management – a solution for information extraction from business process models focusing on BPM Challenges. In: Kő, A., Francesconi, E. (eds.) EGOVIS 2014. LNCS, vol. 8650, pp. 104–117. Springer, Heidelberg (2014)
21. Vas, R.: Educational ontology and knowledge testing. Electron. J. Knowl. Manage. **5**(1), 123–130 (2007)

Semi-automatic Methodology for Compliance Checking on Business Processes

Katalin Ternai([✉])

Department of Information Systems, Corvinus University of Budapest, Fővám Tér 13-15, Budapest 1093, Hungary
katalin.ternai@uni-corvinus.hu

Abstract. The paper aims to provide a semi-automatic methodology, which can be used to validate and improve business processes. The main goal is the process ontology matching, based on ontologies derived from business process models and regulations, rules and policies. The paper introduces a method using ontology building and matching for compliance checking on business processes partway automatically. The objective of this approach is to transform the business process into process ontology and to build reference process ontology from unstructured documents in order to apply ontology matching procedure to restructure, validate and improve the business process. Processes in public administration are also complex and changing fast according to the changes in regulatory environment. In the case study, we illustrate the methodology related to the process of "Assessment of the KICs past performance", to improve the process at the European Institute of Innovation and Technology (EIT).

Keywords: Process ontology · Ontology learning · Ontology matching · Compliance check

1 Introduction

Organizations create enterprise models to represent their structure and dynamics. These enterprise models are used to document the as-is reality of an organization as well as to plan the to-be scenarios. It is common for them to maintain repositories of business process models in order to document and to continuously improve their operations. Business process models play important role in the analysis and improvement of the performance of an organization. The quality of a business process model has a direct effect on the business performance.

In many application domains processes have to comply with regulations, rules and policies as well. Processes in public administration are also complex and changing fast according to the changes in regulatory environment. The rapid growth of the internet led to an enormous amount of machine readable documents online. This increasing text data come from different domains and has been growing exponentially for several centuries. A given organization is likely to be under jurisdiction of several regulations concurrently. These regulations are usually described in a natural language document which is unstructured form, and difficult to understand by non-experts of the field the

© Springer International Publishing Switzerland 2015
A. Kő and E. Francesconi (Eds.): EGOVIS 2015, LNCS 9265, pp. 243–256, 2015.
DOI: 10.1007/978-3-319-22389-6_18

regulation acts on. It is very difficult to extract rules from unstructured documents and therefore, such data cannot be used for any reasonable purpose.

Organizations have to invest a great amount to elaborate their business policies in order to comply with various regulatory requirements. Validating existing process models with business policies are critical issues for recent organizations. Processes have to comply with semantic constraints (e.g. business level rules and policies), however, the currently available tools and techniques for Business Process Management (BPM) lack of semantic description. Analyzing business policies and validating business process models is a critical task in organizations, which is currently done in an ad hoc way due to the lack of systematic methodologies [1].

Semantic technologies provide the foundation for formalizing the complex relationships of a business in a common model using ontology language. Ontologies enable holistic view to a BPM system.

In order to increase quality and reduce the cost in terms of human capacities and time of compliance checking, feasible to use semantic technologies. In our case, it is necessary to deal with semantically extended process models, and regulations have to be structured and expressed using formal means making their automatic processing possible.

The challenge of automated compliance checking can be seen as spreading the business processes model to include semantic aspects and enabling the required automation in checking the business processes model against the regulations. We provide mechanisms to structure and formalize regulations, then the semantics have to be framed into business processes [2, 4]. In the case of Semantic Business Process Management (SBPM), this means creating a reference process ontology to evaluate the compliance with the given process ontology.

In our approach, the reference process ontology directly created from regulations in semi-automated manner, and for the compliance checking we use heuristic ontology matching algorithms.

The paper aims to provide a semi-automatic methodology, which can be used to validate and improve business processes (c.f. Fig. 1). The main goal is the process ontology matching, based on ontologies derived from business process models and regulations, rules and policies. The paper, hence, introduces a method using ontology building and matching for compliance checking on business processes partway automatically. The objective of this approach is to transform the business process into process ontology and to build reference process ontology from unstructured documents in order to apply ontology matching procedure to restructure, validate and improve the business process. The presented methodology has been partly developed, applied and tested in the context of eBest project [3], PROKEX project [4] and on higher education processes.

In the case study, we illustrate the methodology related to the process of "Assessment of the KICs past performance", to improve the process at the European Institute of Innovation and Technology (EIT). The mission of the EIT is to grow and capitalize on the innovation capacity and capability of actors from higher education, research, business and entrepreneurship from the EU and beyond through the creation of highly integrated Knowledge and Innovation Communities (KICs) [5].

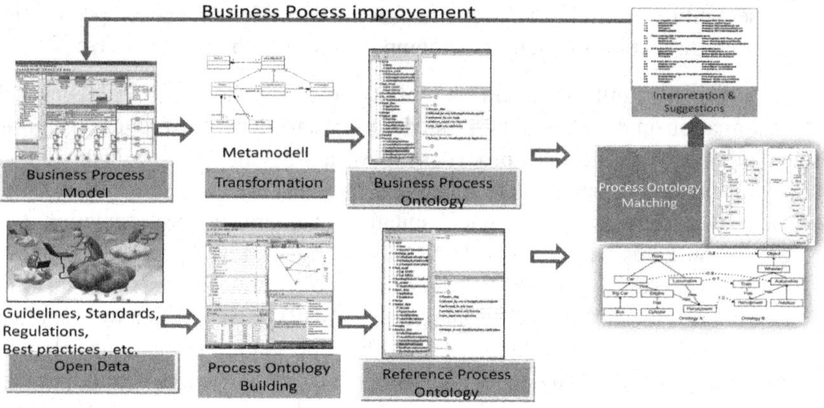

Fig. 1. Compliance checking methodology

2 Theoretical Background

2.1 Semantic Business Process Management

In the new networked economy organizations emphasize the importance of Business Process Management (BPM) and reorganize themselves around their business processes [6]. The Gartner Group predicted that by the year 2015 there will be an explosion of interest in business process management suites and their integration with underlying software infrastructure [7].

By managing processes with continuous improvements, the organization can reduce costs, increase efficiency, and strengthen the ability to respond to change. BPM Systems facilitate the management of business processes using graphical process models [8]. Many organizations already use efficiently BPM to increase their operating agility. Managing business processes means focusing on the important activities and resources of an organization. The aim is to design and control the organizational structures in a very flexible way so they can rapidly adapt to changing conditions.

It is not easy to analyze business processes, to define them and to install them, because a lot of business information, such as information about events, actors, conditions and artifacts, is needed to understand the process. If businesses and business strategies are changing, the underlying business processes also have to be changed and adopted. Once a model of a business process is available, various analytical methods need to be used to check if the process delivers the product or service in the most optimal and cost-effective way [6].

In spite of the great importance of BPM tools and techniques, they include fundamental problems such as:

- difficulty in querying and reusing business processes [9, 10]
- difficulty in integrating business processes across organizations [11]
- inability to transform automatically a business process model to an executable workflow model [12]

- lack of semantic description in business process execution language specifications for dynamic discovery and automatic composition of web services [13],

BPM has gained significant attention by both academy and industry, however the level of automation in BPM is very limited so far and does not provide a uniform representation of an organization's process space on a semantic sphere, which would be accessible to semantic functions, like intelligent queries [11].

Semantic web technologies provide suitable, standardized representation techniques to overcome this barrier. Fensel and his colleagues have proposed to combine semantic web technologies and BPM and provide one consolidated technology, which they call Semantic Business Process Management (SBPM). SBPM is a new approach of increasing the degree of automation of BPM by representing the various spheres of an enterprise using ontology languages and semantic web frameworks. Ontologies have key role in SBPM as well as semantic web [2]. Ontology is responsible for domain conceptualization, structuring knowledge embedded in business processes. It describes not only data, but also the regularity of connection among data. The most important description language of semantic web is the OWL (web ontology language) preferred by W3C [14, 15].

The goal is to be able to apply machine reasoning for the translation between the spheres for the discovery of processes, process fragments and for process composition [10]. The use of ontologies is a key concept that distinguishes SBPM from conventional BPM. Within SBPM two types of ontologies are utilized: domain ontologies and process ontologies. With the semantic description of the data, business process analysis can be semantically enhanced since the semantic meaning of the data is preserved during all phases of the process lifecycle [11].

Ontologies, as general but formalized representation can be used for describing the concepts of a business process. According to our research, process ontologies have no precise definition in the academic literature. Some refer to it simply as a conceptual description framework of processes [16]. In this interpretation process ontologies are abstract and general. Contrary, task ontologies determine a smaller subset of the process space, the sequence of activities in a given process [17].

In this paper the concept of process ontologies is used, where ontology holds the structural information of processes. The solution of establish the links between process model elements and ontology concepts has been prepared in the methodology. The attempt is to provide an extension for the standard ontology definition in the form of an annotation scheme to enable ontologies to cover all the major aspects of business process definition [18]. The approach is identified as a semi-automatic generation of BPM defined ontology.

2.2 Ontology Learning and Matching

The objective of ontology learning is "to generate domain ontologies from various kinds of resources by applying natural language processing and machine learning techniques" [19]. Statistical, rule-based or hybrid ontology learning technique can be distinguished. The goal of the process ontology building and matching tool is to identify process model objects based on their semantic and relations between them using semantic rules. With this object the system uses rule-based ontology learning technique.

Ontology matching procedure can be defined as follows: "given ontologies O1 and O2, each describing a collection of discrete entities such as classes, properties, individuals, etc., we want to identify semantic correspondences between the components of these entities." [20]

The goals of combining ontologies are to merge, transform, integrate, translate, align or map etc. them into a new or an existing ontology. The goal of this paper is to present a solution for executing a compliance check between an actual and an expected process, hence ontology mapping, matching or alignment seemed to be the best method regarding our solution.

The general ontology mapping tools use different kind of method to identify the semantic correspondences between two ontologies [21, 22]. Borbásné Szabó I. (2012) investigated these tools by their dynamism and reusability. [23] Built-in function in Protégé 4.X development environment was found the most appropriate tool to execute an ontology matching within a flexible business environment.

Process specific methods used logical assertions and similarity measures to facilitate the interoperability among processes [24]. Some other research used Petri nets to submit an operational semantics that facilitates composition, simulation, and validation of business processes [25].

3 Our Methodology

The focus in our methodology is given to the extension and mapping the conceptual models to ontology models by using meta-modeling approach and to build reference process ontology from unstructured documents in order to apply ontology matching procedure to restructure, validate and improve the business processes. The usage of semantic technologies does not affect the main phases of the BPM lifecycle, but increases the automation degree within the phases and enhances the BPM functionalities. Meta-models offer intuitive way of specifying modeling languages and are suitable for discussion with non-technical users. Meta-models are particularly convenient for the definition of conceptual models. In our approach the links between model elements and ontology concepts are established.

The main steps of our methodology are:

- Business process modeling
- Semantic annotation of business process models
- Mapping the conceptual models to ontology models
- Ontology building from unstructured documents
- Compliance check using Ontology matching

In the case study, we will illustrate the methodology related to the process of "Assessment of the KICs past performance", highlighting the context of SBPM. To produce an assessment of the KICs past performance the EIT Head Quarter analyze the outputs of the assessment of the reporting for the previous years and give an evaluation based on the rules defined in the previous phase. In the analysis of the past performance the EIT Head Quarter and in particular the KIC Project Officers and Continuous monitor Officer evaluate the KICs past performance by taking in account also the previous assessment on the reporting performed by experts in the previous years and the information collected during the management of the relationship with the KICs. EIT staff need to know if there are knowledge gaps that need to be filled.

3.1 Business Process Modeling

Business process modeling is the first phase of the BPM lifecycle. In the case study discussed in this paper the process models have been implemented using the BOC ADONIS modeling platform [26]. However, our approach is principally transferable to other semi-formal modeling languages [27].

ADONIS is a graph-structured BPM language. The integral model element is the activity. The ADONIS modeling platform is a business meta-modeling tool with components such as modeling, analysis, simulation, evaluation, process costing, documentation, staff management, and import-export. Its main feature is its method independence. Figure 2 presents the “Assessment of the KICs past performance” sample process model in ADONIS.

The next step after the modeling phase is the semantic annotation to explicitly specify the semantics of the tasks and decisions in the process flow. The semantic annotation can either be embedded in the process model itself or can exist as ontology outside the process model. Ontology-based process modeling has to reflect also the semantics of the processes.

3.2 Mapping the Conceptual Models to Ontology Models

For the mapping the conceptual models to ontology models by using meta-modeling approach the models are exported in the structure of ADONIS XML format. The “conceptual model - ontology model” converter maps the Adonis model elements to the appropriate ontology elements in meta-level.

The model transformation aims at preserving the semantics of the business model. To avoid loss of information during the transformation inserting information into annotation attributes of the target elements is needed. The model elements must be annotated to get properly processed by the transformation, model or code generator tools.

There are various languages for the explicit and formal representation of ontology. OWL will be used as the language for representing ontologies due to its increased acceptance. The Portégé-OWL application supports building ontologies.

The general rule used in our approach is to express each ADONIS model element as a class in the ontology and its corresponding attributes as attributes of the class. This transformation is done by means of XSL Extensible Style sheet Language (XSL) translation which performs the conversion.

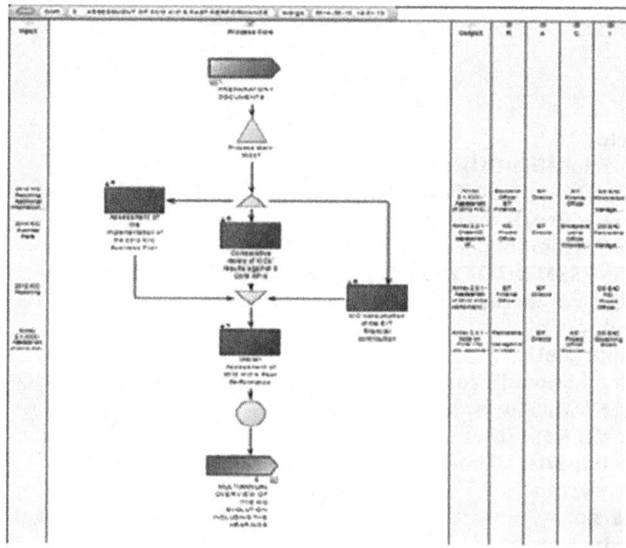

Fig. 2. The ADONIS model of the "Assessment of the KICs past performance" process.

To specify the semantics of ADONIS model elements through relations to ontology concepts, the ADONIS business model first must be represented within the ontology. In regard to the representation of the business model in the ontology, one can differentiate between a representation of ADONIS model language constructs and a representation of ADONIS model elements. ADONIS model language constructs such as "activity", as well as the control flow are created in the ontology as classes and properties. Subsequently, the ADONIS model elements can be represented through the instantiation of these classes and properties in the ontology. The linkage of the ontology and the ADONIS model element instances is accomplished by the usage of properties. These properties specify the semantics of an ADONIS model element through a relation to an ontology instance with formal semantics defined by the ontology. A mapped ontology should define all the entities involved in the business process including how they relate to each other and what properties they have. The converted process is visualized in Fig. 3.

The meta-level mapper has been used to convert the ADONIS model elements to the appropriate ontology elements. The ontology contains all the entities involved in the process, including how they relate to each other and what properties they have.

4 Process Ontology Building

The next architecture presents a solution to build process ontologies from pure texts (best practices, regulations, guidelines etc.) and use them to investigate actual business processes to discover their similarities and discrepancies with business processes extracted from these documents.

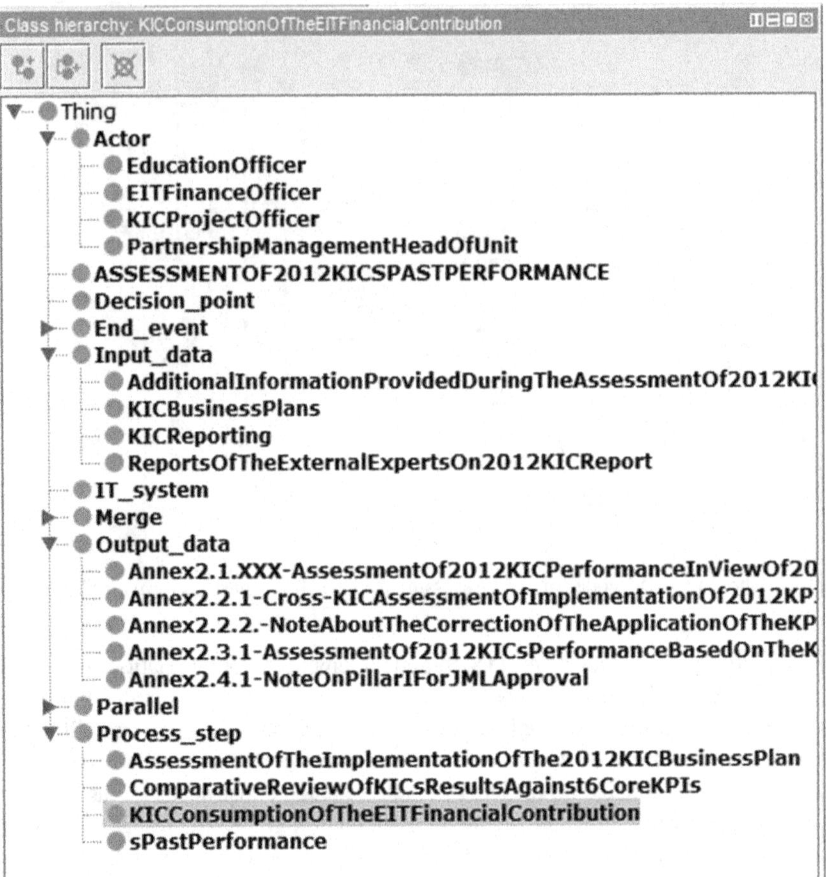

Fig. 3. The process ontology in Portégé

The architecture has two pillars: building process ontologies and matching them to create a report about similarities and discrepancies for process owners. The development of this system is ongoing but some parts are already implemented. XSLT mapper is ready to use. Matching procedure was elaborated and implemented in the SMART project [23, 29] and adapted for SBPM purposes [28, 30]. Hence this paper presents only the process ontology building part (Fig. 4).

4.1 Process Ontology Building

Two ways for process ontology building were taken into our consideration:

- general procedure without any information about the actual business process

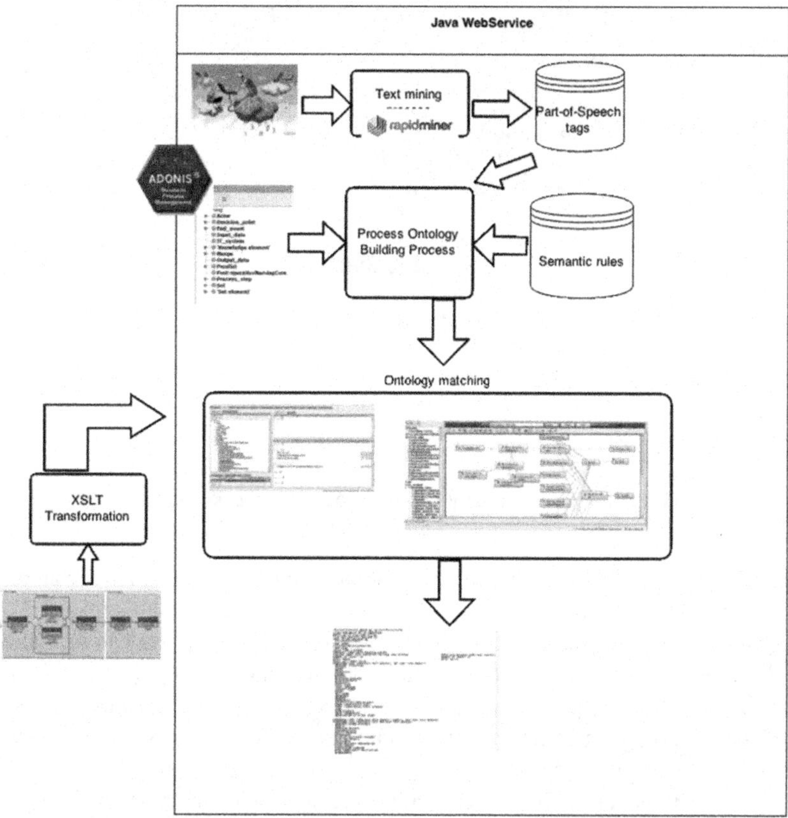

Fig. 4. Process ontology building and matching architecture

- heuristic procedure in that model elements from the actual business process are used to identify them within the unstructured documents and discovering the changes related to these element.

The first one is a very challenging field and the elaboration of accurate algorithm needs a long term period, hence we started to work the second procedure out.

4.1.1 Heuristic Procedure

The input sources of this system are unstructured documents like best practices, standards, protocols, regulations etc., and well-defined classes from the process ontologies transformed from Adonis process models (see Fig. 5).

The heuristic procedure uses the process ontology of the actual business process (actualPO) as basis to create the process ontology of the reference business process (referencePO).

The first step of this system is to identify the actual business process steps within the reference documents. It collects the subclasses of Process_step class one after the other and having split them into words. It finds the sentences containing all words or

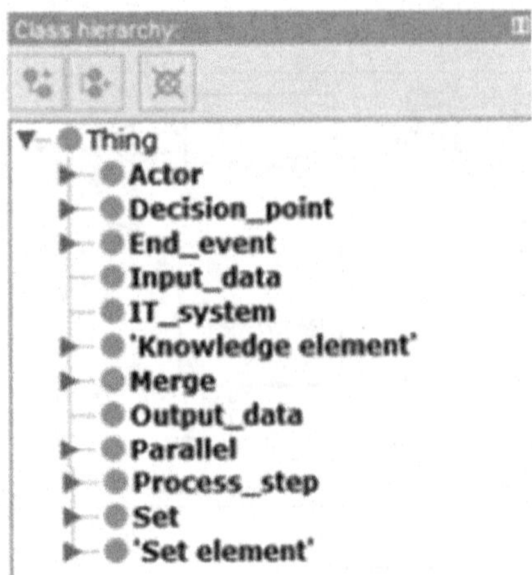

Fig. 5. Class hierarchy based on Adonis process models

some of them within these documents. Around the best fit, it identifies the related Actor using "by the" semantic rule.

In general, tasks are performed by actors. Based on this truth, we can formalize the next rule < task performed > by the < actor >. If we find a sentence whose structure follows this rule, we extract the actor from it. Having identified sentences containing "by the", the algorithm splits these sentences into two parts and the second parts will be the actors.

Having identified an actor, the algorithm create a new subclass of Process_step from the above-mentioned discovered sentence and a new sublcass of Actor and connect them with each other using "performed_by" relation. To elaborate other type of semantic rules is in progress.

These semantic rules can be complemented by grammatical rules that are constructed from part-of-speech tags. A RapidMiner process is responsible for identifying and collecting verbs and nouns from actual document into lists (see Fig. 6).

Process steps are discovered by using expressions represented by combination of verb and noun. Based on this grammatical rule, the identified process steps can be detailed by determine their activities or related other process steps. This algorithm has been implemented in Java. The next section will present the working of this program on the above-mentioned EIT process.

4.1.2 'Assessment of KICs Past Performance' Business Process

Having run the program, the next process ontology was created from the reference documents (Fig. 7).

Having created the reference process ontology by following this procedure, ontology matching procedure will be executed by using built-in ontology matching tool in Protégé 4.X ontology environment. However semantic corresponding checking between the actual and reference process ontology will be executed firstly, if it is needed.

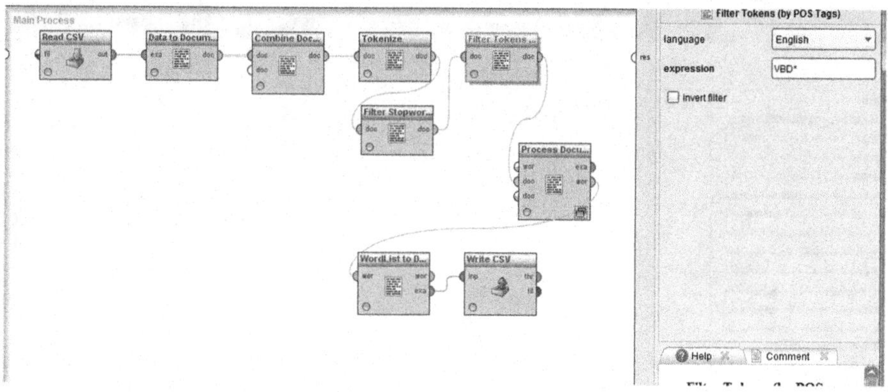

Fig. 6. RapidMiner process

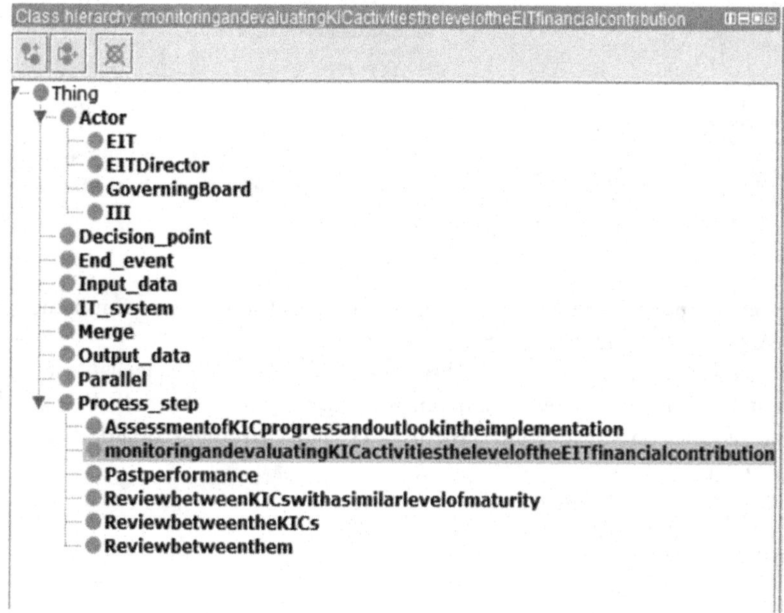

Fig. 7. The process ontology in Portégé

The matching report contains three blocks:

Created blocks show process model elements that are in the reference process, but not in the actual process.

Deleted blocks present process model elements that are in the actual process, but not in the reference process.

Renamed and modified blocks discover process model elements that are in the both processes.

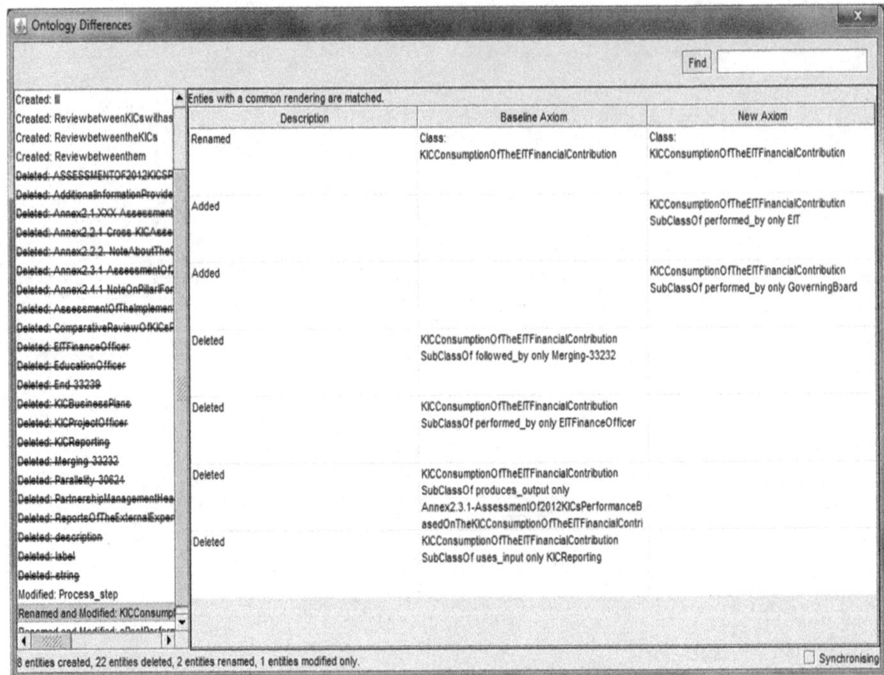

Fig. 8. The matching report

The picture presents an example about what type of information can be delivered for process owners by the report (Fig. 8).

This picture shows that 'KIC Consumption of the EIT Financial Contribution' process step are in the reference and actual business process as well. But the 2016 guideline requires to execute this task by EIT and Governing Board, not by EIT Finance Officer.

5 Conclusion

The paper aimed to provide and elaborate a semi-automatic methodology, which can be used to validate and improve business processes. The main goal is the process ontology matching, based on ontologies derived from business process models and regulations, rules and policies. The paper, hence, introduces a method using ontology building and matching for compliance checking on business processes. The objective of this approach is to transform business processes into process ontologies and to build reference process ontology from unstructured documents in order to apply ontology matching procedure to restructure, validate and improve the business processes.

We illustrated the methodology related to the process of "Assessment of the KICs past performance". We have improved the process on the basis of the 2016 guideline at the European Institute of Innovation and Technology (EIT).

In the future, we plan to test the elaborated tool that creates process ontology from unstructured document with several complex processes in public administration in the dynamic regulatory environment.

References

1. Hoefferer, P.: Achieving business process model interoperability using meta models and ontologies. In: Sterle, H., Schelp, J., Winter, R. (Eds.) Proceedings of the 15th European Conference on Information Systems (ECIS2007), pp. 1620–1631 (2007)
2. Fensel, D., Hepp, M., Leymann, F., Bussler, C., Domingue, J., Wahler, A.: Semantic business process management: using semantic web services for business process management. In: IEEE Conference on e-Business Engineering (ICEBE 2005), Beijing, China (2005)
3. eBEST-Empowering Business Ecosystems of Small Service Enterprises to Face the Economic Crisis. The project co-funded by the European Commission, FP7-SME-2008-2 No. 243554. http://www.ebest.eu/
4. ProKEx: Integrated Platform for Process-based Knowledge Extraction, EUREKA project. http://prokex.netpositive.hu
5. European Institute of Innovation and Technology (EIT). http://eit.europa.eu/
6. Weske, M., van der Aalst, W.M.P., Verbeek, H.M.W.: Advances in business process management. Data Knowl. Eng. **50**(1), 1–8 (2004)
7. Light, A.: Gartner predicts: Nearly Half of IT Jobs will be Lost to Automation by 2015, UsabilityNews.com, 4 Fenruary 2005
8. van der Aalst, W.M.P., Desel, J., Oberweis, A.: Business process management: models, techniques, and empirical studies. Springer, Heidelberg (2000)
9. Hepp, M., Leymann, F., Domingue, J., Wahler, A., Fensel, D.: Semantic business process management: a vision towards using semantic web services for business process management. In: Proceedings of the IEEE International Conference on e-Business Engineering, ICEBE 2005 (2005)
10. Hepp, M., Roman, D.: An Ontology Framework for Semantic Business Process Management. In: Proceedings of Wirtschaftsinformatik 2007, p. 27 (2007)
11. Gábor, A., Szabó, Z.: Semantic technologies in business process management. In: Fathi, M. (ed.) Integration of Practice-Oriented Knowledge Technology: Trends and Prospectives, pp. 17–28. Springer Verlag, Heidelberg (2013). 368 p. ISBN 978-3-642-34470-1
12. Basu, A., Blanning, R.W.: A formal approach to workflow analysis. Inf. Syst. Res. **11**(1), 17–36 (2000)
13. Karastoyanova, D., Lessen, T., Leymann1, F., Ma, Z., Nitzsche, J., Wetzstein, B., Bhiri, S., Hauswirth, M., Zaremba, M.: A reference architecture for semantic business process management systems. In: Multi konferenz Wirtschaftsinformatik GITO-Verlag, Berlin (2008)
14. Berners-Lee, T., Hendler, J., Lassila, O.: The Semantic Web. Scientific American **284**(5), 34–43 (2001)
15. Hepp, M., Cardoso, J., Lytras, M.D.: The Semantic Web: Real-World Applications from Industry. Springer, Heidelberg (2007)
16. Herborn, T., Wimmer, M.: Process ontologies facilitating interoperability in egovernment, a methodological framework. In: Workshop on Semantics for Business Process Management, the 3rd Semantic Web Conference. Montenegro (2006)

17. Benjamins, V.R., Fensel, D., Straatman, R.: Assumptions of problem-solving methods and their role in knowledge engineering. In: Wahlster, W. (Ed.) Poceedings ECAI-1996, pp. 408−412 (1996)
18. Kő, A., Ternai, K.: A development method for ontology based business processes, In: Cunningham, P., Cunningham, M. (eds.) eChallenges 2011: Conference and Exhibition, Florence, Italy. pp. 125−131. Konferencia helye, ideje: Florence, Olaszország, 2011.10.26-2011.10.28. Dublin: International Information Management Corporation, 26–28 October 2011. (ISBN:978-1-905824-27-4)
19. Haase, P., Völker, J.: Ontology learning and reasoning -- dealing with uncertainty and inconsistency. In: da Costa, P.C.G., d'Amato, C., Fanizzi, N., Laskey, K.B., Laskey, K.J., Lukasiewicz, T., Nickles, M., Pool, M. (eds.) URSW 2005 - 2007. ISWC International Workshops, URSW 2005-2007, Revised Selected and Invited Papers, vol. 5327, pp. 366–384. Springer, Heidelberg (2008)
20. Alasoud, A., et al.: An Effective Ontology Matching Technique. In: An, A., et al. (eds.) Foundations of Intelligent Systems, pp. 585–590. Springer, Berlin / Heidelberg (2008)
21. Choi, N., et al.: A survey on ontology mapping. SIGMOD Rec. **35**, 34–41 (2006)
22. Noy, N.F.: Semantic integration: a survey of ontology-based approaches. SIGMOD Rec. **33**, 65–70 (2004)
23. Borbásné Szabó, I.: Design of Higher Education Portfolio, Ph.D dissertation, Corvinus University of Budapest, Hungary (2012)
24. Jung, J.J.: Semantic business process integration based on ontology alignment. Expert Syst. Appl. **36**(8), 11013–11020 (2009)
25. Koschmider, A., Oberweis, A.: Ontology based business process description. In: Proceedings of the CAiSE, pp. 321−333 (2005)
26. BOC ADONIS 4.0 User Manual- Method Manual, BPMS Method (2009)
27. Ternai, K., Török, M.: A new approach in the development of ontology based workflow architectures. In: 17th International Conference on Concurrent Enterprising - Conference Proceedings. Approaches in Concurrent Engineering. Published by: Ralf Zillekens Druck- und Werbeservice, Stolberg, Germany, 20−22 June 2011. ISBN: 978-3-943024-04-3
28. Szabó, I., Varga, K.: Knowledge-based compliance checking of business processes. In: Meersman, R., Panetto, H., Dillon, T., Missikoff, M., Liu, L., Pastor, O., Cuzzocrea, A., Sellis, T. (eds.) OTM 2014. LNCS, vol. 8841, pp. 597–611. Springer, Heidelberg (2014)
29. Castello, V., Mahajan, L., Flores, E., Gabor, M., Neusch, G., Szabó, I.B., Caballero, J.G., Vettraino, L., Luna, J.M., Blackburn, C., Ramos, F.J.: The skill match challenge. evidences from the SMART project. In: Proceedings of the ICERI 2014, pp. 1182−1189 (2014)
30. Ternai, K., Szabó, I., Varga, K.: Ontology-Based Compliance Checking on Higher Education Processes. In: Kő, A., Leitner, C., Leitold, H., Prosser, A. (eds.) EGOVIS/EDEM 2013. LNCS, vol. 8061, pp. 58–71. Springer, Heidelberg (2013)

Management of Large Hydroelectric Reservoirs Surrounding Areas Using GIS and Remote Sensing

Anselmo Cardoso de Paiva[1], Cláudio E.C. Campelo[2(✉)], Lucas Caracas de Figueiredo[1], Julio Henrique Rocha[2], Hugo Feitosa de Figueirêdo[3], and Cláudio de Souza Baptista[2]

[1] Applied Computing Group, Federal University of Maranhão, São Luís, Brazil
paiva@deinf.ufma.br, lucascfxl3@gmail.com

[2] Systems and Computing Department, Federal University of Campina Grande, Campina Grande, Brazil
{campelo, baptista}@dsc.ufcg.edu.br, juliorocha@copin.ufcg.edu.br

[3] Federal Institute of Education, Science and Technology of Paraíba, Monteiro, Brazil
hugo.figueiredo@ifpb.edu.br

Abstract. The management of large water reservoirs is costly. The long perimeter of lakes and the need for an effective control of their surrounding areas prevent the accomplishment of the monitoring task by field engineers. This paper presents a GIS-based corporate IT solution that integrates the management of social, patrimonial and environmental events associated with the land use changes detection methodology. The proposed solution aims to monitor the use and occupation of Permanent Preservation Areas (PPA) around different water reservoirs.

1 Introduction

In Brazil the majority of electrical energy comes from hydroelectric plants, which use water stored in reservoirs as primary energy source. These units when implemented cause several environmental impacts. Thus, the electrical companies are responsible for the environmental management of their area of actuation, aiming to mitigate those impacts. In order to achieve this aim, decision support systems using GIS and Remote Sensing approaches are highly recommended.

Even though hydroelectric plants are one of the most environmentally friendly means of generating electricity, the appropriate management of their surrounding areas has become crucial for a proper planning of land-use around the reservoirs and for harnessing the potential of multiple use of water. This comes from the fact that the use and occupation of reservoir margins and of the stored water have a great influence in the quality and quantity of the hydric resources, reinforcing the importance of an appropriate environmental management of these areas.

© Springer International Publishing Switzerland 2015
A. Kő and E. Francesconi (Eds.): EGOVIS 2015, LNCS 9265, pp. 257–268, 2015.
DOI: 10.1007/978-3-319-22389-6_19

Aware of this context, the Brazilian electric power sector, trough the National Electricity Regulatory Agency - ANEEL regulated these issues to enforce an appropriate management and control of economic, social and environmental information related to areas around water reservoirs. Thus, the Normative Resolution RN-501 establishes procedures to be followed by the concessionaires for mapping the granting areas of hydroelectric plants, which include all properties around the explored reservoirs, max-maximorum curves, Permanent Protection Areas - PPA, among others. This resolution determines that grantees must maintain georeferenced information relating to concession areas and defines that all required information must be sent to ANEEL within twelve months from the beginning of the commercial operation of the first generation unit.

These new rules directly impacts the way companies should acquire, maintain and report information about concession areas, and demand the modernization of the companies' information systems. These systems should contemplate the supervision and correction of illegal situations, preventing the occurrence of new invasions and inadequate use of the reservoir, margins and islands. This involves the preventive patrimonial inspection, aiming the identification and registering of the nearby property areas, their mapping and new critical areas for further analysis. In addition, a continuous verification of the conservation state of those property areas and the execution of social communication programs are required.

This paper presents a GIS-based corporate IT solution to environment management in the San Francisco's Hydro Electric Company (CHESF). CHESF is a unit of Brazil's state-run power utility that generates and transmits electric power to all of the cities in the Northeast of Brazil. This solution is part of a R&D project aimed to facilitate the monitoring of concession areas to meet these new requirements. An important feature of the proposed system is a methodology for automatic detection of land use changes on the reservoirs surround areas, based on the analysis of remote sensing images (orthophotos, high resolution satellite images and LIDAR images).

The reminder of this paper is organized as follows. Section 2 highlights related work. Section 3 focuses on the GIS vector based and mobile solutions for the environment management. Section 4 presents the remote sensing solution and the methodology developed for land use cover change detection based on images. Finally, Sect. 5 addresses the conclusions and discusses further work to be undertaken.

2 Related Work

Land cover change detection can be defined as the identification of changes in the land surface, using images of the same area acquired at different times. This allows the evaluation of spatial dynamics such as urbanization processes, natural disasters, deforestation or other landscape changes, associated with either natural or anthropic causes [8].

The images obtained by remote sensors may be useful to identify the changes in land use and occupation. Furthermore, the multi-temporal aspects of such images contribute to the continuous monitoring of the area over time. There are several techniques for multi-temporal image analysis and each of them has a way to manage the change extraction and classification. There is no universally accepted method. That is, the choice of the method will depend on the objective [3]. These analysis involve the comparison of two or more images, acquired at different times, aiming to detect changes in land-use cover through time. This is usually performed using techniques based on image classification of the spectral signatures of the targets [3].

Many studies proposed the use of remote sensing data to study the problem of land cover change detection [1, 5, 7, 9]. Furthermore, there are some studies that reviewed the various change detection techniques [1, 3, 6, 8]. Jardini et al. [4] proposed the detection of land changes in the reservoir belongs to the Sao Paulo Power Company - CESP - by comparing aerial images (UAV and satellite) of different dates. Zhang Weihong et al. [10] proposed an early warning system for groundwater resources based on "Warning System" theory and GIS technology. The system can be used for groundwater planning, decision-making and water quality management.

It can be seen that a number of existing works have applied remote sensing-based techniques to analyze land cover change. However, their solution do not integrate an information system for the management of social, patrimonial and environmental events associated with the changes detected.

Furthermore, from the analysis of the existing literature, it can be concluded that there is no technique that is suitable for all cases. In some situations, a hybrid approach combining different techniques may be required. In other cases, an existing technique has to be modified. Thus, a method of selecting the appropriate techniques (or the development of a new one) for an specific situation is still an open problem. The techniques used in this work have appeared to be efficient to solve the problem we faced.

3 Vector-Based GIS and Mobile Solutions for Environment Management

The requirements for maintaining Permanent Preservation Areas (PPA) surrounding CHESF's reservoirs surroundings have increased considerably in the last years.

To help the corporation overcome these new challenges facing their business, we developed a corporate TI solution integrating GIS, remote sensing, Web and mobile applications. It allows efficient collection, management and reporting of many different environmental, social and patrimonial information. This integrated solution includes functionalities for managing social and environmental information; registering and tracking events; managing reservoirs and geographic information; handling georeferenced multimedia files; and automatically detecting changes based on satellite images. The solution also comprises modules for mobile collection of information, in loco inspection and auditing.

Figure 1 shows the architecture of the proposed solution showing the functional modules that are described in the following subsections. We used a three tier architecture with the following technologies: Openlayers, Java, Geoserver, Hibernate, Spring, Oracle Locator and Android in the mobile application.

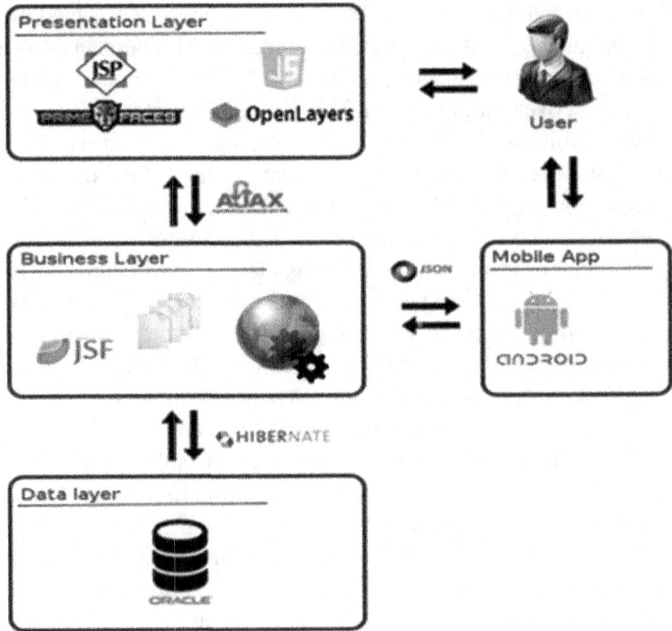

Fig. 1. Architectural view of the proposed system.

3.1 Social and Environmental Information Management Module

The system's module for social and environmental information management, available in both Web and mobile applications, was developed to meet the requirements extracted from a report produced by a specialized company describing a 12-month technical analysis of the physical, biotic, social and economic aspects of the reservoirs surrounding areas.

Georeferenced information managed by the system include climate variables (e.g., rainfall, temperature, humidity, evaporation, evapotranspiration); sites of interest (e.g., historical, cultural, scenic and archaeological remnants, environmental units); characteristics of existing flora and fauna (e.g., biology of species, typologies); soil (e.g., soil type, level of frailty, points of erosion); and water resources (e.g., water abstraction points, irrigation points);

Another important functionality of the system is to be a repository of up to date information about the properties located in the reservoirs' surrounding areas. This is important to facilitate the management and reporting of changes in these areas. This is crucial for the company since this information can be requested by regulatory officials, and meeting the deadlines means avoiding the payment of expensive fines.

The following information about the properties are managed within the system: location; personal, social and economic information about owners/occupiers; legal documents and taxes; economic activities conducted within the properties; and policies of sanitation and waste disposal.

The system provides easy collection of social and patrimonial information via mobile devices. The information collected can then be transferred to the Web server for additional computer-based analysis. This avoids the drawbacks of paper-based methods and makes their business processes noticeably quicker and more reliable. Moreover, georeferenced information can be easily captured with the aid of a GPS-enabled mobile device. The environmental information module of the integrated mobile application is illustrated in Fig. 2.

3.2 Reservoirs and Geographic Information Management

Our system provides a module for visualizing different types of georeferenced information associated with the reservoirs and the properties within the surrounding areas. This feature consists of a graphical user interface based on GIS functionalities. This allows the visualization of a variety of georeferenced files, such as photos, videos, audio, documents and reports by interacting with a digital map. This module of the system offers to the user a more intuitive way to access geographic information, facilitates information management and promotes greater user interactivity with the system.

The main screen of this GIS-based module of the system is shown in Fig. 3. It provides basic GIS navigation features such as zoom and pan (i.e., horizontal and vertical navigation). Other utility tools are also provided, such as a ruler, which allows measuring distance between points or calculating the area of a selected region on the map. It is also possible to load satellite images and add other thematic map layers, such as dams and vegetation. These additional layers can be obtained from external services, through WMS.

Using this interface, the user can select a reservoir of interest either visually, using the interactive map, or using the auxiliary menus shown on the left hand side (Fig. 3). Once a reservoir is chosen, the system retrieves all files associated with the reservoir and organizes them into a hierarchy of folders, so that the user can easily locate the desired file by navigating through the available folders. In addition, all properties located within the surrounding areas of selected reservoir are shown on another menu. By selecting a particular property, another hierarchy of folders is displayed, containing the files associated with that specific property.

Menus and map are properly integrated to facilitate the access and visualization of information resources. For instance, when a reservoir is selected using the menu, the map is automatically zoomed to fit the reservoir and the surrounding area. If a property is selected (either visually or using the menus), it is highlighted in orange as shown in Fig. 3. In addition, when a file is selected by the user, a pop-up window opens to display the metadata associated with the selected file. Then the user can open the file if desired. Furthermore, when a georeferenced file is selected (e.g., a video), the map is automatically zoomed to fit the geographic information associated with the file.

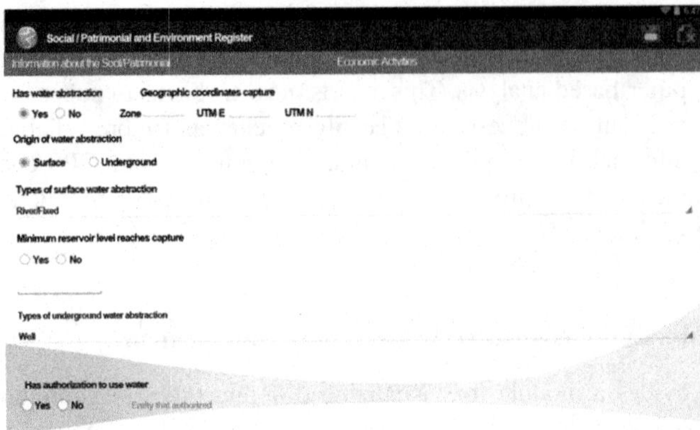

Fig. 2. Recording social and patrimonial information using the mobile application.

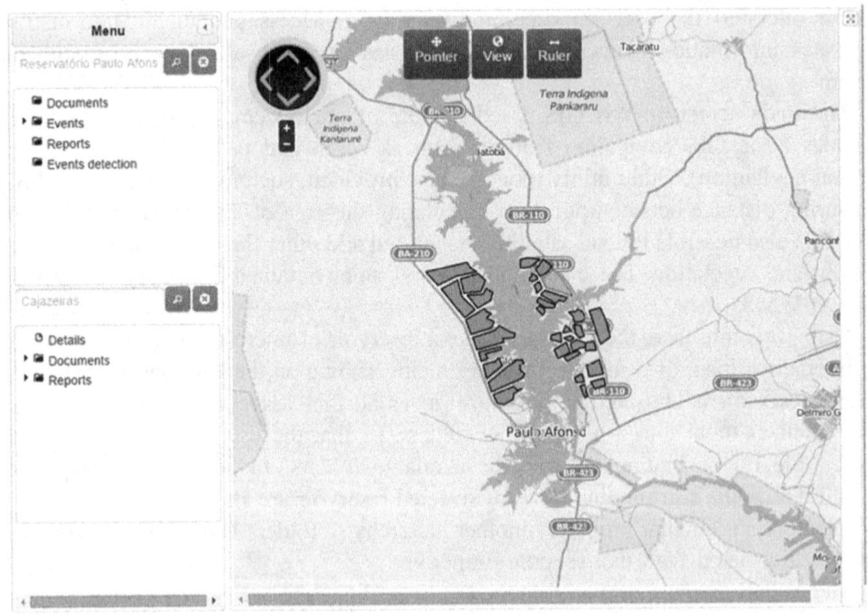

Fig. 3. Main screen of the GIS-based module of the system.

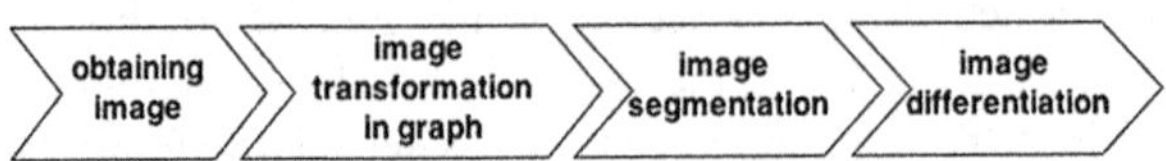

Fig. 4. Methodology of land cover change detection using images

3.3 Managing of Social, Patrimonial and Environmental Events

The main objective of monitoring reservoirs and surroundings of hydroelectric plants is to prevent the occurrence of undesired events of water-use or land-use. These events are illegal activities or accidents observed in the reservoirs, the banks and river islands. These events are classified as social, patrimonial or environmental events.

Social and patrimonial events are characterized by the use of land owned or monitored by CHESF for illegal purposes or without proper authorization by the company. Examples of undesired events of this type with high probability of occurrence are: installation of equipment or construction of buildings; inappropriate abstraction of water; and certain aquaculture activities.

Environmental events may be caused by third parties or natural phenomena, affecting the reservoirs or their surrounding areas. These events impact the environment and involve, directly or indirectly, the modification of water quality of water bodies. Environmental events most likely to occur are: contamination by liquid waste; contamination by solid waste; accident with hazardous chemical; fish mortality; flood; collision, fire, sinking of vessels; fires in vegetation; drowning; slip of marginal slopes; proliferation of aquatic weeds; and removal of timber.

The company must conduct periodic technical inspections in the monitored areas in order to record the occurrence of these events. The information is obtained by face-to-face personal interviews or by observation. Observation are conducted by land, by water, by air or via remote sensing techniques, described in the next section.

Traditionally, all information is collected using pen and paper techniques. However, this paper-form method has a number of drawbacks. Using this new system, all information can be now collected via mobile devices (such as tablets) and automatically downloaded into a data management system specially designed for this project, allowing further computer-assisted analysis of collected data.

The use of this mobile application makes the overall data collection process considerably faster and more accurate, and avoids the need to transport paper forms. In addition, security and confidentiality are ensured through encryption of all information collected and through system access control by authentication. Moreover, georeferenced multimedia information (e.g., photographs) can be attached to the digital forms, and then visualized through the GIS-based user interface.

Another fundamental problem frequently encountered with the traditional paper-based method has been minimized with the use of the new information system: the description of locations. Inspected areas are usually rural, with ill defined addresses, while other target locations have absolutely no formal address, such as a particular portion of a reservoir. Hence, manual descriptions of locations are often imprecise, causing difficulties if the location needs to be revisited. With the use of our mobile application, location can be precisely and automatically determined by the GPS (Global Positioning System) receiver of the mobile device. Additionally, a manual description of the location can still be informed by the user as an auxiliary information or in case of the GPS cannot be used during the inspection.

4 Remote Sensing Land Cover Change Detection

The management of reservoir surroundings requires high investments. Thus, to minimize these costs, the use of automation procedures such as remote sensing has become mandatory. Basically, this is a way to reduce the use of land teams for the inspection of the illegal use of these areas.

4.1 Automatic Detection of Changes Based on Images

Aiming to detect changes in land cover, we developed a computational method based on remote sensing image processing modeled as graph. The proposed method is organized in four steps, as depicted in Fig. 2.

The initial step is the image acquisition that is done using the appropriate technology. After the image acquisition we depicture the image as graph. In this representation each pixel is mapped as a graph vertex and the edges are defined by the pixel neighborhood, associating a weight for each edge based on a specific property associated to the relation between the two pixels connected by it. (Fig. 3).

The graph was implemented as an adjacency list. This was based on the fact that each internal vertex will be connected to eight other vertices and the generated graph will be sparse. In the experiments presented here the weight function was defined by the difference between the pixel values Fig. 5.

After the construction of the graph we apply a depth-first search for segmentation purpose. This will group vertices with similar characteristics, defined by a threshold value. If an edge is discarded, when it has weight above the similarity threshold, the neighbor vertex is not visited. This guaranties that vertex with dissimilar intensities are clustered into different regions. The result is a set of vertices (pixels) clusters. Each cluster has the number of vertices (pixels) counted and associated to it.

For analyze the difference between two images, aiming to detect land cover change, we apply this process in both images. The result group is then submitted to the difference process. This process is done by identifying the pair of clusters in the images that is associated with the same area. Then we subtract the number of vertices of them, which is proportional to the cluster area. If the subtraction result is greater than a threshold value we consider that a change occurred.

Then the system generates a map with areas that should be inspected by land teams to verify whether the changes occurred are adequate or not, to initiate the processes of event identification.

To evaluate the proposed methodology, we applied it in three pairs of images, one of each image class. For the LIDAR images we used the images that corresponds to the first-pulse and to the last-pulse.

In the experiments, the best results were obtained using the parameters presented in Table 1.

The experiments were performed with two Rapideye temporal images. For the Ortophotos and LIDAR data we simulated land cover change through the use of manual editions.

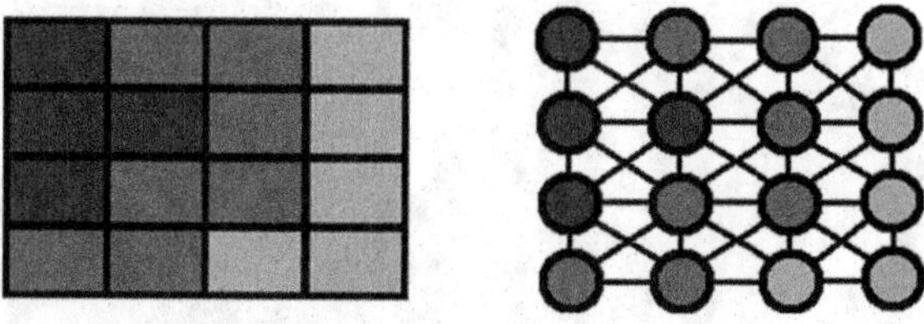

Fig. 5. Graph representation of an image.

Fig. 6. Results applied to ortophoto images.

Table 1. Algorithm parameters used for each data type

Image Class	Similarity Threshold	Area Threshold
Orthofoto	10	0.5 %
LIDAR	4	0.5 %
GeoTIFF	300	0.5 %

Figure 4 presents the application of the land cover change detection methodology for orthophoto images. The first image presents the image at time t1 and the result of the clustering algorithm. The second image presents the same information for an image

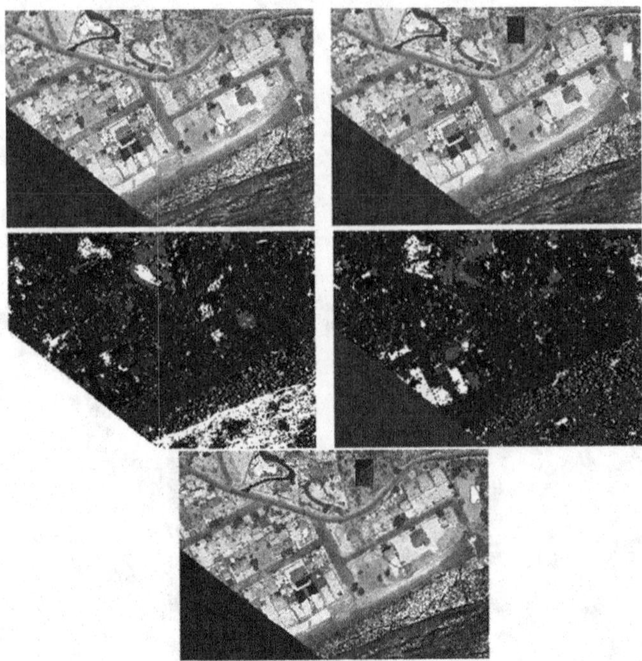

Fig. 7. Results applied to first pulse LIDAR images.

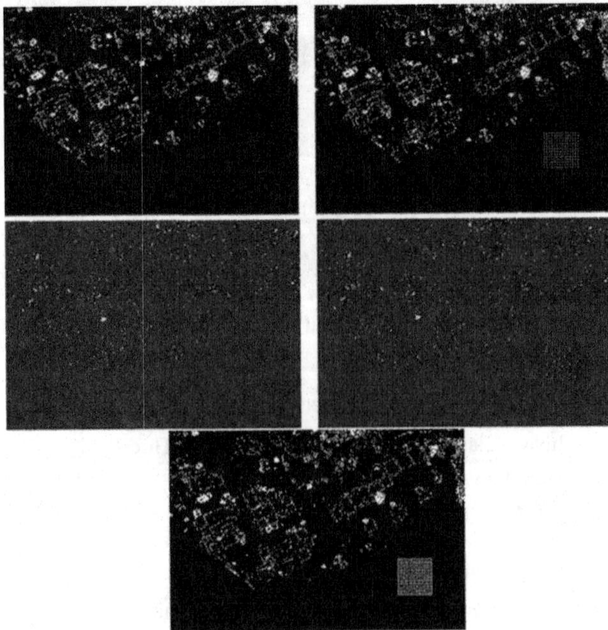

Fig. 8. Results applied to last pulse LIDAR images.

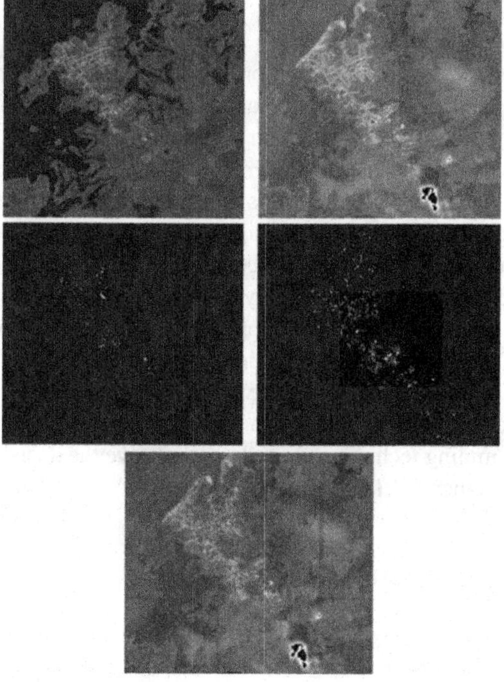

Fig. 9. Experiment with RapidEye images.

taken at time t2 (in this case a simulated image). Finally, the last image presents the results of the detection. We may see that even though the segmentation (clustering) procedure does not segment the visual image in visible detected units, it identifies the changes occurred in the image area.

We noticed that the applied methodology presented similar results obtained in solving the problem of land cover change detection using ortophotos, when applied on LIDAR data, as shown in Figs. 7 and 8. As in Fig. 6, the first image was taken at time t1 and the second at time t2 (simulated image), followed by the result of the clustering procedure.

On the other hand, applying the methodology on RapidEye images required a little more attention to the fact that those data have five bands. With this in sight, we observed that the red, red edge and near infrared bands present greater contrast than the other bands and therefore we decided to use those three in our experiments.

The results obtained with the proposed procedure applied to RapidEye images are shown in Fig. 9. The two images shown on top were taken at times t1 and t2, respectively. The images above shows, respectively, the result of the clustering procedure and the result of the difference process.

As we can see, the result obtained with RapidEye images was a slightly different than the one obtained with LIDAR and Ortophoto images. This difference lies on the fact that it identifies areas that became smaller when applied to the RapidEye images, while in LIDAR and Ortophoto images additional areas are detected.

5 Conclusions

This paper presented a corporate IT solution that integrates Web and mobile applications for managing social, economical, patrimonial and environmental information about large hydroelectric reservoirs and their surrounding areas. This system is part of a R&D project with a major state-run power utility. It could be seen that the system makes the overall data collection process considerably faster and more accurate, avoiding the drawback of paper-based methods and by collecting complex information (such as location) automatically via GPS receivers. Moreover, this new system ensures security and confidentiality, by storing encrypted information access-controlled mobile system. Furthermore, a GIS-based module provides to the user a more intuitive way to access and analyze georeferenced information, which facilitates information management and promotes greater user interactivity with the system.

As future work we plan to develop a GeoBI system, through the use of data warehouse and data mining techniques in order to improve the decision-making process in the field of management of large water reservoirs.

References

1. Alqurashi, F., Kumar, L.: investigating the use of remote sensing and GIS techniques to detect land use and land cover change: a review. Adv. Remote Sens. **2**, 193–204 (2013)
2. Brondizio, E., Moran, E.F., Mausel, P., Wu, Y.: Land use change in the amazon estuary: patterns of caboclo settlement and landscape management. Hum. Ecol. **22**(3), 249–278 (1994)
3. Coppin, P., Jonckheere, I., Nackaerts, K., Muys, B., Lambin, E.: Digital change detection methods in ecosystem monitoring: a review. Int. J. Remote Sens. **09**(05), 1565–1596 (2004)
4. Jardini, M.G.M., Jardini, J.A., Magrini, L.C., Crispino, F., Quintanilha, J.A., Albuquerque, R.W., Pinfari, J.C.: Monitoring system for hydroelectric reservoir using high resolution satellite images. In: 2011 IEEE Trondheim PowerTech, pp. 1–7. IEEE (2011). doi:10.1109/PTC.2011.6019302
5. Kuemmerle, T., Hostert, P., Radeloff, V.C., Perzanowski, K.: Cross-border comparison of land cover and landscape pattern in eastern europe using a hybrid classification technique. Remote Sens. Environ. **103**(4), 449–464 (2006)
6. Mouat, D.A., Mahin, G.G., Lancaster, J.: Remote sensing techniques in the analysis of change detection. Geocarto Int. **8**(2), 39–50 (1993)
7. Pelorosso, R., Leone, A., Boccia, L.: Land cover and land use change in the italian central apennines: a comparison of assessment Methods. Appl. Geogr. **29**(1), 35–48 (2009)
8. Singh, A.: Digital change detection techniques using remotely-sensed data. Int. J. Remote Sens. **10**(06), 989–1003 (1989)
9. Thapa, RB., Murayama, Y.: Urban MappingAccuracy, & Image Classification: A Comparison of Multiple Approaches in Tsukuba City, Japan, Applied Geography, **29**(1), 135–144 (2009)
10. Weihong Z., Yongsheng, Z., Jun, D., Mei, H.: An early warning system for groundwater pollution based on GIS. In: 2011 International Symposium on Water Resource and Environmental Protection, vol. 4, pp. 2773–2776. IEEE (2011). doi:10.1109/ISWREP.2011.5893454

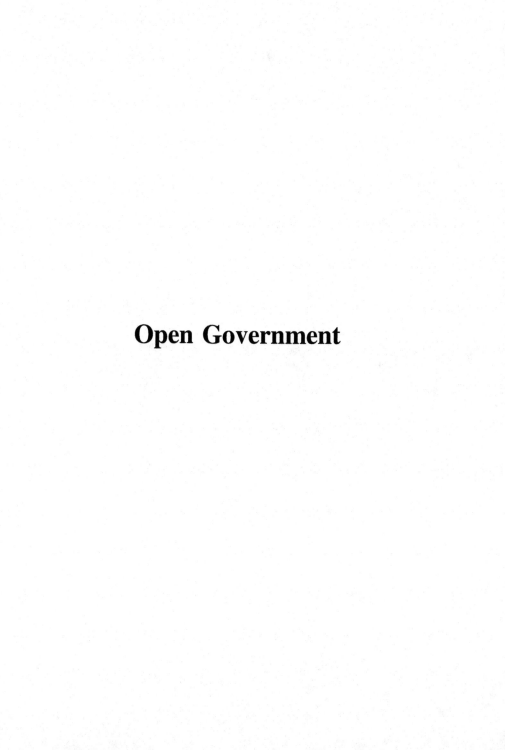

Open Government

Italian Open Government Strategy in National and Regional Regulation

Fernanda Faini(✉)

CIRSFID - Interdepartmental Centre for Research in the History, Philosophy and Sociology of Law and in Legal Informatics, University of Bologna, Bologna, Italy
fernanda.faini@unibo.it

Abstract. In Italy, the division of legislative functions between the central State and the Regions, set out in the Constitution, has allowed the approval of significant Regional *open data* regulations along with the national laws. In the last few years the national legislators have issued specific provisions requiring *open data* to be published and regulated by public authorities. Next to State-issued legislation, some Regions have put in place their own regulations concerning *open data* and *open government*, providing for organization and implementation actions both within the administrations and externally, in their interactions with citizens and businesses. National and regional *open data* regulations have established a virtuous balance, allowing the State to outline the consistent rules necessary to carry out the coordination function attributed to it under the Constitution, and the Regions to play a guiding role in making the digitization of administrative procedures a coordinated process, shared among local public bodies.

Keywords: Open data · Open government · Transparency · Openness · Public sector information · E-Government

1 Italian Open Government

Today's society is experiencing a profound evolution, in which a central role is played by information and communication technology (ICT) and by knowledge, the "raw material" of the new technologies and an essential resource for economic, social and cultural development [3]: this phenomenon is described as "information and knowledge society". The new technologies allow an enormous growth of available information and enable people to use automated tools to acquire it: this leads to a strong reduction in costs and shapes society so as to adopt new forms of cooperation and integration. In the network society, relationships between individuals undergo a deep change, they become simple and immediate once the barriers created by geographic distance no longer exist: this leads the way to the *openness* principle, which promotes a "network" approach able to create unexpected synergies between individuals and to generate ideas, unexplored solutions, new services and products.

The decisive impact of ICT and the central role played by knowledge bring to the fore the need for transparency and *openness* of public information. As a result, in the

© Springer International Publishing Switzerland 2015
A. Kő and E. Francesconi (Eds.): EGOVIS 2015, LNCS 9265, pp. 271–286, 2015.
DOI: 10.1007/978-3-319-22389-6_20

last few years e-government[1] has been evolving into *open government*, a model where the public authorities are expected to be transparent at all levels and their activities to be open and available, so as to promote effective actions and ensure constant control of their conduct by the public through the new technologies.

The *open government* model is characterized by an extensive and integrated use of ICT and the central role attributed to citizens and businesses, which must be granted the right to full access to public information and to informed participation for a dynamic and collaborative interaction between public and private system. Consequently, the new technologies are essential in supporting innovation in the broad sense of the word, i.e. a change in the logic and processes of public administration. *Open government* favours a horizontal dimension characterized by flexibility and emergence of people's needs, where decision making is the result of dialogue and discussion between the public and the private world and decisions can be reached with the contribution of the different stakeholders [5]. The principles of transparency and participation can become a reality in the days of web 2.0, multi-channel communication (PCs, smartphones, tablets etc.), social media and online applications (blogs, forums, sharing platforms, social networks, wiki etc.): these enabling tools reflect a new, dynamic and interactive vision of the network, poised to change the way we think of, use and share information, which becomes independent of its authors and may be used, aggregated and developed by individuals and businesses [9].

A fundamental date for the rise of the *open government* model, after the *Memorandum on Transparency and Open Government* of 21 January 2009, was 8 December 2009, when US President issued the *Open Government Directive* under which the American Government undertook to create an unprecedented level of *openness*, in the belief that this will strengthen democracy, ensure public trust and promote the efficiency and effectiveness of the administration. For this purpose, Barack Obama identified *open data* as a strategic tool for the participation of citizens and businesses, and set out for Government departments and agencies the principles of the open philosophy, consisting of transparency, participation and cooperation, the pillars of the *open government* model:[2] the new technologies are identified as instrumental to ensuring this *openness* process in the public administration [4]. In the area of *open government*, important steps forward have been made in Europe.[3] The strategic

[1] The term e-government refers to the organization of the public administration's activities based on the extensive and integrated adoption of ICT in the performance of their functions and the provision of services, in order to ensure effective actions, increase users' satisfaction, strengthen the democratic process and support public policies.

[2] Cf. Barack Obama, "Memorandum for the Heads of Executive Departments and Agencies on Transparency and *Open Government*" of 21 January 2009 and "*Open Government* Directive" of 8 December 2009, http://www.whitehouse.gov/open/about/policy.

[3] In this respect, the process in Europe started in 2009 with the Open Declaration on European Public Services, sponsored by a group of citizens and associations, which set out the principles of transparency, participation and empowerment, the foundation pillars of *open government*. The contents of the declaration were reiterated in the Declaration of Malmö of 2009, which sets among the objectives for 2015 the development of user-centric services, the engagement of civil society and stakeholders, increased availability of public information and data for re-use, the transparency of administrative processes and the promotion of active participation [4].

framework is currently provided by the European Digital Agenda, one of seven flagship initiatives of the Europe 2020 Strategy.[4] In particular, the objective of the European e-Government Action Plan 2011-2015, adopted in 2010, is to facilitate the transition to a new generation of open and flexible digital administration services at local, national and European level.[5] In December 2011, the European Commission presented a European strategy consisting of a series of measures aimed at promoting *open data* in European countries, which led to a revision of the European Directive on the re-use of public sector information (Directive 2013/37/EU, amending Directive 2003/98/EU).[6]

In Italy, the influence of the international context[7] has resulted in the last few years in significant regulatory actions in the area of *open government*.[8] Following the thorough reform introduced by Legislative Decree no. 235 of 30 December 2010, which involved what can be considered the Italian *Magna Charta* in this matter, i.e. the Digital Administration Code (Codice dell'Amministrazione Digitale, hereinafter also CAD), contained in Legislative Decree no. 82 of 7 March 2005, significant laws have been passed in the last few years, e.g. the act known as Simplifications Decree (Law Decree no. 5 of 9 February 2012, as amended and converted into Law no. 35 of 4 April 2012), which implemented the Italian Digital Agenda;[9] the act known as Development Decree 2012 (Law Decree no. 83 of 22 June 2012, as amended and converted into Law no. 134 of 7 August 2012), containing significant provisions on "open administration"; the act known as Growth 2.0 Decree (Law Decree no. 179 of 18 October 2012, as amended and converted into Law no. 221 of 17 December 2012), which amended several provision of the CAD introducing a stronger focus on *open government*; and lastly the act known as Transparency Decree, i.e. Legislative Decree no. 33 of 14 March 2013, which - in accordance with Law no. 190 of 6 November 2012 (a.k.a. Anti-Corruption Act) - reorganizes the provisions on information publicity, transparency and dissemination. These regulations were accompanied by political strategies put into effect through e-government action plans and most recently the Italian Digital

[4] The Europe 2020 Strategy is aimed at driving intelligent, sustainable and inclusive growth through the achievement by 2020 of employment, productivity and social cohesion goals. The European Digital Agenda is conceived to establish a key role for ICT in achieving the European objectives, and aims to make the most of the potential of these technologies to promote innovation, economic growth and progress.

[5] Cf. European Commission, Communication "The European e-Government Action Plan 2011-2015 - Harnessing ICT to promote smart, sustainable and innovative Government" - COM(2010) 743 final, 15 December 2010. The Plan forms part of the 2020 Digital Agenda.

[6] Cf. European Commission, Communication "Open data. An engine for innovation, growth and transparent governance" - COM(2011) 822 final, 12 December 2011.

[7] On June 18, 2013, the G8 leaders signed the policy paper "Open Data Charter and Technical Annex", which sets out five strategic policy principles for making information open to the public: (1) Open Data by Default; (2) Quality and Quantity; (3) Usable by All; (4) Releasing Data for Improved Governance; (5) Releasing Data for Innovation.

[8] In 2011, the Italian Government asked to participate in the international initiative *Open Government Partnership (OGP)*, aimed at promoting government transparency through the active participation of citizens, trade associations and businesses. In the same year the Government launched a national portal dedicated to *open data* (www.dati.gov.it).

[9] Article 47 of the Simplifications Decree.

Agenda, a strategic framework containing the objectives, actions and initiatives required to implement a digital administration in Italy, increasingly characterized by *open government* elements.

This analysis focuses, in particular, on an essential element of *open government*, i.e. *open data*, and reviews the evolution of State and Regional legislation in this area.

2 The Legislative Jurisdiction of the State and the Regions

In the process through which the Italian public administration is evolving into *open government*, Regional legislation also plays a significant role alongside State legislation. This was made possible by the distinct legislative functions provided for in the Constitution with respect to e-government.

In the Italian constitutional framework, legislative jurisdiction is attributed on the basis of a division between matters on which the State has exclusive legislative jurisdiction; matters on which the State and the Regions have joint jurisdiction, with the State laying out the fundamental principles and the Regions authorized to issue laws in compliance with those principles and of other set requirements; and a residual area, not covered by matters on which the State has exclusive or joint jurisdiction and on which the Regions have exclusive legislative jurisdiction: in fact, Regions have legislative power on any matter not expressly reserved to State legislation.

On matters concerning e-government, the main regulatory reference is contained in article 117, paragraph 2 r), of the Italian Constitution, which attributes to the State on an exclusive basis the jurisdiction on the "coordination of statistical and electronic data of the State, Regional and local administration"; for anything that does not fall within this coordination function, the Regions' legislative power is exclusive (residual). With regard to the content and breadth of the "coordination of statistical and electronic data", disputes have arisen between the State and the Regions and were resolved by the Constitutional Court. According to this body, the coordination of data is to be interpreted as a power of the State, limited as far as the Regions are concerned to a merely technical coordination to ensure common and consistent languages, procedures and standards enabling the public administration's computer systems to communicate with each other.[10] According to the Court's jurisprudence, coordination also legitimates legislative actions aimed at ensuring the quality of services and the rationalization of the public administrations' information technology expenditure, generating significant savings by eliminating duplications and inefficiencies, and directing investments in technologies in accordance with a coordinated and integrated strategy. In addition to laying out technical rules, coordination may also involve organizational aspects whenever this is "deemed necessary to ensure consistency in data processing and transmission".[11] Therefore, coordination contains prescriptive elements which strongly affect the concrete exercise of the functions relating to the "administrative organization

[10] Constitutional Court Judgement no. 17 of 16 January 2004, also referred to in Const. Court Judgement no. 398 of 1 December 2006.

[11] Constitutional Court Judgement no. 31 of 26 January 2005, also referred to in Const. Court Judgement no. 133 of 14 May 2008.

of the Regions and local bodies",[12] and makes it necessary to ensure a forceful involvement of these bodies.[13]

In its decisions, the Constitutional Court has pointed out how the law does not exclude the possibility for the Regions to regulate the implementation within each Region of data collection systems and a jurisdiction of the Regions in regulating and managing their own information networks.[14] The State's exclusive legislative power only concerns coordination of a technical nature, deemed appropriate (cf. Const. Court Judgements no. 31/2005 and 17/2004) and "the exercise of which, in any case, may not exclude the Region's jurisdiction in regulating and managing their own information network (cf. Const. Court Judgement no. 50/2005)".[15] This leaves a wide margin of legislative power to the Regions, also considering the fact that jurisdiction on matters of "legal framework and organization of the Regions and local bodies" is exclusively attributed to the Regions.[16]

The relationship between the State's and the Regions' respective legislative powers, as well as the content of the information coordination, are also the subject matter of various regulations, and in particular of the Digital Administration Code (Legislative Decree no. 82/2005), which in this respect is aligned with the Constitutional Court's jurisprudence: under art. 14, Legislative Decree no. 82/2005, information coordination under State control also includes the issue of the technical rules required to ensure the security and interoperability of information systems and flows for data circulation and exchange and for access to the online services provided by the administrations.[17] In this regard, an important guiding role in the digitization of local bodies is attributed under Legislative Decree no. 82/2005 to the Regions, which are expected to promote local actions to implement a shared, coordinated process for the digitization of administrative procedures.[18]

Within this constitutional and legislative context, the national regulations of the last few years have strongly promoted strategies in support of the *openness* of public information; in this respect, the Regional legislation has also played a major role.

---

[12] As shall be discussed further in this document, this area is under the exclusive legislative jurisdiction of the Regions.

[13] Constitutional Court Judgement no. 31 of 26 January 2005.

[14] Constitutional Court Judgement no. 50 of 28 January 2005.

[15] Constitutional Court Judgement no. 271 of 7 July 2005.

[16] In fact, only the "legal framework and administrative organization of the State and national public bodies" are placed under the exclusive legislative jurisdiction of the State (article 117, paragraph 2 g) of the Italian Constitution).

[17] Article 14, paragraph 1 of Legislative Decree no. 82/2005. The digitization model outlined in the code provides for the "participation" of the different Government levels (State, Regions, local bodies): for this purpose, the code envisages the promotion of understandings and agreements, interregional cooperation, and the establishment of entities tasked with cooperating with the Regions and local bodies (Article 14, paragraphs 2 and 3 of Legislative Decree no. 82/2005).

[18] Article 14, paragraph 2-bis of Legislative Decree no. 82/2005.

3 The Openness Paradigm: Open Data in State Laws

In the recent Italian regulatory process, the principle of transparency has undergone a development in nature: prompted by the European Union, the regulatory evolution has placed increasing emphasis not only on the *amount* of data to be published, but also on *how* transparency is implemented, on its dynamic and active aspect, and on *open data*.

Open data[19] serve multiple purposes, as they are a mean to achieve transparency; allow democratic control by citizens, which ensures greater efficiency and discourage attempts of corruption; help to improve the quality of life of the citizens, enabling them to use, share, update and cross data; and support economic growth, given the great value of public data and their possibility of being re-used for new products and services [6].

In the applicable laws, and in particular in article 68, paragraph 3 (b) of Legislative Decree no. 82/2005, as amended by Law Decree no. 179/2012 in turn amended and converted into Law no. 221/2012, defines *open data*, identifying them in the legal, technological and economic dimensions that characterize them.[20] Under this provision, *open data* are data with the following characteristics:

1. they are available under the terms of a licence allowing use by anyone, for commercial purposes or otherwise, in disaggregated form (legal dimension);[21]
2. are accessible via ICTs, including public and private web networks, in open formats; are suitable for automated use by computer programmes, and are provided with the relevant metadata (technological dimension);
3. are made available free of charge via the ICTs, including public and private web networks, or offered at the marginal costs incurred for their reproduction and dissemination (economic dimension).

This approach explicitly promoting *open data* and *openness* of public information has made great advances in very recent years. The idea is to give the data, which constitute the repository of the public information heritage, back to the community in the form of *open data* and let collective intelligence make use of them, employing them

[19] With reference to the *open data* produced by public authorities, a more specific term is *open government* data.

[20] According to the *Open Knowledge Foundation* (http://okfn.org) a piece of content or data is open if anyone is free to use, re-use, and redistributed it - subject only, at most - to the requirement to attribute and share alike.

[21] The owner of the data is the public administration of public law entity that originally developed for its own use or requested another public or private entity to develop the document that represents the data, or has access to said document. A licence is a contract or other instrument in which are set forth the terms and conditions for reuse of the data (art. 2, paragraph 1 (i) and (h), Legislative Decree no. 36/2006). A distinction to be made among licences is between free and closed licenses. This refers to the different rights granted to users of a work covered by copyright in accordance with Law no. 633/1941: rather than determining the limits of usability of the data, they tend to grant a series of rights to those who come into possession of the information. This model is based on "some rights reserved" and is sometimes referred to as *copyleft*, as opposed to *copyright*. Among the open licences most commonly used in Italy, we should mention *Creative Commons* (CC) (http://www.creativecommons.it/) and *Italian Open Data Licences* (IODL) (http://www.dati.gov.it/iodl/2.0) [1].

for new services and solutions and transforming them into drivers of innovative economic and social potential [10].

Initially, Legislative Decree no. 36/2006, implementing Directive 2003/98/EC (recently amended by Directive 2013/37/EU), did not require the obligation to reuse documents in the public sector, a decision that remained up to the administration - although public data were already viewed as an important "raw material" for digital products and services, to be reused in order to contribute to economic and social growth.

In later years, legislators took a bolder approach and introduced the promotion of the *open data* paradigm among the Italian digital agenda implementation objectives (in art. 47 of the "Simplifications Decree"[22]), "as a model for the enhancement of public information, in order to create innovative tools and services".[23]

Recently, article 9 of the act known as Growth 2.0 Decree (Law Decree no. 179/2012, as amended and converted into Law no. 221/2012), which amended and supplemented the Digital Administration Code (particularly articles 52 and 68 of Legislative Decree no. 82/2005) introduced the definition of *open data* as reported above[24] and introduced a general provision aimed at rationalizing the process for the enhancement of national public information [7]. Specifically, article 52 of Legislative Decree no. 82/2005 provides for online access to data, documents and procedures and the reuse of data and documents to be regulated by public authorities,[25] which are required to publish in their websites a catalogue of data, metadata and the relevant databases in their possession, as well as the regulations that govern the right to online access and reuse, with the exceptions of data contained in the Tax Register information system ("Anagrafe Tributaria").[26]

---

[22] Art. 47, paragraph 2-bis (b), Law Decree no. 5/2012 as amended and converted into Law no. 35/2012.

[23] Subsequently, art. 18 of Law Decree no. 83/2012, as amended and converted into Law no. 134/2012, significantly entitled "Open Administration" (which was later repealed and its content was merged into the Transparency Decree), introduced the obligation, with specific responsibilities and penalties, to publish in open format certain types of particularly important information (the concession of grants, contributions, benefits and financial aid to businesses and the attribution of fees and remuneration to individuals, professionals, private businesses and entities, or otherwise of economic benefits of whatever nature to public and private entities).

[24] Additionally, the regulation introduces the definition of "*open data* format", i.e. a data format made public, exhaustively documented and neutral with respect to the technological means required to use the data (art. 68, paragraph 3 (a), Legislative Decree no. 82/2005), as well as the definition of "reuse" as use of the data as set out in art. 2, paragraph 1 (e) of Legislative Decree no. 36/2006, i.e. use of data owned by a public authority or a public law entity by natural or legal persons, for commercial or non-commercial purposes other than the initial purposes for which the document representing the data was produced for institutional purposes (art. 1, paragraph 1 n-bis), Legislative Decree no. 82/2005).

[25] The obligation concerns all the parties to whom the Digital Administration Code applies, as set out in art. 2, paragraph 2, Legislative Decree no. 82/2005.

[26] Article 52, paragraph 1 of Legislative Decree no. 82/2005.

The provision establishes the important principle of "*open data by default*"[27]: any data and documents published by public authorities by whatever means, without the express adoption of a licence, are understood to be issued as *open data*; the adoption of a licence must be justified in accordance with the national guidelines as defined by the Digital Italy Agency.[28] Art. 52, paragraph 4 of Legislative Decree 82/2005 is conceived to ensure the effectiveness of these provisions, and for this purpose expressly links the activities aimed at providing online access to and reuse of the authorities' data to measurements for the assessment of executives' performance.

For the purpose of enhancing public information, from a governance point of view, the provision assigns a key role at national level to the Digital Italy Agency (Agenzia per l'Italia digitale),[29] a body designated to supervise the correct implementation of the regulations and the transition of Italian public authorities to *openness* of their data through dedicated strategic and technical functions.[30]

Today, this regulatory process is complemented with Legislative Decree 33/2013, which in Article 7, under the significant heading "*Open data* and reuse" sets forth the principle that documents, information and data subject to mandatory publication must be published in open format[31] and be reusable, without further restriction other than the obligation to quote the source and respect their integrity. Transparency, therefore, translates not only in the requirements concerning publication and data quality, but also in their reusability (*open data*) [2, 7, 8].

Thus, in the national legislation transparency combines with data *openness*, configuring administrations characterized by the word "*openness*".

Alongside regulatory provisions, *open data* strategies have taken on the form of specific operating tools and application implementations. In particular, in 2011 the Government launched the Italian *open data* portal (www.dati.gov.it), where the *open data* released by Italian public administrations are made available in a simple, intuitive manner. The website also provides a source of information and awareness *open data* related issues, since it publishes significant news and has a specific section containing documentation and useful links. In addition to the dati.gov.it portal, a number of

[27] Reference to "*open data* by default" is also made in the government portal Dati.gov at http://www.dati.gov.it/content/parte-lopen-data-default (communication of 19 March 2013). It bears pointing out that there needs to be compliance with all applicable provisions of law (with their exclusions and limitations), especially as concerns privacy; intellectual property (including industrial property); public safety and security; state, administrative and statistical confidentiality; and that includes compliance with the legal provisions specific to the subject area at hand (e.g. environmental law).

[28] Article 52, paragraph 2 of Legislative Decree no. 82/2005.

[29] The website of the Digital Italy Agency – AgID is http://www.agid.gov.it.

[30] The Agency is assigned specific tasks to be performed on an annual basis: the National Agenda, in which it defines the content and objectives of the policies for the enhancement of public information, and an annual report on the status of the enhancement process in the country. Alongside its strategic functions, the Agency is also assigned a technical role, as it is tasked with the definition and annual updating of the national guidelines that identify the technical standards, including the determination of the ontologies of the services and data, the procedures and methods for implementing the provisions with a view to making the process consistent nationwide, efficient and effective (Article 52, paragraphs 5, 6 and 7, Legislative Decree no. 82/2005).

[31] Cf. footnote 24.

national and local *open data* platforms have been created over the years; examples include http://www.opencoesione.gov.it (containing *open data* concerning the projects financed by cohesion policies in Italy), http://dati.camera.it and http://dati.senato.it (platforms for the publication and sharing of *linked open data* on the activities and bodies of the Chamber and the Senate).

4 The Regional Open Data Legislation

The Italian Regions have been very active in promoting strategies for the *openness* of public information and, in many cases, have passed specific laws on *open data.*[32]

4.1 The Piedmont and Emilia-Romagna Regions

The Piedmont Region, with Regional Law no. 24 of 23 December 2011, "Provisions for the publication through the Internet and the reuse of documents and public data of the Regional government", issued *open data* regulations earlier than the central State, whose first laws on this matter were passed in 2012. Piedmont's Regional law consists of few but extremely important articles. The first article states the purposes of the law, which coincide with the very objectives that *open data* allow to achieve: social progress, quality of life improvement, and the development of private business initiatives connected to the reuse of public sector information; in detail, the law aims at ensuring maximum freedom of access to public information, promoting the participation of citizens, businesses, foundations and associations in the public administration's decision making processes, encouraging cooperation between the private and the public sector, and making the greatest possible number of documents and data public according to procedures that ensure fair, adequate and non-discriminating conditions. The law justly dedicates a provision to the definitions, in consideration of the technical aspects that characterize the regulation.[33]

In making public documents and data available to the community, the Piedmont Regional law requires compliance with the three dimensions - technological, economic and legal - which connote *open data* and on which the definition of *open data* at national level will later be based.[34]

In addition to public data characteristics, which must be guaranteed for their publication as *open data,* the law includes procedural and implementation aspects to ensure the effectiveness of the provisions. The law provides for implementation

[32] In this analysis I will only be concerned with law, looking at the main regional laws, without taking account of administrative regulations, such as regional resolutions.

[33] Article 2, Piedmont Regional law no. 24/2011.

[34] The Piedmont Regional law prescribes the need for open formats according to international standards, free accessibility via the Internet, and reusability through licences allowing use also for commercial purposes and for profit, guaranteeing equal treatment to reusers and complying with the limits and exceptions set out in the national regulations (Article 3, Piedmont Regional law no. 24/2011).

measures aimed at determining which data, documents and information may be immediately reused; publication procedures; cases in which publication and use are not free of charge; usable open formats, and the procedures to apply for the availability of data and to file complaints; the Region undertakes to process complaints within 30 days, subject to justified extensions.[35]

From an operational point of view, Piedmont was the first Region that released its public information in 2010 and created a regional portal dedicated to *open data* (http://www.dati.piemonte.it). The Emilia-Romagna Region followed the example of Piedmont in 2011, with an *open data* portal (http://dati.emilia-romagna.it). Emilia-Romagna does not have a specific law governing *open data*; however, Regional Law no. 11 dated 24 May 2004 under art. 3, paragraph 1 provides that data accessibility and availability must be ensured through the use of at least one free and/or open standard format.

Subsequently, Lombardy, Lazio, Apulia, and the Autonomous Province of Trento also issued *open data* regulations, specifically in 2012, the same year in which the central State began to pass laws on this matter, prompted not only by European and international pressure but also by the Regions.

4.2 The Autonomous Province of Trento and the Lombardy, Apulia, Umbria, and Marche Regions

Specifically, the Autonomous Province of Trento issued Provincial Law no. 16 of 27 July 2012, named "Provisions on *open data*" within the wider framework of the law containing provisions for the promotion of information society and digital administration and for the dissemination of free software and *open data* formats. In particular, article 9, in line with the Piedmont Regional Law, describes the characteristics of *open data*, which the Province undertakes to guarantee in their legal, technological and economic dimension. The *open data* portal of the Autonomous Province of Trento is http://dati.trentino.it.

The Apulia Regional Law no. 20 of 24 July 2012, "Provisions on free software, data and document accessibility and documented hardware" regulates not only *open data*, but also other aspects related to digital administration and the development of information society. Among its different purposes, the law starts "a process for the dissemination of data freely accessible by all (*open data*) for a Public Administration that is open to the citizens in terms of participation in the decision making process (*open government*)"[36]: the *open data*, an indispensable element of *open government*, are regulated under article 6, whose content is comparable to that of the other Regional laws discussed above. The Apulia Region's *open data* are available at http://www.dataset.puglia.it.

In Regional Law no. 7 of 18 April 2012, Lombardy Region devotes art. 52 to the dissemination and promotion of public data, including data used for commercial

---

[35] Articles 4 and 5, Piedmont Regional law no. 24/2011.

[36] Article 1, Apulia Regional law no. 20/2012.

purposes, referring to specific rules on how to frame databases to be made open; the Lombardy Region's dedicated *open data* portal is found at https://www.dati.lombardia.it. Subsequently, the same approach was taken by Umbria Region in its Regional Law no. 9 of 29 April 2014, which on the question of developing an information society provides for the promotion of *open data* and *open government*, providing as well for the creation of a Training Centre on *Openness*; the Umbria Region's *open data* portal is at http://dati.umbria.it. The Marche Region also dedicates a large portion of Regional Law no. 3 of 16 February 2015 to administrative innovation and simplification, and in one of the provisions (art. 11) undertakes to publish data as *open data* and to promote the dissemination of an *open data* culture; the Marche Region's *open data* are available at http://goodpa.regione.marche.it.

4.3 The Lazio Region

Based on the Piedmont Region model, the Lazio Region issued a specific law (no. 7 of 18 June 2012) on *open data*. The Lazio Regional law, however - alongside the commitment to ensuring *open data* publication and the description of application, reporting and complaint procedures - devotes a great deal of attention to internal organizational aspects and to the need for participation and cooperation with the public and private external world. Therefore, the law "strengthens" the *open data* strategy with actions aimed at implementing a broader regional *open government*.

From the point of view of internal organization, art. 7 of the Lazio Regional law appropriately provides for the planning of training and continuing education courses for the Region's personnel, focusing on the knowledge of electronic tools and use of ICTs. In order to ensure the effectiveness of the provisions, the law sets forth the executives' responsibility for compliance with and implementation of the regulation, linked to the measurement and assessment of the performance of the executives responsible for the relevant functions.[37]

With reference to participation and cooperation with the external world, the Lazio Regional law promotes digital culture in this field by encouraging training and professional qualification initiatives, as well as training and technical support services for the reuse of data based on e-learning systems addressed to the public.[38] The training programmes will be accompanied by dissemination and awareness actions addressed to local institutions and organizations with the involvement of local entities, trade associations and consumers.[39]

The Lazio Region also focuses on businesses and the economic growth driven by the reuse of public data: the law intends to support and promote, in compliance with competition regulations, the entrepreneurial development and competitiveness of the

[37] Article 11, Lazio Regional law no. 7/2012.

[38] E.g. courses for personnel of public and private entities, initiatives for the hiring and development of young people and women, as well as individuals belonging to disadvantaged social groups and minorities.

[39] Article 8, Lazio Regional law no. 7/2012.

Region's industry on national and international markets by implementing different types of initiatives, including the use of guarantee funds, the provision of loans and grants and the creation of a web space for the promotion of innovative technological products related to data reuse. The law also provides for an annual Call for Ideas addressed to young people on specific themes related to the use of innovative digital technologies based on the reuse of public information and data.[40]

The *Open Data* Lazio portal (https://dati.lazio.it) publishes the *open data* of the Lazio Region and of the other local administrations, enterprises and other public and private entities, with the aim to build a body of shared regional information.

4.4 The Campania Region

In 2013, the Campania Region approved a law on administrative transparency and the enhancement of data owned by the Region (Law no. 14 of 13 September 2013). The Campania Region chose to regulate through a secondary act the technological, legal and economic dimensions of *open data*, and in particular the definition of data identification methods, the format, the procedures and means of publication, the assumed costs and rates, the licences and the procedure for accessing data.[41] The Campania Regional law focuses in particular on the technical aspects, specifically on the organization of data into sets, including details on minimum information content: type of licence, data format, date of last update and reference URL.[42]

4.5 The Friuli Venezia Giulia and Veneto Regions

2014 saw the approval of the Regional law of Friuli Venezia Giulia (no. 7 of 17 April 2014), "Provisions on *open data* and reuse thereof". Within the broader framework of the Regional strategy for digital development, the law is aimed not only at the dissemination of data structured into open formats, freely accessible by all, and their reuse, but also to the widest possible collaboration with public and private entities, interaction between the authorities' systems, promotion of the digital culture and development of private economic initiatives connected to data reuse.[43] Art. 4 of the law sets out the technical and legal characteristics of *open data* and their publication, giving special attention to the legal constraints to be complied with, the updating of information and the removal and prevention of any obstacles limiting full accessibility and equal

---

[40] Article 9, Lazio Regional law no. 7/2012. To test the efficiency and effectiveness of the tools provided by these regulations, the Lazio Region undertakes to review the law within one year and to publish the results and any proposed changes through public consultations (Article 14, paragraph 2, Lazio Regional law no. 7/2012).

[41] Article 4, Campania Regional law no. 14/2013.

[42] The data sets will be "encoded and classified preferably as *linked open data*, so as to ensure they are linked to other data sets to increase the value of correlated data." (Article 5, Campania Regional law no. 14/2013).

[43] Article 1, Friuli Venezia Giulia Regional law no. 7/2014.

treatment of reusers. Art. 5 provides for implementation measures to specify which data are subject to immediate reuse, which are released against payment, the methods of publication, the licences, the formats, the systems to facilitate searches and to apply for reuse, which the Region undertakes to process within thirty days subject to delays for justified reasons or impediments of an economic, organizational or legal nature. The Friuli Venezia-Giulia Region's *open data* platform is found at https://www.dati.friuliveneziagiulia.it.

The provisions on *open data* contained in the Veneto Region's Law no. 2 of 24 February 2015 (article 15 *et seq.*), in accordance with the relevant EU directive, recognize the importance of *open data* as a means to achieve transparency and simplification and a resource to promote economic recovery. The law lays down guiding principles and criteria on *open data* from a legal and technological point of view, while referring to a separate regulation for the specific methods to achieve data openness and reuse; the law also requires the *open data* of the Veneto Region and of the other local public entities to be published in a dedicated *open data* portal (http://dati.veneto.it).

4.6 The Tuscany Region

The Tuscany Region has recently approved a law containing provisions on *open data* and reuse thereof (Regional Law no. 19 of 18 February 2015). Despite the reference to *open data* in the heading, the Tuscany Regional law focuses on *open government*, as in the case of the Lazio.

The Tuscany Regional law outlines the characteristics of *open data* in their technological, legal and economic dimensions. From a technological point of view, it provides for platforms dedicated to *open data* and places special emphasis on granularity, interoperability and accessibility.[44] From a legal standpoint, the Tuscany Region encourages licences that promote internationalization, such as Creative Commons, showing a preference for a sort of CC-BY by default.[45] From an economic perspective, the rule is free use, with fees only possible for the costs of making the information available, reproducing it and disseminating it, in compliance with national regulations and through executives decrees.

In addition to *openness*, the Tuscany Regional law gives special attention to the other two principles underlying *open government*: participation and cooperation. These two principles are applied both internally and externally to the Region. Internally, the law sets out the organizational process, for which it refers to a secondary act; clarifies the role of the different structures involved, and assigns responsibility for *openness* to the executives, linking it to performance measurement and assessment.[46] The participation and collaboration principles are also applied to interactions with the external

[44] Articles 4 and 5, Tuscany Regional law no. 19/2015.

[45] Article 5, paragraphs 4 and 5, Tuscany Regional law no. 19/2015.

[46] Article 6, Tuscany Regional law no. 19/2015.

world, with respect to the both public and to the private sphere. In this regard, a significant provision calls for understandings with any individual or entity that "pursues purposes that are instrumental to the achievement of the law's objectives" as well as the promotion of agreements with associations that operate in the areas of *open data*, open services and open knowledge.[47] Participation and cooperation with other administrations is promoted through a series of tools, like *open data* technology platforms developed by the Region and made available to local bodies, the promotion of agreements and incentives.[48]

Participation and cooperation with private subjects is promoted primarily by providing for tools allowing a constant dialogue with the stakeholders, whether citizens, associations or businesses, who are given the possibility to submit proposals and report situations; the Region undertakes to respond with specific procedures and within set time limits. Alongside this proactive role, users also have the possibility to inform the Region of products and services developed thanks to local *open data*, which the Region undertakes to publicize as appropriate.[49] The law calls for initiatives to promote digital culture through information, awareness and training actions, the creation of spaces where systems for the use of *open data* can be set up cooperatively by public and private entities, as well as actions and initiatives for the development of innovative concepts and projects by private subjects on themes related to the use of digital technologies based on data reuse.[50]

To implement its *open government* model, the Tuscany Region created Open-Toscana (http://open.toscana.it), a multi-platform portal intended to bring the administration closer to the citizens and the enterprises by providing easier and more intuitive access to data and services and simplifying their interaction with the administration. The platform consists of six main sections, one of which is dedicated to the *open data* of the Tuscany Region and of the other local administrations (the other sections concern services, participation, apps, the cloud and startups).

In addition to the Regions analysed above, which have issued specific regulatory provisions concerning *open data*, over the years other Italian Regions have also formulated strategies on this matter and created *open data* portals; this is the case, for example, of the Liguria Region (http://www.regione.liguria.it/opendata.html), the Basilicata Region (http://dati.regione.basilicata.it) and the Sardinia Region (http://opendata.regione.sardegna.it).

This analysis shows how the Italian Regions are particularly active in *open data* strategies, issuing regulations to promote *open data* and in some cases, in a broader perspective, *open government* (Table 1).

[47] Article 3, Tuscany Regional law no. 19/2015.

[48] Article 4, Tuscany Regional law no. 19/2015.

[49] Article 7, paragraphs 2 and 3, Tuscany Regional law no. 19/2015.

[50] Articles 7 and 8, Tuscany Regional law no. 19/2015.

Table 1. Chronologically arranged comparative analysis of *open government* in Regional legislation. Legend: *none* (no enacted legislation); *weak* (mention made of need for legislation); *limited* (broadly worded rule, lacking specific provisions); *definite* (definite and specific provisions). The table presents an analysis of Regional law provisions dedicated to *open data*; consequently, it does not include the Liguria, Basilicata and Sardinia Regions which, despite having developed *open data* strategies and created dedicated portals, have not issued specific *open data* provisions.

Region	Law	Promoting open data (open data and open gov principles and objectives)	Technical aspects (standard formats and technical features)	Legal aspects (licences and compliance with legal limits)	Economic aspects (free or fee-basis services)	Internal organization (mode of publication, formation, performance, type of responsibility)	External relations and Open Gov interventions (participation, digital culture, economic development)
Emilia-Romagna	11/2004	weak	limited	none	none	none	none
Piedmont	24/2011	definite	definite	definite	definite	limited	weak
Lombardy	7/2012	weak	weak	weak	none	weak	none
Lazio	7/2012	definite	definite	definite	definite	definite	definite
Apulia	20/2012	definite	definite	definite	definite	limited	weak
Autonomous Province of Trento	16/2012	definite	definite	definite	definite	weak	weak
Campania	14/2013	definite	definite	limited	definite	limited	weak
Friuli Venezia Giulia	7/2014	definite	definite	definite	definite	limited	weak
Umbria	9/2014	definite	none	none	none	weak	limited
Marche	3/2015	definite	none	none	none	none	limited
Tuscany	19/2015	definite	definite	definite	definite	definite	definite
Veneto	2/2015	definite	limited	definite	none	limited	weak

5 Conclusions

In regard to *open data*, the present Italian regulatory framework consists of national and regional regulations. In fact, on matters concerning e-government the Constitution assigns a legislative role to the Regions, which - with the exception of coordination functions, under the exclusive jurisdiction of the central State - have a wide margin for issuing their own laws.

With regard to *open data*, the different Regional laws reviewed in this document are the expression of the guiding role attributed under Legislative Decree no. 82/2005 to the Regions, which are expected to promote local actions to implement a shared, coordinated process for the digitization of administrative procedures.[51] For this reason these laws, in addition to *open data* characteristics in a legal, technical and economic perspective, also focus on organizational and implementation actions to be carried out internally and externally to the Regions. This demonstrates the Regions' awareness an maturity in addressing matters related to *open data*, since in order to be effectively implemented, *openness* strategies require a significant investment in terms of organization to achieve consistency among internal processes and accountability of structures and departments, as well as to create a digital culture in users and encourage them to play a proactive role

[51] Article 14, paragraph 2-bis of Legislative Decree no. 82/2005.

and maintain a constant dialogue with the public authorities. This is especially important in view of the fact that citizens and businesses are reusers of the data, and therefore it is essential to understand which data they like to be open, consider their reports and requests, and be aware of what they can create in terms of products and services through the use of *open data*. From the point of view of local bodies and other local public entities, the Regions play a crucial role in stimulating, providing guidelines and offering tools to launch *openness* strategies, since they are the intermediate local authorities that can effectively perform this function also due to their specific knowledge of the characteristics of the different territories. Consequently, the Regions have a strategic role that they can play in fostering a solid culture across the territory by coordinating open-data initiatives; promoting shared agendas; and supporting local government entities, even the smallest ones, by providing the necessary platforms, resources and skills.

In conclusion, on matters of *open data*, and more in general of *open government*, national and regional regulations have established a virtuous balance, without conflicting but rather complementing each other, allowing the State to set out the consistent rules necessary to achieve information coordination as provided by the Constitution, and the Regions to play a guiding role in making the digitization of administrative procedures a coordinated process, shared among local public bodies.

Acknowledgements. I should like to thank the 30th edition of the Ph.D. Programme in Legal Studies offered by the University of Bologna, under which I have conducted this research, as well as Tuscany Region, for which I am working.

References

1. Aliprandi, S.: Il fenomeno Open Data. Indicazioni e norme per un mondo di dati aperti. Ledizioni, Milano (2014)
2. Carloni, E. (ed.): L'amministrazione aperta. Regole strumenti e limiti dell'open government. Orizzonti di diritto pubblico, Maggioli, Rimini (2014)
3. Castells, M.: The Rise of the Network Society. Oxford University Press, Oxford (2000)
4. Di Donato, F.: Lo stato trasparente. Linked open data e cittadinanza attiva. Edizioni ETS, Pisa (2011)
5. Faini, F.: La strada maestra dell'open government: presupposti, obiettivi, strumenti. Ciberspazio e diritto, 2, pp. 213–240, Mucchi editore, Modena (2013)
6. Faini, F.: Trasparenza, apertura e controllo democratico dell'amministrazione pubblica. Ciberspazio e Diritto, 1, pp. 39–70, Mucchi editore, Modena (2014)
7. Palmirani, M., Martoni, M., Girardi, D.: Open Government Data Beyond Transparency. In: Kő, A., Francesconi, E. (eds.) EGOVIS 2014. LNCS, vol. 8650, pp. 275–291. Springer, Heidelberg (2014)
8. Ponti, B. (ed.): La trasparenza amministrativa dopo il d.lgs. 14 marzo 2013, n. 33. Maggioli, Rimini (2013)
9. Sartor, G.: L'informatica giuridica e le tecnologie dell'informazione – Corso d'informatica giuridica. Giappichelli, Torino (2010)
10. Tiscornia, D. (ed.): Open data e riuso dei dati pubblici. Informatica e diritto, 1-2, Edizioni Scientifiche Italiane, Napoli (2011)

Open Government Data Licensing Framework

Martynas Mockus and Monica Palmirani(✉)

CIRSFID, University of Bologna, Via Galliera 3, 40121 Bologna, Italy
{martynas.mockus2, monica.palmirani}@unibo.it

Abstract. The purpose is to analyze the licensing of Open Government Data (OGD). The problem is that different regimes of regulation of OGD in Europe create extra barriers for re-using OGD. The survey investigated OGD portals around the world and found out which different regulation regimes are applied on datasets and what the most popular licenses are. Compatibility of the leading licenses and legal notices and case analysis of Italy, Lithuania and UK is presented. This paper is organized: (1) definitions, principles and methodology; (2) results of a survey of the licensing of OGD; (3) analysis of the licenses; (4) case analysis; (5) conclusions and future work.

Keywords: Open government data · Licensing of open data · Creative commons license · Copyright of databases · Sui generis database right · Public domain

1 Introduction to the Problem

Since 2009 Open data domain was under the scope of scientists: more than 34,000 of the papers have been published and over 2,200 explicitly focused on *Open Government Data* [1]. But still there are lacks of investigations which focus to the legal side of opening the government data. According to the *Open Data* (OD) community opinion there is not much to discuss about: just "give us the data with an open license" and you will get the first star of five [2, 3]. But this investigation shows that it is not so simple task for the public administration institutions to deal with the legal issues of the open government data concerning the licensing. A lot of the *Open Government Data* (OGD) which is published in the governmental *Open Data* portals does not fulfill the requirements classified by the OD community as the simplest first step (the first star). Several definitions are used in this paper: for favoring the reader they are included in the Annex A below.

1.1 Principles

Analysis of the OD principles provided by Open data community, shows that freely reuse of data is necessary for open data idea.

The Universal Participation principle declares that everyone must be able to use, reuse and redistribute - there should be no discrimination against fields of endeavor or against persons or groups. For example, 'non-commercial' restrictions that would prevent 'commercial' use, or restrictions of use for the certain purposes (e.g. only in education), are not allowed [8].

© Springer International Publishing Switzerland 2015
A. Kő and E. Francesconi (Eds.): EGOVIS 2015, LNCS 9265, pp. 287–301, 2015.
DOI: 10.1007/978-3-319-22389-6_21

The Open Knowledge Foundation suggests the following definition of the open government data: "Data produced or commissioned by government or government controlled entities and it can be freely used, reused and redistributed by anyone" [9].

Why freely reuse is so important? Reuse is one of the pillars of the interoperability and for producing a digital society ecosystem. It is so true that the Directive 2003/98/EC introduced first the concept of the re-use rather than concept of open data. Secondly, the Linked Open Data (LOD) provided a technical framework for supporting the re-use and stressed the freely re-use concept. This characteristic is fundamental for implementing the digital economy. The answer comes from the LOD domain. If there are no legal limitations to connect the datasets, then the LOD principles are satisfied. The LOD first step or first star requires the open license [3].

1.2 Goal, Research Questions and Methodology

Do governments respect the OD principles, or not? What are the tendencies? If not respects, then why? Those questions are too difficult to answer by doing analysis of few countries because the results could be misleading. Data cannot be stopped by borders, so the answers could be found only by the survey of the global OGD domain. The main goal of the Survey is to present the state of art of the current OGD licensing situation. In the paper we address several fundamental questions: does the OGD need legal protection; if so, what kind of licenses should be used; does the CC0 license fulfil the EU regulation? The OD community requires fewer barriers for re-using OD, so should the license be used?

The methodology was to check the legal protection status (license/no license/legal notice) of the datasets provided in the ODG national portals listed in the Annex B below. Because of lack of resources it was not possible to identify the all OGD in every country, so only the key OGD portals have been chosen. The criterions of choosing the portal were those: it should be presented by official public institution as the main OGD portal of the country or the federal state, also OGD portal held by European Commission. Land, state, municipality or other portals held by private and public initiatives were out of a scope of the investigation.

During the survey the condition of the datasets or the links to the datasets was not checked, only metadata was collected. In all cases there were datasets containers (collections of datasets) identified as the singular datasets. All information from the portals was taken as-is. Overall the information of the 435,682 datasets were classified and investigated.

In the absence of specific licenses, we have identified all the legal notices about the obligations, the limitations, the liability, the privacy rules, etc. published on the web in order to understand whether these fragmented legal regulations can fully replace the license instruments. The survey is a representation of the penetration of the license culture in the OGD and also underlines the misuse of the license instrument, which is often adopted as an *admission* rather than a *contract*, especially in the EU. Second, we investigated the principles coming from the OD domain and how they comply with re-use of PSI, copyright law and administrative law principles in the EU-level domain. We also evaluate the impact of the PSI and related licenses on a mashup scenario, presenting a comparative table concerning the compatibility of licenses with the main PSI and OD principles. Thirdly, we have analyzed case studies from Italy, Lithuania and the UK in an effort to model whether it is possible to release OGD without a license, with a CC0 license, with other CC licenses and the like with respect to principles originating from the corresponding jurisdiction and to detect are the OGD of these countries is ready for mash-up in the global OGD domain.

2 The Survey of the Licensing of Open Government Data

In January of 2015 the survey of the licensing of the OGD has been done. The goal of the survey was to collect state-of-art of licenses used in OGD portals to cover datasets.

During the first part of the survey it was checked in the OGD portals: (1) are there datasets covered by any license; (2) if a dataset is not covered by a license, are there any legal notice, conditions for re-use applied to the dataset; (3) are there datasets without the license, or information about the license is not provided.

The results of the first part of the survey are those: (a) 56 % of all datasets from the investigated portals are covered by the license; (b) 17 % of all datasets are not covered by the license, or information about the license in the OGD portal is not provided, or there is any other conditions set of re-use of dataset or is license-free; (c) 27 % of all datasets are covered by legal notice in the portal or in the metadata of the dataset or indicated as legal notice. The legal notice is used in OGD portals of European Union (EU) (100 %), Moldova (100 %), Spain (11 %), US Federal datasets (100 %), other US datasets (0, 3 %) and Germany (only 3 datasets). In Spain and US there are different legal notices.

The second part of the survey is dedicated to multiplicity of the licenses in the global OGD phenomena. The varieties of the licenses were checked and the most popular licenses were identified. The licenses provided by the national authorities and applied only locally are named *local licenses* and it does not include *Creative Commons* localized licenses.

The results are these: (1) the most popular from the licenses are local licenses which covers 90 % licensed datasets (e.g. Open Government License – Canada, License Ouverte, Open Government License (UK), Non-Open Government License (UK), Data license Germany – attribution – version 1.0 and 2.0, Italian Open Data License 2.0 and 1.0, NLOD, Uruguay Open Data License); (2) the second most popular (6 %) from the licenses are CC-BY licenses, including localizations (e.g. CC BY 3.0 AU, CC BY 3.0 NZ, CC BY 3.0 AT, CC BY 3.0 CL, CC BY 3.0 GR and etc.); (3) the third most popular (2 %) are licenses waiving copyrights to public domain CC0 and Open Data Commons *Public Domain Dedication and License* (PDDL); (4) all other licenses covers only 2 % of the datasets. That 2 % pie of the other licenses is divided: Open Data Commons Open Database License (ODbL) (45 %), CC BY-NC (noncommercial) including versions and localizations (38 %), CC BY-SA (attribution, share alike) including versions and localizations (10 %), Open Data Commons Attribution (3 %), GPL (2 %), Against DRM (1 %), CC BY-ND (no derivative works) (1 %), CC BY-NC-ND (attribution, noncommercial, no derivative works), CC BY-NC-SA (attribution, noncommercial, share alike), *GNU Free Documentation License* (GFDL) (cf. Fig. 1).

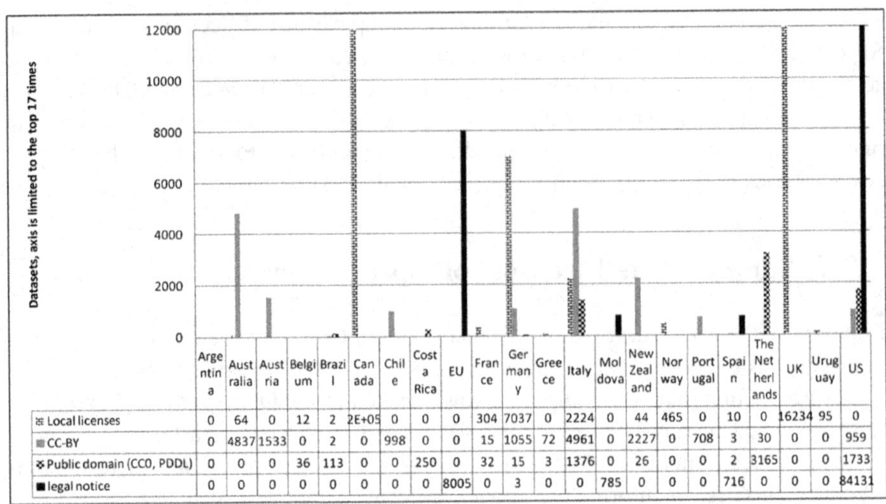

	Argentina	Australia	Austria	Belgium	Brazil	Canada	Chile	Costa Rica	EU	France	Germany	Greece	Italy	Moldova	New Zealand	Norway	Portugal	Spain	The Netherlands	UK	Uruguay	US
Local licenses	0	64	0	12	2	2E+05	0	0	0	304	7037	0	2224	0	44	465	0	10	0	16234	95	0
CC-BY	0	4837	1533	0	2	0	998	0	0	15	1055	72	4961	0	2227	0	708	3	30	0	0	959
Public domain (CC0, PDDL)	0	0	0	36	113	0	0	250	0	32	15	3	1376	0	26	0	0	2	3165	0	0	1733
legal notice	0	0	0	0	0	0	0	0	8005	0	3	0	0	785	0	0	0	716	0	0	0	84131

Fig. 1. Results of The Survey of the Licensing of Open Government Data

Finally, the survey has discovered that in the global licensing scenario the incredibly huge part of the licenses are ruled by the local licenses. Only 17 % of datasets are covered not by the license or the legal notice. Taking to the account that still there is developing stage of the OGD portals and ODG domain, the numbers should change in the coming future. The second important discovery is that CC-BY license is becoming more and more important and is understandable as a standard in the global OGD scenario. From Creative Commons copyright licenses CC-BY has least restrictions to re-use the dataset and is classified as the open license. The third discovery shows, that such countries as The Netherlands, U.S., Italy, Costa Rica, Brazil, Belgium, New Zealand, France, Germany, Greece and Spain release the datasets to the public domain. Last but not least, 27 % of the investigated datasets is "covered" by the legal notices. This is emerging question: how to attach the legal requirements to the dataset in the LOD domain.

3 Analysis of the Licenses for the Datasets Mash-up Scenario

In the datasets mash-up scenario when two different datasets meet, analysis of licenses (or legal regimes applied to datasets) compatibility is needed. No need for it only if dataset is not covered by any license or legal notice or is covered by the license dedicated to the public domain, because these datasets are compatible with any dataset covered by the license.

The survey of the licensing of the OGD showed us 6 most popular legal regimes of the datasets. Compatibility of these licenses and legal notices are shown in a Table 1.[1]

[1] Table 1 must be read from in this manner: licenses in horizontal line meet licenses in a vertical line, and the result represents conclusion of the requirements of two licenses in a mash-up scenario.

Table 1. Top licenses comparison for mashup model

License	Open Government Licence -Canada 2.0.	DATA.GOV Data Policy Statements	Licence Ouverte	Open Government Licence v3.0 (UK)	Legal notice (EU)	CC-BY 4.0.
Open Government Licence - Canada 2.0.	Yes, attribution	Yes, attribution	Yes, attribution	Yes, attribution	Yes, attribution, condition	Yes, attribution
DATA.GOV Data Policy Statements	Yes, attribution	Yes, attribution	Yes, attribution	Yes, attribution	Yes, attribution, condition	Yes, attribution
Licence Ouverte	Yes, attribution	Yes, attribution	Yes, attribution	Yes, attribution	Yes, attribution, condition	Yes, attribution
Open Government Licence v3.0 (UK)	Yes, attribution	Yes, attribution	Yes, attribution	Yes, attribution	Yes, attribution, condition	Yes, attribution
Legal notice (EU)	Yes, attribution, condition	Yes, attribution, condition	Yes, attribution, condition	Yes, attribution, condition	Yes, attribution, condition	Yes, attribution, condition
CC-BY 4.0.	Yes, attribution	Yes, attribution	Yes, attribution	Yes, attribution	Yes, attribution, condition	Yes, attribution

The results are joyful because the most datasets from the investigated OGD portals are compatible because of the correct license regime.

The only problem is to ensure the attribution requirements, which basically are statements about the source of the resource and links to the licenses.

On other hand datasets is not only important by quantity but also by quality. Still there are a lot of datasets which are covered by other licenses. Example of Creative commons licenses compatibility is shown in a Table 2.[2]

In the Table 1 is shown that not CC licenses are compatible, that means not compatible licenses is a barrier for LOD. Datasets covered by not compatible licenses are "out of the cloud of data" in OGD domain and will not create any value in mash-ups of the datasets. Contract type licenses also are a big barrier for LOD.

Only when the contracts made by software agents will be recognized in PSI re-use domain, then the barrier disappears. Otherwise closed platforms as a pools of datasets could be used in specific re-use of PSI projects (e.g. in medicine, where sensual personal data is held and the identification and contracts are needed), or such platforms as ENGAGE [10] could be upgraded to solve contract problems by unifying them.

One of the biggest problems in mash-up scenario is legal notes, which are not unified, does not have common structure. Sometimes it is a document (e.g. EU legal notice), sometimes it is only one sentence (Spain, U.S. datasets) or just a note that legal note is applied (without a reference to that note). Those legal notes usually are placed separately from metadata of the dataset, it means that automatic process of connecting

[2] Table 2 must be read from in this manner: licenses in horizontal line meet licenses in a vertical line, and the result represents conclusion of the requirements of two licenses in a mash-up scenario. Conclusions about mashup possibility is dedicated to the licenses in a horizontal line.

Table 2. Creative commons licenses comparison for mashup model

License	CC-BY4.0	CC-BY-SA 4.0	CC-BY-ND 4.0	CC-BY-NC 4.0	CC-BY-NC-SA 4.0	CC-BY-NC-ND 4.0	Conclusions
CC-BY4.0	YES	YES. BY-SA terms	NO	YES. noncommercial	YES, noncommercial, BY-SA terms	NO	CC-BY 4.0 can be used for mashup with other licenses, except those which doesn't alow to modify
CC-BY-SA 4.0	E: BY-SA terms	YES	NO	NO	NO	NO	CC-BY-SA 4.0 license requires same BY-SA terms for modifications, which doesn't a low to set extra terms as non-commeroal or no modifications.
CC-BY-ND 4.0	NO	NO	NO	NO	NO	NO	CC-BY-ND 40 license can't be used for mashup with other licenses because it doesn't allow mod Ticatlons
CC-BY-NC 4.0	YES, Noncommercial	NO	NO	YES	YES	NO	CC-BY-NC 4.0 license can be used for mashup with other licenses which allow to set extra terms as non-commercia'
CC-BY-NC-SA 4.0	YES, noncommercial, BY-SA terms	NO	NO	YES, noncommercial, BY-SA terms	YES	NO	CC-BY-NC-SA 4.0 license can be used for mashup with other licenses which allow to set extra terms as noncommercial or no modifications.
CC-BY-NC-ND 4.0	NO	NO	NO	NO	NO	NO	CC-BV-NC-ND 4.0 license can't be used for mashup with other licenses because it doesn't allow modifications

legal notes with dataset is very complicated; lifecycle of legal notes in mash-up scenario of datasets is hardly realizable.[3]

To sum up, the most used licenses and unified legal notes to protect OGD are compatible in global scenario. Some licenses (e.g. CC-BY-NC-ND) are not compatible in mash-up scenario. Still there exists a reasonable amount of datasets, especially in Spain, which are covered by not unified legal notes and such legal regime of legal protection of dataset is not suitable for lifecycle of dataset legal regulation.

[3] E.g. In U.S. gov portal there are 350 datasets covered by legal note which provide conditions of re-use: "The Minnesota Department of Natural Resources makes no representation or warranties, express or implied, with respect to the reuse of data provided herewith, regardless of its format or the means of its transmission. There is no guarantee or representation to the user as to the accuracy, currency, suitability, or reliability of this data for any purpose. The user accepts the data 'as is', and assumes all risks associated with its use. By accepting this data, the user agrees not to transmit this data or provide access to it or any part of it to another party unless the user shall include with the data a copy of this disclaimer. The Minnesota Department of Natural Resources assumes no responsibility for actual or consequential damage incurred as a result of any user's reliance on this data.".

4 European Case Analysis

4.1 Italy

4.1.1 OGD Regulation

The Italian Open Government Data Legislation support Public Administrations to release open dataset at national, regional and local levels. The Italian process of open data is quite good at regional (22 bodies) and local level (62 bodies), less important at the ministerial side (26 bodies).[4] The legal framework of the OGD is composed by several different Acts. The fundamental important pillars are: the legislative decree n. 82/2005 *Digital Administration Code* and modifications, the implementation of the Directive 2003/98/EU with the legislative decree n. 69/2009 and the legislative decree n. 33/2013, the *Transparency Act* [11]. The d.lgs. n. 82/2005 defines the Open Government Data modality, but there are two levels for releasing data: (a) to release data using only a technical requirement using open formats (e.g., XML, CSV, etc.); (b) to implement open data paradigm including licenses, reuse without commercial limitations, processes of production of the datasets, quality check. The d.lgs. n. 69/2009 provides the definition of public administration document and the modality and practical means for the public administration that permits the release of documents in open format. In d.lgs. n. 33/2013 we can read a long list of public documents that must be published in digital format in a specific part of the official web site of the public administration, following a strict hierarchical web site tree, but not mandatory in Open Data. The framework is sufficient for implementing a concrete plan of OGD, however the legal scenario is confusing and contradicting.

The Transparency Act is mandatory for each public administration and the prescription is stronger rather than the *Digital Administration Code*. It obliges to release a relevant number of documents/datasets, but limited to cope with the transparency finality (e.g., grant, budget, funds, accountability, performance), limited on time (after three years it is mandatory to move these data in another part of the web site for the *right to be forgotten*) and without any requirement about licenses. So the document/data are released in open format (e.g., XML), but the ownership and the control of the dataset/documents are in the hand of the public administration that can decide to remove all the information from the publication portal in any moment. The *Digital Administration Code* includes wider principles of open data paradigm including the economic benefits produced on the society, the improvement of the quality of life of the citizenships, the effectiveness of the services of the public administration in the governance of the territory. However it imposes to compliance more strict the rules about the privacy related to the *Italian Personal Data Protection Code* (d.lgs. 196/2003 and the connected Guidelines[5]) and so the public administration can (not must) publish a large variety of data (not limited to the accountability matter) using the *Digital Administration Code* rules, but only anonymized. This double track is creating a confuse situation in the public administration about the licenses: the web site of the *Transparency Act* should usually apply *non-open data license* considering that we have

4 http://www.dati.gov.it/content/infografica data related to February 2015.

5 http://www.garanteprivacy.it/web/guest/home/docweb/-/docweb-display/docweb/3134436.

sometime personal data included in the documents (e.g., payments, salaries, grants) and the Open Data portal must publish only using open data licenses. The risk is to have the same data/document released in different format (anonymized and not anonymized) with two different licenses (e.g., funds for natural disasters).

4.1.2 OGD Licensing Review

The Italian situation about the open data licenses is promising [12]. Since the 2010 Formez (the government agency for the public administration training and learning programmers) defined the IODL 1.0 (the Italian Open Data License). It is similar to a *cc-by-sa*, it imposes the same license for the derived works. In the 2012 Formez released the IODL 2.0 that removes *the Share Alike* clause. The current situation of the licenses in the open data portals in Italy is the following: the most adopted license by the public administration is the IODL, but in term of number of datasets the *cc-by* is the larger collection. This variety of licenses criteria creates the problem how to combine them in order to reuse different large datasets coming from different heterogeneous sources (cf. Fig. 2).

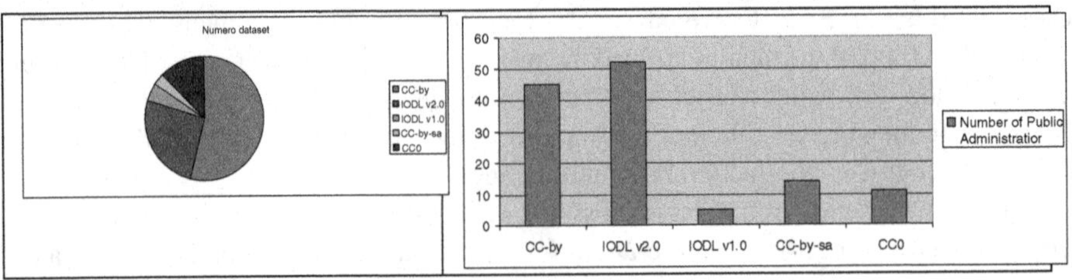

Fig. 2. Table of the statistics concerning the Italian licenses used in open data portals. (Dataset of data.gov.it visited February 2015.)

One of the most used license is the CC0 especially by the technical experts because it resolves the problem of the mush-up of dataset easily. However the CC0 is a waive license and the owner of the dataset frequently is the public administration. Following the public law the owner is the State or the local administration and for this reason the employer does not have the power to waive the rights of the IPR in favour of the community. The artt. 10 and 53 of the Cultural Heritage Code d.lgs., 22 January 2004, n. 42, define the dataset and moreover the digital document as "digital patrimony" of the State and it is inalienable. For this reason is not appropriate to use CC0 for the OGD.

4.1.3 OGD Italian Portal

The data.gov.it portal is the national portal of open data and it hosts all the national, regional, local datasets in a unique central catalogue. We have more than 1,400 dataset and the most used format is CSV, JSON, XML. The license more used is cc-by with

6,527 dataset. The portal permits also to integrate the local open data portal using API in order to share the data and so to build the national catalogue in CKAN.[6]

4.2 Lithuania

4.2.1 OGD Regulation

Public sector information which could be provided for re-use is regulated by the Law on Management of State Information Resources. In Article 10 Sect. 1 part 8 describes important principle for re-use of PSI: *openness of the information resources, which means that favorable conditions for natural and legal persons are created for re-use of information managed by the institutions when carrying out statutory functions independently of the natural and legal persons legitimate operating objectives and legal form thereof.* In the Article 30 Sect. 3 it is noted, that information from state information systems shall prepared for PSI re-use.

The law divides PSI suitable for reuse by 3 parts: 1. data from state registers; 2. Data from state information systems; 3. Other PSI.

Article 26 Sect. 5 introduces obligations to re-users of data of state registers: *the recipient **may not change the data** obtained from the registry and the registry information and **must indicate the data source** when using them.* This obligation means that CC BY-ND 4.0 or similar local license covers data from state registers. Also, by the default information is provided for a charge, except *for the exceptions provided in this law and other laws of the Republic of Lithuania, European Union legal acts and the register's regulations* (Article 29).

Data from state information systems is provided free of charge. Article 35 Sect. 5 sets same requirements as for data of registers: *the data obtained from an institution may not be changed and their source must identified when using the data.*

The conditions of re-use other PSI is not regulated by the law, but regarding openness principle, should be open without any restriction to use it, except if there are special requirements set by other law.

Requirement of the *contract* but not the license come from Article 37 Sect. 3: "When information files containing information managed by the institution that is important for the entire state or several institutions are published on the institution's website and the Republic of Lithuania laws and (or) other legal acts provide for special conditions of the use of such information, the institution shall establish electronic authorization, which includes the terms of use of such information files that must be followed. Such information files shall be provided to persons after their electronically expressed consent with the terms of the electronic authorization."

Data providers must put legal notice according to the Article 37 Sect. 1: "The institution shall disclose on its website the information about its managed information, terms and conditions for the use of this information. In cases when pursuant to the laws of the Republic of Lithuania and other legal acts institution shall not continue to process, update, provide or publish its managed information, it shall announce about the aforementioned on its website no later than two months in advance."

---

[6] http://www.dati.gov.it/content/ckan-datigovit.

Table 3. Requirements to OGD coming from Law on Management of State Information Resources

Type of PSI	Requirement for electronic authorisation	Information is paid or free of charge	Free to adapt or NoDerivatives	Source must identified?
State registers	Yes	Paid, some exceptions	May not change the data	Yes
State information systems	Yes	Free of charge, some exceptions	May not change the data	Yes
Other PSI	No	Free of charge	Free to adapt	In general "no", except when the law requires "yes"

To conclude, OGD can come only from not important states information sources. The most valuable data from state registers and information systems is locked by "electronic authorization" and "click contract" (basically its electronic contract, not a license), re-user has obligation not change the data. Data of state registers is by default provided for a charge; exception can be made by law (Table 3).

4.2.2 OGD Licensing Review

OGD without a license could be released, but there should be legal notice provided. Otherwise, there is a risk that copyright law can be applied automatically.

Copyright law does not cover legal acts, bills, drafts, official translations of law, administrative documents, official symbols and signs, and separate data (Article 5 of Law on Copyright and Related Rights). Therefore, CC0 or other public domain license could be applied only to datasets, which carry data not protected by copyright and not taken from state register or information system (e.g. legal acts register). Other OGD could be covered by CC-BY license, free of charge information from state registers and information systems could be covered by a contract similar to CC BY-ND. There is no law which forbids re-using PSI for commercial purpose. The draft of local license (by restrictions equal to CC-BY) was developed in 2013, but has been never adopted. To sum up, in Lithuania OGD development is a very politically related, most valuable government data has requirement of the re-use contract, cannot be modified, not valuable government data can be re-used freely without restrictions. Public domain license can be applied very rare only cases.

4.2.3 OGD Portal and Other Initiatives

The central OGD portal (http://opendata.gov.lt) actually is not designed as the OGD portal attractive for re-users but as a list of the PSI resources (implements only formally the Article 9 of PSI directive). The portal provides information only in a local language, and consists of 263 links to the data providers of the public data resources available for re-use. There also exist some institutional initiatives, e.g. the Ministry of Economy lead by pro-western politicians started the first in the country OGD portal (http://data.ukmin.lt/duomenys.html) but after 2012 the data is not updated (at that moment was set the new minister representative of Lithuanian Social Democrats Party, which roots comes from ex-communist party). Other initiatives are coming from the NGO's (e.g. "Transparency International" Lithuania collects from the government information about mass media owners and provides it in the open datasets) and private sector (e.g. datasets on CKAN data management system is developed by private person http://atviriduomenys.lt/dataset; popular the OGD visualization project http://freedata.lt/).

4.3 United Kingdom

4.3.1 OGD Regulation

The main act concerning OGD is Protection of Freedoms Act 2012, which has updated Freedom of Information Act 2000. Also important acts are: the Re-use of Public Sector Information Regulations 2005 Act, the Copyright and Rights in Databases Regulations 1997, the Copyright, Designs and Patents Act 1988 and the Copyright and Related Rights Regulations 1996. Freedom of Information Act 2000 regulates right of access to information held by public authorities. The Re-use of Public Sector Information Regulations 2005 Act (PSI Act) implements PSI directive. PSI Act 5(b) establish important exclusion when PSI may not be provided: public information for re-use may not provide if a third party owns: (a) copyright (within the meaning of Sect. 1 of the Copyright, Designs and Patents Act1988), (b) database right (within the meaning of regulation 13 of the Copyright and Rights in Database Regulations 1997), (c) publication right (within the meaning of regulation 16 of the Copyright and Related Rights Regulations 1996), and (d) rights in performances (meaning the rights conferred by Part 2 of the Copyright, Designs and Patents Act 1988). This exclusion shows, that OGD in the most cases will not have related to intellectual property rights (IPR) included material, otherwise IPR holder must give permission for re-use.

Protection of Freedoms Act 2012 (FA) has updated Freedom of Information Act 2000 and is designed for OGD. FA defines dataset in Part 6 Sec 102 Sub 2(c): "means information comprising a collection of information held in electronic form where all or most of the information in the collection (a) has been obtained or recorded for the purpose of providing a public authority with information in connection with the provision of a service by the authority or the carrying out of any other function of the authority, (b) is factual information which (i) is not the product of analysis or interpretation other than calculation, and (ii) is not an official statistic, and (c) remains presented in a way that (except for the purpose of forming part of the collection) has not been organized, adapted or otherwise materially altered since it was obtained or recorded."

FA Part 6 Sec 102 Sub 3 describes how datasets containing copyright works should been released: "When communicating the relevant copyright work to the applicant, the public authority must make the relevant copyright work available for re-use by the applicant in accordance with the terms of the specified licence."

In UK exists also unique Crown Copyright. It is applied to works made by "an officer of the Crown, this includes items such as legislation and documents and reports produced by government bodies. Crown Copyright will last for a period of 125 years from the end of the calendar year in which the work was made. If the work was commercially published within 75 years of the end of the calendar year in which it was made, Crown copyright will last for 50 years from the end of the calendar year in which it was published. Parliamentary Copyright will apply to work that is made by or under the direction or control of the House of Commons or the House of Lords and will last until 50 years from the end of the calendar year in which the work was made" [13]. OGD release also depends from the Data Protection Act 1998, the Freedom of Information (Scotland) Act 2002, the Environmental Information Regulations 2004 and the Environmental Information (Scotland) Regulations 2004. Further information concerning OGD could be found in UK Government Licensing Framework [14].

4.3.2 OGD Licensing Review

There exist 3 types of OGD licenses: the Open Government Licence, the Non-Commercial Government Licence and the Charged Licence. The first license is open license, second – applies limitation for commercial re-use and third is applied for information which is charged by Public body. Open Government Licence v3.0 (UK) satisfies open license criterions and is suitable for LOD domain. According to this, the movement to current versions of Creative Commons license is hardly likely. In 2018 there is planned to revise PSI directive; if decision to have one license in EU will be agreed, there could be changes. Realize of licenses dedicated to public domain or without a license is possible only to those datasets which do not have copyrighted materials or copyright and database rights have expired. E.g., this year Crown copyright is expired to works made until 1890, but taking to account that digitalized copy of work or adaptation of work suitable for OGD dataset also could be protected by Crown copyright, digital copies of works made until 1890 still can be protected by Crown copyright. To conclude, the release of OGD without a license or with public domain license without changing the regulation in this century is not likely.

4.3.3 OGD Portal

At 9th of January 2015 the OGD portal (http://data.gov.uk/) consist of 16234 datasets, 11679 datasets were covered by Open Government Licence v3.0 (UK) and 4555 datasets were covered by Non-Open Government Licence. Also there were 4074 unpublished datasets, which metadata is available in a portal and the reasons of not-publishing are provided. The OGD portal provides more than 350 apps from which the most popular is called Scope Nights: Astronomy Weather Reports.

5 Conclusions and Future Work

The survey underlines some important findings: (i) the majority of the OGD does not fulfil the OD principle of freely re-use of data, but mostly the limitation of re-use ends only with an attribution requirement and the link to the license/legal notice; (ii) the legal notices fragment the legal protection on different parts of the web site containing

OD without any prospect of re-use; (iii) there is the risk that datasets covered without a license in an EU jurisdiction could be automatically protected by the U.S. copyright; (iv) the legal requirements in the different jurisdictions preclude the use of a singular license or contribute to an aversion to the use of the license altogether; (v) the CC licenses are used as brands for communicating an attitude and philosophy rather than a real legal permission or an obligation framework; (vi) the OGD licenses not always comply with PSI re-use policy, e.g. there are restrictions for commercial re-use; (vii) in the global phenomena the most OGD datasets are covered by the licenses which are ready for the mash-up scenario, but in a country level the results could be different.

The regulation of the OGD depends of the national intellectual property, the public law and the database copyright regulation. The CC0 license could be used more as an exception in rare cases, than a rule in investigated EU member countries. The most U. S. federal datasets are in the public domain, but still the U.S. OGD portal sets the attribution requirement in the legal notice. In the EU the most cases copyright is applied automatically to the works without making a notice about copyright or registration. Differently in US, works are protected after making the notice that is copyright work and registration for the extension to copyright term is required.

The interoperability among datasets is fundamental for the economical exploitation of the OD and for developing an inclusive society. Only a good license framework of the OGD can assure legal protection in long-term and guarantee the end-user in the chain of the re-use (e.g. re-use of re-use, derivative works, etc.). In a future, development of the ontology of the global regulation of the OGD domain is required. It could be used as a tool for automatic or semiautomatic mash-up of the licensed and not licensed open government data.

Acknowledgements. This research is funded by the ERASMUS MUNDUS program LAST-JD, Law, Science and Technology coordinated by University of Bologna.

Annex A - Definitions

In this paper the term *Open Government Data* is used for identifying the complex phenomena where the data coming from the government and related bodies (the federal or the state public administration, the region administration, the municipalities, the state enterprises, the police and etc.) are published in open format and with a license in favor of the reuse. In some cases the OGD datasets can include also the copyright works belonging to the private or the public sector.

In the European Union the OGD is coming from the PSI directive 2003/98/EC (updated in 2013, 2013/37/EU) which is known as a re-use of public sector information (PSI) concept implementation. The OGD can be understood as PSI ready for re-use according to the Directive (Art.2 Para4.: "'re-use' means the use by persons or legal entities of documents held by public sector bodies, for commercial or noncommercial purposes other than the initial purpose within the public task for which the documents were produced" [4]). In the US the OGD is coming from the President Obama's initiative [5] and known as *Open Data* for improving participation, transparency and cooperation between citizens and public administrations.

The OGD is as a part of the OD. The other parts of the OD can be identified as the OD coming from private business sector,[7] NGO's[8] and private citizens initiatives[9].

What is an *open licence* is analyzed by *The Open Knowledge Foundation*. One of the conditions of the open license is propagation: the rights attached to the work must apply to all to whom it is redistributed without the need to agree to any additional legal terms [2].

The EU *legal notice* is not a license, but has some attributes of the license, e.g. sets requirements of re-use the data. The requirements are explained in the Commission decision of 12 December 2011 on the reuse of Commission documents 2011/833/EU Article 6 Sect. 2. All requirements satisfy the propagation criteria except one: the obligation *not to distort the original meaning or message of the documents*. This obligation asks to agree an additional legal terms and is a place of wide interpretation in a datasets mash-up scenario. On other hand, 18 July 2015 is the date when Directive 2013/37/EU should be implemented. It supports the open license (recital N. 26) and hopefully irrelevant requirement from the Commission decision 2011/833/EU will be removed.

In the paper the *Creative Commons* (CC) [6] licenses are widely used. CC0 is a license dedicated to public domain. CC-By allows re-distribution and re-use of a licensed work on the condition that the creator is appropriately credited. CC-SA is a license which has the least restrictions to re-use the original creation. There are different versions of CC-SA and localizations adapted to each country law and language. Further information concerning definitions of the CC licenses family are available in the creative common web site and in a previous work [7].

Annex B – Web Site Analyzed for the Survey

Argentina (http://datospublicos.gob.ar), Australia (http://data.gov.au/dataset), Austria (https://www.data.gv.at/katalog/), Belgium (http://data.belgium.be), Brazil (http://dados.gov.br), Canada (http://open.canada.ca/data/en/dataset), Chile (http://datos.gob.cl/datasets), Costa Rica (http://datosabiertos.gob.go.cr/home/), EU (https://open-data.europa.eu/en/data/), France (https://www.data.gouv.fr/en/), Germany (https://www.govdata.de), Greece (http://data.gov.gr), Italy (http://www.dati.gov.it/catalog/dataset), Moldova (http://date.gov.md/en/terms-and-conditions), New Zealand (https://data.govt.nz/catalog/), Norway (http://data.norge.no/), Portugal (http://www.dados.gov.pt), Spain (http://datos.gob.es/catalogo#), The Netherlands (https://data.overheid.nl/data/search), UK (http://data.gov.uk/data/search), Uruguay (https://catalogodatos.gub.uy/dataset), US (http://catalog.data.gov/dataset).

---

[7] E.g. *JC Decaux*, Open data, https://developer.jcdecaux.com/#/opendata/vls?page=static, last accessed 15.12.2014 (2013).

[8] E.g. *"Transparency International" Lithuanian branch*, Open data of mass media owners, http://stirna.info/pages/apie, last accessed 15.12.2014 (2013).

[9] E.g. *Zimnickas, Zemlys, Kilikevičius,* Open dataset of Lithuanian Parliament 2012 election results, https://www.google.com/fusiontables/data?docid=1vOawBGzp_0c-8jiKTyY5sJ8MjiWM8sBlbYoAo6s#rows:id=1 last accessed 15.12.2014 (2012).

References

1. Open Data Research Network, Mapping existing open data research. http://www.opendataresearch.org/news/2015/mapping-existing-open-data-research
2. The Open Knowledge Foundation: Open Definition. http://opendefinition.org/od/index.html
3. Berners-Lee, T.: Linked data-design issues. http://www.w3.org/DesignIssues/LinkedData.html
4. Directive 2003/98/EC of the European Parliament and of the Council of 17 November 2003 on the re-use of public sector information (2003)
5. Obama, B.: Executive order on Making open and machine readable the new default for government information (2013)
6. Creative Commons. https://creativecommons.org/licenses/
7. Mockus, M.: Open Government Data Licenses Framework for a Mashup Model. Jusletter IT, 20 February 2014
8. The Open Knowledge Foundation: Open Data handbook. http://opendatahandbook.org/en/what-is-open-data/
9. The Open Knowledge Foundation: What is Open Government Data. http://opengovernmentdata.org/
10. ENGAGE project. http://www.engagedata.eu
11. Palmirani, M., Martoni, M., Girardi, D.: Open government data beyond transparency. In: Kö, A., Francesconi, E. (eds.) EGOVIS 2014. LNCS, vol. 8650, pp. 275–291. Springer, Heidelberg (2014)
12. Governatori, G., Lam, H.-P., Rotolo, A., Villata, S., Atemezing, G.A., Gandon, F.: LIVE: a Tool for Checking Licenses Compatibility between Vocabularies and Data. In: International Semantic Web Conference (Posters & Demos), pp. 77−80 (2014)
13. UK Copyright Service: UK Copyright Law. http://www.copyrightservice.co.uk/copyright/p01_uk_copyright_law
14. The National Archives: UK Government licensing framework (2014). http://www.nationalarchives.gov.uk/documents/information-management/uk-government-licensing-framework.pdf

Data Visualization: An Untapped Potential for Political Participation and Civic Engagement

Samuel Bohman(✉)

Department of Computer and Systems Sciences, Stockholm University, Stockholm, Sweden
samboh@dsv.su.se

Abstract. This article elaborates on the use of data visualization to promote a more informed and engaged participation in civic and democratic life. First, it outlines the main constraints and challenges in electronic participation research and concludes that the conventional deliberative approach to political participation has been impeding civic engagement. Then, through a couple of recent examples and a brief historical overview, it examines the power of data visualization. Following this, it explores the democratization of data visualization through four interconnected themes that provide new opportunities for political participation and civic engagement research: data storytelling, infographics, data physicalization, and the quantified self. The goal is to call attention to this space and encourage a larger community of researchers to explore the possibilities that data visualization can bring.

Keywords: Data visualization · Political participation · Civic engagement · Electronic democracy · Electronic participation

1 Introduction

For decades, scholars have put their faith in information and communication technology in facilitating a wide civic involvement in democracy [1]. However, despite technological advances and an increasing maturity of electronic participation scholarship, empirical studies suggest that much of the initiatives to date have largely failed to live up to the rhetoric. After an initial phase of excitement and exaggerated expectations, manifested in discourses about empowered individuals and a reinvigorated public sphere, it has become clear that democratic renewal through the telephone, cable TV, or the Internet, is not as straightforward as previously imagined [2]. Whereas the use of information and communication technology to enhance political participation and civic engagement has had a limited impact beyond academia, the last decade has witnessed a rapid popularization and democratization of data visualization. Widely appreciated for its ability to reduce information overload and make complex data accessible,

S. Bohman—The author wishes to thank Yvonne Jansen and Doug Kanter for kindly giving permission to use images of their work in this article.

© Springer International Publishing Switzerland 2015
A. Kő and E. Francesconi (Eds.): EGOVIS 2015, LNCS 9265, pp. 302–315, 2015.
DOI: 10.1007/978-3-319-22389-6_22

data visualization has made its way out of the offices and on to the streets, our homes, and our computer screens and mobile devices. However, there have been few scholarly studies of data visualization that have aimed at promoting citizens' engagement with the institutions of representative democracy. In this paper, we explore how governments could better engage with the public through various forms of data visualization. In the following sections, we first summarize the main constraints and challenges of contemporary electronic participation research. We then, through a couple of recent well-known examples and a brief historical overview, describe the power of data visualization. Following this, we discuss the ongoing popularization and democratization of data visualization through four interconnected themes that represent a hitherto untapped potential for democratic engagement. Finally, some conclusions are drawn.

2 The Challenges to Online Citizen Engagement

Since the advent of the Web in the early 1990s, the prospects for electronic democracy have been viewed as heralding a new era of political participation and civic engagement. However, empirical studies suggest that most initiatives to date have failed to live up to expectations, despite large investments in research. For instance, Chadwick [3] says "the reality of online deliberation, whether judged in terms of quantity, its quality, or its impact on political behaviour and policy outcomes, is far removed from the ideals set out in the early to mid-1990s." Similarly, Norris and Reddick [4] say "few American local governments have adopted e-participation and those that have been adopted, for the most, have not implemented what we would consider meaningful citizen participation". Prieto-Martín, de Marcos, and Martínez [5] even go as far as to argue that "no real breakthrough or even any significant research milestone can be reported for the field." In sum, the proposed methods and technologies of electronic participation such as online deliberation are not perceived to have solved the problem of getting people to participate in the political process. Instead, just as in traditional offline methods of citizen consultation, we typically find a widespread lack of interest, which allows small groups to dominate participatory initiatives [6].

In order to provide a future direction for electronic participation, scholars have attempted to systematize current research and identify its main constraints and challenges. For example, Macintosh, Coleman, and Schneeberger [7] identified six main research challenges, barriers, and needs: the fragmentation of the research, immature research methods and designs, sociotechnical design, institutional resistance, equity, and theory. Other scholars have suggested that the problem with electronic democratic participation goes even deeper. Drawing on the social construction of technology approach, Johnson [8] argued that the concept of electronic democracy is fatally flawed and incompatible with liberal democracy. Electronic democracy is something more than the application of technology to politics: it embodies a particular set of practices and values. He points to three aspects of electronic democracy culture, in particular, that undermine key practices of liberal democracy: commodification (which undermines social equality), popular democracy (which undermines representation and constitutionalism), and individualist publicity (the Internet's infrastructure enables mass surveillance, which undermines the voter's anonymity). Similarly, Coleman and Moss [9] argue that the assumed deliberative citizen is a construction driven by researchers effort to produce responsible, democratically reflexive citizens modeled on Habermas's discursive ideal of deliberative democracy. The authors acknowledge that the deliberative approach to civic dialogue is "unduly restrictive, discounting other important ways of making, receiving, and contesting public claims." They therefore encourage researchers in the field to be more open to a wider range of practices and technologies. This line of argument is supported by other scholars. Wright [10], for example, believes that the study of political deliberation online should be expanded and include different, informal "third spaces" beyond government-run websites and political-party controlled chat-rooms. Coleman and Moss [9] suggest that some of the most innovative participation research is being done in the area of computer-supported argument mapping and visualization. However, the visualization research they are referring to has primarily focused on facilitating large-scale online deliberation on the Web within a conventional rationalistic framework [11]. In general, visualization has been an underused technology in electronic participation research [12].

3 The Power of Data Visualization

Whereas the conventional approach to broadening democratic engagement and participation using the Internet has had a limited impact beyond academic circles, the past decade has seen a significant growth in the use of data visualization to reach a wide target audience. A prime example is Gore's narrated charts in the documentary *An Inconvenient Truth* [13]. In this film, which earned him and the Intergovernmental Panel on Climate Change the Nobel Peace Prize in 2007, Gore outlines the numbers behind man-made climate change by using a wide range of visualizations, including line charts, bar charts, and pictograms. Another prominent example is the approach developed by Rosling, a professor at the Karolinska Institutet, Stockholm, Sweden, and co-founder of the Gapminder Foundation [14]. Using the humor and drama of a sportscaster and a piece of software that turns seemingly dry data into colorful animated graphics, Rosling debunks myths about the developing world while making it an enjoyable experience. These observations, albeit involving only a few examples, suggest that data visualization has the potential for reaching out to a broad audience in innovative ways and facilitate greater citizen engagement in public affairs.

3.1 A Brief Historical Overview

To the casual observer, it would appear that data visualization is a recent phenomenon. In fact, the graphical portrayal of quantitative information has a long and rich history. According to Friendly [15], the beginnings of modern statistical graphics can be found in the scientific discoveries, technological advances, and societal developments in the 17th and 18th centuries, in particular, in analytic geometry and coordinate systems, probability and statistical theory, state statistics, and new technologies for measurement, recording, and printing. Many visualization techniques that are still being used today were introduced during this period, including the line chart, bar chart, and pie chart. The Scottish Enlightenment scientist William Playfair invented or greatly improved these techniques, and is generally referred to as the father of the graphical method in statistics [16].

In the second half of the 19th century, a number of developments combined to produce a "Golden Age of Statistical Graphics" [17]. Three well-known and much-discussed examples from this period that illustrate the power of visual rhetoric include Snow's dot map of a cholera outbreak in London [18], Nightingale's polar area ("coxcombs") charts displaying the mortality rates of British soldiers during the Crimean War [19], and Minard's multivariate display of Napoleon's march on Russia [20]. Snow and Nightingale used their charts successfully as critical evidentiary statements in campaigning for improved sanitation, which eventually led to government healthcare reforms.

In the first half of the 20th century, the earlier enthusiasm for statistical graphs and maps was supplanted by the rise of mathematical statistics [15]. Few graphical innovations were introduced during this period; it was, however, a time for consolidation and popularization. An important factor in the diffusion of this was pictorial statistics, or, pictograms [21]. An influential advocate of pictograms was the Austrian philosopher Otto Neurath, who developed a visual language known as Isotype (International System of Typographic Picture Education), with the purpose of explaining societal developments to the broad, uneducated public [22]. Neurath's own assumption, "to remember simplified pictures is better than to forget accurate figures," captures the general idea [23]. Due to the association of Isotype with left-wing movements and Soviet propaganda, the method disappeared in the Western world during the Cold War, and its legacy has there gone either unnoticed or unappreciated [24]. Nevertheless, the influence of Isotype reverberates through much of our present visual communication, and in the last decade, the method has received renewed interest and increased attention. For example, Mayr and Schreder [25] review Isotype with respect to its potential for today's civic education and participation, and propose we should rediscover its core principles and adapt them to the modern context.

The period from 1950 to 1975 constituted a rebirth for data visualization. Friendly [15] lists three significant events that contributed to this upswing. The first was the publication of Tukey's book *Exploratory Data Analysis* [26], which introduced a new approach to statistics that used the power of visualization as a means to explore and make sense of data. Second, Bertin's book *Sémiologie graphique* [27] was the first attempt to propose a theory of graphical display of data used in maps, diagrams, and networks. The third was the introduction of computers, programming languages, and software for statistical graphs.

In 1983, Tufte published the classic *The Visual Display of Quantitative Information* [28]. In this book, Tufte famously criticized the use of "chartjunk," i.e., unnecessary or distracting visual embellishment included in data graphics. Instead, he advocated the practice of graphical excellence, guided by the fundamental principle: "Above all else show the data" [28]. This principle is formalized in the data–ink ratio rule, which states that the proportion of ink devoted to the non-redundant display of data in the total amount of ink used in the graph should be maximized. Tufte's minimal design aesthetic has had a strong impact on the data visualization community and he is frequently referred to throughout the literature. However, recent empirical studies suggest that visual embellishments can, when properly designed, support the comprehensibility and memorability of a data display [29].

A decade later, Cleveland published two companion volumes, *Visualizing Data* [30] and *The Elements of Graphing Data* [31]. In these books, Cleveland reanalyzes many data sets from the scientific literature and demonstrates the use of graphical methods for studying the structure of data. Similar to Tufte, Cleveland considers clarity a vital aspect of graphing data and suggests the following overall guiding principle: "Make the data stand out. Avoid superfluity [31]." In 1999, Wilkinson published *The Grammar of Graphics* [32] based on his extensive programming experience acquired during writing the SYSTAT and the SPSS statistical packages. The book presented a new multilayered approach to data graphics, later extended and implemented as an open-source R package, ggplot2 [33]. In the same year, Card, Mackinlay, and Shneiderman [34] published a collection of seminal papers under the title *Readings in Information Visualization* which established information visualization as a distinct field separate from scientific visualization.

As previously mentioned, data visualization has exploded in the last ten years. In terms of authorship, one figure perhaps worthy of special note is Stephen Few, author of several approachable textbooks on data visualization that teach fundamental concepts and visualization techniques with a particular focus on the needs of business [35]. If Tufte's 1983 book is the classic on static printed statistical graphics, Few's books are rightly the best practical introductions to computer-based data visualization. Along with an increasing body of literature, the past decade has seen the emergence of a vast array of programming languages, toolkits, and libraries for interactive web-based data visualization. Prefuse, for example, was an early visualization framework using the Java programming language [36]. However, Java is becoming increasingly outdated for interactive and animated web graphics. Instead, JavaScript, the standard language for interactive web content, has become the preferred choice also for data visualization. Today, many web-based data visualizations are often built with D3, WebGL, and other JavaScript frameworks, that use web standards and do not require web browser plug-ins [37].

4 Democratizing Data Visualization

In this section, we explore four interconnected and overlapping themes that contribute to a popularization and democratization of data visualization: infographics (viral visualization), data storytelling (narrative visualization), data physicalization (physical visualization), and the quantified self (personal visualization). Similar to Danziger's [38] four design dimensions for public-facing information visualization, the themes presented here should not be viewed as comprehensive, but rather as stimuli to the research community to begin to ask better questions regarding the design of future technologies and practices for political participation and civic engagement.

4.1 Data Storytelling

Up to now, data visualization beyond the simple pie or bar chart has been the domain of specialists trained in either statistics or computer science. This was particularly true if dynamic and interactive charts and diagrams were required. However, the last few years have seen the emergence of a new class of self-service applications that support the creation of ad hoc visual analysis and dynamic data querying on standard personal computers. This new breed of user-friendly data exploration and visualization tools empowers the average users, as it makes them less dependent on technical expertise. One example is Fusion Tables, a web application by Google for gathering, visualizing, and sharing data. Another example is Tableau Public, from Tableau Software, which features a simple drag and drop interface for creating interactive visualizations. Yet another tool with similar functionalities is Qlik Sense, provided by the company Qlik. This class of applications, which are typically available free, enables a broad audience to tell stories with data using visualization. A typical case is a journalist who wants to use interactive visualization to turn inaccessible data into an engaging story and publish it online. This approach, frequently referred to as data journalism [39], data storytelling [40], or narrative visualization [41], emerged in news organizations, such as *The Guardian* and the *New York Times*, as a response to the disruptive forces of digitization and media convergence. An example of an interactive data-driven story using visualization is the *New York Times*'s dialect quiz "How Y'all, Youse, and You Guys Talk" [42]. By responding to 25 different questions about the language the user is most likely to use in different situations, the quiz builds a profile of the user's dialect. When all the questions have been completed, a heat map indicates where in the United States the user would be most likely to find a person who uses a similar dialect. The user is also given the opportunity to share their map through popular social networks or email. The dialect quiz became a huge success: In just eleven days (it was published on December 21) it became the most visited content of 2013 throughout NYTimes.com, their mobile site, and iOS apps [43].

4.2 Infographics

Information graphics, a popular form of visualization commonly found in news media and often referred to as infographics, has exploded in the digital age. A Google search on the term "infographics" at the time of writing of this article returned 56 million results. To put that number into context, searches on the terms "data visualization" and "information visualization" returned 6.6 million and 0.5 million results, respectively. Businesses use infographics to connect with potential customers, drive website traffic, and increase brand awareness [44].

Non-governmental organizations use them to enhance their communication in outreach and advocacy efforts [45]. Governments release infographics on their websites to convey the current state of public matters [46]. The typical online infographic is a static high-resolution graphic design that attempts to transform abstract or complex information about a specific topic or issue into a format that is visually engaging, easily understood, and easily shared. Infographics combine data with design—numbers, data displays, words, and pictures—in order to inform, entertain, or persuade their audience.

Despite the proliferation of infographics in today's fast-paced digital society, little research has been conducted on them. However, they typically share a number of attributes. Similar to the idea behind micro-blogging services such as Twitter, the main characteristic of infographics is that their purpose is to tell the gist of a story at a glance. They are stand-alone or self-contained visuals that are easy to digest and do not require additional information to be comprehensible. A second important characteristic is that infographics are meant to be aesthetically pleasing: what social media consultant Mark Smiciklas has called the "cool factor" [47], paying particular attention to the use of color, typography, icons, and composition. Indeed, well-executed infographics are often admired for their beauty or for bringing out the beauty in data. A third characteristic of online infographics is that they are viral: easily shared and spread across social networks from person to person through "word of mouse."

Although infographics are generally considered effective for disseminating information to the masses, statisticians and others have criticized them for relying too much on style over substance [48,49]. Clearly, many infographics are nothing more than eye candy that publishers and marketers use to gloss up their content: overly designed and conveying little meaning. A surprisingly large number of infographics deceive their viewers by cherry picking statistics, warping the facts, or providing questionable, vague, or nonexistent data sources [50]. Despite these ethical objections, the sharp increase of online infographics in the last five years suggests that they appeal to a broad audience, a fact that makes them worth investigating further.

4.3 Data Physicalization

Physical data visualization, a lesser known sub-field of data visualization, studies alternative data representations where the data is not represented through pixels on a computer screen, but via physical modalities experienced directly through the eye (not including ink on paper) or other human senses. In contrast to conventional data visualization, where objectivity is the norm, physical representations of data allow of, and sometimes even encourage, the inclusion of subjectivity in order to be evocative and increase the onlooker's engagement. Typically, the alternative data mappings employed in physical visualizations may not be immediately recognizable, but instead be discovered through interaction, association, and reflection. In an overview paper, Vande Moere [51] explores the design space of physical data visualization in casual or non-professional contexts. He lists five genres: data sculptures, ambient displays, pixel sculptures, object augmentation, wearable visualization, and alternative modalities. Data sculptures are data-driven physical artifacts that can be touched and explored through a tangible user interface. In the first study of its kind, Jansen, Dragicevic, and Fekete [52] compared data sculptures to screen-based visualizations, using three-dimensional bar charts as an example, and found that the physical bar charts improved the users' efficiency at information retrieval tasks, see Fig. 1.

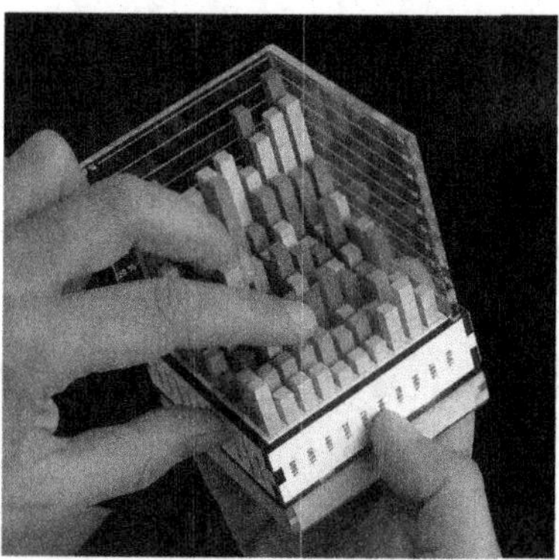

Fig. 1. A physical three-dimensional bar chart made of laser-cut acrylic automatically generated from data. Each bar was spray-painted and mounted on a base together with two scales made from transparent acrylic sheets on which axis labels and lines were engraved. Country and year labels were engraved on all four sides of the base using a vertical orientation.

Ambient displays turn architectural spaces into a data display through subtle changes in light, sound, movement, solids, liquids, or gases that can be processed in the background of awareness. Envisioned as being all around us, ambient displays blur the boundary between the physical and digital worlds to create an interface between people and digital information. Pixel sculptures use non screen-based visual units for representing information. For example, there are the synchronized mass games or gymnastics, often seen at the Olympic Games, where each individual makes up an element in a giant mosaic picture. Object augmentation refers to superimposing everyday objects with information. Visual animated projections on building facades and sidewalks are common examples. Wearable visualization draws on miniature computing devices that fit in clothing, jewelry, and other things that can be worn over long periods. The last category, alternative modalities, uses non-visual representations of data that can be experienced through sound (sonification or auditory displays), touch (tactile or haptic displays), smell (olfactory displays), or taste (palatable interfaces). For instance, an experimental workshop called Data Cuisine explored food using culinary means as an alternative medium for representing data [53].

4.4 Quantified Self

Self-knowledge through numbers, the motto of the quantified self grassroots movement [54], is quickly becoming a mainstream phenomenon. Currently it

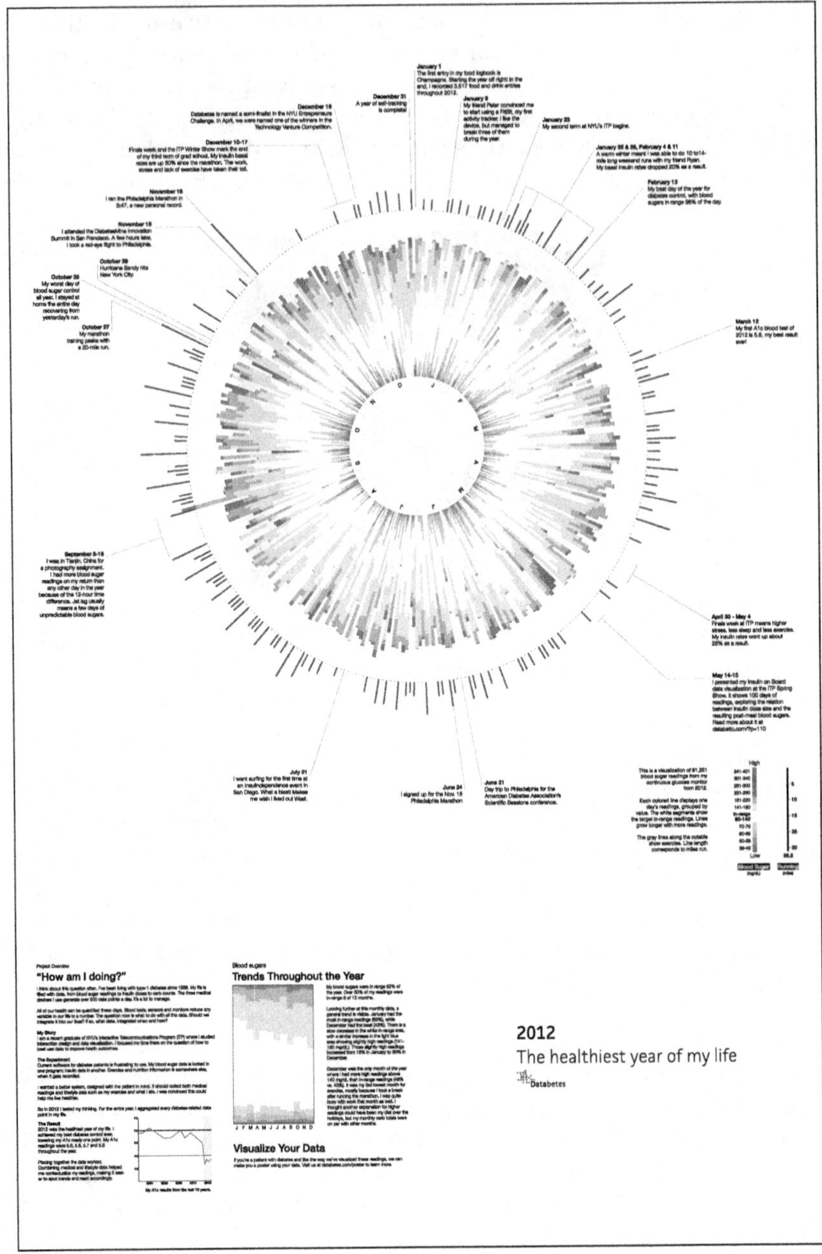

Fig. 2. The poster *2012 The healthiest year of my life* by Doug Kanter. The main circular graph displays 91,251 blood sugar readings from his glucose monitor with each line indicating one day. High blood sugar levels are shown in colder colors, and low blood sugar levels are in warmer colors. Along the outside of the circle are dark gray lines showing how much he ran each day. Notes for significant events are listed throughout the year in order to contextualize the medical readings.

is estimated that one in five adults in the United States are tracking their physical activity, sleep pattern, nutritional intake, and many other things related to their lives, through a portable or wearable computing device such as a smartphone, smartwatch, or activity tracker [55]. The basic idea is simple: Through more granular around-the-clock quantified monitoring, people can make smarter lifestyle choices and live healthier, more active lives.

Anyone interested in measuring their well-being and becoming more self-reflexive through the prism of performance data can choose from a variety of consumer-oriented products on the market or simply download and install a health and fitness application on their smartphone. Large technology companies, as well as more established producers of navigation and fitness equipment, are presently investing heavily in personal health and wellness technologies. Typically, these applications and devices are paired with a website for data management and visualization, social networking, personal recommendations, and action plans. Some services also include gamification features, such as challenges, leader-boards, and virtual awards, drawing on theories of behavioral economics to keep users motivated and engaged [56].

The reasons for self-surveillance are numerous and varied and range from those of the causal fitness-tracker who monitors their own exercise, to those of tech-savvy patients and citizen scientists who share their medical and lifestyle data online to help others and advance research, to those of life-logging enthusiasts with a passion for self-discovery through personal analytics. The story of Doug Kanter, who blogs about living with diabetes at databetic.com, offers a glimpse of what the future of personal data quantification might look like [57]. In 2012, he used a suite of medical devices, activity trackers, smartphone applications, and PC software to record all his diabetes data and physical activities. Kanter visualized his yearlong quantified self project as a poster displaying every blood sugar reading, every insulin dose, and every meal, as well as all activity data he tracked in 2012, see Fig. 2. Kanter's systematic self-tracking approach helped him become more aware of his behavior and provided an opportunity for change. As a result, his diabetic control improved considerably, making 2012 the healthiest year of his life.

5 Conclusions

In this article, we have explored the potential of using data visualization to promote political participation and civic engagement. First, we reviewed the main constraints and challenges of contemporary electronic participation research and found that it cautions us to reduce our expectations of the conventional approach to online participation since there is little evidence of its success. In particular, it suggests that the rationalistic model based on deliberative theory has become a straightjacket, impeding wide civic involvement. This predicament has prompted some scholars to rethink their earlier views, and to suggest that the study of online participation should be expanded to incorporate a wider range of technologies and practices. As a response to this call, we examined the power of data visualization through a couple of recent examples and a brief historical overview. We then explored four overlapping themes that contribute to an ongoing popularization and democratization of data visualization: data storytelling (narrative visualization), infographics (viral visualization), data physicalization (physical visualization), and the quantified self (personal visualization). All four themes suggest that data visualization has a yet untapped potential for promoting a more informed and engaged participation in civic and democratic life. An important aspect of this technological transformation is the empowerment that visualization can bring about through a more direct and personal interaction with data. When people are given the opportunity to explore data on their own, they become empowered to take responsibility and enact change, both individually and collectively. Moreover, as people adapt to new flows and contours of data, statistical literacy is likely to become increasingly important and eventually a necessity for efficient citizenship in information-laden societies. Data visualization, in all its various forms and expressions, may prove to be an important factor in developing this competence.

The themes and examples discussed in this paper are suggestive (but by no means conclusive) evidence that the time is ripe for scholars to consider the use of data visualization in electronic participation research. However, the versatility and potential applications of data visualization in the service of democracy remain to be explored. I would like, therefore, to invite my colleagues to join me in exploring and reflecting on the following research questions:

- Techniques of storytelling focus on people, motives, and contexts, rather than on numbers. How can stories help bring data to life?
- Aesthetics reaches us at a different level than words and numbers alone. How can data be combined with art and design to evoke emotional engagement?
- In today's networked society, harnessing the power of human connections is key. How can we make data conversational and sharable?
- Beyond-the-desktop visualizations may be effective in engaging hard to reach groups. How can we unlock the hidden potential of tangible data?
- Smartphones and other connected devices bring visualization closer to people than ever before. How can we leverage the ubiquity of data in people's lives?

Acknowledgments. This research has received funding from The Swedish Research Council for Environment, Agricultural Sciences and Spatial Planning (FORMAS) under grant agreement no. 2011-3313-20412-31.

References

1. Arterton, F.C.: Political participation and teledemocracy. PS Polit. Sci. Polit. **21**, 620–627 (1988)
2. Vedel, T.: The idea of electronic democracy: origins, visions and questions. Parliam. Aff. **59**, 226–235 (2006)
3. Chadwick, A.: Web 2.0: new challenges for the study of e-democracy in an era of informational exuberance. J. Law Policy Inf. Soc. **5**, 9 (2008)

4. Norris, D.F., Reddick, C.G.: E-participation among American local governments. In: Wimmer, M.A., Tambouris, E., Macintosh, A. (eds.) ePart 2013. LNCS, vol. 8075, pp. 37–48. Springer, Heidelberg (2013)
5. Prieto-Martín, P., de Marcos, L., Martínez, J.J.: A critical analysis of EU-funded eparticipation. In: Charalabidis, Y., Koussouris, S. (eds.) Empowering Open and Collaborative Governance, pp. 241–262. Springer, Berlin (2012)
6. Kloby, K., D'Agostino, M.J.: Citizen 2.0: Public and governmental interaction-through Web 2.0 technologies. IGI Global, Hershey (2012)
7. Macintosh, A., Coleman, S., Schneeberger, A.: eParticipation: the research gaps. In: Macintosh, A., Tambouris, E. (eds.) ePart 2009. LNCS, vol. 5694, pp. 1–11. Springer, Heidelberg (2009)
8. Johnson, J.A.: The illiberal culture of e-democracy. J. E-Gov. **3**, 85–112 (2007)
9. Coleman, S., Moss, G.: Under construction:the field of online deliberation research. J. Inf. Technol. Polit. **9**, 1–15 (2012)
10. Wright, S.: Politics as usual? revolution, normalization and a new agenda for online deliberation. New Media Soc. **14**, 244–261 (2012)
11. Benn, N., Macintosh, A.: Argument visualization for eparticipation: towards a research agenda and prototype tool. In: Tambouris, E., Macintosh, A., de Bruijn, H. (eds.) ePart 2011. LNCS, vol. 6847, pp. 60–73. Springer, Heidelberg (2011)
12. Bohman, S.: Information technology in eparticipation research: a word frequency analysis. In: Tambouris, E., Macintosh, A., Bannister, F. (eds.) ePart 2014. LNCS, vol. 8654, pp. 78–89. Springer, Heidelberg (2014)
13. Guggenheim, D., Gore, A.: An Inconvenient Truth: A Global Warning [Motion picture]. Paramount Classics, United States (2006)
14. Gapminder: Unveiling the beauty of statistics for a fact-based world view. http://www.gapminder.org
15. Friendly, M.: Handbook of Data Visualization. In: Friendly, M. (ed.) A Brief History of Data Visualization. Springer Handbooks Comp.Statistics, vol. II, pp. 15–56. Springer, Heidelberg (2008)
16. Funkhouser, H.G.: Historical development of the graphical representation of statistical data. Osiris **3**, 269–404 (1937)
17. Friendly, M.: The golden age of statistical graphics. Stat. Sci. **23**, 502–535 (2008)
18. Koch, T., Denike, K.: Essential, illustrative, or ... just propaganda? Rethinking John Snow's Broad Street map. Cartographica **45**, 19–31 (2010)
19. Magnello, M.E.: Victorian statistical graphics and the iconography of Florence Nightingale's polar area graph. Bull. J. Br. Soc. Hist. Math. **27**, 13–37 (2012)
20. Friendly, M.: Visions and re-visions of Charles Joseph Minard. J. Educ. Behav. Stat. **27**, 31–51 (2002)
21. Beniger, J.R., Robyn, D.L.: Quantitative graphics in statistics: a brief history. Am. Stat. **32**, 1–11 (1978)
22. Cat, J.: Otto Neurath. In: Zalta, E.N. (ed.) The Stanford Encyclopedia of Philosophy (2014). http://plato.stanford.edu/archives/win2014/entries/neurath
23. Neurath, O.: From Vienna method to Isotype. In: Neurath, M., Cohen, R.S. (eds.) Empiricism and Sociology, pp. 214–248. Springer, Netherlands (1973)
24. Jansen, W.: Neurath, Arntz and Isotype: the legacy in art, design and statistics. J. Des. Hist. **22**, 227–242 (2009)
25. Mayr, E., Schreder, G.: Isotype visualizations. A chance for participation and civic education. JeDEM **6**, 136–150 (2014)
26. Tukey, J.W.: Exploratory Data Analysis. Addison-Wesley, Reading (1977)
27. Bertin, J.: Sémiologie Graphique: Les Diagrammes, Les Réseaux, Les Cartes. Gauthier-Villars, Paris (1967)

28. Tufte, E.R.: The Visual Display of Quantitative Information. Graphic Press, Cheshire (1983)
29. Bateman, S., Mandryk, R.L., Gutwin, C., Genest, A., McDine, D., Brooks, C.: Useful junk?: the effects of visual embellishment on comprehension and memorability of charts. In: Proceedings of the SIGCHI Conference on Human Factors in Computing Systems, pp. 2573–2582 (2010)
30. Cleveland, W.S.: Visualizing Data. AT&T Bell Laboratories, Murray Hill (1993)
31. Cleveland, W.S.: The Elements of Graphing Data. AT&T Bell Laboratories, Murray Hill (1994)
32. Wilkinson, L.: The Grammar of Graphics. Springer, New York (1999)
33. Wickham, H.A.: Practical tools for exploring data and models (2008). http://had.co.nz/thesis
34. Card, S.K., Mackinlay, J.D., Shneiderman, B.: Readings in Information Visualization: Using Vision to Think. Kaufmann, San Francisco (1999)
35. Few, S.: Show Me the Numbers: Designing Tables and Graphs to Enlighten. Analytics Press, Oakland (2004)
36. Heer, J., Card, S.K., Landay, J.A.: Prefuse: a toolkit for interactive information visualization. In: Proceedings of the SIGCHI Conference on Human Factors in Computing Systems, pp. 421–430. ACM, New York (2005)
37. D3.js–Data-driven documents. http://d3js.org/
38. Danziger, M.: Information visualization for the people. Master thesis (2008)
39. Gray, J., Chambers, L., Bounegru, L., Ruetten, W.: The Data Journalism Handbook. O'Reilly Media, Sebastopol (2012)
40. Kosara, R., Mackinlay, J.: Storytelling: the next step for visualization. Computer **46**, 44–50 (2013)
41. Segel, E., Heer, J.: Narrative visualization: telling stories with data. IEEE Trans. Vis. Comput. Graph. **16**, 1139–1148 (2010)
42. How y'all, youse and you guys talk. http://www.nytimes.com/interactive/2013/12/20/sunday-review/dialect-quiz-map.html
43. The New York Times's most visited content of (2013). http://www.nytco.com/the-new-york-timess-most-visited-content-of-2013
44. Visual.ly: Original visual content for brands. http://www.visual.ly
45. Emerson, J.: Visualizing Information for Advocacy: An Introduction to Information Design (2008). http://backspace.com/infodesign.pdf
46. The White House: Infographics. http://www.whitehouse.gov/share/infographics
47. Smiciklas, M.: The Power of Infographics: Using Pictures to Communicate and Connect with Your Audience. Que Pub, Indianapolis (2012)
48. Cairo, A.: Graphics lies, misleading visuals. In: Bihanic, D. (ed.) New Challenges for Data Design, pp. 103–116. Springer, London (2015)
49. Tufte, E.R.: Beautiful Evidence. Graphics Press, Cheshire (2006)
50. Krum, R.: Cool Infographics: Effective Communication with Data Visualization and Design. Wiley, New York (2013)
51. Vande Moere, A.: Beyond the tyranny of the pixel: exploring the physicality of information visualization. In: 12th International Conference on Information Visualisation, pp. 469–474 (2008)
52. Jansen, Y., Dragicevic, P., Fekete, J-D.: Evaluating the efficiency of physical visualizations. In: Proceedings of the SIGCHI Conference on Human Factors in Computing Systems, pp. 2593–2602. ACM, New York (2013)
53. Data cuisine. Exploring food as a form of data expression. http://data-cuisine.net
54. Quantified self–Self knowledge through numbers. http://quantifiedself.com

55. Fox, S., Duggan, M.: Mobile health (2012). Pew Research Center. http://www.pewinternet.org/2012/11/08/mobile-health-2012
56. Singer, E.: The measured life. Technol. Rev. **114**, 38–45 (2011)
57. Kanter, D.: A year in diabetes data. http://www.databetic.com

e-Government Solutions and Approaches

A Document Centric Approach for Analysis and Design of E-government Systems

Bálint Molnár[1(✉)] and András Benczúr[2]

[1] Information Technology Foundation of Hungarian Academy of Sciences, Konkoly-Thege út 29-33, 1121 Budapest, Hungary
molnarba@inf.elte.hu

[2] Information Systems Department, Eötvös Loránd University of Budapest, Pázmány Péter Sétány 1/C, 1117 Budapest, Hungary
abenczur@inf.elte.hu

Abstract. As the computer literacy spreads among public servants, the focus of communication between system analysts and users is moved on specification forms that appears formal and semi-formal documents, and spreadsheet like descriptions. The documents are going to be planned to serve both clients and officers of government, both external and internal processing. For system and business analyst, there is a new situation that requires the polishing and improving the readily available methods and methodologies. For accurate interpretations of valid requirements, the system analyst needs approaches that are grounded in formal methods. In *e-government* environment, the specification of requirements happens through calculation spreadsheet and/or office document. So that there is a need for a systematic and at least semi-formal approach that focuses on the *ubiquitous documents*. The models deduced from the document-centric point of view should be placed into an overall Information Systems Architecture. The linkage between the models provides the opportunity for cross validation and verification to keep up the integrity and consistency. The convoluted relationships among the models can be adequately represented by generalized hypergraphs that offer the chances a disciplined and correct systems analysis and design procedure.

Keywords: Document-centric · Modelling · Information systems · Analysis · Design

1 Introduction

In an e-government environment, the electronic documents play important roles. The recent tendencies highlight the fact that the document handling within governments cannot be equaled with Web pages on the specific sites of local and central governments. Even in the case when the documents show active behavior, the users/clients of e-government services create, modify, manipulate, retrieve and put in persistent stores documents. The not active documents will be stored in the public administration secure domain and either by the solution or the constraints of available technology they are semi-structured (form-like) and unstructured documents that contain important instructions for public administration. In Hungary, a set of legal rules has been created

© Springer International Publishing Switzerland 2015
A. Kő and E. Francesconi (Eds.): EGOVIS 2015, LNCS 9265, pp. 319–333, 2015.
DOI: 10.1007/978-3-319-22389-6_23

for supporting the electronic based processes of public administration. There is a set of legal rules so called "Controlled Electronic Public Administration Services" that provide options for both the external and internal partners of local and central governments to use the electronic documents for business processes of public administration in a wide area in official matter. The documents can be perceived as reification of business objects that are the subject matter of business processes. A generic business process handles the citizen's "Instructions to Public Administration" that is in itself an electronic document that contains information as whether which communication channel can be used between a specific authority and the citizen e.g. electronic mailing; furthermore what type of official procedures can be initiated at which authority etc. At the commencing of the "Instruction to Public Administration", the appearance in person in front of the authority is required. However, all of the updating and upgrading of the instructional documents may happen through electronic means with the authorization and access right that is obliged by the rules. When such an instructional document achieves a certain state of completeness and it is approved by the stakeholders it will be moved into a content repository for permanent storage and ensuring its retrieval. The document repository provides the opportunity for authorities to access and process the instructional documents whenever their back-end business processing needs them. The completed documents may contain instructions to several authorities according to specific official procedures and processes and to the related communication channel (e.g. electronic), consequently the instructions may result in several database operations at various authorities taking into account the specific standards of procedures at a certain point of time. As we can see from the example that was described above, the document centric approach becomes ubiquitous in e-government as. Moreover, the requirements originated from public servant conceptualized in document either semi-structured textual (XML) or calculation sheets. Another important aspect that emerges is the electronic mailing system that should offer a secure, reliable and trusted communication channel that should be integrated into the electronic document handling processes. This paper outlines a perception of documents that assist to formalize the life-cycle of documents, from the instantiation of empty template during processing to accomplishing a fairly stable state that makes allowance for further updating. The life cycle of documents is strongly coupled to the business processes, workflows the roles and actors of the organization. The complex networks of interactions and information exchange can be mapped through using appropriate graph structures that can reflect the various and different relationships among the entities that are affected by the procedures.

2 Literature Review

The use of semi-structured and dynamic documents represented in the form of XML and an engineering proposal to create web-based applications is discussed in [14]. Another article [1] describes a methodology for a methodized design process to organize and store large amounts of data in a Web site. For large-scale Web Information System design [28] includes a method. Zachman ontology and TOGAF was developed for information systems to assist understanding the complex set of relationships within Information systems [25, 27, 31]. The service orientation is appeared as new enterprise and software architecture approach and SOA (Service Oriented Architecture) is a loose framework that is independent of technology. The *Service Oriented Computing* (SOC), *Cloud Computing* focuses on services as an information interchange medium dedicated to end-users. There are diverse input data format for information exchange between services: (1) HTML pages, (2) SOAP messages, (3) structure, semi-structured and unstructured documents in XML format (e.g. textual office documents tagged only at the meta-data level). The semi-structured documents embracing hypermedia or hypertext document has essential function in IS (Information systems) [2, 5, 23]. The *adaptive documents* (ADocs) can be grasped as a piece of design work that depends on the status of environment. The relevant properties of ADoc [15]: dynamically varying data environment; state-dependent behavior as the piece of design work reacts to business events; assist in the collaboration between "*pieces of design work (so called artifacts)*" and "*services*". The *adaptive business objects* (ABOs) [24] stands for and abstracts a business entity. The life cycle of entities is mirrored in the history of adaptive business objects. The changes of state are described by a *finite state machine* (FSM) formally. The external and internal events affect entities depicted by state transitions. The data items are not included in an ABO notwithstanding, it uses a notion, and namely *data graph* that task is to actively gather information from various resources. The ABO can be understood as a holistic perception. The *business artifact* can be comprehended as combination of the process and document perspectives [6, 11]. A business artifact is composed of requirements originated from business necessities. The *business artifact* is different analysis and design method that treats information entities along with processing objectives. The business *tasks* impacts on business artifacts conforming to business rules. The tasks of business processes have goals and algorithms that incorporate business rules, pre- and post-conditions. In [17, 15], a conceptual framework is outlined to propose an all-embracing and cohesive set of definitions for business notion. The alignment and fitting between Business Processes and organization can be analyzed on the base of ontologies and semantic approaches [8]. The previously outlined approach can be regarded as holistic approaches that make an attempt to unite various aspects of information systems and the related documents. In spite of this, the practice needs an analytical approach that allows treating with the dichotomy and opposing viewpoints of documents and single information systems model.

3 A Model for Documents in E-government

The semi-structured and even the unstructured documents contain data in their variables or placeholders. For effective and efficient processing of data, the data should be placed into some structured database. Although, the data within documents can be queried and retrieved through tools as XQuery of XML technologies the successful application of these technologies require several pre-conditions. The structured databases as e.g. relational databases demand a disciplined organization of data. The documents based on XML permit a loose structure, however the underlying database and the documents should be coupled to each other. At theoretical level for this reason we define the *collections of data*, each collection has a given name, contains a set of or multi-set of data. The data belong to *data types* that own well-defined attributes, properties and structure. The collections and certain parts of documents can be mapped on each other and through this mapping the data within documents can be paired to partitions of the underlying database. The life cycle of documents that reflects the manipulation over time can be mirrored in the structured database.

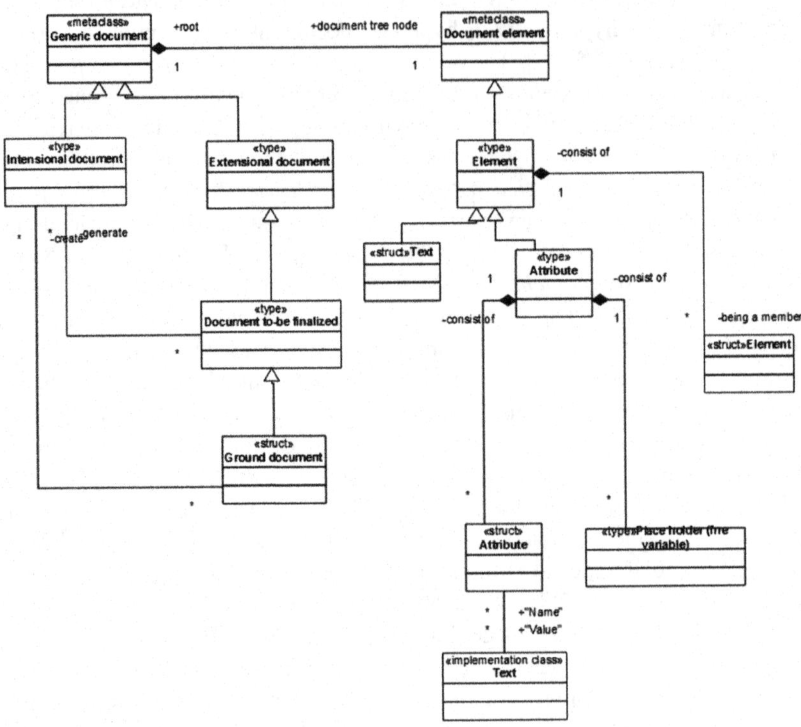

Fig. 1. Representation of document structure by UML-like visual language

3.1 Model of Documents

In e-government procedures we may encounter three major types of documents: forms-like strictly structured, semi-structured and para-semi-structured (hardly structured). The document formats that move through activities of business processes typically industrial standards such as PDF, DOC/ODF, HTML and XML and its dialects. The semi-structured documents can be categorized into two types: data-centric documents and document-centric [7]. The data-centric documents are basically contains primarily data, and their main purpose is to support information interchange between application systems. In *e-government environment*, we can identify e.g. income statements - documents related to taxes as form-like, spreadsheet like documents -, moreover documents for initiating specific official procedures. The data-centric document can be characterized as strictly structured or semi-structured documents.

The document-centric documents can be perceived as textually heavy that can be considered the electronic version of conventional paper documents that may contain very few structured data, and only the necessary "meta-date" to describe the document. We can categorize documents as being static or dynamic. Static documents basically are not changed during processing. At the beginning of processing, they may contain some free variables that later on are to be filled in, the navigation structure is fixed, and the underlying configuration of documents cannot be altered. The meta-data of documents should indicate – in principle – the significant facts in correspondence to the variables that were set within the document.

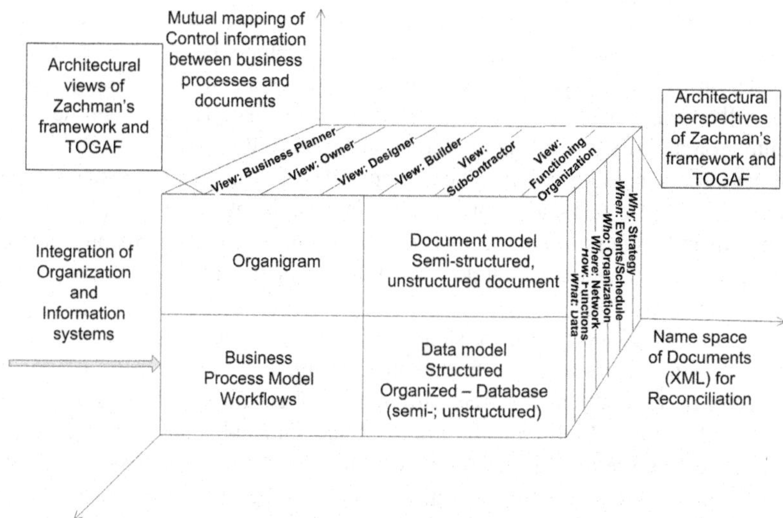

Fig. 2. An enterprise architecture viewpoint for collaboration between information systems and documents

The dynamic documents make allowances for changing both content and structure. We can set up taxonomy for dynamic documents. A generic document can be considered as a hierarchy of documents. The variables that are contained in generic documents are all free. A generic document can be perceived as a general template that permits some structural changes under some constraints that are formulated in logical statements. The documents that contain free variables and a pre-defined overall composition can be called as *free-documents*. During the processing of documents, the free variables valuated through several steps until the document achieves a finalized or a finished state. All of the variables have a value in the finalized state. However, the finalized state allows for minor modifications until the document reaches a finished state. We can define the version of documents in which all variables are valuated as *ground-document*.

We may assume that there exists a generalized document for each organization that embraces all of generic types or classes of documents, this document may be called as overarching document. Beside the above mentioned document type, we may categorize documents into intensional and extensional types. A certain collection of the dynamic, semi-structured documents can be comprehended as intensional document type that can be defined as a super-type or super class of the bag of certain possible documents that can be instantiated in the form of extensional document instances; the instantiation procedure is governed by certain logical rules and constraints. The subjects of inferences that are performed by the rules are as follows: (1) the collections of data related to documents, (2) data-centric and semi-structured document types. The originating document type can be a generic document, a template, or a free-document partly or fully valuated variables. During processing of an instance of a specific intensional document type, the inference procedure may create (1) totally new free-document, (2) a template for instantiation, (3) an extension to a free-document. An extension to a free-document means a definite new part of free-documents. The free-documents can be in any state during its life-cycle according to its variables, i.e. no variables are valuated, partly or fully valuated, finalized, and even may be finished. The attached new part of the document may initiate a connection to a collection of data, to a set of activities and tasks of certain business processes. The responsibilities for the newly generated part of the document join the tasks and roles within the organization. After the logical reasoning based on business rules, the instance generated from an intensional document can be considered as an extensional document that are subject for further processing by business activities.

The *extensional documents* as instances of more generic ones can be grasped as free-documents that are ready for further processing, i.e. as a member of document hierarchy can be refined and the free variables can be valuated. During the business process we differentiated between the finalized and finished states. The reason is that the finalized state represents a document without free-variable, the finished state represents a document that cannot be modified, and the integrity of the content should be safeguarded. The necessity for alteration of a finished document leads to new instance of the document and the related document hierarchy as well.

3.2 A Document-Centric Analysis of Business Processes

The business processes in an e-government or e-public-administration environment are triggered by documents and concluded in documents. To analyze the business processes we should start at the structure of organization and the related document hierarchies. The structure of documents, variables, data place holders as syntactical structures are getting strongly coupled to *semantic* information during the business and system analysis. Figure 2 contains an overall information system architecture model that embraces specific, single models in the cells of the cube [3, 27, 31]. Following the diagonal on the front face of the cube, from left to right and down we move through the different level of abstraction. On the upper face of the cube, the same diagonal shows the steps of transformation from business concepts to physical representation. This process can be perceived as a refinement procedure. The lateral face on the right side manifests the essential perspective of enterprise architecture. The intersection of perspectives with the other two viewpoints features as specific model at a certain point of abstraction and granularity. From the Business Planner viewpoints and Strategy perspective, the related models contain only the essential roles, actors and connection between them. The organigram section contains the models and analysis artifacts for describing that set of relationships among roles and actors. Business analysis concentrates on business processes that are modeled within the domain of Function perspective. The artifacts in the cross-section of Organigram, Business Planner, perspective of Organization and Function can depict the links among the processes, documents, actors and roles. The work process model explores the tasks that are carried out by particular individuals. The tasks represent a piece of work that can be grasped by certain steps of scenarios within use cases. The tasks can be perceived as an algorithm owning pre- and post-conditions. The tasks can be coupled to user interfaces or to interfaces of other applications.

Table 1. A cross-section of three-dimensional matrix to represent models and their transformations [31]

	what	*how*	*where*	*who*	*when*	*why*
Planner (*Contextual*)	Business Documents	Business Processes	Business Locations	Organizations	Events	Business Motivations - Goals, Strategies
Owner (*Conceptual*)	Collection of Data within *Documents*	Business Process Model	Business Information and Document Logistics System	Work Process Model	Master Schedule	Business Plan
Designer (*Logical*)	Logical Data Model *Mapped Documents*	Information System' Services, Documents	System Geographic Deployment Architecture e.g. Distributed System Architecture	Human Interface Architecture. *Documents*	Task Structure *Documents as subject of algorithms*	Business Rules *Part of Documents is Governed by*
Builder (*Physical*)	Physical Data Model *Valuated Variables of Documents*	System Design, *XML Documents and Operations*	System Architecture/Technology Architecture	Presentation Architecture *HTML/XML interface*	Task Control Structure *Documents as input-output for regulation*	Rule Design *Intensional Documents* and *Inferences, Logical Predicates for safeguarding consistency and integrity*
Subcontractor (*Implementation*)	Data Definition Repository	Programs	Network Architecture	Security Architecture, *Identity, Authentication, Authorization,*	Timing Definition	Rule Specification
Models	Data Model	Business Process Model	Network	Organigram	Behavior	Business Rules
	Document Model					

The user interfaces connected to access and manipulation rights in this way to roles and actors within the organization. The scenarios may consist of scenes; the scenes are built up out of steps that represent the elementary activities and acts of users that compose of the overall algorithm that can be depicted by use cases or stories. The user interfaces can be implemented by dynamic or active document that should be joined to specific tasks. The subjects of activities and acts are documents being at different levels of structuring and in various levels of processing. Hence, it is clear that analysis of tasks and documents are strongly related. The document analysis highlights the collection of data that final destination are databases within the system. The technology of database should fit to the requirements deduced from documents for effective and efficient processing. The combined analysis of tasks and documents expose business rules, the intended usage of documents and their data (Fig. 3).

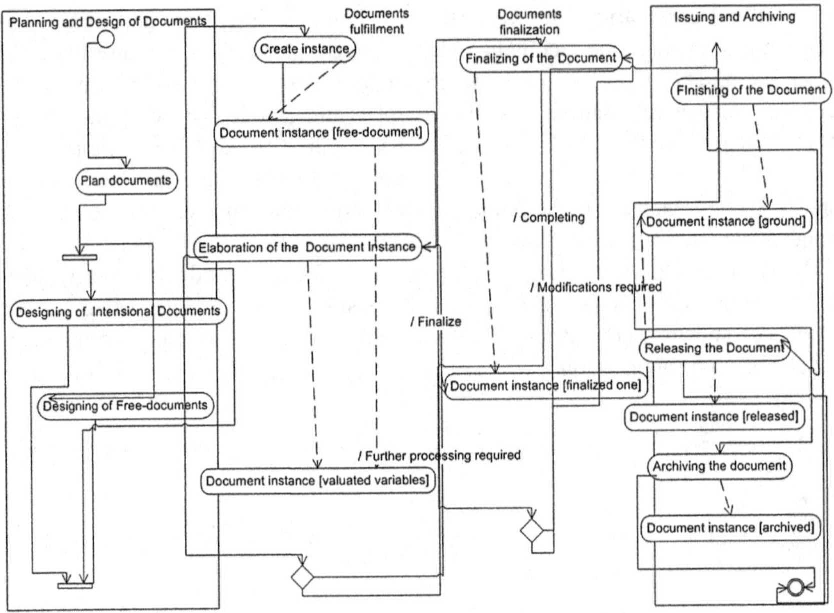

Fig. 3. Functions of organization and processes for document handling at upper-level

Document analysis concentrates on the element of document hierarchies as intensional documents, free-documents and finally the ground documents. On the front and left hand side within the three dimensional matrix represented in Fig. 2, the document analysis should be carried out along with data modeling that creates a mapping between documents and data models. There are two mainstream paradigms of data modeling: structured one that is based on entity-relationship approach and object centered that makes use object-oriented method and UML visual language. Both approaches commence with conceptual modeling. On the left hand side of lateral side of cube, the Data perspective appear that intersects the Document and Data Model, moreover the Business Planner and Owner views. The models represented by the intersections aims at domain modeling to set up an abstract representation of data collections that were revealed during document analysis. The main goal of modeling methodologies is to populate the three dimensional matrix (Fig. 2) with pieces of modeling and design. These pieces contain documents, their models, set of modeling and design patterns that provide assistance to build models. The document-centric method can be perceived as complex path described by a graph structure through the three dimensional matrix (Fig. 2); furthermore the method can be explicated as a chain of model transformations (Table 1) Naturally, a life cycle of specific project may give emphasis to particular part of possible paths through the matrices. From a theoretical viewpoint we do not make differences and devote more weight to any models. A Strategic Planning or top-down analysis put a heavy burden on the upper, left hand side of matrix (Table 1), and the first two rows. The objective of this analysis is generally to align business process model, organization, their manipulated documents and the technology. From an Information Technology viewpoint, these models are abstract and have coarse granularity as the models bundle up the major concepts to yield an image of the context. The Designer (Logical Model) and Builder (Physical Model) views as rows of models may produce more detailed descriptions for representing data and processes at transactional level.

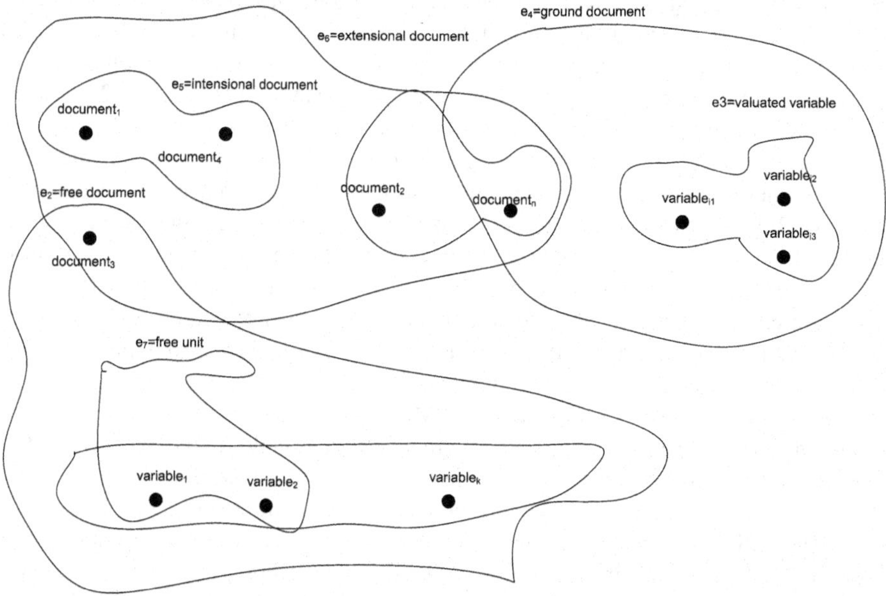

Fig. 4. Representation of document structure by hypergraph

The subjects of transactions are documents that exhibit differing structuring principles and at various stages of fulfillment; and that are generated or used up by tasks within transactions. The arrangement of document-centric modeling into a three dimensional matrix provides an opportunity for a dynamic reconciliation, integration, verification and validation between models. The high level models do not have enough granularities to give clues how to implement the models and integrate them. The lower-level models do not support the alignment exercise between high-level business objectives, opportunities of technologies and decisions for implementation. That is the reason why we should use the Zachman, TOGAF and Blokdijk approaches [3, 27, 31] for describing and representing the complex networks of models. In this way, producing various models with differing details and focus points secures that the new models covering business processes and documents are complete, consistent, dependable and implementable in information systems that comply with business requirement.

3.3 Construct a Formal Structure for Verification and Validation

The cells of the three dimensional matrix (Fig. 2, Table 1) contain models. The models and the representations of related documents can be characterized by meta-data and data that describe the cross-references and links between different models and related documents. The matrix exposed in Table 1 can be interpreted as a state transition matrix. Each element has some linkage to other ones. In our first attempt, we concentrate on meta-data of models and the essential arguments of relationships' description. The basic descriptive information of models and their relationships among them can be represented as vectors. The vectors can be transformed by matrices that reflect the transition, integration, modification rules, and consistency checking. The axiomatic design framework provides a basic tool set that can be applied in the document-centric information systems analysis and modeling [21, 20, 22, 29]. However, the vector and matrix representations seems feasible to use for specifying constraints and prescribing alteration methods; the complex network of relationships, the cross-referencing needs an adequate mathematical structure for an accurate mapping of linkages. Our proposal is that the generalized hypergraph is an appropriate mathematical formalism. The hypergraphs allow that a hyperedge may contain several nodes. A node may belong to more than one hyperedge. In the generalized hypergraph, a hyperedge can be considered as a node embedded into other hyperedges [4, 12].

The first row can be perceived as various views of *requirements* from the viewpoint of the analysis (Table 1). The requirements can be – beside the enterprise level, comprehensive document – formulated by UML 2.0 sequence, upper-level activity and use case diagrams. The relevant models can represented as nodes in the hypergraph, the basic properties can be placed into the nodes as significant attributes. The general organization of documents (Fig. 1) and the hypergraph representation can be seen in Fig. 4. The difficulties to represent the complex relationships can be sensed out of the to figures (Figs. 1 and 4). The upper level UML diagram indirectly covers the relevant functions of organizations that involve implicitly the organizational unit, roles and actors. To render the whole picture, the description by a hypergraph seems to be adequate. Moving across the perspectives or columns in the matrix (Table 1), the cross references between documents, activities and other components can be depicted by hyperedges; meanwhile a "cell" in the matrix embodies an appropriate model, e.g. activity diagram. The links between particular elements and models can be expressed by directed hyperedges (Fig. 5). The decisive components as *interfaces* between the various elements of the system are the documents that belong to the document hierarchy. The meta-structure of documents (Fig. 1) and their instances can be shown in UML like class and object diagram. Further details can be described by Document Object Model and proper XML structure [18]. The composite structure diagram (UML) can be used to create links between components of documents to activities and then map them into hypergraph structure. During the model refinement, constituents of the second and third row (system analyst and design view) in the matrix can be decomposed to mirror the relationships more precisely.

The governance and control of the overall activities and actions within the organizations appear in perspectives as Business Processes, Organization, Events and Motivations. To describe controls, the activity, state transition and sequence UML models can be used. All the diagrams should reference the documents, parts of documents and consequently the related collection of data in the underlying logical database. Beside control, the representation of concurrency among organizational functions, unit, roles and actors is an essential aspect that shows the compositional

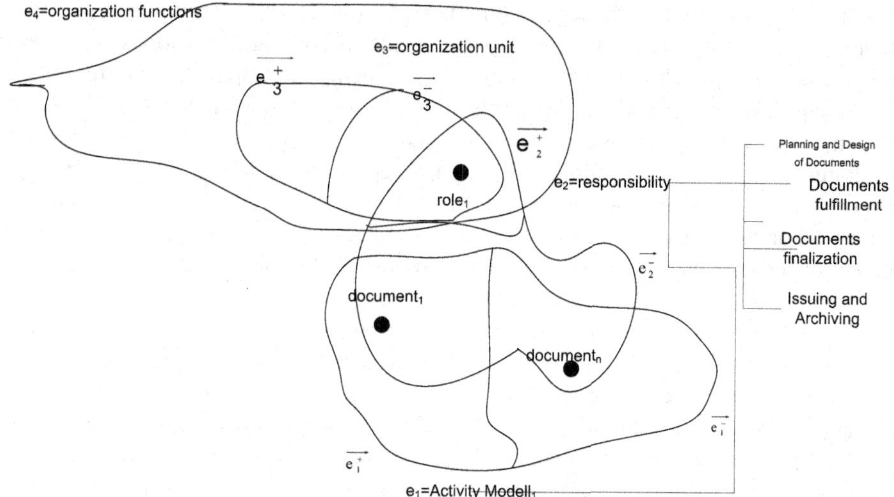

Fig. 5. Representation of cross-references between the significant models and their Elements

structures of activities, events and business processes. The basic structures are as follows: sequence, branching, alternative or optional branches, parallel structures as forks and joins. Reasonable parts of business processes and tasks can be grouped into scenarios and within them into scenes to provide some structuring principle.

The time perspective (when and Events column) can be displayed by sequence and state transition diagram. In the case of real-time requirements, the timing diagram in UML can be utilized. The models provide a description how the documents and their integral parts go through changes and interaction with the business process, tasks, activities and collection of data in the database. The granularity of the related models indicates that they surface especially in the System Builder or Physical viewpoint.

The last row, the subcontractor and operations are responsible for the performance issues essentially. The architecture solution related the documents should respond a set of non-functional criteria, quality of service levels as e.g. response time, throughput and latency. The refinement and accurate extension of the previously mentioned diagrams (timing and activity diagram expanded by timing parameter) can exhibit the performance behavior. The structure and parts of free-documents emerge in the diagrams as subjects of manipulation and state transition.

4 A Motivating Example

In a *public administration*, the requirement for a *secure* and *reliable* document and message interchange method has emerged. A business process model was created that focuses on documents and their manipulation. The most important business processes for treatment of documents are as follows: (1) Documents intended to be part of officials procedures are mailed by individuals;(2) Recording the delivered documents and identification(of the sender party; (3) Assigning the electronic document to the responsible public officer;(4) Public administration processes for taking care of documents;(5) The storing, archiving of documents according to various pre- and post-conditions; (6) Production of official documents as responses and reactions; (7) Amendment, authorization, digital/electronic signing of documents; (8) Electronic document interchange among Offices and Agencies; (9) Obtaining, recording and cataloguing paper-based documents; (10) Safekeeping in the record office, archiving, disposal and demolition. A system for transmitting of messages and documents is planned. For the reason of the standardized management, the paper-based documents are converted into electronic ones. There are two sorts of e-documents: registered and certified one. The basic methods for handling them are as follows: (1) Transmitting/obtaining e-documents; (2) Returning receipts; (3) Acknowledging the reception of envelope and/or content of the message. The business processes can be performed through Web interfaces that are integral parts of man-machine interface as interactive documents. Through the Web interfaces, Web services are available. The Web services are accessed through Message–oriented Middleware as basic Web services can be as follows (1) requesting for obtaining a document, (2) fetching the received documents, (3) inquiring the content of meta-data of received documents, (4) cataloguing and storing documents into office record system etc. [30].

The conceptual level contemplating of end-users concentrates on documents. The public officers express the business processes of public administration in terms of documents. The analysis concentrated on the possible, various documents. The heterogeneity of documents were decreased by a sort of clustering that is based on the meta-data of documents. In both cases of electronic and originally paper ones, the information that can be gained from the documents and later on handled a structured or semi-structured way is embodied in the form of meta-data. The messages are document-oriented in the automated systems.

The workers at postal services talk about the life cycles of postal matters, firstly paper-based, secondly electronic ones. The Web interface that is itself an interactive document provides services for managing electronic postal matters and their document content. The meta-data related to a particular document are keyed in through the Web interface, the core of the document transformed into electronic form to transmit it electronically.

The basic analysis and design questions was how to solve the accurate registering, monitoring, tracking of documents that are received and expedited by public administration. The reception point of documents is a general registering service with a massive underlying database that stores the electronic documents along with their descriptive information. The starting point of subsequent workflow is the document registering and expedition service. Within the workflow that is specific to an office or authority the document life cycle is monitored, the responsibilities mapped to documents, activities and finally onto the schema of logical database.

The described document-centric analysis method assisted to structure of the anarchic relationships between varieties of documents. The free variables within free documents as the subject of data processing activities can be allocated to roles. This analysis and abstraction laid the groundwork for role based access right system. The meta-data of documents comprise a specific collection of data that represented as definite a part of the related logical database. The other free variables – both in a single document and in an interactive document within the web interface – mapped onto another specific collection of data in the database. The convoluted links that appear at the different layers of architecture and models can be decomposed and traced steadily exploiting the proposed method. The method during the refinement of design creates opportunity for verification and validation, furthermore for taking advantage of the dichotomy of contrasting perspectives for quality assurance.

5 Evaluation Method

Our goal was to create an approach that may be used as a methodology designing a document based information systems in an e-government environment. The characteristic property of methodology development is that the usability of proposed method can be studied by examples in the form of case studies. The applicability of the method can be appraised by qualitative analysis instead of statistical or any other quantitative assessment [9]. The case study as a research method and evaluation approach is correct analytical tool the study of formal methodologies and models that aimed at understanding of Information systems [19]. A suggested methodological approach can be appraised by its bearing on the functional and non-functional requirements of information systems. Up to now, we had the chance to carry out only one case study and to observe it. Our center of evaluation was not a meticulous investigation of the recommended method by statistical methods. Although, as a collateral result of the case study, we have detected the dissimilarity between our method and the software product line that was pursued by the programming group, and valuated only on a fuzzy scale to provide a perception. The employed software engineering methodology used by the programmers' team pursued Java-based object-oriented and API methods, although with ignorance of Web service based approaches. Our proposed model gives attention to most modern information systems that present as decisive feature: the document-centric communication and user-interfaces, extensive exploitation of Web technologies and a selection of functionalities provided for Service Oriented Architecture. Our proposed method supports reducing the *complexity* of systems, assisting in the *transformation* of the models during the software production process. Furthermore, the conceptualization of *Business Rules* that is based on the syntax and semantics of documents can be improved. The step-by-step alteration of models can be *tracked* for verification, validation and controlling.

6 Conclusion

We have outlined a method and its formal representation that grounded in the documents, their structures and their interaction with a public administration environment. The official procedures of *governments* can be perceived as business processes that are triggered by documents and finally produce documents to be released. The recent technologies allow putting into the focus point the documents as the subject of the analysis. The document-centric analysis fits to the general principles of operations in *public administration*. The presented architecture-based, model driven approach provides a way to build up information systems. The mathematical based representation in an adequate underlying database technology, namely hypergraph database gives the opportunity for a systematic verification and validation across the whole life cycle of Information systems. The contribution of the paper is the proposal for a document-centric system analysis, the provision the required models and their formal and semi-formal representation.

References

1. Atzeni, P., Merialdo, P., Mecca, G.: Data-intensive web sites: design and maintenance. In: World Wide Web, vol. 4, pp. 21–47 (2001)
2. Bernauer, M., Schrefl, M.: Self-maintaining web pages: from theory to practice. Data Knowl. Eng. **48**, 39–73 (2004)
3. Blokdijk, A., Blokdijk, P.: Planning and Design of Information Systems. Academic Press, London (1987)
4. Bretto, A.: Hypergraph Theory: An Introduction. Springer, Heidelberg (2013)
5. Chiua, C.-M., Bieber, M.: A dynamically mapped open hypermedia system framework for integrating information systems. Inf. Softw. Technol. **43**, 75–86 (2001)
6. Cohn, D., Hull, R.: Business artifacts: A data-centric approach to modeling business operations and processes. IEEE Data Eng. Bull. **32**, 3–9 (2009)
7. Thomas, ERL.: SOA design patterns. Pearson Education (2008)
8. Gábor, A., Kö, A., Szabó, I., Ternai, K., Varga, K.: Compliance check in semantic business process management. In: Demey, Yan Tang, Panetto, H. (eds.) OTM 2013 Workshops 2013. LNCS, vol. 8186, pp. 353–362. Springer, Heidelberg (2013)
9. Gerring, J.: Case study research: principles and practices. Cambridge University Press, Cambridge (2006)
10. Gorton, I.: Essential Software Architecture, 2nd edn. Springer, Heidelberg (2011)
11. Hull, R.: Artifact-centric business process models: brief survey of research results and challenges. In: Meersman, R., Tari, Z. (eds.) OTM 2008, Part II. LNCS, vol. 5332, pp. 1152–1163. Springer, Heidelberg (2008)
12. HyperGraphDB. http://www.hypergraphdb.org/index. Last visited: 08 March 2015
13. Kim, S.J., Suh, N.P., Kim, S.-K.: Design of software systems based on axiomatic design. Robot. Comput.-Integr. Manuf. **3**, 149–162 (1992)
14. Köppen, E., Neumann, G.: Active hypertext for distributed web applications. In: Proceedings of The Eighth IEEE International Workshops on Enabling Technologies: Infrastructure for Collaborative Enterprises (WET-ICE 1999), pp. 297—302 (1999)
15. Kő, A., Ternai, K.: A development method for ontology based business processes. In: eChallenges e-2011 Conference Proceedings. IIMC International Information Management Corporation Ltd., Florence (2011)
16. Kumaran, S., Liu, R., Wu, Frederick Y.: On the duality of information-centric and activity-centric models of business processes. In: Bellahsène, Z., Léonard, M. (eds.) CAiSE 2008. LNCS, vol. 5074, pp. 32–47. Springer, Heidelberg (2008)
17. Kumaran, S., Nandi, P., Heath, T., Bhaskaran, K., Das, R.: ADoc-oriented programming. In: Symposium on Applications and the Internet (SAINT), pp. 334–343 (2003)
18. Marini, J.: The Document Object Model: Processing Structured Documents. McGraw-Hill, New York (2002)

19. Miles, M.B., Huberman, A.M.: Qualitative Data Analysis: An Expanded Sourcebook. Sage, Thousand Oaks, London (1994)
20. Molnár, B.: Applications of hypergraphs in informatics: a survey and opportunities for research. Ann. Univ. Sci. Budapest. Sect. Comput. **42**, 261–282 (2014)
21. Molnár, B., Tarcsi, A.: Architecture and System Design Issues of Contemporary Web-based Information systems, In: Proceedings of the 5th International Conference on Software, Knowledge Information, Industrial Management and Applications (SKIMA 2011), September 8–11, 2011, Benevento, Italy (2011)
22. Molnár, B., Benczúr, A.: Facet of modeling web information systems from a document-centric view. Int. J. Web Portals (IJWP) **5**(4), 57–70 (2013). IGI Global
23. Nama, C.-K., Jang, G.-S., Ba, J.-H.: An XML-based active document for intelligent web applications. Expert Syst. Appl. **25**, 165–176 (2003)
24. Nandi, P., Kumaran, S.: Adaptive business objects – a new component model for business integration. In: Proceedings of International Conference on Enterprise Information systems, pp. 179–188 (2005)
25. OASIS 2006. A reference model for service-oriented architecture, White Paper, Service-Oriented Architecture Reference Model Technical Committee, Organization for the Advancement of Structured Information Standards, Billerica, MA, February 2006
26. OASIS. ebXML Business Process Specification Schema Version 1.01. http://www.ebxml.org/specs/ebBPSS.pdf
27. Open Group, 2010. TOGAF: The Open Group Architecture Framework, TOGAF® Version 9 (2010). http://www.opengroup.org/togaf/
28. Rossi, G., Schwabe, D., Lyardet, F.: Web application models are more than conceptual models. In: Kouloumdjian, J., Roddick, J., Chen, P.P., Embley, D.W., Liddle, S.W. (eds.) ER Workshops 1999. LNCS, vol. 1727. Springer, Heidelberg (1999)
29. Suh, N.P.: Axiomatic Design: Advantages and Applications. Oxford University Press, New York (2001). 2001
30. W3C 2001. Web Services Description Language (WSDL) 1.1. Web Site (2001). http://www.w3.org/TR/wsdl
31. Zachman, J.A.: A framework for information systems architecture. IBM Syst. J. **26**(3), 276–292 (1987)

Elliptic Curve Array Ballots for Homomorphic Tallying Elections

Maria dels Àngels Cerveró[1(✉)], Víctor Mateu[1,2], Santi Martínez[1], Josep Maria Miret[1], and Francesc Sebé[1]

[1] Dept. of Mathematics, Universitat de Lleida, Jaume II, 69, 25001 Lleida, Spain
{mcervero,vmateu,santi,miret,fsebe}@matematica.udl.cat
[2] Scytl Secure Electronic Voting, Tuset, 20, 08006 Barcelona, Spain

Abstract. Remote voting systems implementing the homomorphic tallying paradigm have proven to be the best option for elections with a small range of candidates. In this paper, we propose a new homomorphic tallying remote voting system that makes use of elliptic curve cryptography. The proposed system is suitable for multiple choice elections. Detailed security and performance analysis are provided.

Keywords: Electronic voting · Elliptic curve cryptography · Homomorphic cryptosystem · Security

1 Introduction

Remote voting systems allow the participants to cast their ballots from any place with an available Internet connection. At the end of the voting period, the votes can be tallied automatically, reducing the economic cost while improving the speed and accuracy of the process. Unfortunately, the fact that the voting platform is accessible through the Internet makes it vulnerable to attacks coming from the network. Hence, security is a key aspect to consider. A remote voting system must provide the following security properties:

Authentication: only the votes cast by eligible voters are taken into account.
Unicity: a participant can vote once at most.
Privacy: vote content cannot be related to the identity of its caster.
Fairness: partial results are not revealed.
Verifiability: correctness of the voting process can be checked. A voting system is *universally verifiable* if any external entity can verify that all votes have been properly counted. If voters can only verify that their own vote has been taken into account, the scheme is *individually verifiable*.
Uncoercibility: a voter cannot prove she voted in a particular way.

The aforementioned security requirements are achieved by making use of advanced cryptographic techniques. According to the way in which cryptography

© Springer International Publishing Switzerland 2015
A. Kő and E. Francesconi (Eds.): EGOVIS 2015, LNCS 9265, pp. 334–347, 2015.
DOI: 10.1007/978-3-319-22389-6_24

is used, remote voting schemes can be classified into three main paradigms: *mix-type*, *blind signature-based* and *homomorphic tallying*.

The *mix-type* paradigm [16,18,21] resembles paper-based traditional voting using a ballot box. Eligible voters generate their votes, encrypt them using the election public key and sign their encrypted vote (ballot) before sending it to the polling station. In order to authenticate each voter, the polling station verifies the signature of the received ballots. Once the voting period is concluded, the ballots are mixed (shuffled and remasked) in order to break the link between them and the identity of voters who cast them. Finally, they are decrypted and tallied. Ballot mixing has to be performed verifiably. To that end, the polling station computes a zero–knowledge proof to demonstrate that the cleartexts of the received ballots are equal to the cleartexts of the mixed ballots. Such proofs are usually hard to generate and verify in terms of computational effort. Their conceptual complexity is also very high so that it is very difficult for observers to get convinced about the security they enforce.

In *blind signature-based* voting schemes [10,17], a participant composes her vote, encrypts it and then authenticates herself to a trusted authority (the authentication server) who manages the electoral roll. That trusted authority checks whether this is the first time the participant is authenticated. In that case, the authentication server blindly signs [4] the participant's ballot. Next, the participant transmits her blindly signed ballot to the polling station through an anonymous channel. The voting platform will only accept ballots that have been signed by the authentication server. Once the voting period is concluded, votes are decrypted and tallied. The process needs a verifiable anonymous channel if universal verifiability is needed.

The *homomorphic tallying* paradigm, first proposed in [6], is constructed over a homomorphic public key cryptosystem. In this paradigm [3,12,14,15,23], participants cast their votes encrypted under the homomorphic cryptosystem. After collecting all the ballots, the polling station aggregates them using the homomorphic operation. As a result, a single ciphertext is generated. Its decryption will provide the homomorphic addition/multiplication of the cleartext votes. An appropriate coding of votes permits to obtain the global vote tally from this message. In such a system, the participants are required to prove in zero-knowledge that their ballots have been properly composed [8,11]. These proofs can be verified as ballots are being received by the polling station. However, their complexity renders this paradigm to be only applicable to elections in which choices can be coded in a very simple way.

Homomorphic cryptosystems can be additive or multiplicative. The problem when operating with a multiplicative homomorphism is that cleartext multiplication easily overflows the cryptosystem cleartext range. To avoid that, proposals like [19,20] aggregate the ballots in small groups so that cleartext overflowing is avoided. After that, the resulting aggregated ciphertexts are mixed. Although such hybrid systems are more efficient that mix-type schemes, they are not as fast as classic homomorphic tallying schemes.

Helios 2.0 is a remote voting system that belongs to the homomorphic tallying paradigm. The original Helios 1.0 was presented in [1] and has been successfully used for small elections [2]. Our proposal is an improvement to Helios 2.0. It enhances that system by allowing a better perception of blank ballots, especially in elections in which voters can vote for more than one candidate. In addition, the use of elliptic curve cryptography provides a better performance.

Motivation and Contribution. Although elliptic curve cryptography provides very fast encryption and decryption methods, it is rarely used within the homomorphic tallying remote voting paradigm due to the elevated computational cost of the process required to obtain the election result from the cleartext of the aggregated ciphertext. Furthermore, there exist some zero- knowledge proofs that do not work with elliptic curves while others just do not provide the security of their multiplicative group version. Although the proposal in [3] is completely functional and meets all the security requirements listed before, the proof and the verification of ballots as well as its homomorphic decoding step have an elevated computational cost. In this paper we exploit the additive homomorphic property of the Elliptic Curve ElGamal cryptosystem to create an efficient remote voting protocol suitable for real elections. The proposal allows to aggregate all the ballots into a single ciphertext, so a mixing step is not needed.

The paper is structured as follows. Section 2 recalls some theoretical aspects of elliptic curve cryptography, focusing on the Elliptic Curve ElGamal cryptosystem. Our proposal is described in Sect. 3. The security of the presented system is discussed in Sect. 4. Finally, Sect. 5 is devoted to provide some details about the performance together with some concluding remarks.

2 Elliptic Curves

An elliptic curve E over a prime finite field $\mathbb{F}_p$ is an algebraic curve given by the reduced Weierstraß equation [22],

$$E : y^2 = x^3 + ax + b,$$

with nonzero discriminant $4a^3 + 27b^2 \neq 0$. We denote by $E(\mathbb{F}_p)$ the set of points $(x, y) \in \mathbb{F}_p \times \mathbb{F}_p$ that satisfy the curve equation, along with the point at infinity $\mathcal{O}$. An addition operation can be defined over $E(\mathbb{F}_p)$ using the chord-tangent method. This operation endows the set $E(\mathbb{F}_p)$ with an abelian group structure in which $\mathcal{O}$ is the identity element. Considering this group law, the *Elliptic Curve Discrete Logarithm Problem* (ECDLP) consists in, given two points P and Q, find an integer d that satisfies $Q = dP$. This is a computationally hard problem when the cardinality of $E(\mathbb{F}_p)$ has a large prime factor.

2.1 Elliptic Curve ElGamal Cryptosystem

In this paper, we use an analogue of the ElGamal cryptosystem [9] using elliptic curves, the Elliptic Curve ElGamal (EC-ElGamal). For simplicity, only elliptic curves defined over a prime order finite field are considered.

Setup and Key Creation. The setup of the cryptosystem requires choosing a prime p, which defines a finite field $\mathbb{F}_p$, and two parameters a and b defining an elliptic curve E over $\mathbb{F}_p$. We also need an order m point $P \in E(\mathbb{F}_p)$, such that m is a large prime of the same size as p.

A private key is created by taking a random integer $d \in \{1, \ldots, m-1\}$. The corresponding public key is $Q = dP$.

Encryption and Decryption. A point $V \in E(\mathbb{F}_p)$ is encrypted under public key Q as follows:

$$Enc_Q(V) = C = (A, B) = (rP, V + rQ),$$

where r is a random integer in $\{1, \ldots, m-1\}$.

A ciphertext $C = (A, B)$ can be decrypted when the private key d is known. The cleartext V is recovered by computing:

$$Dec_d(C) = V = B - dA.$$

A ciphertext $C = (A, B)$ can be *verifiably decrypted* by publishing its cleartext V and proving in zero-knowledge that $\log_P Q = \log_A (B - V)$ by means of Chaum-Pedersen's proof [5]. However, there is an alternative way to reveal the cleartext of C. This can be done if the random value r generated for encryption is known. First, we have to check whether rP equals A and next compute:

$$Rev_r(C) = V = B - rQ.$$

Homomorphic Property. The EC-ElGamal cryptosystem has a homomorphic property with respect to the point addition operation. Two ciphertexts $C_1 = (A_1, B_1)$ and $C_2 = (A_2, B_2)$, encrypting V_1 and V_2, can be aggregated as

$$C_3 = C_1 + C_2 = (A_1 + A_2, B_1 + B_2) = ((r_1 + r_2)P,\ (V_1 + V_2) + (r_1 + r_2)Q).$$

The decryption of C_3 provides $V_3 = V_1 + V_2$ as a result.

3 E-voting Scheme

In this section, we present a remote voting system implemented using the EC-ElGamal cryptosystem. Our proposal can be extended to accommodate multi-candidate elections, as shown in Sect. 3.4.

3.1 Participating Parties

We assume there exists a publicly readable Bulletin Board (BB) on which only some specific authorities can write. Our protocol involves the following parties:

Registrar: it publishes the electoral roll on the BB.

Key Storage Trusted Party (KSTP): it generates and stores the election private key and publishes the election public key on the BB. It will perform a verifiable decryption when required. It may be a distributed entity.

Voters: eligible voters are those appearing in the electoral roll.

Polling Station (PS): it collects the ballots and, after verifying their correct composition and checking the people casting them are listed in the electoral roll, publishes them on the BB so that anyone can check their validity.

The BB is publicly accessible for reading, but only the Registrar, the KSTP and the PS can write on it.

3.2 Voting System

The forthcoming system description assumes a single-choice election (see Sect. 3.4 for multi-candidate elections). The system description is divided into three phases: *setup*, *vote casting* and *tallying*. Each stage starts when the previous one ends.

Setup Phase. Let n be the amount of eligible voters in the electoral roll. First of all, the Registrar publishes the electoral roll and the list of candidates $L = \{L_1, L_2, \ldots, L_k\}$ on the BB. The electoral roll consists of a list of all the eligible voters $\{v_1, v_2, \ldots, v_n\}$ and their public keys $pk_1, pk_2, \ldots, pk_n$, which could be certified by some certificate authority.

Next, the KSTP chooses a suitable elliptic curve and chooses a secret key d. Next, it publishes an order m point $P \in E(\mathbb{F}_p)$ together with the election public key $Q = dP$ on the BB.

Reliability on the KSTP can be increased by distributing it into a set of entities $\{\text{KSTP}_1, \ldots, \text{KSTP}_t\}$. Thus, each KSTP_i generates its own private key d_i and publishes $Q_i = d_i P$. Then, the election public key is $Q = \sum_i Q_i$. A message encrypted under Q can only be decrypted if all the entities composing the KSTP do collaborate.

Finally, the PS publishes a point V of the same curve. It also precomputes and stores the points $V, 2V, \ldots, \lfloor n/2 \rfloor V$. Each point iV is stored together with the corresponding integer i in a hash table $\mathcal{T}$.

Vote Casting Phase. A voter v_i creates her ballot for a candidate L_j by generating a ciphertext array $(C_{i,1}, \ldots, C_{i,k}, C_{i,k+1})$ in which the cleartext of $C_{i,j}$ is $2V$ while the remaining ciphertexts are an encryption of V. Ciphertext $C_{i,k+1}$ would accommodate and eventual blank vote. Assuming the chosen candidate was L_k, v_i would randomly select $r_{i,1}, \ldots, r_{i,k}, r_{i,k+1} \in_R \{1, \ldots, m-1\}$ and would generate:

$$C_{i,j} = (r_{i,j}P,\ \ V + r_{i,j}Q), \quad \text{for } j \neq k,$$
$$C_{i,k} = (r_{i,k}P, 2V + r_{i,k}Q).$$

Next, v_i signs her ballot and creates a zero-knowledge proof proving a proper composition of it. This is done by means of the procedure described in Sect. 3.3. Finally, she sends $(C_{i,1}, C_{i,2}, \ldots, C_{i,k}, C_{i,k+1})$, her signature and the zero-knowledge proof to the PS.

When the PS receives a ballot, it, firstly, verifies the signature using the voter's public key, available on the BB. Then, it checks that the voter has not voted before and that no other ciphertext with the same ciphertexts has been cast before by some other voter. Finally, it verifies the zero-knowledge proof. If all the verifications are satisfied, it publishes the ballot, its zero-knowledge proof and its signature on the BB. Otherwise, the ballot is discarded.

Vote Tallying Phase. When the vote casting phase has ended, the PS aggregates the received ballots into a ciphertext array $(T_1, \ldots, T_k, T_{k+1})$ by computing,

$$T_j = \sum_{i=1}^{z} C_{i,j} = \left(\sum_{i=1}^{z} A_{i,j}, \sum_{i=1}^{z} B_{i,j} \right), \quad \forall j \in \{1, \ldots, k+1\},$$

where z is the amount of voters that have cast a vote. Then, the PS asks the KSTP to perform a verifiable decryption of each ciphertext T_j, obtaining

$$Dec_d(T_j) = \sum_{i=1}^{z} y_{i,j} V, \quad y_{i,j} \in \{1, 2\}.$$

The value $\sum_{i=1}^{z} y_{i,j}$ ranges between z and $2z$. Therefore, the PS computes $Dec_d(T_j) - zV = x_j V$ and searches for $x_j V$ in the precomputed table $\mathcal{T}$. If candidate L_j has received more than $\lfloor n/2 \rfloor$ votes, then $x_j V$ will not be found in the table. In that case, the PS computes $x'_j V = x_j V - \lfloor n/2 \rfloor V$ and checks $x'_j V$ against $\mathcal{T}$ again. Thus, the number of votes for candidate L_j is $x_j = x'_j + \lfloor n/2 \rfloor$. This operation generates the amount of votes for candidate L_j, *i.e.* x_j, as a result.

3.3 Zero-Knowledge Proof of Correct Ballot Composition

During the vote casting phase, the voter must provide a zero-knowledge proof proving her ballot has been properly composed. To that end, we have adapted a non-interactive proof presented in [8], to operate with EC-ElGamal ciphertexts.

This proof proves in zero-knowledge that a given ciphertext is an encryption of a point in a set $\{V_1, V_2, \ldots, V_\ell\}$. In our system, we prove that each component of a ballot is an encryption of V or $2V$. Moreover, by making use of the reveal operation, presented in Sect. 2.1, we guarantee that a voter cannot vote for more candidates than she is allowed. This is done by revealing the cleartext of the ciphetext obtained from the aggregation of all the ballot components.

Prover. The prover (voter v_i) has to prove in zero-knowledge that each ciphertext $C_{i,j} = (A_{i,j}, B_{i,j})$ in vector $(C_{i,1}, \ldots, C_{i,k}, C_{i,k+1})$ is an encryption of either

V or $2V$. Thus, for each j, if $C_{i,j}$ is an encryption of V, the prover randomly generates the values $w''_j, u''_j, s_j \in_R \{1, \ldots, m-1\}$ and computes

$$\begin{array}{ll} A'_j = s_j P, & B'_j = s_j Q, \\ A''_j = w''_j P + u''_j A_{i,j}, & B''_j = w''_j Q + u''_j (B_{i,j} - 2V). \end{array}$$

He also computes

$$\begin{array}{rll} chall_j &= \mathcal{H}(A'_j, A''_j, B'_j, B''_j) & \pmod{m}, \\ u'_j &= chall_j - u''_j & \pmod{m}, \\ w'_j &= s_j - u'_j r_{i,j} & \pmod{m}, \end{array}$$

where $\mathcal{H}$ is a cryptographic hash function like SHA-256 [7]. Recall that $r_{i,j}$ is the random integer taken to generate $C_{i,j}$. On the other hand, if $C_{i,j}$ is an encryption of $2V$, the prover will generate A''_j, B''_j as A'_j, B'_j and vice versa, taking into account that the computation of B'_j will involve V instead of $2V$. The generation of u'_j and w'_j will also be swapped with the generation of u''_j and w''_j, respectively.

After that, the prover computes $r_i = \sum_{j=1}^{k+1} r_{i,j} \pmod{m}$ and sends

$$A'_j, A''_j, B'_j, B''_j, u'_j, u''_j, w'_j, w''_j$$

for each j, $1 \leq j \leq k+1$, together with r_i to the verifier.

Verifier. For each j, $1 \leq j \leq k+1$, the verifier checks that

$$\begin{aligned} A'_j &= w'_j P + u'_j A_{i,j}, \\ A''_j &= w''_j P + u''_j A_{i,j}, \\ B'_j &= w'_j Q + u'_j (B_{i,j} - V), \\ B''_j &= w''_j Q + u''_j (B_{i,j} - 2V), \\ u'_j + u''_j &= \mathcal{H}(A'_j, A''_j, B'_j, B''_j). \end{aligned} \tag{1}$$

Then, in order to prove the voter has voted for only one candidate, the verifier aggregates $C_i = \sum_{j=1}^{k+1} C_{i,j}$ and uses r_i to reveal $C_i = (A_i, B_i)$. Then it checks that,

$$Rev_{r_i}(C_i) = B_i - r_i Q = (k+2)V.$$

All these verifications ensure that v_i has voted for just one candidate.

3.4 Multi-candidate Elections

Some elections allow voters to vote for more than one candidate or to choose up to a number of candidates. Our scheme can accommodate this kind of elections by slightly changing the ballot composition and the proof of correct composition.

Setup Phase. The system is configured and the information is published as described in Sect. 3.2. Moreover, the PS also publishes *max* and *min*, the maximum and minimum amount of candidates to be voted in each ballot.

Vote Casting Phase. A voter v_i generates a ballot in which f ciphertexts, $0 < min \leqslant f \leqslant max < k$, are an encryption of $2V$ (the chosen candidates), while the $k - f$ remaining ones are an encryption of V (non-chosen candidates). A blank vote is always permitted regardless of the value of min. Assuming that the chosen candidates are indexed between $k - f$ and k (with the blank subvote at position $k + 1$), v_i generates:

$$\begin{aligned} C_{i,j} &= (r_{i,j}P, V + r_{i,j}Q) && \text{for } j \notin \{k-f, \ldots, k\}, \\ C_{i,l} &= (r_{i,l}P, 2V + r_{i,l}Q) && \text{for } k - f < l \leqslant k, \\ C_{i,k+1} &= (r_{i,k+1}P, r_{i,k+1}Q) && \text{and} \\ C_{i,aux} &= (r_{aux}P, (max - f)V + r_{aux}Q). \end{aligned}$$

If the voter v_i wants to cast a blank ballot, she will need to generate k ciphertexts encrypting V, $C_{i,k+1}$ encrypting $maxV$, and $C_{i,aux}$ encrypting $\mathcal{O}$:

$$\begin{aligned} C_{i,j} &= (r_{i,j}P, V + r_{i,j}Q) && \text{for } 1 \leqslant j \leqslant k, \\ C_{i,k+1} &= (r_{i,k+1}P, maxV + r_{i,k+1}Q) && \text{and} \\ C_{i,aux} &= (r_{aux}P, r_{aux}Q). \end{aligned}$$

After that, the ballot is signed by v_i.

When computing the proof of correct ballot composition, v_i now generates a proof that the cleartext of ballot $C_{i,k+1}$ is either $\mathcal{O}$ or $maxV$. Moreover, the ciphertext $C_{i,aux}$ is proven to encrypt a point in the set $\{\mathcal{O}, V, \ldots, (max - min)V\}$ [8]. Finally, she sends the values,

$$(C_{i,1}, \ldots, C_{i,k+1}), C_{i,aux},$$

their signature and the proofs to the PS. The PS will proceed as in a one-candidate election, but the verification of the proof has to take into account that the aggregated components ciphertext is computed as, $C_i = (A_i, B_i) = \sum_{j=1}^{k+1} C_{i,j} + C_{i,aux}$ so that,

$$Rev_{r_i}(C_i) = B_i - r_iQ = (k + max)V,$$

with $r_i = \sum_{j=1}^{k+1} r_{i,j} + r_{i,aux} \pmod m$. The new ranges of $B_{i,k+1}$ and $B_{i,aux}$ have to be also taken into account. Notice that when $min = max$ there is no need to generate $C_{i,aux}$, since it will always correspond to an encryption of $\mathcal{O}$.

Tallying Phase. Although in a multi-candidate election more than one candidate may receive more than $\lfloor n/2 \rfloor$ votes, the tallying phase remains the same except for the blank votes. When the PS computes $T_{k+1} = \sum_{i=1}^{z} C_{i,k+1}$, it will obtain $x_{k+1}V = (max + 1)^{-1}Dec_d(T_{k+1})$. Thus, it will search for $x_{k+1}V$ in the table $\mathcal{T}$. Notice that the values $C_{i,aux}$ do not need to be aggregated nor decrypted.

4 Security

In this section, we prove that the presented e-voting system fulfills the security requirements enumerated in Sect. 1. Our proofs assume a one-candidate election. Their extension to multi-candidate elections is straightforward.

Authenticity. Only people in the electoral roll are able to cast a ballot since each ballot is digitally signed by the participant casting it. The electoral roll, which includes the public key of each voter, and the received ballots are publicly available on the BB. Thus, any one can check ballot signatures.

Unicity. Our system has to ensure that each voter has not voted more than once. As we have pointed out above, each ballot comes signed, so that two ballots cast by the same voter are easily linked through the public key that permits to verify their signature. The system must also ensure that the content of a ballot represents a vote for just one candidate. This is proven by the following two lemmata.

Lemma 1. *Assuming $\mathcal{H}$ a secure cryptographic hash function, there is no ciphertext $C_{i,j}$ able to pass the zero-knowledge proof unless it is an encryption of either V or $2V$.*

Proof. Let us assume $C_{i,j} = (A_{i,j}, B_{i,j}) = (r_{i,j}P, X + r_{i,j}Q)$ with $X \notin \{V, 2V\}$. According to the verifications that will be performed by the verifier (Eq. 1) the attacker has to generate four points A'_j, A''_j, B'_j, B''_j and four integers u'_j, u''_j, w'_j, w''_j satisfying

$$\begin{aligned} A'_j &= w'_jP + u'_jA_{i,j}, \; B'_j = w'_jQ + u'_j(B_{i,j} - V), \\ A''_j &= w''_jP + u''_jA_{i,j}, B''_j = w''_jQ + u''_j(B_{i,j} - 2V). \end{aligned}$$

One possibility is to generate first u'_j, u''_j, w'_j, w''_j at random and compute A'_j, A''_j, B'_j, B''_j according to the previous formulas. In that case, the verifier performs an additional checking requiring that $\mathcal{H}(A'_j, A''_j, B'_j, B''_j)$ outputs exactly $u'_j + u''_j$, which is unlikely because $\mathcal{H}$ is a secure hash function, so it is preimage resistant.

Another possibility is to generate $w'_j, u'_j, s_j, s'_j \in_R \{1, \ldots, m-1\}$ at random and compute

$$\begin{aligned} A'_j &= w'_jP + u'_jA_{i,j}, \; B'_j = w'_jQ + u'_j(B_{i,j} - V), \\ A''_j &= s_jP, \qquad\qquad\quad B''_j = s'_jQ. \end{aligned}$$

Next, compute $chall_j = \mathcal{H}(A'_j, A''_j, B'_j, B''_j) \pmod m$ and $u''_j = chall_j - u'_j \pmod m$, and find a value w''_j such that:

$$A''_j = w''_jP + u''_jA_{i,j}, \; B''_j = w''_jQ + u''_j(B_{i,j} - 2V).$$

Let $X = 2V + tQ$. From the equality involving A''_k we get

$$w''_j = s_j - u''_jr_{i,k} \pmod m.$$

By substituting w''_k in the equality involving B''_k we get

$$s'_j = s_j + u''_jt.$$

If $s_j = s'_j$, the previous equality is satisfied if $t = 0$, in which case, $C_{i,j}$ would be an encryption of $2V$ or $u''_j = 0$ in which case, the output of $\mathcal{H}(A'_j, A''_j, B'_j, B''_j)$

should be exactly u'_j which is very unlikely. If $s_j \neq s'_j$, then it is required that $u''_j = (s'_j - s_j)t^{-1} \pmod m$ in which case, the output of $\mathcal{H}(A'_j, A''_j, B'_j, B''_j)$ should be exactly $(s'_j - s_j)t^{-1} + u'_j$ which is very unlikely.

First generating $w''_j, u''_j, s_j, s'_j \in_R \{1, \dots, m-1\}$ and next computing

$$\begin{aligned} A'_j &= s_j P, & B'_j &= s'_j Q, \\ A''_j &= w''_j P + u''_j A_{i,j}, & B''_j &= w''_j Q + u''_j (B_{i,j} - 2V), \end{aligned}$$

leads to an equivalent situation. Hence, the claim follows.

Lemma 2. *Assuming Lemma 1 is true, a voter can only vote for one candidate.*

Proof. From Lemma 1, each $C_{i,j}$ is an encryption of either V or $2V$. Hence, $C_i = \sum_{j=1}^{k} C_{i,j}$ is an encryption of a point in the set $\{kV, (k+1)V, \dots, 2kV\}$. Revealing C_i outputs $(k+1)V$ if, and only if, all the ciphertexts $C_{i,j}$ encrypts V except one of them, whose plaintext is $2V$.

Both lemmata remain true when changing the points V and $2V$ for any other point pair. Furthermore, they are both true if the amount of possible points increases.

Privacy. This property requires that the candidate chosen by each voter must remain secret. In our system the vote is encrypted under the EC-ElGamal cryptosystem, which is assumed to be a semantically secure cipher. Therefore, no information can be obtained from an encrypted ballot. Assuming the KSTP only deciphers the aggregated ballot, an attacker could only obtain information from the proof of correct ballot composition. That proof, given in Sect. 3.3, is composed of two parts. The first one proves that the cleartext in each of the ciphertexts $C_{i,j}$ is either V or $2V$. The second one is a proof to validate that just one candidate is voted in the ballot.

First, we will prove that the proof corresponding to the first part is zero-knowledge. This is formalized by showing that there exists a simulator that can produce a transcript that looks like a proper interaction in its interactive version. That transcript is easy to generate if the challenge was known in advance.

Lemma 3. *The proof correct ballot composition is zero-knowledge.*

Proof. Given a value $chall'_j$ a simulator can generate a proof for any ciphertext $C_{i,j} = (A_{i,j}, B_{i,j})$ by generating $u'_j, w'_j, w''_j \in_R \{1, \dots, m-1\}$ at random and next computing $u''_j = chall'_j - u'_j$. After that, it is easy to generate the points:

$$\begin{aligned} A'_j &= w'_j P + u'_j A_{i,j}, & B'_j &= w'_j Q + u'_j (B_{i,j} - V), \\ A''_j &= w''_j P + u''_j A_{i,j}, & B''_j &= w''_j Q + u''_j (B_{i,j} - 2V). \end{aligned}$$

These values would satisfy the conditions given in Eq. 1, regardless of the cleartext of $C_{i,j}$. Hence, the claim follows.

In the second part of the proof, the prover reveals an integer r_i, computed as $r_i = \sum_{j=1}^{k+1} r_{i,j} \pmod m$. The value r_i reveals information about some $r_{i,l}$ if, and only if, all the other values $r_{i,j}$ with $j \neq l$ are known. Hence, no information about any $r_{i,l}$ is leaked and no ciphertext $C_{i,l}$ can be revealed.

Fairness. Assuming the KSTP behaves correctly, our system provides fairness because no vote is decrypted until the vote casting phase has ended.

Verifiability. Our proposal offers universal verifiability because any entity can check that all the ballots are cast by people who appear in the electoral roll by verifying its digital signature. Additionally, the proof of correct vote composition can also be verified by any entity who can also aggregate the received ballots by itself and check that the PS performed this operation properly. Finally, the aggregated ciphertexts are decrypted verifiably by the KSTP.

Coercion-Resistance. Our proposal is compatible with several coercion-resistance solutions which are able to send a fake vote without the coercer noticing it. Solutions like [13] can be adapted and included in our protocol.

5 Performance Analysis and Conclusion

Remote voting systems should provide both security and efficiency at the same time. The cost of some parts of the system are more critical than the cost of others. For example, in our proposal, during the vote casting phase, the voters are required to prove in zero-knowledge a proper composition of their ballots. These proofs are validated by the PS. It is desirable that the generation and verification of these proofs are as fast as possible but, since the vote casting phase usually takes a long time, and the proofs can be validated while the ballots are being received, these validations are not a problem as long as the PS can handle them.

In contrast, the best efficiency is required for the tallying phase. This is because a long tallying phase would cause a delay in the publication of the election result.

In our performance analysis, we have first compared the encryption and decryption costs of ElGamal and EC-ElGamal cryptosystems. Table 1 shows the results for different security levels. It can be seen that EC-ElGamal is more efficient than ElGamal. The difference in cost between the two cryptosystems increases with the security level. From the obtained results, we can state that by using EC-ElGamal we can achieve a 50 % efficiency gain, at least.

Next, we have compared the current proposal with an implementation of a similar remote voting scheme presented in [3]. The system in [3], which will be called *redundant scheme* from now on, is also implemented over elliptic curves. It includes a redundancy system in order to decrease the time required for obtaining the election result from the aggregated ciphertext. In the simulation of that scheme, we have used homomorphic packages of 500, 1000 and 100000 aggregated ballots, depending on the number of voters (5000, 10000 and 1000000, respectively). Our current proposal is able to homomorphically aggregate all the ballots into a single ciphertext with just a slight increase in the preprocessing time. Hence, the presented simulations create packages with 5000, 10000 and 1000000 aggregated ballots.

Table 1. Comparison between encryption and decryption times (ms) of ElGamal and EC-ElGamal.

Bits	ElGamal		EC-ElGamal	
	Encryption	Decryption	Encryption	Decryption
1024 — 160	1.5889	0.8787	0.8968	0.4837
2048 — 224	11.8224	6.2014	1.3105	0.6617
3072 — 256	61.2937	32.5329	1.6502	0.8429

Although the redundant scheme is more efficient at ballot creation, Table 2 shows it is twice as fast as the current one, in most phases it requires more time than the new proposal. In the redundant scheme, a ballot is composed of $2 \cdot \lceil k/4 \rceil$ ciphertexts while the current proposal contains k, being k the number of candidates. However, this fact is not enough to consider the redundant scheme is better. Table 2 shows that the zero-knowledge proof validation is twice slower in the redundant scheme than in the current proposal. Proof generation requires the computation of $47 \cdot \lceil k/4 \rceil + 18 \simeq 12 \cdot k$ multiplications in the redundant scheme while the current proposal only needs $6 \cdot k$. On the other hand, the verification requires $56 \cdot \lceil k/4 \rceil + 20 \simeq 14 \cdot k$ multiplications in the redundant scheme, while the current scheme only needs $8 \cdot k$. The time required for ballot validation is more critical. This is because each voter has to create just one ballot while the PS has to validate all of them.

Finally, we have also compared the time required for decryption and tally. Table 3 shows the current proposal is faster in both cases. In the new proposal, decryption only requires the computation of k multiplications. In contrast, in the redundant scheme, it involves $\frac{z}{t}\lceil k/4 \rceil$ multiplications, where z is the number of ballots and t is the capacity of the homomorphic packages (500, 1000 and 100000, as mentioned above). On the other hand, obtaining the result from the aggregated cleartext, in the new method, involves a point multiplication, a point subtraction and a query to the hash table $\mathcal{T}$. In contrast, the redundant scheme involves n subtractions and $(n + 1)$ hash queries (see [3] for a detailed description).

As a conclusion, we state that the remote voting protocol presented in this paper is efficient and, therefore, suitable for its use in real remote voting processes. All the simulations have been implemented in *C++*, using the *Crypto++* library and have been run on a PC with an *Intel Core i5 650 3.2GHz*

Table 2. Time (ms) spent to compose and prove a ballot (voter) and verify it (PS).

k	Current scheme			Redundant scheme		
	Compose	Prove	Verify	Compose	Prove	Verify
4	3.427865	10.572475	14.481125	1.70986	29.911125	33.099075
16	13.66835	42.384625	56.62975	6.78942	95.844325	106.35025
64	54.5824	169.35675	224.8665	26.9671	359.72	400.34225

Table 3. Time (ms) spent to decrypt and tally the aggregated ballots.

k	Voters	Current scheme		Redundant scheme	
		Decryption	Tally	Decryption	Tally
4	5000	1.7595	0.273	8.64875	60.494
	10000		0.273		120.721
	1000000		0.424		12084.549
16	5000	6.85625	1.079	34.6022	60.139
	10000		1.092		124.119
	1000000		1.61		12218,945
64	5000	27.434	4.273	137.5085	61.47
	10000		4.26		121.982
	1000000		6,284		12245,186

CPU and 4GB of RAM, running a *Debian 7.8 Wheezy* OS. Additionally, the times shown in Tables 2 and 3 have been obtained using 160 bit elliptic curves.

Acknowledgement. Research of the authors was supported in part by grants MTM2013-46949-P (Spanish Ministerio de Ciencia e Innovación), 2014SGR-1666 (Generalitat de Catalunya) and IPT-2012-0603-430000 (Spanish Ministerio de Economía y Competitividad).

References

1. Adida, B.: Helios: web-based open-audit voting. USENIX Secur. Symp. **17**, 335–348 (2008)
2. Adida, B., Pereira, O., Marneffe, O.D., Quisquater, J.J.: Electing a university president using open-audit voting: analysis of real-world use of helios. In: Electronic Voting Technology/Workshop on Trustworthy Elections (EVT/WOTE) (2009)
3. Cerveró, M.À., Mateu, V., Miret, J.M., Sebé, F., Valera, J.: An efficient homomorphic E-Voting system over elliptic curves. In: Kő, A., Francesconi, E. (eds.) EGOVIS 2014. LNCS, vol. 8650, pp. 41–53. Springer, Heidelberg (2014)
4. Chaum, D.: Security without identification: transaction systems to make big brother obsolete. Commun. ACM **28**(10), 1030–1044 (1985)
5. Chaum, D., Pedersen, T.P.: Wallet databases with observers. In: Brickell, E.F. (ed.) CRYPTO 1992. LNCS, vol. 740, pp. 89–105. Springer, Heidelberg (1993)
6. Cohen, J.D., Fischer, M.J.: A robust and verifiable cryptographically secure election scheme. In: 26th Annual Symposium on Foundations of Computer Science (FOCS), pp. 372–382 (1985)
7. US Department of Commerce, N.I.o.S., Technology: Secure hash standard. Federal Information Processing Standard# 180–2 56, 57–71 (1994)
8. Cramer, R., Damgård, I.B., Schoenmakers, B.: Proof of partial knowledge and simplified design of witness hiding protocols. In: Desmedt, Y.G. (ed.) CRYPTO 1994. LNCS, vol. 839, pp. 174–187. Springer, Heidelberg (1994)

9. El Gamal, T.: A public key cryptosystem and a signature scheme based on discrete logarithms. In: Proceedings of CRYPTO 84 on Advances in Cryptology. pp. 10–18. Springer-Verlag, New York (1985)
10. Fujioka, A., Okamoto, T., Ohta, K.: A practical secret voting scheme for large scale elections. In: Zheng, Y., Seberry, J. (eds.) AUSCRYPT 1992. LNCS, vol. 718, pp. 244–251. Springer, Heidelberg (1993)
11. Groth, J.: Non-interactive zero-knowledge arguments for voting. In: Ioannidis, J., Keromytis, A.D., Yung, M. (eds.) ACNS 2005. LNCS, vol. 3531, pp. 467–482. Springer, Heidelberg (2005)
12. Hirt, M., Sako, K.: Efficient receipt-free voting based on homomorphic encryption. In: Preneel, B. (ed.) EUROCRYPT 2000. LNCS, vol. 1807, pp. 539–556. Springer, Heidelberg (2000)
13. Juels, A., Catalano, D., Jakobsson, M.: Coercion-resistant electronic elections. In: Proceedings of the 2005 ACM workshop on Privacy in the electronic society. pp. 61–70. ACM (2005)
14. Katz, J., Myers, S., Ostrovsky, R.: Cryptographic counters and applications to electronic voting. In: Pfitzmann, B. (ed.) EUROCRYPT 2001. LNCS, vol. 2045, pp. 78–92. Springer, Heidelberg (2001)
15. Kiayias, A., Yung, M.: Self-tallying elections and perfect ballot secrecy. In: Naccache, D., Paillier, P. (eds.) PKC 2002. LNCS, vol. 2274, pp. 141–158. Springer, Heidelberg (2002)
16. Mateu, V., Miret, J.M., Sebé, F.: Verifiable encrypted redundancy for mix-type remote electronic voting. In: Andersen, K.N., Francesconi, E., Grönlund, Å., van Engers, T.M. (eds.) EGOVIS 2011. LNCS, vol. 6866, pp. 370–385. Springer, Heidelberg (2011)
17. Ohkubo, M., Miura, F., Abe, M., Fujioka, A., Okamoto, T.: An improvement on a practical secret voting scheme. In: Zheng, Y., Mambo, M. (eds.) ISW 1999. LNCS, vol. 1729, pp. 225–234. Springer, Heidelberg (1999)
18. Peng, K.: An efficient shuffling based evoting scheme. J. Sys. Softw. **84**(6), 906–922 (2011)
19. Peng, K., Aditya, R., Boyd, C., Dawson, E., Lee, B.: Multiplicative homomorphic e-voting. In: Canteaut, A., Viswanathan, K. (eds.) INDOCRYPT 2004. LNCS, vol. 3348, pp. 61–72. Springer, Heidelberg (2004)
20. Peng, K., Bao, F.: Efficient multiplicative homomorphic e-voting. In: Burmester, M., Tsudik, G., Magliveras, S., Ilić, I. (eds.) ISC 2010. LNCS, vol. 6531, pp. 381–393. Springer, Heidelberg (2011)
21. Sebé, F., Miret, J.M., Pujolàs, J., Puiggali, J.: Simple and efficient hash-based verifiable mixing for remote electronic voting. Comput. Commun. **33**(6), 667–675 (2010)
22. Silverman, J.H.: The Arithmetic of Elliptic Curves, vol. 2. Springer-verlag, Heidelberg (2009)
23. Yi, X., Okamoto, E.: Practical internet voting system. J. Netw. Comput. Appl. **36**(1), 378–387 (2013)

E-Government Cases II

Proposal for Effective Planning of Cooperation Activities in a Company

Viliam Lendel(✉), Josef Vodák, and Jakub Soviar

Department of Management Theories, Faculty of Management Science, University of Žilina, Univerzitná 8215/1, 010 26 Žilina, Slovak Republic
{viliam.lendel, josef.vodak, jakub.soviar}@fri.uniza.sk

Abstract. Aim of this article is to offer a proposal for effective planning of cooperation activities in a company, based on a comprehensive analysis of scientific literature and performed empirical research. This work enabled authors to describe the planning process of cooperation activities. The article thus offers a tool that can be used by company managers in their efforts to manage cooperation projects and activities. The article also deals with the specifics of planning in cooperation management as well as of planning a cooperation project in a company. Use of effective planning is meant to help minimize occurrence of conflicts and to support problem-free course of the cooperation activities, particularly from the project perspective.

Keywords: Cooperation · Cooperation management · Planning · Process

1 Introduction

In the present day are cooperations seen as an elementary prerequisite for development of a company and for ensuring stable place on the market. Establishing of a company cooperation with suitable partners is a distinct process which involves multiple activities and necessary decisions. It is therefore important to use the methods and techniques of project management for managing this process. Specifically, these would be creation and realization of a cooperation project, ensuring employee motivation towards cooperation tasks, leading the cooperation team and setting the cooperation goals. Otherwise it may happen that the cooperation initiatives in a company fail. The cooperation means the establishment of long-term relations of production between economically and legally independent enterprises [5].

The purpose of the article is to offer, in a comprehensible form, a coherent overview of managing cooperation activities in a company. This includes a methodology of planning company cooperation activities, which is based on a detailed mapping of theoretical and practical knowledge in the area of cooperation management and a performed research of the level at which it is used in Slovak enterprises.

2 Objectives and Methodology

The main objective of the article is to obtain new knowledge in the area of cooperation management, with particular focus on its definition within management. Another goal of the article is to highlight the possibility to use the managerial function of planning

© Springer International Publishing Switzerland 2015
A. Kő and E. Francesconi (Eds.): EGOVIS 2015, LNCS 9265, pp. 351–363, 2015.
DOI: 10.1007/978-3-319-22389-6_25

for the purpose of managing company cooperation activities. Identification of the specifics and suitable methods for planning may significantly help minimize occurrence of conflict situations related to cooperation activities.

In order to address the points in question, as set by this article, it was necessary to use several methods, depending on and fitting to the character of the individual parts of the solution. In order to accumulate necessary data, we used the method of document analysis (for analysis of current as well as historical data about the topic), the questionnaire method and the method of semi-structured interview (gathering data in an empirical research) and the method of observation (used during visits of selected companies).

For processing the data, we mainly used the method of quantitative evaluation (statistical methods and tools were applied) and the method of comparison (for comparing the data gathered by empirical research and the data from the analysis of secondary information sources).

The performed research focused on medium and large enterprises active in the Slovak Republic. The actual respondents were company managers on the mid to top management level within the managerial hierarchy of companies. In total, 273 respondents took part in the research focused on diagnostics of the level of use of cooperation management.

Research included companies active in multiple sectors of the Slovak economy. Companies included were categorized by the Statistical Office of the Slovak Republic as medium or large enterprises. The actual respondents were company managers on the mid to top management level within the managerial hierarchy of companies. Size of the sample was 345 respondents, with the required 95 % interval of reliability and the maximum allowable error of 5 %. Since 273 respondents actually took part in the research, the maximum allowable error reached 5.72 %. Data was gathered exclusively via personal interview.

The following methods were used for approaching and solving the research goals: induction, deduction, synthesis (for identification of suitable organizational structures and the proposed matrix of cooperation organizational structures), abstraction and model building.

3 The Current State of Dealing with the Issue

We identified an ongoing scientific discussion regarding the term cooperation management, its definition and the scope of use. Several definitions of cooperation management can be found in the scientific literature, however, these typically address only a subset of the whole task of cooperation management. High variability in interpretation of the term can be supported by the following examples. Lafleur (2005) understands cooperation management as a way of managing and developing collaboration in a competitive environment [12]. According to Ray (2002), cooperation management represents a term for integrated management of company networks [21]. Staatz (1983) sees cooperation management as cooperative decision making within heterogeneous preferences [26]. He highlights the need for a model of cooperation based on a defined group choice.

Similar view is held by Watzlawick, whose idea of cooperation management is that of a complex decision making process, ongoing on three levels of the managerial pyramid, whose goal is to reach suitable balance between company success within cooperation as a business unit and as a social institution. Mendoza sees cooperation management as an effective use of resources within cooperation as a business organization, focused on satisfying needs of its members, according to the accepted cooperation principles [32]. Zhang (2011) believes that cooperation management represents a basis for solving all managerial problems [36]. According to him, cooperation management provides conditions for creating a system of cooperation based on effective use of resources and technologies. Veerakumaran (2006) summarized the most important characteristics of cooperation management into the following points: [32]

- Cooperation management is a complex decision making process and the decisions are made on all managerial levels.
- Primary goal of cooperation management is to satisfy the needs of the members of cooperation.
- All activities need to occur according to the agreed principles of management and cooperation.
- Suitable balance needs to be established between the efforts for commercial success and maintaining goals of the cooperating parties.
- Management focused on reaching a goal via effective use of resources.

Based on the abovementioned comprehensive analysis we can provide a more precise definition of this term: Cooperation management is effective and efficient management of relationships in a cooperation between separate and relatively independent organizations or individuals, with the goal of improving their competitiveness [25, 33].

Building of relationships based on cooperation and having the following attributes (see [6, 7, 14, 15, 20]): cooperation and partnership; seriousness; non-disturbance of mutual competitive relationships; focusing particularly on long-term time horizons – long-term cooperation.

Based on the performed analysis and evaluation of various approaches to managing company cooperation activities, as presented by multiple authors, we are able to proceed to systematization of these findings. Here we provide a summary of the main contributions of each approach to managing cooperation activities. These represent a basis of the proposal for effective planning of cooperation activities in a company (see Table 1).

Based on the performed analysis of the current state of dealing with this issue and related aspects, it can be concluded that effective planning of cooperation activities in a company should take into account the following attributes:

- *Innovations:* a suitable environment should be established in a company that would support entrepreneurship and innovations, characterized by determination and close collaboration between the cooperating parties.
- *Trust:* this aspect is an important part of strategic decision making. Managers who use optimal trust in the relations with the involved parties improve performance of the company. For this reason it is necessary to correctly understand the character of

Table 1. Summary of the contributions of individual approaches to managing company cooperation activities.

Author(s)	Emphasis	Contribution
Sahut and Peris-Ortiz [23] Díaz Piraquive, F.N. et al. [2]	Role of innovations in planning cooperation activities	Basis = favourable environment for entrepreneurship and innovations
Ritala and Sainio [22]	Determination and close collaboration between cooperating parties	Application of the business model
Mustak [17], Kultti [11]	Creation of cooperation networks	Application to the area of innovation of services
Felzensztein et al. [4]	Portfolio of the areas of collaboration and its gradual expansion	Application to marketing activities and innovations
Weck and Ivanova [34]	Trust between cooperating parties	Gradual adaptation of business cultures of partner organizations
Wicks et al. [35]	Company performance	Cooperation process based on trust
Fawcett et al. [3]	Correct understanding of trust	Dynamics of trust building in cooperation
Monczka et al. [16]	Information background of cooperation processes	Quality of information and their sharing
Biggiero [1]	Relation of knowledge	Use in managing critical activities
Szekely [28]	Specifics of the region	Taking into consideration specifics of the region when establishing cooperations
Kowalski and Marcinkowski [10]	Motivation for starting a cooperation	Main motivation = existing market potential within the regional economy
Nemcová [18]	Uniqueness of cooperation	Influence of the uniqueness in managing a cooperation
Perry [19]	Process of control	Establishing suitable metrics
Jassawalla and Sashittal [9]	Organizational factors	Organizational structure that supports cooperation
Staber [27]	Imitation within cooperation	Behavior of partners
Schmoltzi a Wallenburg [24]	Organizational and strategic complexity in building cooperation management	Efficient planning of cooperation activities
Valenzuela and Villacorta [29]	Expected effects of cooperation	Effective cooperation management
Lehtonen, T.; Salonen A. [13]	Partnering relationships	The task of top management is to provide the shared values and visions.

trust and the dynamics of building trust within cooperation, and to pursue gradual adaption of the business cultures of the cooperation partners.

- *Information background:* it is necessary to ensure the quality of information in the company, as well as its sharing for the needs of managerial decision making. Effective work with information within a collaboration can help prevent conflicts and aid with solving complex cooperation tasks.
- *Organizational factors:* this aspect involves change of organizational structures to support cooperation, interest and support from top management of the partners, openness to changes while maintaining mutual goals of the partner companies.

4 Situation in Slovak Enterprises – Results of the Empirical Research

Between September 2012 and February 2013 we conducted a research, with the primary goal to gather and interpret information about the level of use of cooperations in the environment of Slovak enterprises. The main goal of the research was to identify the key aspects of efficient management and functioning of cooperations, related issues, degree of satisfaction of companies within cooperation and the opportunities for improvement of already functioning cooperations. Data that was gathered provided complete picture about readiness of Slovak enterprises to use (implement) cooperation management. In total, 273 managers of medium and large enterprises took part in the research, from companies active in Slovak republic. Data from the respondents was gathered via personal interviews.

The areas with the most developed cooperations are supplier relationships (68.13 %), purchasing relationships (52.38 %), technical cooperation (44.32 %), education (35.16 %), advertising and promotion (24.18 %). Respondents indicated that the major benefits of the cooperation are good mutual relations (26.62 %), increased profit (20.78 %), lower costs (20.13 %) and improved competitiveness (15.58 %). In contrast, the areas specified as those where improvement is necessary were better communication (31.78 %), adherence to contractual terms (23.08 %) and improved effectivity of collaboration (22.14 %).

The main challenges and problems that were listed by respondents to occur in the process of cooperating with companies and organizations were mainly insufficient adherence to the agreed contractual terms (58.39 %), financially demanding (35.04 %), distortion of information (34.41 %), low effectiveness of cooperation (29.56 %), unwillingness to provide internal information by a cooperating company, i.e. concerns about providing internal information to a company (28.83 %).

It could be considered positive that almost half of the respondents (47.62 %) plans in the near future (within one year) to establish a more intense cooperation with a company or an organization. When choosing partners for cooperation, companies make decisions using the following factors: costs (8.12 points), insolvency (8.03 points), market position (7.25 points), profitability (7.18 points), certificates (7.05 points). In contrast, the lowest perceived importance have company legal form (4.16 points) and company location.

Based on the Chi-squared test we identified a dependence between the level of satisfaction of a company with a cooperation, and its size (number of employees). We also identified a dependence between the level of satisfaction with a cooperation and the time that a company has been active on the market.

Using cluster analysis (statistical software SPSS) we identified two clusters (see Fig. 1). The first cluster (A) includes respondents who, when considering partners for cooperation, consider as very important the factors of market position and insolvency. These factors influence to a high degree their final decision. This cluster/segment can be considered significant, and it includes 189 companies, i.e. 69.23 %. The second cluster (B) includes respondents who, when considering partners for cooperation, also consider as important the factors of market position and insolvency. However, while these factors contribute to the final decision, it is not to as significant degree as in the case of the cluster A. This cluster/segment is fairly large, and it includes 84 companies, i.e. 30.77 %.

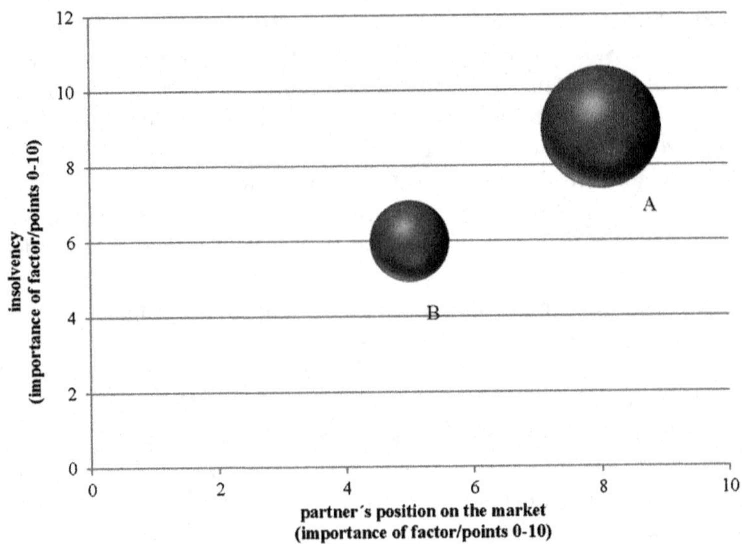

Fig. 1. Graphical representation of the clusters.

5 Proposal for Effective Planning of Cooperation Activities in a Company

Planning in the management of cooperation activities represents a significant group of activities, using which are set cooperation goals and by which are determined resources and ways for achieving them. Complexity and demanding character of this process increases with size of the company, with the increasing hierarchical level on which it is performed, with the length of the time horizon and the number of involved parties (partners). Planning of cooperation activities in a company requires:

- to anticipate future development of external and internal environment and the changes that occur in them (development of customers, change in segments, new communication tools, development of customers' demands, development of factors that influence customers' purchasing decisions…),
- to take into consideration interests of the various involved parties who take part on the cooperation activities (employees, top management, suppliers, banks, partners, surroundings); interests of individuals, groups and society,
- to consider economic as well social conditions and their criteria,
- to arrange in hierarchy goals and tasks of cooperation activities, which create conditions for internal harmony of relationships and processes and occurrence of synergistic effects; also to identify relationships and processes related to future cooperation and to arrange them in hierarchy,
- to consider limitations of resources, their suitable allocation and efficient use for supporting cooperation activities,
- to choose suitable methods and techniques that enable creation of cooperation ideas and their evaluation and selection, establishment of cooperation and support for its development.

Planning of cooperation activities in a company (see Fig. 2) can be also defined as a process of setting cooperation goals for the company, their further elaboration, specifying resources and ways for reaching them.

5.1 Setting Cooperation Goals

This step represents a key element of planning cooperation activities in a company. Role and significance of this process is major, because by it we also establish basis for effective cooperation management and for achieving successful results in the form of fulfilled cooperation activities. It also gives direction to all efforts placed into managing cooperation activities in a company. Cooperation goals define the course of a cooperation process and are one of the prerequisites for its development.

Cooperation goals in general represent future situations that are to be achieved by a certain time-specific moment. All of the future company cooperation activities should be directed towards achieving these goals. Achieving cooperation goals is realized through achieving individual tasks, into which are the goals structured.

Company that decides to manage its cooperation activities needs to understand that its goals indicate where is the company heading in the process of creating the cooperation, and what it seeks to achieve or how it wishes to develop the cooperation. Cooperation goals are also the basis for the whole planning process and are the source of motivation for the employees engaged in the cooperation activities. Finally, cooperation goals represent the basis for control and evaluation of the realized cooperation activities.

5.2 Resources for Achieving Goals

The other key step in planning cooperation activities is the organization of resources. Resources are the limiting factor for taking advantage of opportunities in the external environment that are identified while seeking ways for achieving the set goals. The defined cooperation goals can be achieve using the following resources:

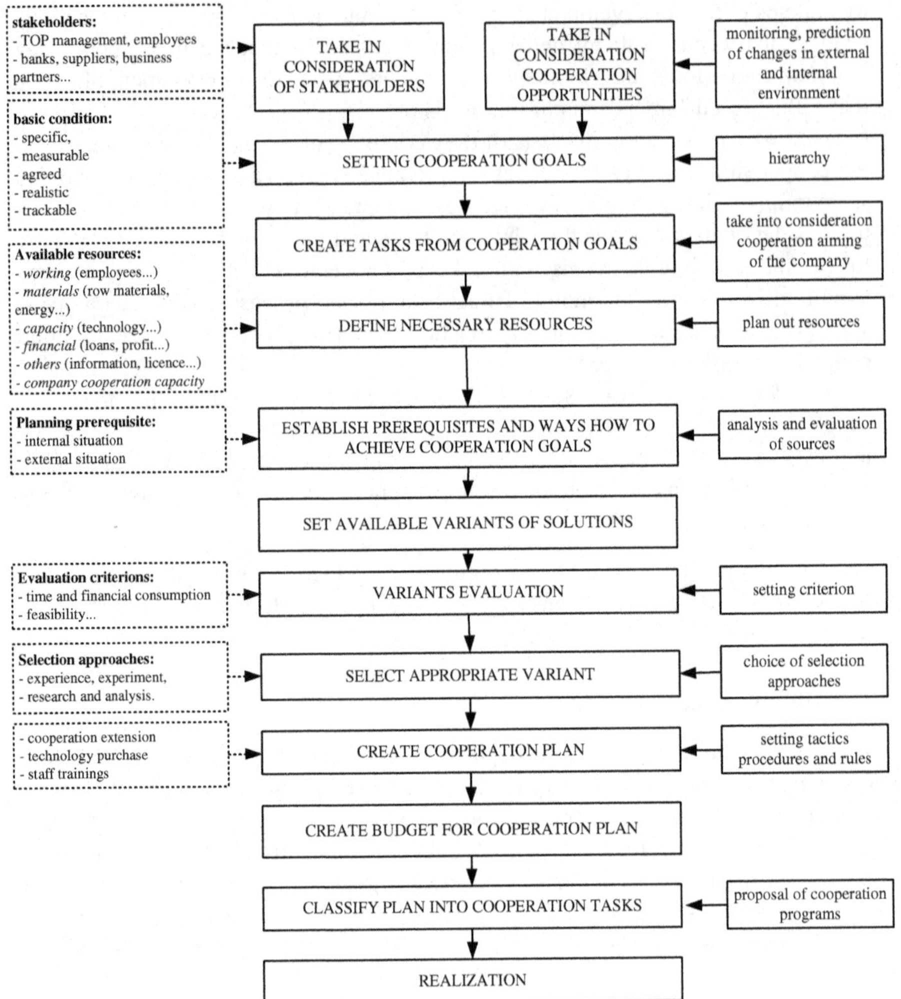

Fig. 2. Planning of cooperation activities in a company.

- labor (employees, managers, owners…),
- material (material, energy…),
- capacity (technology, machinery, IT equipment…),
- financial (loans, profit, share capital…),
- other (information, time, licenses…).

In addition to the listed resources we could also add cooperation capacity of the company. It is based on and interconnected with the total of knowledge, resources, experience, managerial capabilities and skills that the company has at its disposal for the purpose of managing cooperation activities.

5.3 Ways for Achieving the Set Goals

It is also highly important to specify the ways by which should be the previously set goals achieved. Typically there are several options – possible solutions. Here we talk about so called variants that may be formed by a combination of various resources in such a way that all of the goals are optimally achieved in their logical interconnectedness.

6 Discussion

Current state of dealing with the topic of cooperation management (in more detail in Chapter 3) indicates a key role of the attributes such as: cooperation and partnership; seriousness; non-disturbance of mutual competitive relationships; focusing particularly on long-term time horizons – long-term cooperation. We focused on these attributes also in our research, which confirmed their significance. These attributes are particularly important for effective and successful development of cooperation management. An interesting finding of our research was the dependence between the level of satisfaction of a company with a cooperation and its size (in more detail in Chapter 4). This finding suggests that companies with certain history, reputation and size are more attractive for cooperation. Related to this, particularly small and young companies appear to be less attractive as cooperation partners. Such companies (small, young) have the option to use cooperation management and to start cooperations among themselves – with similar entities. Consequently, they could use such alliances to better compete with more established competitors who had been active on the market longer or are larger. This situation can also be influenced by interventions of state, e.g. subsidies for start-ups can improve their position when joining cooperation relationships with established companies. Such situation could, under certain circumstances, represent an opportunity for large / established companies. Their cooperation strategy could also focus on identification of potential partners e.g. among start-ups. There exists the assumption that the start-ups will be more willing to efficiently cooperate with an established partner.

Existence and justifiability of cooperation management is strongly influenced by the dynamic development of the market environment. For this reason planning represents a crucial part of all important processes here. Planning is ongoing on all levels of the goals – long-term (strategic goals, ca. 3–5 years), mid-term (tactical goals, ca. 1–3 years) as well as short-term (operational goals, ca. less than 1 year) (see [8]). In case of the planning within already existing cooperation connection, this is in the theoretical sense the case of standard methods. Specific situations arise in two cases:

- *Planning as part of facilitation:* Start and establishment of cooperation is a separate and specialized managerial process labeled as facilitation. Here is planning focused on the activities needed for start and successful launch of cooperation (analyses, agreements, negotiations…). This specialized managerial activity then ends.
- *Planning in dynamic environment:* Decline or significant change of a cooperation bond is a frequent occurrence. Planning then becomes specific to the situation such

as successful termination of the cooperation (division of shares, settlements etc.) or a transformation in relation to the set goals.

Strategic planning relates to the start of cooperation and to setting parameters of its existence. The term "existence" here means that on the strategic level exact parameters of competitiveness of the cooperation bond are specified. If it happens that these cease to be achievable in a given situation, termination or modification of the cooperation follows. Tactical planning relates to specific cases of facilitating cooperation and its termination or transformation. Operational planning is used in the standard meaning as well as in the case of the mentioned specific cases.

Competitiveness and efficiency (power and reciprocity) are in general the long-term strategic goals of cooperation groups [30, 31]. In concrete cases – strategic goals adjusted to fit given situation. Other goals (tactic and operational) are managed by mutual agreement of the cooperating parties and are primarily dependent on the market situation.

When establishing a cooperation, it is not enough only to define the vision and goals as represented by a concrete future cooperation opportunity, but also to adopt the ability of its practical realization. In order for the company to be able to create and realize a successful cooperation, it needs to use project management. Above all, it is necessary to realize that the process of establishing a cooperation is an extensive cooperation project that involves multiple processes. Basic rule for managing a cooperation project is to set:

- Goal of the project
- Content of the project
- Time plan of the project
- Financial budget

Every cooperation project is unique because it is realized only once, is temporary and a group of people is working on it – cooperation team. In order to be able to afterwards evaluate success rate of the goals or changes, it is necessary to:

1. Clearly defined goals of the cooperation project
2. Comparison of potential benefits of possible variants for solving a cooperation project
3. Establishment of a model of metrics that will enable monitoring and control of the evaluation of project effects
4. Model of metrics interconnected with the whole system for evaluating company performance; evaluation of relationships between the results of measuring
5. Determine responsibility for results of the cooperation project
6. Set time horizon for monitoring and evaluation of reaching cooperation goals using suitable metrics
7. Establishment of a communication channel for sharing results of measuring among all responsible people that influence results of the measuring, including definition of corrective actions

Planning of cooperation projects is shown in Fig. 3.

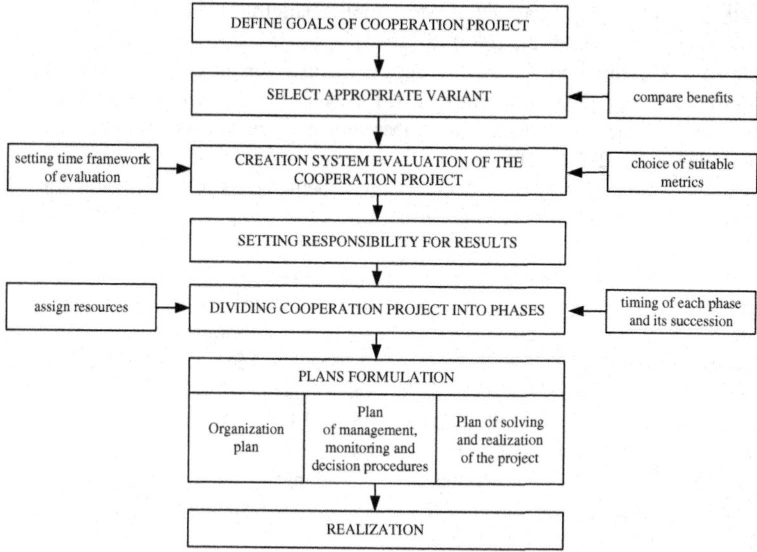

Fig. 3. Planning of cooperation project in a company.

7 Conclusion

Ideas about complexity of managing cooperation activities in a company are justified. The topic of managing cooperation activities is currently very relevant among Slovak enterprises. Managers in Slovak enterprises strive to build cooperation management in their companies, aiming to enable creation of successful cooperations and fulfillment of set cooperation tasks. In order for this initiative to be successful, it is needed to use elements of project management and to establish such environment that will support new cooperations, enable communication and effective work with information within created partner relationships. For this purpose, the presented methodology of planning cooperation activities of a company could be helpful to company managers.

Acknowledgments. This paper was partially supported by the Slovak scientific grant VEGA 1/0621/14 Marketing management in cooperative environment – Proposal of strategic cooperation management implementation model.

References

1. Biggiero, L.: Industrial and knowledge relocation strategies under the challenges of globalization and digitalization: the move of small and medium enterprises among territorial systems. Entrepreneurship Reg. Dev. **18**(6), 443–471 (2006)
2. Piraquive, F.N.D., García, V.H.M., Crespo, R.G., Liberona, D.: Knowledge management, innovation and efficiency of service enterprises through ICTs appropriation and usage. In: Uden, L., Oshee, D.F., Ting, I.-H., Liberona, D. (eds.) KMO 2014. LNBIP, vol. 185, pp. 300–310. Springer, Heidelberg (2014)

3. Fawcett, S.E., Jones, S.L., Fawcett, A.M.: Supply chain trust: The catalyst for collaborative innovation. Bus. Horiz. **55**(2), 163–178 (2012)
4. Felzensztein, C., Gimmon, E., Aqueveque, C.: Cluster or un-clustered industries? Where inter-firm marketing cooperation matters. J. Bus. Ind. Mark. **27**(5), 392–402 (2012)
5. Ginevičius, R.: The effectiveness of cooperation of industrial enterprises. J. Bus. Econ. Manag. **11**(2), 283–296 (2010)
6. Gumilar, V., Zarnić, R., Selih, J.: Increasing competitiveness of the construction sector by adopting innovative clustering. Inzinerine Ekonomika-Engineering Econ. **22**(1), 41–49 (2011)
7. Gurrieri, A.R.: Networking entrepreneurs. J. Socio-Econ. **47**, 193–204 (2013)
8. Hittmár, Š.: Management. EDIS - vydavateľstvo ŽU, Žilina (2006). (in Slovak)
9. Jassawalla, A.R., Sashittal, H.C.: An examination of collaboration in high-technology new product development processes. J. Prod. Innov. Manage **15**(3), 237–254 (1998)
10. Kowalski, A,M., Marcinkowski, A.: Clusters versus cluster initiatives, with focus on the ICT sector in poland. Eur. Plan. Stud. **22(1)**, 20–45 (2014)
11. Kultti, K.: Sellers like Clusters. J. Theor. Econ. 11(1), 1–26 (2011)
12. Lafleur, M.: A Model for Cooperative Challenges. Cooperative Grocer Network, No. 116 (2009). http://www.cooperativegrocer.coop/articles/2009-01-21/model-cooperative-challenges. Cited 17 November 2014
13. Lehtonen, T., Salonen, A.: An Empirical Investigation of Procurement Trends and Partnership Management in FM Services – A Finish Survey. Int. J. Strateg. Property Manage. **10**, 65–78 (2006)
14. Lydeka, Z., Adomavičius, B.: Cooperation among the competitors in international cargo transportation sector: key factors to success. Inzinerine Ekonomika-Engineering Economics **51**(1), 80–90 (2007)
15. Malakauskaite, A., Navickas, V.: Relation between the level of clusterization and tourism sector competitiveness. Inzinerine Ekonomika-Eng. Econ. **21**(1), 60–67 (2010)
16. Monczka, R.M., Petersen, K.J., Handfield, R.B., Ragatz, G.L.: Success factors in strategic supplier alliances: The buying company perspective. Decis. Sci. **29**(3), 553–577 (1998)
17. Mustak, M.: Service innovation in networks: a systematic review and implications for business-to-business service innovation research. J. Bus. Ind. Mark. **29**(2), 151–163 (2014)
18. Nemcova, E.: The function of clusters in the development of region. Ekonomicky casopis **52**(6), 739–754 (2004)
19. Perry, M.: Business environments and cluster attractiveness to managers. Entrepreneurship Reg. Dev. **19**(1), 1–24 (2007)
20. Ramanauskienė, J., Ramanauskas, J.: Economic management aspects of cooperatives. Econ. Eng. Decis. **49**(4), 15–21 (2006)
21. Ray, P.K.: Cooperative Management of Enterprise Networks. Kluwer Academic Publishers, New York (2002)
22. Ritala, P., Sainio, L.M.: Coopetition for radical innovation: technology, market and business-model perspectives. Technol. Anal. Strateg. Manag. **26**(2), 155–169 (2014)
23. Sahut, J.-M., Peris-Ortiz, M.: Small Business, innovation, and entrepreneurship. Small Business Econ. **42**(4), 663–668 (2014)
24. Schmoltzi, C., Wallenburg, C.M.: Operational governance in horizontal cooperations of logistics service providers: performance effects and the moderating role of cooperation complexity. J. Supply Chain Manage. **48**(2), 53–74 (2012)
25. Soviar, J.: From Cooperation to Management – Cooperative management. Habilitation thesis. University of Zilina, Faculty of Management Science and Informatics (2012). (in Slovak)

26. Staatz, J.M.: The Cooperative as a Coalition: A Game-Theoretic Approach. Am. J. Agric. Econ. **65**(5), 1084–1089 (1983)
27. Staber, U.: Imitation without interaction: how firms identify with clusters. Org. Stud. **31**(2), 153–174 (2010)
28. Szekely, V.: Regional industrial clusters and problems (not only) with their identification. Ekonomicky casopis **56**(3), 223–238 (2008)
29. Valenzuela, J.L.D., Villacorta, F.S.: The relationship between the companies and their suppliers. J. Bus. Ethics **22**(3), 273–280 (1999)
30. Varmus, M.: Comparison of selected concepts strategies. In: Hittmar, S., et al. (eds.) Theory of Management 1, pp. 169–173. University of Zilina, Žilina (2009)
31. Veber, J. et al.: Management. Foundations, Prosperity, Globalization. Management Press, Praha. (2006). (in Slovak)
32. Veerakumaran, G.: COCM 511 - Management of Cooperatives and Legal Systems, Faculty of Dryland Agriculture and Natural Resources. Mekelle University, Mekelle (2006)
33. Vodak, J., Soviar, J., Lendel, V.: Identification of the main problems in using cooperative management in Slovak enterprises and the proposal of convenient recommendations. Communications – Scientific letters of the University of Žilina 15(4), 63–67 (2013)
34. Weck, M., Ivanova, M.: The importance of cultural adaptation for the trust development within business relationships. J. Bus. Ind. Mark. **28**(3), 210–220 (2013)
35. Wicks, A.C., Berman, S.L., Jones, T.M.: The structure of optimal trust: Moral and strategic implications. Acad. Manage. Rev. **24**(1), 99–116 (1999)
36. Zhang, W.: Cooperation system constructing and model of its operation mechanism. In: Proceedings of the International Conference on Business Management and Electronic Information (BMEI), vol. 3, pp. 784–787 (2011)

A Lazy Approach for Filtering Parliamentary Documents

Luis M. de Campos, Juan M. Fernández-Luna, and Juan F. Huete(✉)

Departamento de Ciencias de la Computación e Inteligencia Artificial, ETSI de Informática y de Telcomunicación, CITIC-UGR, Universidad de Granada, 18071 Granada, Spain
{lci,jmfluna,jhg}@decsai.ugr.es

Abstract. We propose a lazy approach to build a content-based recommender system for parliamentary documents. Given a new document to be recommended, the system will decide what Members of the Parliament could find interesting such a document, in order to deliver it to them. Our approach is lazy because we do not build an elaborated profile of each deputy, but collect all the text of his/her speeches within the parliament debates and generate a document collection where we can search through queries. In this way we transform a recommender system problem into an information retrieval problem. Our proposals are tested using the documents of the regional Parliament of Andalusia at Spain.

Keywords: Content-based recommender systems · Information filtering · Information retrieval · Parliamentary documents

1 Introduction

The increasing application of Information and Communications Technologies (ICT) to our daily life has changed our habits: we are connected everytime and everywhere and producing a vast amount of information which is uploaded to the Web and can be consumed by other people. But this revolution is not only focused on individuals, but also on public and private organizations as well as companies, which are involved in a global competition where ICT are crucial for their development.

Governments all around the world are trying to not miss the boat, adapting their administrative processes to the current technology context. This application of ICT to the government framework is called *e-government* [13], and it refers to the ways in which the public administrations of a territory are adopting ICT to serve better to the citizens.

One of the main concerns of the e-government is to facilitate the citizens the access to the information that these administrations generate, as a way of promoting the participation of people and keeping them informed (service *Government to Citizen* in the taxonomy given in [15]). But the problem is that the amount of available information is huge and increasing exponentially, so it is not easy to find what a citizen would need.

© Springer International Publishing Switzerland 2015
A. Kő and E. Francesconi (Eds.): EGOVIS 2015, LNCS 9265, pp. 364–378, 2015.
DOI: 10.1007/978-3-319-22389-6_26

More specifically, the problem presented in this paper is framed in the context of regional or national parliaments, where, again, the problem is how to move closer all the matters discussed in this assembly to the citizens. The generated volume of data should be more accessible than it is. The communication deficit is not only related to the people to whom they have a duty of explanation, the citizens, but also the Parliament staff and the Members of the Parliament (MP) themselves [4]. Then effective applications are required to save this gap. This paper presents an approach to tackle this problem, focusing on the concept of parliamentary initiatives[1]: Given a new initiative, and in order to filter it, the system must evaluate and decide, among the potential MPs (or staff, media or users in general) to whom we send it. But our approach can also be useful to tackle another task, i.e. to help the citizens to circulate their petitions. In this case, a person can submit a request to the system, using its title and a summary that describes the topic (the most important parts since they would capture the MPs attention), and the system can show him those MPs that can be helpful at solving it.

With these ideas in mind, our research may be contextualized within the field of content-based recommender/filtering systems [2,17], i.e. systems that recommend an item (an initiative) to a user based on a description of the item and a profile of the user's interests. There exist many content-based recommender systems for a variety of domains [7,12], as web pages, news, music, movies, books, emails, scientific literature and digital television, among others. However, we are not aware of any such a system in a parliamentary context.

In this paper, we are going to adopt a lazy approach, where we do not build an elaborated profile of each MP (each user) but collect (in several different ways) all the text of his/her speeches within the parliament debates. We consider this information as a kind of document collection and use an Information Retrieval System (IRS) operating on this collection to retrieve the MPs (the "documents") that are more similar to the document to be recommended (or the citizen's topic of interest), which acts as a query to the system. The underlying assumption is that the speeches of an MP can reveal the topics he/she is interested in, and a new document similar in textual content to these speeches probably will also be of interest. Hence we shall recommend the document to the top ranked MPs.

The proposed system is lazy in the sense that it does not build an explicit model of each MP using for example an automatic classifier (based on training data composed of the documents that the user has previously considered as relevant and irrelevant, see for example [3,9,16], where K-NN, decision trees and Naive Bayes, respectively, are used). Instead of learning a user model, our system compares the new document (or topic of interest) with the speeches of the MPs and recommends it to the MPs which seem to be more similar. It works in a way that loosely resembles to a k-NN algorithm [18], which does not train a model based on relevant and irrelevant documents but simply compares the new document with all the documents previously classified. It should be noticed

[1] An initiative is the literal transcription of the discussion in the parliament of a petition presented by the MPs or groups.

that in our case we do not have previous information about irrelevant documents but only about relevant ones (the speeches of each MP). Thus, from a machine learning perspective, it should be tackled using positive unlabeled learning[2] [11].

If we are going to transform our recommender system problem into an information retrieval problem, we must address two main questions: which are the documents that compose our document collection and which are the queries submitted to the IRS against this collection (and how to process them).

The rest of the paper is organized in the following way: in Sect. 2 we consider several proposals to build our document collection from the MP's speeches within the parliament debates. Section 3 studies different alternatives to transform the new document to be recommended (or the topic of interest for a citizen) into a query to the IRS. In Sect. 4 we describe the experiments designed to validate our proposals and the obtained results. Finally, Sect. 5 explains our conclusions and proposals for future work.

2 Document Collection

As we have already mentioned, the source of information about the interests of the MPs will be the textual transcriptions of their speeches within parliamentary debates. These debates are organized around the concept of *parliamentary initiative*, whereby an action taken by an MP or political party is discussed in a plenary or specific area committee session. The transcription of the discussion of an initiative is identified by means of a code, and contains a title (short description of the matters being discussed), a general information section (e.g. type of session, term of office, date and presidency), a summary that includes a detailed description of the agenda (proposer and the list of MPs participating), created once the session has finished. And finally the transcriptions of all the speeches are included and set out like a script for a play or a film (see Table 1).

In this paper we are going to consider and analyze three different configuration alternatives of the document collection. In any case, these documents will be indexed by a search engine and used to find the requested relevant information. In our particular case, the objective is to know either who are the MPs that should receive the new document to be recommended or (for the other possible use of our system) who MPs should be contacted in order to discuss or seek advice for some particular point. Therefore, in both cases the output of our system will be a ranked list of MPs.

2.1 Initiative-Based Collection

This is the simplest approach since initiatives correspond to the original format of the parliamentary documents, i.e. each document represents a whole initiative (Table 1 presents an XML example of an initiative). For that reason this approach

[2] A type of binary classification problem where we have a set of positive examples and another larger set of unlabeled examples, but there is no set of negative examples.

Table 1. Example of the documents' initiative view in the collection encoded in XML, in this case the document represents the initiative with ID *ini1234*.

```
<initiative>
<iniID> 1234 </iniID>
<summary> a short summary representing the initiative.</summary>
<intervention>
  <deputy> Mr. XXX </deputy>
  <speech> the first intervention of Mr. XXX in the initiative 1234 </speech>
</intervention>
<intervention>
  <deputy>Mr. YYY </deputy>
  <speech> reply to Mr. XXX proposals </speech>
</intervention>
<intervention>
  <deputy>Mrs. ZZZ </deputy>
  <speech> new request to the government </speech>
</intervention>
<intervention>
  <deputy>Mr. XXX </deputy>
  <speech> this is the answer to Mrs. ZZZ</speech>
</intervention>
<intervention>
  <deputy>Mr. WWW </deputy>
  <speech> ..... </speech>
</intervention>
</initiative>
```

will be considered the baseline. In this paper we shall denote this collection *c_INI*, acronym of collection of initiatives.

In this case, the retrieval system will match the query (i.e. the new initiative to be recommended or the citizens' request) to the set of initiatives previously discussed in the parliament, finding the most similar ones. Thus, when the system returns an initiative as relevant, then we shall assume that all the MPs participating in this initiative are the right MPs we are looking for, because they took part in an initiative similar to the new document or to the citizen's information need (for the initiative with code 1234 in Table 1, these MPs are Mr. XXX, Mr. YYY, Mrs. ZZZ and Mr. WWW).

2.2 Profile-Based Collection

Since MPs usually participate in several initiatives (depending on the specific MP, it can be only a few or many initiatives), we thought that an alternative representation could be to construct a document collection of MP profiles, where we store the interests of the MPs. In this paper, we shall explore a lazy way of representing the MPs profiles. Particularly, in this case we propose to collect, for each MP, the text of his/her speeches within all the initiatives in only one document, thus obtaining a document collection with as many documents as MPs.

Table 2. An XML profile view of the documents in the collection. In this case, one profile is build for each MP in the parliament.

```
<profile>
<deputy>Mr. XXX </deputy>
<initiative>
   <iniID> 1234 </iniID>
   <summary> a short summary.</summary>
   <intervention>
      <speech> the first intervention of Mr. XXX in the initiative 1234 </speech>
   </intervention>
   <intervention>
      <speech> this is the answer to Mrs. ZZZ</speech>
   </intervention>
</initiative>
<initiative>
   <iniID> 5678 </iniID>
   <summary> the summary.</summary>
   <intervention>
      <speech> the speech in this initiative </speech>
   </intervention>
   <intervention>
      <speech> another speech </speech>
   </intervention>
</initiative>
<initiative>
   ....
</initiative>
....
</profile>
```

In this case we have few documents but rather large, as Table 2 illustrates. We shall denote this collection as *c_PRF*, acronym of collection of profiles.

2.3 Discourse-Based Collection

After looking at the MP profiles, we found out that some MPs used to participate in a range of initiatives that are related to different areas of interest, for example, agriculture, fishery, economy, food, and so on. Putting all this information together in a common user profile could bias the profile towards the most frequent areas, diminishing the importance of the uncommon ones. So that, we propose a different way (but still lazy) to represent the MP's profiles. Particularly, we divide the document representing an initiative in different documents containing the text of the speeches of each MP who participated in the initiative (in other words, we collect, for each MP, the text of its speeches within each initiative in a different document). As a consequence we have a larger set of documents but with shorter length, as it is illustrated in Table 3, where we show the discourses of Mr. XXX, Mr. YYY and Mrs. ZZZ extracted from our

Table 3. A discourse view of the collection, in this case the discourses of each MP in an initiative are considered as isolated documents. In this example, the original initiative with ID 1234 can be split into four different documents, representing each one of the MP's interventions.

XXX_ini1234.xml

```
<discourse>
<iniID> 1234 </iniID>
<deputy> Mr. XXX </deputy>
<summary> initiative short summary.</summary>
<intervention>
  <speech> the first intervention of Mr XXX ... </speech>
</intervention>
<intervention>
  <speech> this is the answer to Mrs. ZZZ</speech>
</intervention>
</discourse>
```

YYY_ini1234.xml

```
<discourse>
<iniID> 1234 </iniID>
<deputy>Mr. YYY </deputy>
<summary> initiative short summary.</summary>
<intervention>
  <speech> reply to Mr. XXX </speech>
</intervention>
</discourse>
```

ZZZ_ini1234.xml

```
<discourse>
<iniID> 1234 </iniID>
<deputy>Mrs. ZZZ </deputy>
<summary> initiative short summary.</summary>
<intervention>
  <speech> new request to the government</speech>
</intervention>
</discourse>
```

WWW_ini1234.xml

```
<discourse>
<iniID> 1234 </iniID>
<deputy>Mrs. WWW </deputy>
<summary> initiative short summary.</summary>
<intervention>
  <speech> ... </speech>
</intervention>
</discourse>
```

toy initiative with ID 1234. The collection obtained following this approach will be denoted *c_DIS*, acronym of collection of discourses.

2.4 Transforming the IRS Output

In case of using the *c_PRF* collection, when we formulate a query (associated either to the document to be recommended or to a citizen information need) against this document collection, we obtain a ranking of documents, each one representing an MP, i.e. we directly obtain a ranking of MPs whose profiles are more similar to the query.

However, in the other two cases, *c_INI* and *c_DIS*, the IRS does not directly return a ranking of MPs but a ranking of complete initiatives (each one associated to several MPs) and discourses (each one associated to only one MP), respectively. Then, to obtain a ranking of MPs, we substitute a discourse in the ranking by its associated MP, and an initiative by the set of MPs who participated in it (preserving the scores). In both cases the problem is that, as the same MP can appear in different initiatives or discourses related to the query, the obtained ranking of MPs can contain duplicate MPs (each duplicate having a different score). Therefore, we must use some strategy for aggregating the scores associated to the same MP into a single score, in order to re-rank the list of (non duplicate) MPs according to this score. The best strategy found in our preliminary experiments was to use the maximum as the aggregation operator.

3 Query Approaches

As we have already said, our model can be used for two different, but related tasks. For the first one, which could be considered as a *filtering* task, we have to tackle the internal needs of the parliament, where it is necessary to filter (possibly by e-mail) new initiatives to those MPs who might be interested in the discussed topics. For this task, the query is an initiative, which implies that its internal structure is known (the query source is the XML file). The second one, which could be considered as a *recommendation* task, is related to an external use in the sense that there exists a citizen who wants to know which are the MPs being concerned about a given topic. In this case, the citizen expresses his/her information need by means of a query which includes those terms that might be related to the topic, and the system will recommend the most appropriate MPs. Thus, in this case, the structure of the query has no relationships with the way in which the topics are discussed in the parliament. Therefore, two different types of queries can be considered:

q_SGL: In this case, there is a single query being just a set of terms that should be given directly by the user (when recommending MPs) or extracted considering all the speeches in an initiative (in the case of filtering). Note that in this last case we shall obtain very large queries, possibly with hundreds of terms, although it does not represent a big handicap since filtering is a task that can be done offline.

q_CMP: One of the problems of the previous approach is that all the interventions are considered as a whole, being unable to differentiate the particularities of the MPs discourses. In order to solve this problem we propose the use of the structure of the initiative to obtain a compound query, and therefore this approach can only be applied for filtering purposes.

Particularly, we shall divide the initiative by grouping all the text associated to the speeches of each MP who participated in the discussion of the initiative (as illustrated by Table 3), thus obtaining as many subqueries as MPs participated. Ideally, in this case each subquery should represent the point of view of an MP in the initiative, since it is focused in her own intervention. Then, these queries can be executed independently, being necessary a method to fuse the different rankings obtained for each query into a final ranking. The rationale for this proposal is that each subquery may possibly more accurately identify the corresponding MP who participated in the initiative. So, we hope that the compound query is more effective than the single one, in those cases where both can be applied. The ranking fusion strategies considered will be discussed in the next Subsection.

3.1 Ranking Fusion

Ranking fusion has to be applied when considering compound queries, where a set of n different (sub)queries, $\{q_1, \ldots, q_n\}$, are used in order to find the relevant MPs. In this case, for each query q_i we have computed a sorted list of MPs, $L_{q_i} =< m_1, m_2, \ldots, m_i >$, being $s_i(m_j)$ the score of the jth-MP for the query q_i. Therefore, it becomes necessary to merge the different ranked lists into a single one which represents the relevance of each MP to the compound query.

In the literature several methods to tackle data fusion problems can be found [19]. They mainly try to estimate the relevance of all the retrieved documents for a given query via combining these retrieved documents from multiple information retrieval systems into a single list. Although our problem is different, i.e. different queries are launched into one retrieval system, the same techniques for ranking combination can be applied. As we have access to the scores given by the IRS to each result, and it has been reported [1,20] that in these cases is preferable to use a ranking fusion method that takes the scores into account, instead of methods based exclusively on the ordering, we shall use the score information.

Previously to any combination, since each query represents a speech of an MP in an initiative, it is usual that they differ in length. Therefore, in the case that the retrieval system does not give normalized scores as output, it might happen that those (sub)queries with greater length have larger scores. This situation has a negative impact in the retrieval performance because it could bias the output towards the MPs having large speeches, reducing the relevance of those MPs that with less words are able to express their opinion. Therefore, previous to any combination, a score normalization step is indispensable, in order to make the scores, which are obtained from different queries, comparable to each other. Particularly, in this paper we shall normalize them by considering the score of the top MP for a particular query, i.e.

$$s_i(m_j) \leftarrow s_i(m_j)/s_i(m_1)$$

Focusing on the combination strategies, in this paper we shall explore the following alternatives, proposed originally in [6], which have been reported as good methods for ranking fusion in several studies.

- *CombMAX*: choose the maximum of the relevance values, i.e. $s(m_j) = \max_{i=1,\dots,n} s_i(m_j)$
- *CombSUM*: the sum of the score values in the different rankings, i.e. $s(m_j) = \sum_{i=1}^{n} s_i(m_j)$.
- *CombMNZ*: this methods tries to promote those MPs appearing more frequently and is computed as $s(m_j) = k \sum_{i=1}^{n} s_i(m_j)$, being k the number of lists where the MP appears.

In the previous formulas, in the case an MP m_j does not appear in a list L_{q_i}, then a zero score is used, $s_i(m_j) = 0$.

4 Evaluation Framework and Results

In this section we describe the components of the evaluation framework, as well as the obtained results and conclusions. The evaluation framework is composed by the following components: a document collection formed by all the initiatives (5258) from the eighth term of office of the Parliament of Andalusia at Spain[3], marked up in XML [5]. These initiatives contain a set of 12633 interventions of the MPs (and a total of 28706 different speeches). In order to evaluate the

[3] http://www.parlamentodeandalucia.es.

performance of our proposals, we have used the repeated holdout method [10]: the set of initiatives is randomly partitioned into training (80 %) and test (20 %), and we repeat this process five times (the results presented in the study are the averages over the different rounds). With respect to the initiatives in the test set, we remove the information related to the MPs who participate in their discussion, being totally anonymous.

We have carried out experiments with both, filtering and recommending problems (see Sect. 3):

1. *Filtering* task is simple, since we can use either all the text in the initiative to build a simple query (*q_SGL*), or formulate a compound query (*q_CMP*), using the different discourses of the MPs. In the last case we shall experiment with three different ranking fusion methods (MAX, SUM and MNZ).
2. *Recommending MPs* implies that there exists a user who expresses his/her information need by means of a set of terms. In this experimentation we shall not use real users, but simulated ones instead. Particularly, we shall use as (*q_SGL*) queries the titles of the initiatives (typically one or two lines of text[4]) which are hand-made brief descriptions of their contents (we shall denote this type of queries as *hm*). We shall also experiment with automatic summaries of the initiatives which, in order to be able to capture the initiative topics, have been constructed by selecting the best 25 and 50 terms[5] (these queries will be denoted as *au*25 and *au*50, respectively). Note that these numbers are under the limits of words in the summary of a citizen's request, which for example is set to 75 words in some US states, as indicate the National Conference of State Legislature (www.ncsl.org).

Thus, independently on the query, the purpose of our model is to predict those MPs who would be relevant to its content and, as a consequence the output has to be a ranking of MPs. In this experimentation we have considered, as the ground truth that an initiative, i, will be relevant only to those MPs that participate in it, its number being denoted as ni. This is a rather conservative assumption, because it is quite reasonable to think that an initiative can also be relevant to other MPs.

In order to evaluate the accuracy of our approach, we shall measure the quality of the ranking at fixed low levels of retrieved results, particularly we present the recall values considering the top 10 MPs, rec@10. This metric measures how many among the relevant MPs appear in the top positions of the ranking, measuring the capability of the system at finding these MPs. We also show the Normalized Discounted Cumulative Gain [8] over the top 10 positions, NDCG@10, which measures the ranking quality. Moreover, considering that the number of relevant MPs varies with the initiative (on the average there are 2.4 interventions per initiative) we shall also measure the accuracy on the top ni positions using MAP@ni (Mean Average Precision) and the R-precision

[4] An example of the title of an initiative is *"Non-legislative proposal on social and employment situation of women in Andalusia"*.

[5] Using the *MoreLikeThis* facility in Lucene.

(that represents the precision over the ni top MPs). These results were obtained when considering three different information retrieval models, namely BM25, Language Model (LM) and vectorial (VECT), using the implementation in the search engine library Lucene[6]. All the results obtained from our experiments for the different metrics are displayed in Tables 4 and 5. More specifically, the former contains the values of the metrics for the filtering task, while in the latter, the results shown are related to the recommending task.

4.1 Analyzing Filtering Results

The baseline filtering approach to compare our proposals is to use the initiative-based collection, c_INI, and the single queries, q_SGL (i.e. the whole content of the test initiatives to be filtered). That is to say, we use the documents as they are already stored in the parliament, without any processing for both collection and queries. In Table 4 we present the obtained results, where we highlight in bold and underlined fonts the results obtained with the baseline and best approaches, respectively.

From these results we can obtain several interesting conclusions:

1. All the metrics point in the same direction, i.e. what is better from the perspective of one metric is also better from the perspective of any other metric. This means that the differences in performance between different configurations are consistent across the different metrics.
2. With respect to the collection, the best results are obtained for the profile-based collection, c_PRF, followed by the discourse-based one, c_DIS (the worst collection is c_INI), and this happens almost independently on the type of query being selected.
3. For the queries, the best alternative is to submit a compound query, q_CMP, using the different discourses, instead of using a single query, q_SGL, and this is also independent on the type of collection being used.
4. In the case of compound queries, how we aggregate the rankings matters, being in general CombMax the strategy with the best results (except when we consider the initiative-based collection, where it is better to aggregate the results using the other strategies). The results obtained using the CombMNZ and CombSUM strategies are very similar. We think this is because the different subqueries tend to get the same set of MPs[7] (although in different orderings). This may be because all the subqueries are about the same topic (the one discussed in the initiative). Although it has been established [14] that CombMNZ provides best results in the general case, here the situation is different, as CombMax is clearly the best ranking fusion method. This would deserve further analysis. Nevertheless, it should be noticed that our ranking fusion problem is different from the usual one: we have different queries submitted to a single retrieval system, whereas the usual problem is the converse, with a single query launched into several retrieval systems.

[6] https://lucene.apache.org.

[7] Note that we have set to 200 the number of documents returned by the search engine.

Table 4. Accuracy metrics for filtering with the selected retrieval models. The baseline approach is the one obtained processing neither collection nor queries, i.e. $c\_INI \times q\_SGL$ (in bold fonts for each retrieval model). The best results for each retrieval model have been highlighted using underlined values.

Coll.	Query	Comb	rec@10	NDCG	MAP	R-prec
Filtering Task: BM25						
c_INI	**q_SGL**	—	**0.7563**	**0.5790**	**0.3367**	**0.3996**
c_INI	*q_CMP*	MAX	0.7507	0.5674	0.3184	0.3774
c_INI	*q_CMP*	SUM	0.7575	0.5968	0.3610	0.4152
c_INI	*q_CMP*	MNZ	0.7574	0.5968	0.3610	0.4152
c_DIS	*q_SGL*	—	0.7537	0.6253	0.3929	0.4427
c_DIS	*q_CMP*	MAX	0.8237	0.7114	0.5147	0.5703
c_DIS	*q_CMP*	SUM	0.7832	0.6646	0.4430	0.4917
c_DIS	*q_CMP*	MNZ	0.7816	0.6637	0.4428	0.4915
c_PRF	*q_SGL*	—	0.7770	0.6778	0.4568	0.4959
c_PRF	*q_CMP*	MAX	<u>0.8648</u>	<u>0.7786</u>	<u>0.6190</u>	<u>0.6677</u>
c_PRF	*q_CMP*	SUM	0.7983	0.7017	0.4917	0.5339
c_PRF	*q_CMP*	MNZ	0.7983	0.7017	0.4917	0.5339
Filtering Task: LM						
c_INI	**q_SGL**	—	**0.7627**	**0.5750**	**0.3270**	**0.3915**
c_INI	*q_CMP*	MAX	0.7595	0.5689	0.3207	0.3801
c_INI	*q_CMP*	SUM	0.7519	0.5953	0.3581	0.4121
c_INI	*q_CMP*	MNZ	0.7519	0.5954	0.3581	0.4121
c_DIS	*q_SGL*	—	0.7386	0.6081	0.3726	0.4235
c_DIS	*q_CMP*	MAX	0.8057	0.6777	0.4637	0.5253
c_DIS	*q_CMP*	SUM	0.7752	0.6438	0.4112	0.4643
c_DIS	*q_CMP*	MNZ	0.7730	0.6427	0.4110	0.4640
c_PRF	*q_SGL*	-	0.7421	0.6176	0.3867	0.4329
c_PRF	*q_CMP*	MAX	<u>0.8421</u>	<u>0.7171</u>	<u>0.5110</u>	<u>0.5706</u>
c_PRF	*q_CMP*	SUM	0.7780	0.6384	0.4024	0.4544
c_PRF	*q_CMP*	MNZ	0.7773	0.6382	0.4025	0.4544
Filtering Task: VECT						
c_INI	**q_SGL**	—	**0.6814**	**0.5277**	**0.3110**	**0.3685**
c_INI	*q_CMP*	MAX	0.6837	0.5237	0.2993	0.3543
c_INI	*q_CMP*	SUM	0.6980	0.5552	0.3384	0.3915
c_INI	*q_CMP*	MNZ	0.6979	0.5552	0.3384	0.3915
c_DIS	*q_SGL*	—	0.6906	0.5844	0.3716	0.4170
c_DIS	*q_CMP*	MAX	0.7814	0.6735	0.4744	0.5315
c_DIS	*q_CMP*	SUM	0.7241	0.6183	0.4085	0.4562
c_DIS	*q_CMP*	MNZ	0.7186	0.6157	0.4081	0.4554
c_PRF	*q_SGL*	—	0.7971	0.6876	0.4584	0.5030
c_PRF	*q_CMP*	MAX	<u>0.8757</u>	<u>0.7737</u>	<u>0.5911</u>	<u>0.6462</u>
c_PRF	*q_CMP*	SUM	0.8222	0.7089	0.4853	0.5319
c_PRF	*q_CMP*	MNZ	0.8222	0.7089	0.4853	0.5319

5. It is also interesting to note that all these results are also independent on the information retrieval model being used, which implies that our lazy approach could be used independently on the particular search engine implemented in a given parliament[8].

Focusing on the best results, i.e. the combination of c_PRF &q_CMP &Comb-MAX, we obtain significant improvements with respect to the baseline for those metrics which consider the top 10 retrieval results: 14 %, 10 % and 29 % for the recall@10 and 34 %, 25 % and 47 % for the NDCG@10, considering the BM25, LM and VECT retrieval models, respectively. Similarly, if we consider those metrics that focus on the *ni* top positions, the improvements are even more significant. Particularly we obtain improvements of 67 %, 46 % and 75 % for the R-precision and 84 %, 56 % and 90 % for MAP@*ni*, considering the BM25, LM and VECT retrieval models, respectively. This implies that this approach not only finds out more relevant MPs, but also in better positions.

Finally, if we focus on the time needed to perform the queries, the time for compound queries is 68 % greater than for single queries. But this is due to the fact that we have executed each single subquery sequentially. Taking into account that the different subqueries should be executed in parallel, we could also expect to obtain significant improvements (around 30 %) with respect to the baseline, because of the smaller size of the single subqueries.

4.2 Analyzing Recommending Results

In this case (see Table 5, where the best results have been underlined), the results are worse than those obtained for the filtering task, although they are not directly comparable. Its counterpart in the filtering task might be the case where we perform a single query, *q_SGL*, which includes all the content in an initiative. Nevertheless, we shall distinguish between hand-made and automatic summaries, being considerably worse the hand-made queries. One reason for this behavior is that hand-made summaries have a relative large proportion of terms which are common to many other initiatives in the collection (they are used to place the initiative within the parliamentary workflow), whereas automatic terms have been selected according to their retrieval capabilities. Another reason is that the number of terms in the hand-made summaries tends to be considerably smaller than those in the automatic summaries. In fact, we can observe a clear tendency towards obtaining better results as the number of terms used in the queries increases (from the hand-made short summary, to 25 terms, to 50 terms, to all the terms in the initiative). This suggests that users should be rather wordy when expressing their main points in the petition's proposals.

In general, it seems that the best results are obtained using the initiative-based collection when the number of terms in the query decreases (hand-made and au25). This may be explained because it can be guaranteed that all the selected terms belong to the initiative, whereas this is not the case when querying

[8] Although it is not important for our purposes, the best performing model is BM25.

Table 5. Accuracy metrics for recommending with the selected Retrieval Models. The best results for each retrieval model have been highlighted using underlined values.

Query	Coll.	rec@10	NDCG	MAP	R-prec
Recommending Task: BM25					
hm	*c_INI*	0.5515	0.3871	0.1942	0.2377
hm	*c_DIS*	0.5434	0.3818	0.1831	0.2266
hm	*c_PRF*	0.4849	0.3522	0.1763	0.2119
au50	*c_INI*	0.7733	0.5955	0.3491	0.4126
au50	*c_DIS*	0.7521	0.6148	0.3734	0.4250
au50	*c_PRF*	0.7532	<u>0.6299</u>	<u>0.3978</u>	<u>0.4455</u>
au25	*c_INI*	<u>0.7755</u>	0.5988	0.3561	0.4218
au25	*c_DIS*	0.7350	0.5886	0.3471	0.3994
au25	*c_PRF*	0.7232	0.5882	0.3518	0.4000
Recommending Task: LM					
hm	*c_INI*	0.5331	0.3620	0.1689	0.2085
hm	*c_DIS*	0.5020	0.3560	0.1709	0.2117
hm	*c_PRF*	0.4766	0.3414	0.1674	0.2025
au50	*c_INI*	<u>0.7598</u>	0.5734	0.3247	0.3884
au50	*c_DIS*	0.7331	<u>0.5948</u>	<u>0.3575</u>	<u>0.4112</u>
au50	*c_PRF*	0.7129	0.5739	0.3416	0.3915
au25	*c_INI*	0.7575	0.5708	0.3229	0.3880
au25	*c_DIS*	0.7185	0.5762	0.3350	0.3876
au25	*c_PRF*	0.6892	0.5553	0.3290	0.3800
Recommending Task: VECT					
hm	*c_INI*	0.6390	0.4707	0.2590	0.3137
hm	*c_DIS*	0.5882	0.4273	0.2129	0.2610
hm	*c_PRF*	0.6046	0.4633	0.2474	0.2950
au50	*c_INI*	0.7373	0.5906	0.3491	0.4126
au50	*c_DIS*	0.7218	0.6154	0.3810	0.4304
au50	*c_PRF*	<u>0.7795</u>	<u>0.6383</u>	<u>0.3962</u>	<u>0.4462</u>
au25	*c_INI*	0.7719	0.6028	0.3652	0.4308
au25	*c_DIS*	0.7434	0.5997	0.3594	0.4108
au25	*c_PRF*	0.7467	0.6073	0.3638	0.4154

against the different speeches isolately. However, as we increase the number of terms (au50 and all the terms in the initiative), the profile-based collection becomes preferable.

Nevertheless, we can say that using the right number of terms we can recommend a good set of top 10 MPs (the recall@10 values are almost equivalent to their counterparts using all the terms in the initiative) but with a worse ranking (as the other metrics indicate).

5 Conclusions

In this work we have proposed a system to either filtering parliamentary documents to MPs that could be interested in reading them, or recommending those

MPs that could be more involved in any given topics of interest to citizens. We followed a lazy approach that avoids learning an elaborated profile of each MP. We simply collect all the text of his/her speeches within the parliamentary debates and build an information retrieval system that returns a ranked list of MPs as a response to a query, which is formed from either the document to be filtered or the citizen's topics of interest.

We have carried out experiments with a collection of documents from the Parliament of Andalusia to test several alternative proposals. These proposals are relative to what document collection should be used by the IRS and how the document to be filtered (or the topics of interest of the citizen) should be transformed into a query against the IRS. Our experiments confirm that some of our proposals obtain significant improvements in performance with respect to a baseline approach.

The best results are obtained when we build a lazy profile for each MP, consisting of collecting all his/her speeches into a single large document. For future research we would like to study more elaborated (not so lazy) ways of building the MPs' profiles. We are also planning to tackle the problem from a machine learning perspective, using positive unlabeled learning methods to deal with the problem of having only positive examples to train the model of each MP (the own speeches of this MP). We shall also try to deploy the filtering/recommendation system within the Andalusian Parliament.

Acknowledgements. Paper supported by the Spanish "Ministerio de Ciencia e Innovación" and "Ministerio de Economía y Competitividad" under the projects TIN2011-28538-C02-02 and TIN2013-42741-P.

References

1. Aslam, J.A., Montague, M.: Models for metasearch. In: Proceedings. of the 24th Annual International ACM SIGIR Conference, pp. 24–37 (2003)
2. Belkin, N.J., Croft, W.B.: Information filtering and information retrieval: two sides of the same coin? Commun. ACM **35**, 29–38 (1992)
3. Billsus, D., Pazzani, M., Chen, J.: A learning agent for wireless news access. In: Proceedings of the International Conference on Intelligent User Interfaces, pp. 33–36 (2002)
4. Busby, A., Belkacem, K.: Coping with the Information Overload: An Exploration of Assistants' Backstage Role in the Everyday Practice of European Parliament Politics. European Integration online Papers. vol. 17 (2013)
5. de Campos, L.M., Fernández-Luna, J.M., Huete, J.F., Martin-Dancausa, C.J., Tur-Vigil, C., Tagua, A.: An integrated system for managing the andalusian parliament's digital library. Program Electron. Libr. Inf. Syst. **43**, 121–139 (2009)
6. Fox, E.A., Shaw, J.A.: Combination of multiple searches. In: Proccedings of the Second Text REtrieval Conference (TREC-2), pp. 243–252 (1994)
7. Hanani, U., Shapira, B., Shoval, P.: Information filtering: overview of issues, research and systems. User Model. User-Adap. Inter. **11**, 203–259 (2001)
8. Jarvelin, K., Kekalainen, J.: Cumulative gain-based evaluation of ir techniques. ACM Trans. Inf. Syst. **20**, 422–446 (2002)

9. Kim, J., Lee, B., Shaw, M., Chang, H., Nelson, W.: Application of decision-tree induction techniques to personalized advertisements on internet storefronts. Int. J. Electron. Commer. **5**, 45–62 (2001)
10. Lantz, B.: Machine Learning with R. Packt Publishing Ltd, Birmingham (2013)
11. Li, X., Liu, B.: Learning to classify texts using positive and unlabeled data. In: Proceedings of the 18th International Joint Conference on Artificial Intelligence, pp. 587–592 (2003)
12. Lops, P., de Gemmis, M., Semerano, G.: Content-based recommender systems: state of the art and trends. In: Ricci, F., Rokach, L., Shapira, B., Kantor, P.B. (eds.) Recommender Systems Handbook, pp. 73–105. Springer, New York (2011)
13. Marchionini, G., Samet, H., Brandt, L.: Digital government. Commun. ACM **46**, 25–27 (2003)
14. Montague, M., Aslam, J.A.: Relevance score normalization for metasearch. In: Proceedings of the 2001 ACM CIKM International Conference on Information and Knowledge Management, pp. 427–433 (2001)
15. Palvia, S.C.J., Sharma, S.S.: E-government and e-governance: definitions/domain framework and status around the world wide web. foundations of e-government. In: 5th International Conference on E-Governance, pp. 1–12 (2007)
16. Pazzani, M., Billsus, D.: Learning and revising user profiles: the identification of interesting web sites. Mach. Learn. **27**, 313–331 (1997)
17. Pazzani, M.J., Billsus, D.: Content-based recommendation systems. In: Brusilovsky, P., Kobsa, A., Nejdl, W. (eds.) Adaptive Web 2007. LNCS, vol. 4321, pp. 325–341. Springer, Heidelberg (2007)
18. Soucy, P., Mineau, G.W.: A simple KNN algorithm for text categorization. In: Proceedings of the IEEE International Conference on Data Mining, pp. 647–648 (2001)
19. Wu, S.: Data Fusion in Information Retrieval. Adaptation, Learning, and Optimization, vol. 13. Springer, Heidelberg (2012)
20. Wu, S., Crestani, F.: Data fusion with estimated weights. In: Proceedings of the 2002 ACM CIKM International Conference on Information and Knowledge Management, pp. 648–651 (2002)

Relations Between Marketing and Innovation in Brazilian Universities

Dalton de Sousa, Ricardo Braga Veroneze(✉), André Luiz Zambalde, and Paulo Henrique de Souza Bermejo

Federal University of Lavras, Lavras, Minas Gerais, Brazil
{dalton.sousa,rbveroneze}@gmail.com,
{zamba,bermejo}@dcc.ufla.br

Abstract. In the 21st century, the engine of economic development has been the knowledge and, the universities are increasingly being seen as key actors in this process. The interaction between the university and the market, promoted by the transfer of technology, has been the subject of several studies in the literature. However, few studies have worried on relating marketing with this process. From these studies it is suggested that the marketing exerts an important role in the understanding and development of technology transfer activities from Brazilian universities to the market. We propose, for such argument, a theoretical model of marketing from the view of Kotler and Keller [1], covering relationship marketing, integrated marketing, internal marketing and performance marketing. It was realized a theoretical essay from the review of published articles in Brazilian and international journals.

Keywords: Innovation management · Technology transfer · Universities · Marketing

1 Introduction

In the 21st century the economic development engine has been the knowledge and the universities are increasingly being seen as key actors in this process. And these organizations can contribute significantly through technology transfer. Several studies have worried about researching the interactions based on knowledge exchange between university and market, especially because of the strong influence that inventions have to the innovation capacity of companies.

Public institutions of higher education in Brazil (Federal, State and City, the last with less prominence) are responsible for over 90 % of the scientific production in the country and, together, have billionaire budget, as well as an incalculable patrimony under their direct responsibility. They have a very important role in the Brazilian economic, cultural and social development as well as in the improvement of national technical competitiveness in the international context. This brings innovation to the center of the discussions [2, 3].

This concern intensified especially after the major Western economies created specific laws to support innovation, whit the purpose that universities could commercialize the intellectual property resulting from researches funded by the government [4].

© Springer International Publishing Switzerland 2015
A. Kő and E. Francesconi (Eds.): EGOVIS 2015, LNCS 9265, pp. 379–389, 2015.
DOI: 10.1007/978-3-319-22389-6_27

In this new context of expansion of knowledge, the current time is of academic structures adequacy aiming the improvement of technology management of the university to the exploitation of the results of academic research [5].

Complementing this view, according to studies by Swamidass and Vunasa [6], Dalmarco [7]; Dias and Porto [8] these academic adjustments are necessary, because Brazilian universities are giving too much emphasis on the phases of registration and obtainment of a patent, regardless if there is, in fact, the licensing of that technology. Such act is a null value in terms of innovation and revenue for universities, because if there is no real transfer of the technology to the market, there is no return of the public resources investment used throughout the process.

From this line of thought, some studies, such as Malvezzi, Zambalde and Rezende [9], Stal and Fujino [10] and Garnica and Torkomian [11] suggest that the university intensify its marketing actions if they want to succeed in this innovation process.

So, in this work, it is suggested that marketing plays an important role in the understanding and development of technology transfer activities from the Brazilian universities to the market, even if the researchers in the field has not yet intensely dedicated to understand this context.

Thus the guiding question in this article is: "Which marketing relationships should be investigated in transfer activities of intellectual property from Brazilian universities to the market?"

Aiming to explore the theoretical possibilities of marketing relationships in technology transfer activities for innovations (MTTI) and propose a general theoretical model, this work is characterized as a theoretical essay, made by the review of published articles in Brazilian and international journals.

This paper is organized as follows: theoretical framework presenting the main authors and approaches related to innovation from intellectual property, first internationally and after focused on Brazil. Subsequently it is presented the theoretical marketing currents related to technology. Then we present the theoretical model with the proposals of Marketing influences in the technology transfer process. Finally, it is presented the final considerations and the references used throughout the text.

2 Theoretical Framework

2.1 Innovation from the Intellectual Property: The Role of North American Universities

Companies primarily depend on technological innovation, as much to stay in the market, as to contribute to the growth and development of the country. Innovate in a continuous manner is the key to create and maintain the competitive advantage of an organization, despite the technological, social or marketing conditions involved [12]. Such innovation can be primarily achieved through partnerships between private organizations and universities, which contribute to technical and managerial advances in companies.

It is worth noting the enactment of the Bayh-Dole Act Law of 1980 in the United States, as an important point for the current relational stage between company, university and innovation [13]. Since then, universities in several countries, besides having to promote teaching, research and extension, won an active role in the dissemination process and knowledge transformation in new technologies.

This active role of the university is called by some authors as the "commercialization" of academic knowledge as it involves the patenting and licensing of inventions, besides the academic entrepreneurship, which attracted great attention in the literature [14, 15]. This global trend is strongly linked to the legitimacy of the importance that universities have to face contexts of fast economic changes experienced by the national research and innovation systems [16].

US universities, in general, have always sought practical purposes on the achievements of their researches. Several innovative advances came from the North American academy, beyond the collaboration between industry and university have influenced the advances in engineering and applied sciences areas [13].

From that greater interaction between research and market, US universities began to expand its efforts to license and market their inventions from the 1970s. As Henderson [17] argue, this expansion of activities have led to an increase of the commercial interest in academic research, because there was a contribution to the growth of industrial funding in research, implying the desire of many universities to explore new sources of income and growth.

It is also worth mentioning that in addition to the benefits related to the advances in science to the North American universities, as well as institutions of countries that already have a practical commercialization of mature intellectual property, guarantees billion dollars revenue derived from such new sources of incomes [18].

However, despite the American universities are in a more developed stage of innovation, Siegel et al. [19] report that they are criticized for engaging in the development of new technologies, but do not occupy to take them to a private application, leading makers of public policy to state that this gap could seriously damage the global competitiveness of US companies.

Siegel and Phan [20] argue, collaborating with the exposed arguments, that there are some issues that must be addressed to universities, administrators and other policy makers in order to improve the effectiveness of technology transfer. According to the researchers, universities should adopt a strategic approach emphasizing technology transfer mechanisms that are more focused on stimulating economic and regional development.

From the exposed international theory, is noticed that even the North American universities, which are at the forefront in the technology transfer process to the market, there are still problems related to communication, so they should pay attention to strategic and management issues, and from this be able to achieve innovation.

After showed the current stage of international literature on the subject, the next session will be focused on a literature review about the material dealing with Brazilian universities regarding innovation from the intellectual property.

2.2 Innovation from the Intellectual Property: The Long Path of Brazilian Universities

In most studies found in Brazilian literature on the subject of intellectual property there is a tendency by the academy to study the relationship between patents, licenses and spin-offs, from the perspective of the university, seeking to reveal in which way these intellectual properties may contribute to the transfer of knowledge to the market.

Unlike happened in the United States, a law to encourage innovation was enacted in Brazil only in 2004. The Innovation Law is intended to encourage interaction between universities and the productive sector, being in charge of the universities to adequate to certain requirements, including, among other things, the creation of Technological Innovation Centers (NIT), responsible for the link between academy and the market [5].

Since then began to establish a set of incentives to strengthen the interaction between companies and the NIT's, recognizing that the presence of the inventor is essential in the process of technology transfer, especially in developing countries, such as Brazil, due to the low technology absorption capacity of the companies [21].

On the other hand, according to Couto [22], throughout history, universities have failed to develop coordinated and systematic policies that would ensure the property rights of their inventions.

To protected these rights and succeed in the transfer, from the logic presented by Póvoa and Rapini [21], it should have an effort by the inventor to make his idea become an innovation and not just a unilateral effort by the university. Corroborating this view, according to Jensen and Thursby [23], the vast majority of North American licensed inventions demanded cooperation between the inventor and the company, so that it would succeed in marketing.

We should also consider that the context experienced by Brazil is even more complex because of the roles assumed by public universities. The organizational culture of these organizations is sustained on the one hand, through ideological values that defend the unrestricted access to the results obtained from the researches developed, and on the other hand, antagonistic, that prizes the standards that maintain the bureaucratic administrative hierarchy [24].

Seen the inadequacy of most universities in the management capacity, even after the creation of the NIT, it is necessary to manage the patents because of the strategic importance that they have for universities and also to Brazil, due to the benefits derived from innovations. There was a deep and rapid change in the role of science forward to Brazilian society, which expects much more public investment in research [25].

These changes influenced the way in which the NIT's should adapt, especially in relation to its structure in order that, through their actions, it is possible to return public investments for its operation. Reinforcing this view, as shown in studies [5, 8, 26] the relative number of patents that underlie the deposit stage and turn into innovation is no more than 10 %, and in some public universities of São Paulo that number is even lower, not exceeding 6 %. This low number of patents in the market represents high expenditures for the institutions due to the annual fees for maintaining other patents that are not bringing financial return to universities.

This whole scenario shows that Brazilian universities should be strengthened and prepared to face the challenges for improving technology transfer, improving, among other things, the marketing of its technologies [5]. Such action may contribute to an increase in technology transfer, which could directly increase universities' income.

2.3 Marketing and Its Possibilities of Research on Technology Transfer

The effects of marketing strategies on business performance are poorly studied in specific contexts of business, such as marketing in the technology transfer activities for innovation in Brazilian universities. One explanation for this is due to the fact that marketing activities are very exposed to numerous internal and external influences, turning the identification of cause and effect relations a complex task [27].

According to Jaakkola et al. [27], it is assumed that the impact of marketing factors is constant in different business contexts, which is a strong assumption, despite the lack of knowledge about the effects of strategic marketing factors in some business contexts and, thus define strategic marketing "as a concept deeply oriented to stakeholders that focuses on long-term view of a company for competitive advantage and value aggregation through innovation" (p. 1301).

It is a concept strongly aligned to the Marketing conceptualization of the American Marketing Association: "Marketing is the activity, set of institutions, and processes to create, communicate, deliver and exchange offers that have value for customers, clients, partners and the society in general" [28].

When such concepts are considered, itshould not be neglected the fact that a more comprehensive view of the influences of marketing activities on the organizations needs to be placed under discussion.

In the context of Brazilian universities, marketing in the technology transfer activities to innovations (MTTI) must take place in an environment that seeks high integration between technology transfer offices (TTOs), other formal structures of institutions and researchers/inventors. What is here called MTTI is the ability of institutions of higher education, in the Brazilian case, especially the public ones, have to use marketing efforts to catalyze the transfer of applied knowledge, produced by its researchers in innovative products or services.

Although it has not yet been operationalized and applied systematically by the academy, it is believed that the vision proposed by Kotler and Keller [1] about the orientation of holistic marketing complement this important gap in research coverage in marketing and presents numerous possibilities for theoretical and empirical exploration.

To Kotler and Keller [1], the holistic marketing is an alternative marketing that expands the possibilities of analysis. They introduce the concept of holistic marketing as based on the development, structuring and implementation of programs, processes and marketing activities, considering its scope and interrelations.

According to Zandberg [29], there are five marketing guidelines usually reported in the literature, which are: production orientation, product orientation, sales orientation, marketing orientation and holistic marketing orientation. Points out, however, that in a world of increasing competition, the first three guidelines have been considered limited by researchers, while the holistic marketing has emerged as the most complete proposal today.

Kotler and Keller [1] state that "the holistic marketing […] recognizes and reconciles the scope and complexities of marketing activities" and present, through the Fig. 1, the overview of the four components that characterize it: relationship marketing, integrated marketing, internal marketing and performance marketing (p. 17).

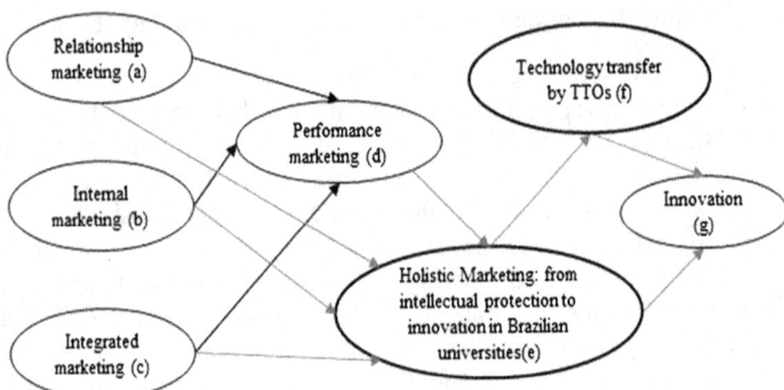

Fig. 1. Theoretical model of marketing relations in the technology transfer process in Brazilian universities

Thus, Kotler and Keller (2012) have the following definitions for the dimensions of the components of Holistic Marketing:

1. Relationship Marketing: seeks to develop deep and lasting relationships with those people or organizations that may affect the success of the company's marketing activities and aims to build long-term relationships mutually satisfactory with its main components;
2. Integrated Marketing: is that in which the company plans marketing activities and rides marketing programs in order to create, communicate and deliver value to consumers, so that 'the whole is greater than the sum of its parts'. Two key issues are: 1.Various marketing activities can create, communicate and deliver value, and; 2. Professionals should plan and implement all marketing activity considering all the other activities of the organization.
3. Internal Marketing: is that oriented hire, train and motivate employees who want to be able to serve the customers well. "Smart Marketing professionals recognize that marketing activities inside the company can be as important as marketing activities directed outside the company - if not more" (KOTLER; KELLER, 2012, p. 20);
4. Performance Marketing: It has as assumption the understanding of financial and non-financial returns to society from activities and marketing programs. Not only does it analyze results through financial returns, but also consider the marketing scorecard and the interpretation of what happens with the market share, customer loss rate, customer satisfaction level, quality of products or services and other indicators.

In this sense, Brettel et al. [30] highlight that the development of new technologies (products, services, etc.) is an multidisciplinary effort in which, in different circumstances, a high level of cross-functional integration can not lead to more effective and efficient results.

On the other hand, they should take a position of products/services provider able to achieve success front their customers, which usually are quite diverse. In this sense, Čater et al. [31] claim that customers and customer relationships are considered as the most important assets of organizations and are related to the long-term success, thereby emerges the need to understand the elements of marketing relationship in the activities of TTOs.

In this sense, it appears that the pressure for results, whether economic or social, private or public, makes many organizations to seek implementing new strategies to improve the quality of service and to position strategically in its area of operation, what generates substantial emphasis on relationship marketing strategies.

At the same time, the nature of interactions, especially the behavior of employees, affects the perceived quality of service, customer satisfaction and their future intentions. New strategies require that the culture of an organization is able to align the attitudes of workers with new strategies, which may require a change. As an organization is a group of people, its culture depends on how the employees see their organization and its goals. In this sense, the Internal Marketing is useful in developing and maintaining a culture within which customer-oriented behavior must be recognized and rewarded reported [32].

According to Gounaris [33], the Internal Marketing Guidance is the company's commitment measure in producing value for its employees and is an orientation that emerged in the 1970 s as an alternative to the development and provision of superior service to customers. For him, the internal marketing orientation must be consistently enhanced by the organizations, so that, they can respond effectively to market demands (external).

As presented above, there is a relevance to understand two major subdivisions of study in marketing (relationship marketing and internal marketing) in MTTI study proposal. Similarly, another area has presented fundamental importance, named the Integrated Marketing. In this sense, Mumel Hocevar and Snoj [34] state that:

Companies use different marketing activities to communicate with the environment. These decisions are often a result of past experiences, habits or a certain influences. Measuring the efficiency of a communication mix as well as analyzing the effect of using a specific marketing communication activity on different business performance determinants are usually neglected (p. 83).

For Mumel, Hocevar and Snoj [34], countless studies have even investigated the relationship between what, in this work, was adopted under the perspective of Integrated Marketing and other theme of interest, which is the Performance Marketing in accordance with the proposal of Kotler and Keller [1].

According to Mumel, Hocevar and Snoj [34], a large number of studies have investigated the relationship between certain marketing tools and the resulting business performance and are presented effects on sales, customer satisfaction and the efficacy of a particular marketing activity.

In this sense, Jaakkola et al. [27] state that, the market orientation and the innovation orientation tend to affect more the marketing performance of an organization in the long term than their internal capabilities (inside-out). These authors consider that a good strategy will only have greater effects on the business performance if its implementation is effective.

Therefore, it is assumed that Brazilian universities must understand and develop their marketing skills in a holistic manner, covering all possibilities to create competences that provide a more effective and natural relationship with the market.

From these considerations, it is believed that only a holistic model can handle to help understanding the marketing relations in the technology transfer activities to innovations (MTTI) and it is presented the proposal by Fig. 1.

Performance Marketing will be influenced by different capacities [1, 27, 31–34] developed by the TTOs in the relationship with external and internal customers and through communication actions capable of catalyzing its services (propositions: a => d, b => d; c => d).

Holistic Marketing (from intellectual protection to innovation in Brazilian universities), according to Kotler and Keller [1], will be positively influenced by the guidelines of relationship marketing, internal marketing, integrated marketing and performance marketing (propositions: a => e; b => e; c => e; d => e).

According to the perspective presented by Bradley, Hayter and Link [35], only one enhanced capability of relationship with the market will be able to make that the TTOs assume an effective role in innovation. In turn, the Holistic Marketing [1] will also exert positive influence on market innovations generated from academic researches (propositions: e => f; e => g; f => g).

This proposal comes in this scenario where there is an evolution of the role of universities in Brazilian innovation, which is confirmed in Malvezzi [36], who states that discussions are being conducted aiming to find alternatives for the conversion of patents in innovation, in order to obtain results that go beyond the generation of knowledge and that can also produce social and economic benefits to the university and society.

In this sense, Costa, Porto and Plonski [37] state that the cooperation between universities and companies can not be set aside by the three stakeholders segments: business, academic and government, as this may delay the technological development of companies and countries.

Thus, it is considered that the academics of the marketing area should move toward understanding the scenario and marketing relationships in technology transfer processes in Brazilian universities, with a view that it is an unexplored context in the area, but presents numerous opportunities for research and management.

In the following section, will be presented the final considerations, the limitations of the study and future study proposals.

3 Final Considerations, Research Limitations and Future Studies

The answer to the research problem presented in this paper, after the discussions, leads to the consideration that, in the context of Brazilian universities, only a holistic marketing approach will be able to provide answers that can help to understand the marketing relations from the role of TTO's to the innovation.

Thus, it was proposed the theoretical model of relationship marketing in the technology transfer process in Brazilian universities, which aims to encourage researches to be conducted to understand the influences of internal marketing, relationship marketing, integrated marketing and marketing performance on the activities of TTO's and on the generation of innovations through Brazilian universities.

The proposed objective to hold this theoretical essay was achieved, since the raised literature demonstrates the feasibility and the need that researchers in marketing consider the issue as relevant to empirical studies, which, until now, is still incipient.

A relevant consideration, which points to an important gap in the literature, is the fact that most studies have been interested only on the final result of the work of TTO's or to analyze and criticize its structures, without, however, point out a framework that considers the relationships between people, processes, organizations from a strategic perspective of marketing.

In Brazil, in particular, public universities still face the difficulty of most of its researchers and intellectuals to understand and accept that teaching and research should not just be an end in itself, but that universities need to take a highlighted position in economic and social development. And it naturally leads to the need to understand that marketing relationships can not be excluded or marginalized by these institutions, by the simple and naive claim of neutrality and impartiality of the academy.

After all, to assume the defense of academic purity opens a fruitless and partial ideological debate that, at the same time, creates and stimulates the transfer of technology to be performed in a shy way and without the participation of the university, through consulting firms and other forms of direct relationships between researchers and the various industries.

More than ever, universities should make use of all alternatives to understand the environment that surrounds it, which also includes considering the impacts that globalization of the economy, science and the media have on its role in society.

Regarding the limitations of this work, it should be considered the low interest of the marketing area about the studies of the roles of TTO's, either in Brazil or abroad, what was evident in the survey of the references used in the paper. Another limitation is the restriction on the use of holistic marketing orientation in empirical research, which indicates a lack of boldness of researchers of this area.

Therefore, it is suggested that future studies can empirically test models that seek this holistic marketing vision, not only in the processes of marketing innovation in universities, but that in other segments can be developed models that are able to launch a more comprehensive understanding of the various factors that influence the daily lives of organizations and that are competence of marketing studies.

Acknowledgement. The authors thank the Minas Gerais State Foundation for Research Development (FAPEMIG), the Brazilian Council for Scientific, Technological Development (CNPq) and Federal University of Lavras for their financial support.

References

1. Kotler, P., Keller, K.L.: Administração de marketing, 14th edn. Pearson Education do Brasil, São Paulo (2012)
2. Ristoff, D.: Os desafios da educação superior na Ibero-América: inovação, inclusão e qualidade. Avaliação: Revista da Avaliação da Educação Superior **18**(3), 519–545 (2013)

3. Santos, Dos, F.S.: Financiamento público das instituições federais de ensino superior – IFES um estudo da Universidade de Brasília – UnB. Dissertação (Mestrado) – Universidade de Brasília, Brasília (2013)
4. Sampat, B.B., Mowery, D.C., Ziedonis, A.: Changes in University Patent Qualiy after the Bayh-Dole Act: A Re-Examination. Int. J. Ind. Organ. **21**, 1371–1390 (2003)
5. Garnica, L.A., Oliveira, R.M., Torkomian, A.L.: Vitale. Propriedade intelectual e titularidade de patentes universitárias: um estudo piloto na Universidade Federal de São Carlos – UFSCar. In: Simpósio De Gestão Da Inovação Tecnológica, 24, 2004, Gramado. Anais… Gramado: Associação Nacional de Pós-Graduação e Pesquisa em Administração (2006)
6. Swamidass, P.M., Vulasa, V.: Why university inventions rarely produce income? Bottlenecks in university technology transfer. J. Technol. Transfer **34**, 343–363 (2009)
7. Dalmarco, G., et al.: Universities' intellectual property: path for innovation or patent competition? J. Technol. Manage. Innov. **6**, 159–170 (2011)
8. Dias, A.A., Porto, G.S.: Como a USP transfere tecnologia? Organizações & Sociedade **21** (70), 489–507 (2014)
9. de Malvezzi, F.A., Zambalde, A.L., de Rezende, D.C.: Marketing de Patentes à Inovação Um Estudo Multicaso em Universidades Brasileiras. Revista Brasileira de Marketing **13**(5), 109–123 (2014). e-ISSN: 2177-5184
10. Stal, E., Fujino, A.: RAI:revistade administração e inovação. As Relações Universidade-Empresa No Brasil Sob A Ótica Da Lei De Inovação **2**(1), 5–19 (2005). doi:10.5585/rai.v2i1.30
11. Garnica, L.A., Torkomian, A.L.V.: Gestão de tecnologia em universidades: uma análise do patenteamento e dos fatores de dificuldade e de apoio à transferência de tecnologia no Estado de São Paulo. Gestao & Produção **16**(4), 624–638 (2009)
12. Amadei, J.R.P., Torkomian, A.L.V.: As patentes nas universidades: análise dos depósitos das universidades públicas paulistas. Ciência da Informação **38**(2), 9–18 (2009)
13. Mowery, D.C., Nelson, R.R., Sampat, B.N., Ziedonis, A.A.: The growth of patenting and licensing by US universities: an assessment of the effects of the Bayh-Dole act of 1980. Res. Policy **30**(1), 99–119 (2001)
14. O'shea, R.P., Chugh, H., Allen, T.J.: Determinants and consequences of university spinoff activity: a conceptual framework. J. Technol. Transfer **33**(6), 653–666 (2008)
15. Phan, P., Siegel, D.S.: The effectiveness of university technology transfer. Foundations and Trends in Entrepreneurship, **2**(2), 77–144 (2006)
16. Curi, C., Daraio, C., Llerena, P.: University technology transfer: how (in) efficient are French universities?. Cambridge Journal of Economics, p. bes020 (2012)
17. Henderson, R., Jaffe, A.B., Trajtenberg, M.: Universities as a source of commercial technology: a detailed analysis of university patenting, 1965–1988. Rev. Econ. Stat. **80**(1), 119–127 (1998)
18. AUTM. Association of University Technology Managers (2010). http://www.autm.net/FY_2010_Licensing_Survey/9337.htm
19. Siegel, D.S., Waldman, D.A., Atwater, A.N., Link, A.N.: Toward a model of the effective transfer of scientific knowledge from academicians to practitioners: qualitative evidence from the commercialization of university technologies. J. Eng. Technol. Manage. **21**(1), 115–142 (2004)
20. Siegel, D.S., Phan, P.: Analyzing the effectiveness of university technology transfer: implications for entrepreneurship education. Adv. Study Entrepreneurship, Innov. Econ. Growth **16**, 1–38 (2005)

21. Póvoa, L.M.C., Rapini, M.S.: Technology transfer from universities and public research institutes to firms in Brazil: what is transferred and how the transfer is carried out. Sci. Public Policy **37**(2), 147–159 (2010)
22. Couto, A.: Universidade e sistemas regionais de inovação – da periferia para o centro da dinâmica económica?. Tese (Doutorado). Universidade da Beira Interior, Covilhã (2000)
23. Jensen, R., Thursby, M.: Proofs and prototypes for sale: The licensing of university inventions. Am. Econ. Rev., pp. 240 − 259 (2001)
24. Fujino, A., Stal, E.: Gestão da propriedade intelectual na universidade pública brasileira: diretrizes para licenciamento e comercialização. Revista de Negócios **12**(1), 104–120 (2007)
25. Perucchi, V., Mueller, S.P.M.: Estudo com as patentes produzidas e o perfil dos inventores dos Institutos Federais de Educação. Ciência e Tecnologia. RDBCI **12**(1), 191–213 (2014)
26. Dias, A.A., Porto, G.S.: Gestão de transferência de tecnologia na Inova Unicamp. RAC. Rio de Janeiro **17**(3), 263–284 (2013)
27. Jaakkola, M., Moller, K., Parvinen, P., Evanschitzky, H., Muhlbacher, H.: Strategic marketing and business performance A study in three European 'engineering countries'. Ind. Mark. Manage. **39**(8), 1300–1310 (2010)
28. American Marketing Association AMA definition of marketing (2007). https://www.ama.org/AboutAMA/Pages/Definition-of-Marketing.aspx
29. do Zandberg, M.C.: A importância da gestão de marketing em empresa inovadora: estudo de empresa do Prime-Programa Primeira Empresa Inovadora. Dissertação (Mestrado) – Escola Brasileira de Administração Pública e de Empresas, Fundação Getúlio Vargas, Rio de Janeiro (2012)
30. Brettel, M., Heinemann, F., Engelen, A., Neubauer, S.: Cross-Functional Integration of R&D, Marketing, and Manufacturing in Radical and Incremental Product Innovations and Its Effects on Project Effectiveness and Efficiency. J. Prod. Innov. Manage **28**(2), 251–269 (2011)
31. Čater, B., Zabkar, V., Čater, T.: Commitment In Marketing Research Services: Two Alternative Models. J. Bus. Econ. Manage. **12**(4), 603–628 (2011)
32. Huang, M., Chen, M.Y.: Internal Marketing, customer orientation, and organizational commitment: moderating effects of work status. Psychol. Rep. **113**(1), 180–198 (2013)
33. Gounaris, S.P.: Internal-market orientation and its measurement. J. Bus. Res. **59**(4), 432–448 (2006)
34. Mumel, D., Hocevar, N., Snoj, B.: How marketing communications correlates with business performance. J. Appl. Bus. Res. (JABR), **23**(2) (2011)
35. Bradley, S.R., Hayter, C.S., Link, A.: Models and methods of university technology transfer. Found. Trends Entrepreneurship, **9**(6) (2013)
36. de Malvezzi, F.A.: Marketing de patentes à inovação: um estudo multicaso em universidades brasileiras (2013)
37. Costa, P.R., Porto, G.S., Plonski, G.A.: Gestão da cooperação universidade-empresa nas multinacionais brasileiras. Revista de Administração e Inovação. **7**(3), 150–173 (2010)

Author Index

Printed in the United States
By Bookmasters